Personality and Social Behavior

FRONTIERS OF SOCIAL PSYCHOLOGY

Series Editors:
Arie W. Kruglanski, *University of Maryland at College Park*
Joseph P. Forgas, *University of New South Wales*

Frontiers of Social Psychology is a new series of domain-specific handbooks. The purpose of each volume is to provide readers with a cutting-edge overview of the most recent theoretical, methodological, and practical developments in a substantive area of social psychology, in greater depth than is possible in general social psychology handbooks. The Editors and contributors are all internationally renowned scholars, whose work is at the cutting-edge of research.

Scholarly, yet accessible, the volumes in the *Frontiers* series are an essential resource for senior undergraduates, postgraduates, researchers, and practitioners, and are suitable as texts in advanced courses in specific sub-areas of social psychology.

Published Titles

Negotiation Theory and Research, Thompson
Close Relationships, Noller & Feeney
Evolution and Social Psychology, Schaller, Simpson, & Kenrick
Social Psychology and the Unconscious, Bargh
Affect in Social Thinking and Behavior, Forgas
Science of Social Influence, Pratkanis
Social Communication, Fiedler
The Self, Sedikides & Spencer
Personality and Social Behavior, Rhodewalt

Forthcoming Titles

Attitudes and Attitude Change, Crano & Prislin
Social Cognition, Strack & Förster
Political Psychology, Krosnick & Chiang
Social Psychology of Consumer Behavior, Wänke
Social Motivation, Dunning

For continually updated information about published and forthcoming titles in the *Frontiers of Social Psychology* series, please visit: **www.psypress.com/frontiers**

Personality and Social Behavior

Edited by Frederick Rhodewalt

Psychology Press
Taylor & Francis Group
New York London

Psychology Press
Taylor & Francis Group
270 Madison Avenue
New York, NY 10016

Psychology Press
Taylor & Francis Group
27 Church Road
Hove, East Sussex BN3 2FA

© 2008 by Taylor & Francis Group, LLC

Printed in the United States of America on acid-free paper
10 9 8 7 6 5 4 3 2 1

International Standard Book Number-13: 978-1-84169-450-4 (Hardcover)

Except as permitted under U.S. Copyright Law, no part of this book may be reprinted, reproduced, transmitted, or utilized in any form by any electronic, mechanical, or other means, now known or hereafter invented, including photocopying, microfilming, and recording, or in any information storage or retrieval system, without written permission from the publishers.

Trademark Notice: Product or corporate names may be trademarks or registered trademarks, and are used only for identification and explanation without intent to infringe.

Library of Congress Cataloging-in-Publication Data

Personality and social behavior / edited by Frederick Rhodewalt.
    p. cm. -- (Frontiers of social psychology)
Includes bibliographical references and index.
ISBN-13: 978-1-84169-450-4 (alk. paper)
ISBN-10: 1-84169-450-9 (alk. paper)
    1. Personality. 2. Social psychology. I. Rhodewalt, Frederick Thomas.

BF698.P47 2008
155.2--dc22
                                                                                            2007035776

Visit the Taylor & Francis Web site at
http://www.taylorandfrancis.com

and the Psychology Press Web site at
http://www.psypress.com

Contents

About the Editor   vii
Contributors   ix

1. Personality and Social Behavior: An Overview   1

    Frederick Rhodewalt

2. Beyond Person and Situation Effects: Intraindividual Personality Architecture and Its Implications for the Study of Personality and Social Behavior   9

    Daniel Cervone, Tracy L. Caldwell, and Heather Orom

3. The Self and Social Behavior: The Fragile Self and Interpersonal Self-Regulation   49

    Frederick Rhodewalt and Benjamin Peterson

4. Contextual Variability in Personality: The Case of the Relational Self and the Process of Transference   97

    Susan M. Andersen, S. Adil Saribay, and Christina S. Kooij

5. Ties That Bind: Linking Personality to Interpersonal Behavior Through the Study of Adult Attachment Style and Relationship Satisfaction   117

    W. Steven Rholes, Ramona L. Paetzold, and Mike Friedman

6. Different Toolkits for Different Mind-Readers: A Social-Cognitive Neuroscience Perspective on Personality and Social Relationships   149

    Geraldine Downey, Jamil Zaki, and Jason Mitchell

7. Personality, Individuality, and Social Identity   177

    Michael Hogg

8.	Leadership as Dynamic Social Process	197
	Martin M. Chemers	
9.	Personality and Prejudice in Interracial Interactions	223
	Patricia G. Devine, Frederick Rhodewalt, and Matthew Siemionko	
10.	Social Psychological Processes Linking Personality to Physical Health: A Multilevel Analysis With Emphasis on Hostility and Optimism	251
	Bert N. Uchino, Allison A. Vaughn, and Sonia Matwin	

Author Index — 285

Subject Index — 299

About the Editor

Frederick Rhodewalt received his PhD in social psychology from Princeton University in 1979. His primary research explores the interpersonal construction and maintenance of self and includes topics such as self-handicapping and narcissism. He is Professor of Psychology and Associate Dean of the Graduate School at the University of Utah. Dr. Rhodewalt is a former editor of *Personality and Social Psychology Bulletin* and *Basic and Applied Social Psychology*. In 2003, he was awarded the Distinguished Service Award to the Disciplines of Social and Personality Psychology by the Society for Personality and Social Psychology.

Contributors

Susan M. Andersen
New York University
New York, New York

Tracy L. Caldwell
North Central College
Naperville, Illinois

Daniel Cervone
University of Illinois at Chicago
Chicago, Illinois

Martin M. Chemers
University of California, Santa Cruz
Santa Cruz, California

Patricia G. Devine
University of Wisconsin–Madison
Madison, Wisconsin

Geraldine Downey
Columbia University
New York, New York

Mike Friedman
Texas A&M University
College Station, Texas

Michael Hogg
Claremont Graduate University
Claremont, California

Christina S. Kooij
New York University
New York, New York

Sonia Matwin
University of Utah
Salt Lake City, Utah

Jason Mitchell
Harvard University
Cambridge, Massachusetts

Heather Orom
Karmanos Cancer Institute
Detroit, Michigan
and
Institute of Gerontology
Wayne State University
Detroit, Michigan

Ramona L. Paetzold
Texas A&M University
College Station, Texas

Benjamin Peterson
University of Utah
Salt Lake City, Utah

Frederick Rhodewalt
University of Utah
Salt Lake City, Utah

W. Steven Rholes
Texas A&M University
College Station, Texas

S. Adil Saribay
New York University
New York, New York

Matthew Siemionko
University of Utah
Salt Lake City, Utah

Bert N. Uchino
University of Utah
Salt Lake City, Utah

Allison A. Vaughn
University of Utah
Salt Lake City, Utah

Jamil Zaki
Columbia University
New York, New York

1

Personality and Social Behavior
An Overview

FREDERICK RHODEWALT
University of Utah

This volume is about personality and social behavior. It surveys a wide variety of research domains with roots in the two disciplines in an attempt to understand the transactions between persons and their social worlds. The organizing questions are (a) How do characteristics of the person drive and shape interpersonal behavior? and (b) How do features of the social environment constrain and elicit behaviors from the individual? These are not new questions. However, there are new and evolving answers. It can be argued that the "emerging symbiosis" (Swann & Selye, 2005) between the disciplines of social and personality psychology is evidenced in the new and exciting approaches to addressing the personality and social behavior questions put forth in the following chapters.

Evidence for such symbiosis between the fields of personality and social psychology may be found in current textbook definitions of the two disciplines. Consider the following:

> Personality is the complex organization of cognitions, affects, and behaviors that gives direction and pattern (coherence) to the person's life. ...personality consists of both structures and processes and reflects both nature (genes) and nurture experience. (Pervin, 1996, p. 414)

> Social psychology is the scientific study of how people think about, influence, and relate to one another. (Myers, 2007, p. 4)

As these two representative definitions suggest, contemporary views of personality and social psychology share much overlap in their central concerns. Although social psychology places greater emphasis on the interpersonal aspects of the person, both fields are interested in systematic study of the thoughts, emotions, and behaviors of the person, and both acknowledge that people behave in contexts. This rapprochement is a marked departure from more classic definitions of the respective fields, personality being the study of individual differences and social psychology being the investigation of the impact of the situation on the individual.

Such "balkanization" of the disciplines set the stage for the person-situation debate of the 1970s and 80s. Ignited by Walter Mischel's (1968) trenchant critique of traditional trait approaches, specifically that behavior is highly situation-specific and not cross-situationally consistent, the ensuing discussion and research contributed to a number of useful and some not so useful developments in the fields of personality and social psychology. First, it forced trait theorists and social psychologists to be more precise in defining their constructs and to clarify what their theories contended about the control and coherence of behavior. For example, did trait theorists ever suggest that one could predict an individual's behavior in a single instance with only person information? Of course not. Did their conception of traits suggest levels of cross-situational and temporal consistency in individual behavior that was greater than that suggested by the data? Yes.

Second, it led to a renewed interest in interactionist frameworks in which to account for person and situation factors. In particular, reciprocal interactionist views (Bandura, 1986; Cantor & Kihlstrom, 1987; Endler & Magnusson, 1976; Smith & Rhodewalt, 1986) depict person, situation, and behavior as unfolding over time and reciprocally influencing one another. For example, in their description of Type A coronary-prone behavior as a challenge-engendering behavioral style, Smith and Rhodewalt argued that Type As—through their choice of situations, appraisals of situations, and interpersonal behaviors—created situations that were objectively more challenging and stressful than were the situations encountered by non-coronary-prone Type Bs.

Most important, I would argue, is that the person-situation debate and subsequent revisiting of interactionist ideas has led to the development of new "dispositional constructs" (Cervone, 2004; Mischel & Shoda, 1996) that have importantly reframed the person-situation debate (see Cervone, Caldwell, & Orom, this volume). The person-situation question became virtually irrelevant when the social environment was represented within the individual difference variable. For example, a major challenge for dispositional approaches has been the issue of variability in responding across situations. A person who possesses the trait of assertiveness may be very assertive with family members but deferential with strangers. Mischel and Shoda (1995) propose that one can observe consistency in variation if one defines dispositions as containing the elements of behavioral (or cognitive/affective) responses, situations, and conditional *if-then* linking rules. Thus, the trait of assertiveness becomes the dispositional construct of "if with family then behave assertively, if with strangers then show deference." I will return to the appeal and applicability of this conceptualization of "disposition" later in this essay; my point for now is that the person-situation debate did not end in a stalemate in which each side grudgingly conceded the other's validity. Rather, it advanced our basic understanding of what is meant by the term disposition in ways that integrated and enriched both fields.

On the downside, however, one can argue that the person-situation controversy distracted personality psychology away from its rich conceptual history that construed personality as an interpersonal process, one that recognized the individual as an active interpersonal being. A goal of this chapter is to remind readers of these earlier frameworks so that one may appreciate the exciting work on personality and social behavior represented herein.

THE INTERPERSONAL PERSPECTIVE

The classic view of personality is that people possess psychological characteristics that give patterning and coherence to their behavior. However, although the focus is on qualities of the person, it is correct to say that these classic positions, be they psychodynamic, phenomenological, or dispositional, all specify to some extent that their putative characteristics have interpersonal origins and, often, orientations. Patterns of anxiety and defense, inauthentic self-perceptions, and traits develop through a set of fairly regular and routine interpersonal experiences. A few examples are mentioned here to illustrate this point. These examples by no means reflect an exhaustive or in depth review of the interfaces between personality and interpersonal processes and situations (see Kiesler, 1996 for a more in depth resource). Also, to say that a characteristic describes patterns of behavior in interpersonal situations does not mean that it is not also viewed as a static descriptor of the person. For example, the Big Five trait (Digman, 1990; Goldberg, 1993) of agreeableness refers to a friendly and pleasant interpersonal style, a style that is temporally stable and cross-situationally consistent, but says nothing about the processes by which the person uniquely perceives, selects, and acts upon interpersonal events.

Perhaps the earliest example of an interpersonal approach to personality is Freud's (1925) theory of psychosexual development. Clearly one of the most controversial elements of his theory, in essence it specifies a series of interpersonal learning affordances in which the child, when physically mature enough, can learn something about navigating his or her social world in order to meet biological and psychological needs. To paraphrase in contemporary terms, what is taken away from each learning affordance is a set of strategies for getting what one wants (or avoiding what one does not want) in various social contexts. It is interesting to note that in Freud's view, the flexible and appropriate use of strategies and defenses is adaptive. It is the rigid use of a particular coping behavior invariantly across situations that is maladaptive. Had he been available to comment on the person-situation debate, I suspect that Freud would have been more Mischelian than Cattellian.

As described by Rhodewalt and Peterson (this volume), Alfred Adler (1927) continued the interpersonal element in psychodynamic theory with his statements that individual differences, a person's *style of life*, are the result of developmental, interpersonal relationships, including factors such as birth order and correlated family roles. For Adler, *style of life* included interpersonal goals and orientations as well as strategies for pursuing them. A common theme across interpersonal perspectives is the idea that a significant part of personality is organized in the service of two social motives, agency and communion (Wiggins & Trapnell, 1996). Adler's concepts of striving for superiority (agency) and social interest (communion) anticipated this idea.

Clearly the most interpersonal of the psychodynamic positions was Harry Stack Sullivan's (1953) view that "personality is the relatively enduring pattern of recurrent, interpersonal situations which characterize a human life" (Sullivan, 1953, pp. 110–111). For Sullivan, personality was observed at the intersection of the person with others. Interpersonal behavior referred, "to the recurrent patterns of reciprocal relationships present among two persons' covert and overt actions and reactions studied over the sequence of their transactions with each other." Consistency and patterning, to the extent that it was an issue, was found in the fact that we tend to interact with the same individuals in a limited set of contexts. Although Sullivan's is clearly a psychodynamic theory in the sense that behavior is driven by a desire to avoid or reduce anxiety, the source of anxiety is rooted in a set of internalized representations of previous interactions that were affectively positive or negative and the interpersonal behaviors associated with them. People behave in their current social settings in ways that produced the least anxiety in the past.

In contemporary personality theory, Sullivan's influence is most clearly seen in the dyadic interactional perspective of Wiggins and colleagues (Pincus &Wiggins, 1992; Wiggins & Pincus, 1994). They argue that personality is organized around the social motives of the need for independence (a variant of the meta construct agency) and the need for security (a variant of the meta construct communion, see Wiggins & Trapnell, 1996). In this view the meaningful "interpersonal dispositions" of the person are in the service of meeting these social motives and can be depicted in an interpersonal circumplex space along the orthogonal dimensions of dominance-submissiveness and love-hate.

An interesting extension of these ideas is that the unit of analysis is not individual behavior but rather human transactions at the level of dyad or group (Kiesler, 1996). Thus, for example, the way in which persons view themselves, what we typically define as the self, can only be understood in terms of the acted-out claims that a person places on others with regard to the kinds of reactions or acknowledgement the person wants others to provide. These ideas are well illustrated in the writings of Paul Wachtel, who has focused on cyclical processes in psychopathology. Wachtel (1994) notes that people behave in ways that draw predictable responses from other people; in effect, the person shapes the interpersonal environment. As the interpersonal environment changes, so to does the psychological state of the individual. For Wachtel, "internal states and external events continually recreate the conditions for the reoccurrence of each other" (1994, p. 51). More recently, Cantor and Kihlstom (1987) have offered the term "skewed interactionism" to capture the idea that personality structures and processes have a greater impact on social situations than social situations have on personality (see also Swann, 1985).

CONVERGENT INTERESTS

In the late 1970s and continuing to the present, the cognitive revolution has swept through the fields of social and personality psychology. Fiske (2003) cites Markus' (1977) paper on self-schema and Cantor and Mischel's (1977) paper on prototypes in person perception as among a small group of papers that triggered the field of social cognition. Social psychologists now had metaphors and paradigms for studying what was going on in the head of the individual during persuasion attempts, interracial interactions, social comparisons, and the like and could address more precisely the reciprocal effects of the social situation and the individual.

The cognitive wave also washed over the field of personality. In describing interactional perspectives on personality, Wachtel (1994) stated that they "concern themselves with persistent individual differences, but the emphasis in the cyclical version is on the process that maintains these differences" (p. 53). Again, the importation of theory and research paradigms from cognitive psychology has been hugely important because the processes of greatest interest to personality researchers are most often those going on inside the head of the individual. Cantor (1990) describes three types of units—schemas, tasks, and strategies—as constituting the cognitive substrate of personality. It is an analysis of these units in social context that occupies most of the authors contributing to this volume.

Perhaps the cognitive approach to personality process is best illustrated by Mischel's (Mischel & Shoda, 1999: Wright & Mischel, 1987) definition of dispositions as if-then contingencies for behavior in specific situations. This notion has been particularly generative and is being applied to an increasingly broad set of topics within personality and social psychology. For example, Baldwin (Baldwin, 1997; Baldwin & Sinclair, 1996) has described the "relational self" as a set of cognitive representations of the person as he or she is in specific relationships with others. These representations are in the form of if-then contingencies such as "if with mom, then be dependent." This approach contextualizes the self so that it changes as a function of the relational context. This view of the relational self has been used to frame Andersen's (Andersen & Chen, 2002; Andersen, Saribay, & Kooij, this volume) social cognitive model of transference.

More recently, Murray, Holmes, and Collins (2006) have applied the if-then contingency framework in their risk-regulation system in close relationships. They propose that in balancing the goal of closeness with a romantic partner against the goal of avoiding rejection and hurt, the risk regulation system is engaged. This system is comprised of three interconnected if-then contingency rules involving cognitive, affective, and behavioral responses to perceptions of the partner's behavior, particularly the partner's regard. One of the appealing aspects of this model is that it accommodates individual differences in risk regulation and allows for a contextualized understanding of relationship viability. Rholes, Paetzold, and Friedman (this volume) cast attachment theory's notion of working models of self and others as relational if-then schemas that have different specifics as a function of having secure versus insecure attachment styles.

The examples provided above are but a few of many that illustrate what I believe to be the convergence of personality and social psychology at the social behavior interface. As one final illustration, the reader is reminded of how often one encounters in our best journals what might be called the prototypical three-study package. The first study demonstrates the phenomenon of interest; the second manipulates the putative independent variables; and the third is a replication of the second, in which an individual difference measure is substituted for the manipulated variable. For example, a paper might report that people perform more poorly in the presence of an audience and speculate that self-awareness is the causative factor. Then Study 2 shows that a manipulation of self-awareness produces the effects on performance observed in Study 1, and Study 3 shows the individual difference measure of self-consciousness moderates the performance effects. This research strategy has become ubiquitous in the social psychology research literature, such is the convergence of personality and social psychology.

THE CURRENT VOLUME

The chapters included in this volume chronicle the multiple ways in which the interplay between attributes of the person and features of the interpersonal context can be conceptualized and investigated. Rather than provide a collection of chapters reporting research on individual differences that have been related in one way or another to social situations, the goal was to draw on work from both social psychology and personality that focuses on the processes by which the person and situation transact with one another. Regardless of whether their primary identification was in the area of personality or social psychology, contributors were asked to think about their work simultaneously in intraindividual and interpersonal terms. They were asked to discuss how individual differences serve as markers for differences in cognitive, motivational, emotional, behavioral, and interpersonal processes.

Several chapters begin with what may considered traditional topics in personality. Cervone, Caldwell, and Orom trace the evolution of the field since the person-situation debate erupted in the 1970s. Cervone et al. extend the Mischel and Shoda (1995) approach to dispositional constructs by elaborating on the cognitive mechanisms and processes that underlie the if-then dispositional framework. Rhodewalt and Peterson place self-esteem, a classic topic in personality, in an interpersonal context. They present a dynamic process model of self-esteem that specifies the way in which individuals interact with others for the purposes of self-esteem regulation. Rholes et al. take another classic personality construct, attachment style, and describe a broad program of research that illuminates the ways in which self and other schema translate into interpersonal behaviors that channel relationship satisfaction. And finally, Andersen et al. return to the issue of contextual influences on personality through their analysis of social cognitive, affective, and behavioral processes illustrated in transference effects.

A second set of chapters begins with what may be considered a set of topics traditionally associated with social psychology. Michael Hogg tackles the problem of the friction between social identity theory's focus on group behavior, intergroup relations and the context-dependent *collective self* and the traditional personality position of stable, context-free dispositions. He traces developments in both social identity theory and the way that personality is now conceptualized and suggests areas for future integrations. Leadership has been a daunting topic to both personality and social psychologists. Fiedler's (1967) contingency model of leadership was arguably one of the first person-situation interaction models found in psychology. Martin Chemers, a protégé of Fiedler's, expands on this early work to describe leadership as a bidirectional, dynamic process unfolding between leaders and group members. Prejudice is another subject that has been approached from both personality and social psychology perspectives. Devine et al. review Devine's work on individual differences in the motivation to control prejudice and outline the cognitive, affective, and behavioral processes that shape interracial interactions.

Two very provocative chapters link personality processes and social behavior to emerging areas in psychology. Downey, Zaki, and Mitchell lay out the implications and cautions offered by taking a social cognitive neuroscience approach to the study of personality and social behavior. They call for additional combinations of behavioral and neuroimaging studies to more fully understand how personality dispositions reflect the basic set of social-cognitive tools that people bring to contextualized interactions with other people. The field of health psychology has grown rapidly in the past quarter century. Central to this growth have been attempts to connect personality to physical well-being. In their chapter, Uchino, Vaughn, and Matwin explore the connections among personality, social behavior, and physical health.

In total, the set of essays included in this volume represents a broad but far from exhaustive sampling of the exciting advances being realized as a result of the convergence of personality and social psychology.

REFERENCES

Adler, A. (1927). *The practice and theory of individual psychology*. New York: Harcourt, Brace, Jovanovich.

Andersen, S. M., & Chen, S. (2002). The relational self: An interpersonal social-cognitive theory. *Psychological Review, 109*, 619–645.

Baldwin, M. W. (1997). Relational schemas as a source of if-then self-inference procedures. *Review of General Psychology, 1*, 326–335.

Baldwin, M. W., & Sinclair, L. (1996). Self-esteem and "if...then" contingencies of interpersonal acceptance. *Journal of Personality and Social Psychology, 71*, 1130–1141.

Bandura, A. (1986). *Social foundations of thought and action*. Englewood Cliffs, NJ: Prentice Hall.

Cantor, N. (1990). From thought to behavior: "Having" and "doing" in the study of personality and cognition. *American Psychologist, 45*, 735–750.

Cantor, N., & Kihlstrom, J. F. (1987). *Personality and social intelligence*. Englewood Cliffs, NJ: Prentice Hall.

Cervone, D. (2004). The architecture of personality. *Psychological Review, 111*, 183–204.

Digman, J. M. (1990). Personality structure: Emergence of the five-factor model. *Annual Review of Psychology, 41*, 417–440.

Endler, N. S., & Magnusson, D. (1976). Toward an interactional psychology of personality. *Psychological Bulletin, 83*, 956–974.

Fiedler, F. E. (1967). *A theory of leadership effectiveness.* New York: McGraw-Hill.
Fiske, S. T. (2003). The discomfort index: How to spot a really good idea whose time has come. *Psychological Inquiry, 14,* 203–208.
Freud, S. (1925). *Collected papers, Vol. 2.* London: Institute for Psychoanalysis and Hogarth Press.
Goldberg, L. R. (1993). An alternative "description of personality": The big-five factor structure. *Journal of Personality and Social Psychology, 59,* 1216–1229.
Kiesler, D. J. (1996). *Contemporary interpersonal theory and research: Personality, psychopathology, & psychotherapy.* New York: Wiley.
Mischel, W. (1968). *Personality and assessment.* New York: Wiley.
Mischel, W., & Shoda, Y. (1996). A cognitive-affective system theory of personality: Reconceptualizing situations, dispositions, dynamics, and invariance in personality structure. *Psychological Review, 102,* 246–286.
Mischel, W., & Shoda, Y. (1999). Integrating traits and processing dynamics with a unified theory of personality. The cognitive-affective personality system. In L. Pervin & O. P. John (Eds.), *Handbook of personality: Theory and research* (pp. 197–218). New York: Guilford.
Murray, S. L., Holmes, J. G., & Collins, N. L. (2006). Optimizing assurance: The risk regulation system in relationships. *Psychological Bulletin, 132,* 641–666.
Myers, D. (2007). *Social psychology* (8th ed.). New York: McGraw-Hill.
Pervin, L. (1996). *The science of personality.* New York: Wiley.
Pincus, A., & Wiggins, J. S. (1992). An expanded perspective on interpersonal assessment. *Journal of Counseling and Development, 71,* 91–94.
Smith, T. W., & Rhodewalt, F. (1986). On states, traits, and processes: A transactional alternative to the individual difference assumptions in Type A behavior and physiological reactivity. *Journal of Research in Personality, 20,* 229–251.
Sullivan, H. S. (1953). *The interpersonal theory of psychiatry.* New York: Norton.
Swann, W. B. (1985). The self as architect of social reality. In B. Schlenker (Ed.), *The self and social life* (pp. 100–125). New York: McGraw-Hill.
Swann, W. B., & Selye, C. (2005). Personality psychology's comeback and its emerging symbiosis with social psychology. *Personality and Social Psychology Bulletin, 31,* 155–165.
Wachtel, P. (1994). Cyclical processes in personality and psychopathology. *Journal of Abnormal Psychology, 103,* 51–54.
Wiggins, J. S., & Pincus, A. (1994). Personality structure and the structure of personality disorders. In P. Costa & T. Wideger (Eds.), *Personality disorders and the five-factor model of personality* (pp.73–93). Washington, DC: American Psychological Association.
Wiggins, J. S., & Trapnell, P. D. (1996). A dyadic-interactional perspective on the five-factor model. In J. S. Wiggins (Ed.), *The five-factor model of personality: Theoretical perspective.* (pp. 88–162). New York: Guilford.
Wright, J., & Mischel, W. (1987). A conditional approach to dispositional constructs: The local predictability of social behavior. *Journal of Personality and Social Psychology, 53,* 1159–1177.

2

Beyond Person and Situation Effects:
Intraindividual Personality Architecture and Its Implications for the Study of Personality and Social Behavior

DANIEL CERVONE
University of Illinois at Chicago
TRACY L. CALDWELL
North Central College
HEATHER OROM
Karmanos Cancer Institute and Institute of Gerontology, Wayne State University

The study of personality and social behavior, as conducted by card-carrying personality and social psychologists, historically has been sustained by a narrative familiar to all. As in many classic tales, there are three characters: There are persons; there are situations; and there are social behaviors. The plot is a whodunit: Who—or perhaps "what"—caused those social behaviors? Was it the persons? Or—unbeknownst to the naive, unsuspecting persons—was it the situations?

The story has been sustaining in three respects. When theoretical paradigms pose questions that are simple, it is easy to formulate theory-driven research. To evaluate person versus situation causes, all one needs to do is round up some persons, classify them according to some commonly accepted dimension of variation, observe their behavior in different situations, and see if variation in social behavior is relatively predictable from variations among persons or among situations.

In addition to ease, the narrative has heightened interest in the field, thanks primarily to a dramatic turn in the plot. People appeared to be in peril! Variations among persons seemed to leave more than 90% of the total variance in social behavior unexplained (Mischel, 1968).

Finally, sustenance has been derived from a third feature of the story: a happy ending. The cavalry arrived with more data, and persons were saved. Person effects were not only detectable, but equal in size to situation effects (e.g., Funder & Ozer, 1983). Personality psychologists and social psychologists could rest secure in the knowledge that "situation and disposition are about equally effective in predicting behavior" (Baumeister, 1999, p. 368).

Like other classic stories, this one is still told. One might have guessed that the widespread acceptance of person-situation interactionism would have brought the telling to an end. However, as Funder has noted, it "is something of a mystery...everybody is an interactionist. Still, the argument persists" (Funder, 2006, p. 22).

Here in a handbook of personality and social behavior, this persistent story about the relative size of person and situation effects should be scrutinized. Its conclusions and, perhaps more importantly, the presuppositions made in formulating questions about which conclusions could be drawn are fundamental to many issues: the interpretation of research findings, the formulation of novel research, the relation between social and personality psychology, and the nature of situations and persons.

OVERVIEW: PERSONALITY ARCHITECTURE AND ITS IMPLICATIONS

We thus begin our chapter by revisiting this story and considering some potential rewritings. This opening section (immediately below) is itself a preamble to the main story that we ourselves wish to tell. We advance an alternative perspective on personality and social behavior, specifically, a perspective that features a conception of personality that is an alternative to the one that is embedded within the traditional narrative and that was particularly prominent in personality psychology in the latter two decades of the century past. We outline that perspective here.

Much past work in personality psychology has embraced a conception of personality that has two defining features: (a) Persons are construed in terms of behavioral tendencies, or dispositions; a "personality variable" is a construct that describes what people tend to do, and (b) persons are conceptualized using constructs that are global; that is, personality constructs refer to generic, situation-free attributes of persons. Combining the two points yields a conception in which personality is a collection of situation-free tendencies to display a certain class of behavior. Recent writing conveys the position clearly: "A person...can be thought of as the sum total of all of his or her behaviors" (Funder, 2006, p. 31), and "a definitive task for personality psychology" is to identify "broader traits" that capture "behavioral invariance or behavioral consistency...irrespective of the situation" (Funder, 2006, p. 26).

Both of these features are severely limiting if one wants to construct a science of persons (Cervone & Mischel, 2002). If one defines persons merely as "sum totals of behaviors," one fails to capture the distinction between persons and non-persons (cats, dogs, zombies...) who also behave (cf. Gosling & John, 1999). If one defines personality psychology as the study of what people do irrespective of the situations they encounter, one removes personality psychology from the broader science of psychology, whose findings repeatedly document that psychological systems can be understood only if one refrains from computing situation-free averages and instead examines the functioning of persons in context (e.g., Kagan, 2003, 2007).

The alternative, then, is the following. It is to base an understanding of personality on the study of the human mind (cf. Kelly, 1955). We strive to understand personality and social behavior by exploring the mental systems—the social-cognitive and affective structures and processes—that contribute to the coherent and distinctive patterns of experience and action that are the hallmarks of personality. Our overall effort is grounded in a conceptual model of these intra-individual cognitive and affective systems, or a model of personality architecture (Cervone, 2004a).

In this alternative, people are not aggregates of behavior. They are self-reflective agents who possess a mental architecture that enables them to plan courses of action, to self-regulate their behavior and emotions, to acquire knowledge and skills, and thereby to contribute to the course of their development (Bandura, 2006; Caprara & Cervone, 2000, 2003). People are not understood by positing personality variables that function irrespective of context. Instead, one understands personality by studying persons *in* context, for the reasons explained by Lewin long ago: Scientific understanding (of persons or of other complex entities) does not progress by positing abstract "Aristotelian" qualities that correspond to what things tend to do on average; it progresses by elucidating enduring structures and dynamic processes whose functioning can be understood only by examining how an entity interacts with its surrounding environment (Lewin, 1935; also see Cervone, 2006).

In grounding the study of personality and social behavior in the study of intra-individual personality architecture, we are not alone. As Kuhl and colleagues have noted, "there exists a new breed of theories of *personality architecture*, which analyze the mental systems that shape the individual's enduring, distinctive patterns of experience and action" (Kuhl, Kazén, & Koole, 2006, p. 409). Numerous investigators contribute to the development of models of personality architecture (e.g., Cloninger, 2004; Kuhl & Koole, 2004; Matthews, Schwean, Campbell, Saklofske, & Mohamed, 2000; Mischel 1973, 2004; Mischel & Shoda, 1995, 1998; Morf & Rhodewalt, 2001). This new breed of theories is an exciting development for those who seek a truly integrated personality and social psychology. Once one construes personality in terms of the intra-individual architecture of cognitive and affective systems, personality psychologists and social psychologists become true partners in the explanation of behavior. The social psychologist's models of affect and social cognition directly inform the personality psychologist's quest to understand personality systems and their coherence (see Higgins, 1999).

REWRITING THE NARRATIVE

Let us reconsider our opening narrative as a means of airing conceptual issues that surely recur throughout this volume. Our opening story about persons, situations, and the relative size of their effects on social behavior may elicit objections of two types.

Rewriting the Ending: The Relative Size of Person and Situation Effects

Some may object to the happy ending. Objections could come from either direction. "No, no," some might argue, "person and situation effects are not equal; situation effects really are bigger." A well-known basis for the claim of equality, a comparison of situation effect sizes in classic social psychology experiments to person effect sizes in personality-and-prediction studies (Funder & Ozer, 1983), could be turned on its head. As Ross and Nisbett (1991) have explained, in many classic social psychological studies investigators did not try to maximize effect sizes. They tried to maximize the subtlety of manipulations and unexpectedness of results while obtaining effects that merely reached standard significance levels. In personality psychology, in contrast, bigger person effects are the "coin of the realm" (Bem & Allen, 1974, p. 512); no one drops an item from a personality scale because the item's predictive strength is unsurprising. The comparison of person and situation effect sizes (Funder & Ozer, 1983), then, is not so much a comparison of apples to oranges as apples to Palm™ Pilots: It's nice the farmer could get the one to be so big; it's surprising the engineer could get the other one to be so powerful while keeping it small; oh, and they happen to be about the same size.

"No," others might contend, "person effects really are bigger." In naturally-occurring circumstances, a highly significant person effect is that people choose environments they encounter. Standard research paradigms do not detect this phenomenon. In laboratory experiments, people are assigned to situations at random. In observational studies, people often are observed across a set of situations that is fixed (e.g., Mischel & Peake, 1982). These procedures are necessary to some scientific goals. Yet they deflect attention from a potentially large "person effect" by giving people no say in the situations they encounter or in which they are observed. Our databases thus may systematically underestimate the effects of persons by reducing their role in the selection of situations. This underestimation could be severe; persons sometimes select themselves into long-lasting situations that can alter personal attributes enduringly. If people choose to enroll in a socially liberal college to expand their horizons, they encounter, year upon year, social situations and reference groups that may enduringly affect their basic value systems (Newcomb, 1952/1965).

This last example raises a broader question: Maybe, through mislabeling, situations are getting credit for person effects. If the situation "liberal college" shifts one's values but one has chosen to expose oneself to this situation, with the choice partly determined by one's enduring personal attributes, might the shift not be called a person effect? Investigators who equate person effects with stability in personal attributes may underestimate the effects of persons. For example, in developing mathematically formal models of the stability of inter-individual differences, Fraley and Roberts (2005) aptly note that, "the environmental influences that come to influence the person are caused, in part, by the person" (p. 64) but add that "To the extent to which such transactions take place, the effect of the environment on the person is likely to sustain existing psychological qualities" (p. 65). Based on this reasoning, they construct a system of linear equations in which the "pathway...from the person to the environment...represents the effect that the person has on shaping, selecting, or influencing his or her environment in ways that are consistent with the preexisting psychological quality" (p. 66, emphasis added). What about—the defender of person effects may ask—people's potential to select environments that are inconsistent with their preexisting qualities: to enroll in the military to toughen one's weak self; to travel to become more open to experiences; to engage in meditative practice to lessen one's anxieties; to hire a life coach to become more conscientious? Putting "potentials" back into personality psychology (Caprara & Cervone, 2000) expands one's conception of person effects.

Deconstructing the Narrative

The above objections accepted the overall story structure, questioning only its conclusions. The narrative still depicted a person-versus-situation contest for a slice of behavioral-variance pie. The objections questioned merely whether the "situation and disposition" pieces really are "about equally" (Baumeister, 1999, p. 368) large. An alternative objection would question the entire storyline by examining its presuppositions. What is logically entailed in asking about the relative size of person and situation effects?

Any discussion of the relative magnitude of person, situation, and interactive person-x-situation effects presupposes that there exist such things as "person effects" and "situation effects." That is, it presupposes that one can discuss situation-independent persons and their effects as well as person-independent situations and their effects. At the level of theory, to pit persons versus situations one must posit person constructs that are defined independently of situations and situational constructs defined independently of any persons. If person constructs include situational components—e.g., if one explains social behavior by reference to cognitive schemas that are representative of one versus another sociocultural context and that are activated by situational cues (Wong & Hong, 2005)—then it makes no sense to discuss pure person effects that compete with pure situation influences in a variance-pie eating contest. Person and situation factors become collaborators, rather than competitors, in the prediction or explanation of behavior.

What Are the Situation-Free Attributes of Persons? At first glance, this two-sided assumption—pure persons, pure situations—may not appear problematic. Our normal conception of a person does not inherently include any situations. One can easily imagine situations with no persons in them. Problems do arise, however, when one gets down to details. What personal attributes can be conceptualized in a situation-free manner? That is, for what psychological attributes of persons can one reasonably posit constructs that make no reference whatsoever to situations?[1]

In response to this question, consider the range of psychological attributes people generally are thought to have. A typical list would include desires, motives, interests, and goals; beliefs, attitudes, preferences, and evaluative standards (i.e., criteria used to evaluate the goodness of entities or occurrences); and skills and competencies. One might add traits, but that would not change the list substantively if traits are defined to include "attitudes, interests, and other more or less stable psychological characteristics" (de Raad, 2005, p. 185). The question then is: Which of these attributes can be defined in a situation-free manner? That is, for which can one posit constructs that are entirely situation-free? Not desires, motives, interests, or goals. These refer not to isolated attributes of a person, but to the person plus something else: the aim of the desire, interest, or goal. It makes no sense to say "I desire [period]" or "I have a goal, but not to do or get any thing." Not beliefs, attitudes, and standards. Attitudes are attitudes *about*, beliefs are beliefs *in*, and standards are criteria for evaluating *some thing*. If one eliminates "the thing," the construct loses its meaning. One cannot "just believe" without believing something. The general point is that these personal attributes have the quality of intentionality (e.g., Searle, 1983); that is, they are directed entities in the world (including oneself as an object in the world). Finally, not skills and competencies. Kagan (2007) explains that to understand competencies one must focus a Wittgenstein lens on concrete cases rather than engage in Platonic speculation about abstract, context-free essences that are hidden from view. This focus reveals the role of context. This is true even for simple competencies. Children's ability to categorize objects presented visually is inherently context-linked "because the child's perceptual schemata for many objects/events (in contrast to their semantic representations) represent the object together with its usual settings" (p. 4). For complex socially-acquired skills, the need for person-in-context constructs is only more obvious (Cantor & Kihlstrom, 1987).

It would be a mistake to conclude that only those who embrace a "social" or "cognitive" (or some mixture of those words) orientation to personality require contextualized person constructs. Research on biological foundations of personality and individual differences similarly requires constructs that embed persons in situations. An understanding of temperament requires that one construe temperament contextually (Kagan, 2003) and consider cultural factors in the development of temperament and social behavior (Fox, Henderson, Marshall, Nichols, & Ghera, 2005). The search for evolved mechanisms that subserve social behavior features context- or domain-linked constructs and research strategies (Sugiyama et al. 2002). Toulmin (1985) has explained that it was Darwinian principles that shifted scientists' attention from timeless context-free laws to historically contingent relations between organisms and environments. More recently, Costall (2004) explains that Darwinian principles imply organism–environment "mutuality," where "mutuality is most emphatically *not* 'interactionism'" (p. 191). The conception is not of separate, encapsulated organisms and environments that occasionally bump into each other. One can distinguish organisms from environments, of course, but the "distinction...presupposes their relation, just as riverbeds and rivers, and beaten-paths and walkers imply one another's existence" (Costall, 2004, p. 191).

Other approaches lead similarly to the conclusion that psychological functioning cannot meaningfully be divorced from social context. Research and theory by McAdams and colleagues (McAdams, 2006; McAdams, Diamond, de St. Aubin, & Mansfield, 1997) highlight the role in personality functioning of life stories, that is, personally constructed narratives that integrate aspects of the self with socioculturally situated events from the past as well as goals for the future. Life stores are attributes of persons, yet they inextricably combine the personal, interpersonal, and situational. Hermans' (1996, 2001) dialogical approach to personality dynamics recognizes that the inner mental life of even seemingly isolated individuals consists heavily of multi-voiced dialogues in which people adopt different narrative positions. As a result, "the form of an interpersonal relationship" is used to study "the inner world of one and the same individual" (Hermans, 1996, p. 32). Finally, work inspired by the later writings of Wittgenstein (1953, 1980) on language, social action, and the philosophy of psychology (e.g., Geertz, 2000; Hacker, 1996; Harré, 2002; Harré & Tissaw, 2005; Toulmin, 1985) reminds one that much of mental life is the production of flows of thought using linguistic symbols. Language acquisition, understanding, and production, in this view, is understood metaphorically as a "game," that is, a social activity featuring rules that are shared by a community of participants. The meaning of words and sentences—even when they are spoken to oneself—resides in their shared social usages. There is the little room for an asocial mental life. "A *mental process* can be called 'mental' at all," Toulmin (1985, p. 18) summarizes, "only if it is called into play on relevant occasions as one element in a constellation of activities that manifest human mindedness." Such thinking deeply questions psychology's tendency to begin theorizing about persons and social behavior by typing the word "person" onto a computer screen and then placing an encapsulating box around it.

Where then did our field's story about situation-free person effects and person-free situation effects originate? Is determining the separate contributions of "persons" versus "situations" to a psychological outcome simply a blunder, akin to determining the separate contributions of light versus shadow to the effect of a chiaroscuro painting? Is a story about situation-free persons and their effects a story about unicorns?

Things are not quite so bad. There exists one set of assumptions under which the computation of person and situation effects is sensible. Specifically, there are two distinct classes of referents for the word "personality" in the scientific literature in personality and social psychology (Cervone, 2005). Under one meaning of the term "person" or "personality," predicting overt social behavior via separate person and situation factors is at least sensible. Under the other, it is not.

ALTERNATIVE CONCEPTIONS OF PERSONALITY: INTER-INDIVIDUAL DIFFERENCES AND INTRA-INDIVIDUAL ARCHITECTURE

Like most words, the word personality can take on a various meanings. In the scientific literature on personality psychology, two have predominated. As a result, the field houses two sets of conceptual units of analysis that differ qualitatively. These alternative units of analysis are best suited to solving scientific problems that may be complementary, yet are distinct. In this sense, the professional field harbors "two disciplines" (Cervone, 1991). Any failure to grasp this distinction breeds confusion and misunderstanding in the study of personality and social behavior.

Inter-Individual Differences

For many personality psychologists, the primary target of empirical inquiry is inter-individual differences. Theoretical constructs are formulated by analyzing variations in personality styles in the population at large. In such work, it is most common that (a) as noted above, personality constructs describe average, or global, dispositional tendencies; (b) factor-analytic methods are used to identify primary dimensions of variation in these tendencies; and (c) five (Goldberg, 1993; John & Srivastava, 1999; McCrae & Costa, 1996) or six (Ashton et al., 2004) factors are required to summarize between-person differences. The resulting n-dimensional systems commonly are called a "personality structure" or "the structure of personality" (e.g., Ashton & Lee, 2005a, b; Digman, 1990; Paunonen et al., 1996; Wiggins & Pincus, 1992).

In this usage of the phrase personality structure, personality refers to ways in which people differ on average. Each personality construct—that is, each of the five or six constructs identified via factor analysis—refers to an aspect of variation in the population at large. Whatever one thinks of this approach to the study of personality—brilliant, bankrupt, or anything in between—it is critical to recognize what its constructs are and are not doing. They are summarizing differences among people. They are not modeling psychological structure in the head of an individual person or describing behavioral tendencies displayed by each of a series of individual persons. This is clarified by investigators who themselves advance this inter-individual differences tradition: "The lexical approach to personality structure [i.e., the approach to inter-individual differences that is grounded in the assumption that significant differences among persons are encoded in the natural-language lexicon as individual words] *makes no assumption about* the equivalence of interindividual and intraindividual structures...these structures might be rather different" (Ashton & Lee, 2005a, p. 16, emphasis added). In the inter-individual differences meaning of the term personality, then, one cannot assume that the "personality structures" are psychological structures within the psyche of any individual person.[2]

The n-dimensional inter-individual difference structures commonly are treated as taxonomies (John & Srivastava, 1999). Again, however, it is critical to recognize that the taxonomic structure is not a structure *of*, or *in*, the individual who is classified; the inter-individual differences structure is not a structural model in the sense that id/ego/superego is a structural model. The dimensions cannot be equated with the study of personality because they describe variations in the population, not mental entities in the head of each person. As Saucier, Hampson, and Goldberg (2002) explain, a lexical model of global personality attributes may yield "a useful and highly generalizable classification system for personality traits" but it "should not be reified...the study of personality lexicons should not be equated with a study of personality" (p. 28). This is not in any way a critique of taxonomic models such as the Big Five; it is simply a natural feature of any taxonomy for classifying entities. Individuals do not each possess the constructs that comprise a taxonomy. Taxonomically, a snake is a reptile and, at a higher level of classification, an animal, but "reptile" and "animal" are not things to be found in any given snake. Taxonomic constructs are nominal (Harré, 2002); they specify features that lead one versus another individual in a population of beings to be called one versus another type of thing. Taxonomic constructs are not simultaneously models of the inner workings of each individual being who is classified.

Intra-Individual Personality Architecture

The other meaning of personality is one that does, quite explicitly, reference intra-individual structure. Indeed, in this second meaning of the term, personality refers to intra-individual structure and dynamics, or personality architecture (Cervone, 2004a).

Although the term "personality architecture" may be new, the substantive scientific focus is not. When scholars of the early-mid 20th century crafted comprehensive theories of personality, the central phenomenon about which they were theorizing was not variation in the population in average dispositional tendencies. It was the organization of personality structures and dynamics in the head of the individual. It was only in the second half of the century, with the advent of computer-based factor analyses of inter-individual differences, that the primary referent for the word personality became between-person variation (see Kagan, 2002). In the old days, the target of investigation was the individual. That "the objects of study are individual organisms, not aggregates of organisms" is the first proposition—"Primary Proposition" "A.1."—in the classic work of Murray and colleagues (Murray, 1938, p. 38). The theories of Freud (1923) and Lewin (1935) were quite obviously meant to model intra-individual mental dynamics, not dimensions of variation in the population. The reason that the models of Freud and Lewin look nothing like the Big Five model (e.g., Goldberg, 1993) is not that the older theorists lacked computer programs for running factor analysis; it is that they were studying an entirely different topic: intra-individual mental structure and dynamics.

Personality psychology has recently seen a resurgence of interest in its original mission (Swann & Selye, 2005). Numerous investigators in personality psychology and beyond contribute to the understanding of intra-individual personality architecture (see Cervone, 2005; Cervone & Mischel, 2002; Mischel, 2004). Theoretical analyses have advanced in a two-pronged line of attack. Some theorists have provided broad principles within which specific explanatory models of personality functioning could then be formulated. Others have capitalized on these foundations while providing specific explanatory models of one or more aspects of personality functioning, development, and individual differences. This two-step approach is natural to the sciences. Scientific explanation generally is achieved by identifying general principles that guide inquiry in an area of investigation and then formulating specific conceptual models of the structures or systems that underlie, and generate, observed phenomena of interest (Harre, 2002; Giere, 1999; Morgan & Morrison, 1999).

General Principles: Cognitive and Affective Systems and Their Expressions. An encouraging sign for the study of personality construed the old fashioned way, as the study of intra-individual personality architecture, is that there exists much consensus at the level of broad principles. Numerous writers view personality as a complex dynamical system (e.g., Carver & Scheier, 2002; Cloninger, 2004; Dimaggio & Semerari, 2006; Kuhl & Koole, 2004; Morf & Rhodewalt, 2001; Nowak & Vallacher, 1998; Read & Miller, 2002). An exceptionally generative systems formulation is the Cognitive-Affective Personality Systems (CAPS) model of Mischel and Shoda (1995, 1998; also see Mischel, 2004; Shoda, Cervone, & Downey, in press). The CAPS model views the individual as a complex system of psychological processes that function within distinct, but highly interconnected, cognitive and affective subsystems (Metcalfe & Mischel, 1999).

An implication of the CAPS model that is crucial for understanding personality and social behavior is its construal of dispositional tendencies. The question being addressed is: What is the nature of the distinctive and enduring behavioral tendencies that distinguish persons from one another? As Mischel and Shoda emphasize, once the individual is construed as a dynamic cognitive–affective system, there is no reason whatsoever to limit the notion of disposition or trait to average, mean-level behavioral tendencies. For any complex system, the system's properties may be revealed in *patterns* of behavior displayed over time and context. Mean level of behavior, aggregated across some set of times and contexts, is just one parameter through which the system can be described. Other descriptions may be equally or more informative.

This abstract point is supported concretely by a wealth of research. In everyday social behavior, patterns of variation around the mean are temporally stable; these stable patterns are distinctive signatures of an individual's personality (Mischel, 2004; Mischel & Shoda, 1995). The findings of Mischel, Shoda and colleagues are complemented by numerous lines of research that similarly document the importance of parameters of personality other than the mean (Eid & Langeheine, 2004; Fleeson, 2001; Fleeson & Leicht, 2006; Moskowitz & Zuroff, 2005; Vansteelandt & Van Mechelan, 2004). In light of these developments, the belief that "the most fundamental problem of the field" (Goldberg, 1993, p. 26) is to identify constructs that describe mean-level tendencies now appears not only arbitrary but potentially detrimental in that it deflects attention from much that is interesting about persons.

Intra-Individual Structure and Dynamics: A Knowledge-and-Appraisal Personality Architecture (KAPA). In addition to guiding principles, the study of intra-individual personality structure and dynamics requires well-specified models. One needs a theoretically-grounded, comprehensive system of personality structure and process variables. Such a variable system would serve as a heuristic guide for assessing intra-individual personality architecture and explaining personality consistency, coherence, and change. Note that one cannot meet this need by importing the trait variables identified in factor analyses of variation in the population; on psychometric grounds, these between-person factors cannot be assumed to function as causal psychological structures at the level of the individual (Borsboom, Mellenberg, & van Heerden, 2003).

One of us recently has attempted to meet this challenge by providing a theoretical system of intra-individual personality structure and dynamics. This system builds on past efforts in the social-cognitive tradition in personality psychology (Cervone & Shoda, 1999), especially the work of Bandura (1986, 1999), Mischel (1973; 2004), Dweck and colleagues (Dweck & Leggett, 1988; Grant & Dweck, 1999, 2003), Cantor and Kihlstrom (1987), Markus and colleagues (Markus, 1977; Markus & Wurf, 1987), and Higgins (1996, 1999). The result is a conceptual model referred to as a *Knowledge-and-Appraisal Personality Architecture* (KAPA; Cervone, 2004a).

The KAPA model distinguishes among intra-individual personality variables via three conceptual principles. The first, noted above, is the principle of *intentionality*. Some mental contents do, and others do not, possess a feature that philosophers refer to as intentionality: the internal mental content is directed beyond oneself to objects in the world (Searle, 1983). Propositional knowledge has this quality; propositions refer to something beyond themselves. For example, if one is feeling tired and thinks, "I'll get a cup of coffee," the proposition about the coffee and any associated mental imagery are internal mental states, but they refer beyond oneself to an entity in the world. In contrast, feelings states such as moods or "core affect" (Russell, 2003) do *not* have the quality of intentionality. For example, the sheer feeling of being "tired" does not, in and of itself, refer to the outer world; one can be tired without being tired about or of something. A fundamental distinction in modeling intra-individual personality variables, then, differentiates mental contents that do have the quality of intentionality from those that do not (Cervone, 2004a). Although this point may seem obvious, it is noteworthy that the variable systems in theories that originated in the study of inter-individual differences (e.g., McCrae & Costa, 1996) lack this basic distinction.

The other two principles (Cervone, 2004a) differentiate among attributes that do have the quality of intentionality, or are cognitive or social-cognitive. One differentiates between *knowledge* and *appraisal*. The distinction is drawn by Lazarus (1991) in his classic analyses of cognition and emotion. Lazarus explained that knowledge refers to "our understanding of the way things are and work" (Lazarus, 1991, p. 144). Knowledge then consists of enduring mental representations of persons or the physical or social world. In any given setting, however, actions and emotional experiences are based not on abstract stored knowledge, but on processes of meaning construction that occur within a given encounter. These meaning-construction processes are referred to as appraisals. In navigating day-to-day events, people engage in appraisals, that is, "continuing evaluation[s] of the significance of what is happening for one's personal well-being" (Lazarus, 1991, p. 144). People appraise whether and how encounters are significant to them and whether and how they can cope with them. In the KAPA model, appraisal processes are proximal determinants of experience and action, whereas knowledge structures are more distal determinants that influence emotion and action through their influence on appraisals.

The third principle differentiates among alternative forms of knowledge and of appraisal. Analyses in the philosophy of mind by Searle (1983, 1998) distinguish among mental propositions with different directions of fit. Some mental states either fit or do not fit a current state of the world; they are true versus false *beliefs*. Others represent the goal or intention to bring about a future state of the world; they are not currently true/false but become fulfilled when a future state of the world fits the current mental content. Finally, some mental contents of particular interest to the personality/social psychologist are neither true/false facts nor personal intentions but, instead, are criteria for evaluating the goodness or worth of an entity. In psychology, we commonly refer to these as evaluative standards (Bandura, 1986; Higgins, 1987). This third principle applies to both knowledge structures and appraisals processes, and in combination; the combination of these two principles thus yields a system of social-cognitive personality variables (Figure 2.1).

The KAPA model is a tool for moving from abstract declarations that persons and situations interact to concrete specifications of distinct psychological processes involved in such interactions. The model suggests four classes of processes

Intentional States with Alternative Directions of Fit

	BELIEFS	EVALUATIVE STANDARDS	AIMS/GOALS
APPRAISAL	Beliefs about one's Relation to an Encounter (e.g., self-efficacy appraisals)	Standards for Evaluating an Encounter (e.g., standards for evaluating ongoing performance)	Aims in an Encounter (e.g., intentions-in-action, personal goals during a task)
KNOWLEDGE	Beliefs about Oneself and the World (e.g., self-schemas, situational beliefs)	Standards for Evaluating Oneself and the World (e.g., ethical standards, criteria for self-worth)	Personal, Interpersonal, and Social Aims (e.g., personal goal systems)

Knowledge vs. Appraisal

Figure 2.1 The KAPA system of social-cognitive personality variables. In the variable system, the distinction among beliefs, evaluative standards, and aims holds at both the knowledge and the appraisal levels of intra-individual personality architecture, yielding six classes of social-cognitive variables; from Cervone, 2004a.

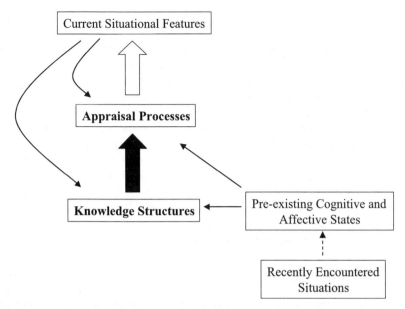

Figure 2.2 Schematic representation of relations among knowledge and appraisal mechanisms (indicated by a solid block arrow) and four classes of situational influence on knowledge-and-appraisal personality architecture (KAPA) mechanisms (indicated by smaller regular arrows) and of the influence of recently encountered situations on cognitive and affective states (indicated by a dashed arrow) that, in turn, may influence KAPA mechanisms. The open block arrow represents the assignment of personal meaning to situational features via appraisal processes; from Cervone, 2004a.

involving knowledge and appraisals (Figure 2.2). Two involve features of a current encounter. First, as long studied in the field of social cognition (e.g., Higgins, 1990; Markus & Wurf, 1987), current situational features activate enduring knowledge structures to which they are semantically linked. Second, situational features may prompt people to engage in certain types of appraisal processes; for example, if an encounter contains authority figures who may evaluate one's attainments, people are more likely to appraise the quality of their ongoing performance and their capacity to improve (Elliott & Dweck, 1988; Grant & Dweck, 1999; cf. Bandura & Cervone, 1983; Cervone, Jiwani, & Wood, 1991). The other two involve situations that have recently been encountered, rather than one's present circumstances. Recent encounters may activate knowledge or induce affective states that influence the knowledge that is most accessible in a subsequent encounter. Alternatively, past encounters may generate affects that directly influence subsequent appraisals (Lerner & Keltner, 2001; Schwarz & Clore, 1983; Scott & Cervone, 2002). Note that these are not the only forms of person–situation interaction in the KAPA model; situational features may activate affective systems through relatively non-cognitive routes (LeDoux, 1996), and the resulting affective states may, in turn, affect subsequent cognitive processing (Phelps, 2006).

Using the KAPA Model to Identify and Explain Cross-Situational Coherence. A task of defining interest to personality psychology is to identify and explain cross-situational coherence in psychological response (see, e.g., Allport, 1937). The KAPA model suggests an approach to this problem that differs fundamentally from most prior approaches and that, in so doing, illustrates the theme of this chapter. Traditionally, investigators have studied cross-situational consistency by selecting for study a global dispositional construct and gauging the degree to which people's actions, across distinct situations, are consistent with respect to this construct. This strategy implicitly pits person versus situations; one concludes that there is personality consistency to the degree to which the person attribute overrides the potential influence of situations. The KAPA strategy is entirely different. In the KAPA model, personality consistency is the result of psychological structures and processes that are inherently contextual. People possess enduring knowledge about aspects of the world and about themselves in that world, and these knowledge structures foster consistent patterns in people's appraisals of encounters.

Specifically, it is hypothesized that enduring beliefs about the self, or self-schemas (Markus, 1977), will come to mind and guide appraisal processes across multiple circumstances of an individual's life. An important aspect of this hypothesis is that the content of self-schemas and the circumstances in which any given schematic knowledge structure comes to mind may vary idiosyncratically. Idiographically-tailored methods thus are required to identify patterns of personality consistency that are potentially idiosyncratic.

In our research, open-ended assessment methods are used to tap the content of both self-schemas and situational beliefs, specifically, beliefs about the relevance of schematic attributes to everyday social contexts (see Cervone, 2004a, b). Subsequent to these assessments, we assess an aspect of self-appraisal that, we hypothesize, should be influenced by the personal and situational beliefs assessed earlier: appraisals of self-efficacy (Bandura, 1986) or appraisals of one's capability for performance in a given setting. Four aspects of our results (Cervone, 1997, 2004a; Cervone, Orom, Artistico, Shadel, & Kassel, 2007) are of note.

First, people display highly significant patterns of consistency in appraisal across diverse social situations. High and low self-efficacy appraisals are found across sets of situations that, in people's subjective construals of the world, are related to schematic positive and negative attributes they possess. Second, similar results are *not* obtained via nomothetic methods. People do not display significant cross-situational consistency in situations linked to generic, aschematic personality attributes (Cervone, 1997, 2004a). Third, the patterns of cross-situational coherence identified at the level of the individual often violate the structure of traditional inter-individual difference categories. People's situational- self-knowledge, and contextualized appraisals, may, for example, include beliefs that are semantically inconsistent with respect to a global trait category (e.g., people might possess the belief that they are hard working in some contexts and lazy and unreliable in others). Fourth, assessments at the knowledge level of the KAPA architecture predict not only the content of self-appraisals, but the speed of these appraisals. The speed with which people appraise their efficacy for coping with challenges varies significantly across situations in which schematic attributes earlier were judged to be an aid versus a hindrance to coping efforts (Cervone et al., in press).

Our initial research applying the KAPA model to the study of cross-situational coherence consisted of basic laboratory-based investigations that explored a diverse range of everyday social behaviors. An additional challenge is to apply the model to a specific domain in which, in the past, traditional assessment practices have proven to be insufficient for investigators' needs. One such domain is smoking. The study of smoking and cessation is particularly ripe for novel personality assessment methods because traditional methods commonly fail to predict outcomes of interest (Cervone, Shadel, Smith, & Fiori, 2006). For example, when Big Five constructs were related to seven smoking-related variables (e.g., motivation to quit, nicotine dependence, self-efficacy for quitting, indices of quitting history) in a sample of 130 regular smokers, four of the Big Five were completed uncorrelated with any smoking-related variables (i.e., all 28 correlations were nonsignificant), and the fourth (openness/intellect) exhibited only two significant correlations, both r's < .25 (Shadel, Cervone, Niaura, & Abrams, 2004).

Thus we have recently applied our idiographic, contextualized KAPA-based methods to personality assessment in the domain of smoking. We assess smokers' schematic self-knowledge, specifically, their beliefs about personal attributes that they possess that may be important to smoking and their efforts to quit. We also assess their beliefs about the relevance of these attributes to specific situations that, based on past research, are known to be high-risk circumstances for people trying to avoid relapse. Findings indicate these assessments of self-knowledge and situational beliefs robustly to predict intra-individual variation in self-efficacy for avoiding smoking across high-risk smoking-related situations (Figure 2.3; Cervone et al., 2007). Related work has provided experimental tests of the link from

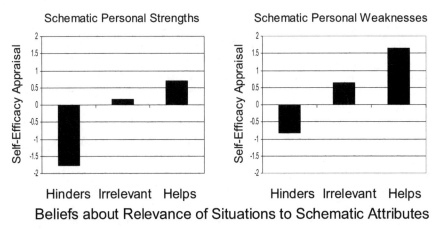

Figure 2.3 Mean levels of self-efficacy for avoiding smoking in high-risk situations, plotted as a function of self-knowledge (self-schemas involving attributes judged as personal strengths and as personal weaknesses) and situational knowledge (beliefs about the relevance of the given self-schema to abstinence efforts in the given situations: hinders, irrelevant, helps) among smokers who were motivated to quit; from Cervone et al., 2007.

knowledge structures to personality dynamics among smokers by priming alternative aspects of self-knowledge. Priming schematic self-knowledge alters smokers' appraisals of self-efficacy and their craving for cigarettes (Shadel & Cervone, in press). Our intra-individual conception of personality structure and dynamics thus enables significant predictions of health-relevant outcomes and yields insights into psychological mechanisms that contribute to smoking and cessation. Importantly, it does so in a domain in which an alternative perspective on personality—the classification of persons via global inter-individual difference variables—provides no insights into psychological dynamics and yields predictions that commonly are quite weak.

ALTERNATIVE CONCEPTIONS OF PERSONALITY: IMPLICATIONS FOR PERSON EFFECTS AND SITUATION EFFECTS

The Intra-Individual View

What are the implications of the alternative conceptions of personality—inter-individual and intra-individual—for the construal of person and situation effects? As should be apparent at this juncture, if by person one is referring to intra-individual personality structure and dynamics, then there are no pure person effects or pure situation effects. If one asks about the determinants of a given intentional act or set of acts engaged in by an individual person, then there are no situation-free personal qualities that cause the person's actions independently of the situation in which he or she acts and no situational influences that cause the actions independently of the individual's enduring personal qualities and dynamic here-and-now psychological processes. There also are no person-by-situation interactions in the traditional sense of the term, since the traditional statistical meaning of the term interactions presupposes pure person effects and pure situation effects and asks whether, in addition to these effects, there is an additional effect in which one main effect is dependent on another. From an intra-individual perspective, questions about pure person or situation effects dissolve. There is, instead, a synthetic interplay of the situational and the personal.

This synthesis of the situational and the personal results from two factors, either of which is sufficient to make the field's traditional discourse of "person effect size versus situation effect size" an inadequate grammar for understanding the social interactions of individual persons. These factors are highlighted above. First, people generally act on, and react emotionally to, the meaning they construct in a given encounter. Features of the encounter activate the cognitive structures that come into play in this process of meaning construction (2.2). Processes of meaning construction, then, cannot be considered as forces that explain behavior independent of context since the meaning-construction processes are themselves shaped by features of the social context. Second, even if (hypothetically) cognitions were to spring forth from one's head independently of situational influence, those cognitions have the quality of intentionality; that is, they refer to features of the environment. They thus cannot be conceptualized in a situation-free manner.

Some may lament this synthetic approach to the personal and the situational. It prevents one from formulating simple and broadly generalizable statements about person and situation effects (statements such as that the effects are about equal). If one views science as a search for such lawful generalities, then the perspective advanced here may be unwelcome. However, readers inclined toward this view should recall that a complex synthesis of the personal and the situational is demanded not only from an intra-individual psychological perspective, as pursued here, but from an analysis of intra-individual biological processes as well. Consider the role of genes in biological development. From a between-person perspective, one can partition the effects of genes and the environment. But if one inquires about an individual organism, this partitioning simply doesn't make sense. Genes do not influence development independently of the environment, such that one can compute the size of their independent effects. Biologists recognize that separating the effects of genes from the environment is like separating "the contributions of length and width to the area of a rectangle" (Ehrlich, 2000, p. 6). Rather than an old picture in which genes were portrayed as a program that determines development, research shows them to be "little more than puppets," with "the strings, telling the genes when and where to turn on or off" being pulled by "an assortment of proteins and, sometimes, RNA's" (Pennisi, 2001, p. 1064). Cells *"respond to environmental signals"* conveyed by hormones, growth factors, and other regulatory molecules" (Pennisi, 2001, p. 1064, emphasis added; also see Gottlieb, 1998).

Our basic thesis, then, is not merely that it is desirable to move beyond the computation of separate person versus situation effects. It is that one has no choice but to do so if person and its neighboring term, personality, refer to intra-individual personality structures and dynamics. The KAPA model (Cervone, 2004a) provides one set of tools for conceptualizing this interplay of the situational and the personal.

Views Complementary to the KAPA Model

Having stated this thesis and embedded it within the KAPA model of personality architecture, we should broaden our view by relating it to past and recent perspectives in personality and social psychology. Our provision of a model of person-in-situations—rather than persons *and* situations—surely is not unique (see, e.g., Smith & Rhodewalt, 1986). Yet it is surprisingly uncommon. Roberts and Pomerantz (2004) explain that although "the person and the situation are inseparable," in a wide variety of recent models of person–situation interaction they continue to be "treated as separate entities" (p. 413). We suggest that this is because of the persistent equation of personality with "what the person does on average." Once the term takes on this meaning, average dispositional tendencies, one is left with no conceptual tools for understanding the situationally embedded person. By computing the average, one sacrifices information about situational variability. By adopting dispositional constructs, one is left merely with descriptions of behavior rather than an explanatory model of the psychological functioning of the individual.

Though less common, the call for synthetic accounts of persons-in-situations has been sounded, loud and clear, in the past. Perhaps the loudest and clearest call was that of Mischel (1973). His provision of a set of social-cognitive person variables commonly is construed as a study of personality "processes" that can be aligned next to a study of trait "structures." But that reading vastly underestimates the goals and implications of Mischel's work. As his title indicated, Mischel (1973) was calling for a "reconceptualization of personality." In the alternative conceptualization, personality does not refer to what the person does on average. It refers, instead, to the enduring mental structures and dynamic psychological processes through which people interpret the world, interact with others, and plan and regulate their own experiences and actions. In this analysis of the mental life of the individual, there is no splitting of the person from the situation; the social-cognitive variables develop and function through interaction with the social world. Mischel (2005) recently has underscored this point, while judging that the persistent "person-situation split" has been "destructive to the building of a cumulative science of mind and social behavior."

A similar perspective is Bandura's (1978) principle of reciprocal determinism. In this formulation, which is foundational to Bandura's social cognitive theory of personality (1986, 1999), personal and situational factors are mutually determinative. Social behavior similarly is seen as influenced by, and as influencing, the nature of the person and the environments that he or she encounters.

In the study of personality development, Magnusson and colleagues have long provided a framework in which the personality and social behavior is understood in terms of "an integrated person–environment system" (Magnusson, 2003, p. 5). Magnusson's focus is similar to the KAPA model presented here in that Magnusson explicitly begins by analyzing the individual, rather than inter-individual differences (see, e.g., Magnusson & Törestad, 1993). The intra-individual focus eliminates the separateness of persons and situations.

The study of purposive behavior and "personal projects" by Little and colleagues (e.g., Little, 2004, in press) also dissolves the person/situation divide. A distinguishing feature of the personal projects approach is the unit of analysis through which social behavior is understood. Rather than positing separate person and situations factors, Little and colleagues study "how both person characteristics and situation characteristics... [interact] *within the single case* to determine what a person was negotiating in his life, or which direction she intended to take at the next important intersection" (Little, in press, p. x).

Shweder (2007) recently has provided a perspective on personality and social behavior that rids one of the person–situation split in a manner that is complementary to Mischel's (1973) earlier analysis. Shweder urges personality psychologists and social psychologists to replace their trait/situation vocabulary with a language of preferences and constraints. In this view, people are active agents who construct meaning in social encounters and act according to their goals and preferences. Action commonly is constrained by the opportunities available in the encounter or by norms that constrain certain behavioral options. This formulation lends itself readily to an analysis of meaning construction and personal agency, in the way that a language of average dispositional tendencies does not (Shweder, in press; also see Shweder & Sullivan, 1990).

Assessing Person and Situation Effects: Computations Based on an Inter-Individual Conception of Personality

Despite this range of arguments and findings, some investigators surely will persist in computing separate person and situation effects. It thus is important to assess these efforts. We will do so by asking two questions. First, does the computation of a separate "person effect" even make sense; that is, what can the word person mean for there to be an effect "of person" on social behavior that is independent of the effect of situations?

The computation of independent person effects is perfectly reasonable as long as one recognizes that, in these computations, the word person does not refer to the psychological experiences of any one person. It refers to classifications of differences between people. It is these between-person variations—not the personality dynamics of any individual person—that are the person effect in most studies of personality and social behavior. As long as one does not make the mistake of thinking that a person effect refers to the psychological life of any particular person, the literature is readily interpretable.

Since the semantics here are a bit unusual, an example is in order. On intuitive grounds, nothing could be more consequential for the life of a person than his or her social relationships. Relationships with friends, family, professional colleagues, romantic partners, etc. are integral to personal development (e.g., Park, 2004) and emotional life (e.g., Ayduk et al., 2000) and have long been the centerpiece of theories of personality (Sullivan, 1953). Asendorpf and Wilpers (1998) studied personality and social relations by assessing the nature of people's relationships—the experience of social conflict, of social support, of falling in love, etc.—over a period of 18 months. They found that although "personality affects... social relationships, relationships had no effect on personality" (Asendorpf & Wilpers, 1998, p. 1543). What could this mean? Is it possible that none of the 132 persons in this research was in any way affected psychologically by the experience of social conflict, of falling in love, etc.? Surely that can't be. As the investigators themselves were keenly aware, personality in this study does not refer to the inner mental life of any person. It refers to a taxonomic classification of differences among persons, specifically, the Big Five taxonomy. The ease with which one may inadvertently shift back and forth from one meaning of the term personality (a classification of inter-individual differences) to another (the psychological structure and dynamics of the individual) is apparent from these scientists' own writing. In their view, their null result "warns against" the "theoretical discussion of personality development [and] reciprocal effects" (Asendorpf & Wilpers, 1998, p. 1543) in the writing of theorists such as Magnusson (1990; cited by these authors as a prototypical dynamic interactionist). But these results have little if anything to do with the theoretical position of Magnusson. Magnusson (1990) quite explicitly views personality development as the study of "the individual as an organized whole, functioning as a totality" (p.

197) and judges that assessments of between-person factors such as the Big Five "make only limited contributions to an understanding of individual functioning" (p. 216). To Magnusson, the notion of personality, then, has little to do with the between-person variables assessed by Asendorpf and Wilpers (1998). These writers are employing alternative, inter- versus intra-individual referents for the term. If one fails to recognize this, one may be led by the ambiguity of the term personality to the inappropriate and frankly bizarre conclusion that the research findings indicate that "relationships [have] no effects on" (Asendorpf & Wilpers, 1998, p. 1543) the "functioning...[of] the individual as an organized whole (Magnusson, 1990, p. 197).

The second question is: What are the benefits and the limits of computing the magnitude of between-person effects, that is, computing the degree to which between-person classifications predict psychological outcomes? For many applied purposes, this form of research may be quite meritorious. Psychologists often are asked to classify individual differences in a manner that may enable members of society to predict psychological outcomes. If "any nonzero effect of a personality characteristic" in such applications is viewed as "a large effect in practical terms" (Ozer & Benet-Martinez, 2006, p. 416), then these applied efforts are bound to be seen as a success! However, there also are limits to this strategy. As Toulmin (1961) explained years ago, such predictions are not the heart of the scientific enterprise. Science seeks to understand phenomena, not merely to predict them, and prediction and understanding often fail to go hand-in-hand. It is here, in the effort to develop scientific understanding of the social behavior of individuals, that the limits of the between-person approach show.

These limits may be made clear by an analogy. Suppose one were interested in a personal attribute other than one involving personality, for example, physical attractiveness. One research strategy would be to classify people as being more or less physically attractive and to correlate the classifications with people's degree of success in various social contexts. If one calls the correlation a person effect, then surely the person effect will be nonzero. More attractive persons might be more successful not only in contexts such as "meeting people in bars" but in domains in which attractiveness might not be expected to play a role (cf. Dion, Berscheid, & Walster, 1972). But whatever the effect size, the approach has three limits: (a) One obtains no understanding of how or why physical attractiveness influences social outcomes. (b) One cannot conclude that there is any single process through which attractiveness influences social outcomes; although one computed a single person effect, it may reflect a multiplicity of different processes (e.g., automatic emotional responses, stereotype-driven thinking; deliberate calculated thinking) at the level of the individual in context. The finding thus provides no firm guidance for a subsequent search for underlying processes. (3) One cannot conclude that physical attractiveness itself is a unitary entity. Physical attractiveness may be, like SES, merely an index that summarizes diverse features, with different people who share no significant single physical attribute being classified as equally (un)attractive. The computation of a single effect size then in no way guarantees that attractiveness itself is a single thing, that is, a unitary physical entity that exerts a single type of effect.

These then are the limits of studying personality and social behavior by classifying people within global trait taxonomies and computing person effects: The approach (a) yields no understanding of the processes through which personal attributes influence social behavior, (b) is an unsure guide in the search for such processes because any single person effect, computed across multiple persons and settings, could reflect a multiplicity of such processes, and (c) does not enable one even to conclude that the personality attribute is a unitary quality at the level of the individual. On this last point, decisive data are available. Consider the two most prominent global trait variables: neuroticism and extraversion. Anxiety, a central feature of neuroticism, is not biologically unitary; instead, different brain regions are involved in anxious arousal during a task versus anticipatory anxiety, or worrying, prior to a task (Heller et al., 2002; Hoffman et al., 2005). Positive emotion, a central feature of the between-person construct of extraversion, is found to have at least two components—anticipatory versus consummatory pleasure—that are psychometrically distinct (Gard, Gard, Kring, & John, 2006) and may be subserved by different brain systems (Berridge & Robinson, 2003).

There can be little doubt that if one (a) classifies people according to any taxonomy of global individual differences, (b) correlates the classifications with a psychological outcome, and (c) calls the correlation a person effect, one will obtain person effects that are non-zero. The challenge for personality science is not to demonstrate this repeatedly until society closes us down (see Mischel, 2005) but to advance the science of personality and social behavior by gaining an understanding of the specific psychological capacities through which people interpret, influence, and act within the social world. This requires that one investigate the structure and dynamics of intra-individual personality architecture. In the remainder of this chapter, we illustrate how this can be done in two specific domains of study.

PERSONALITY AND RELATIONSHIPS: RELATIONAL REPRESENTATIONS

Among our most consequential social contexts are our relationships. Relationships with close others—romantic partners, family, friends—impact our lives and well-being. A challenge for personality psychology then is to shed light on the social behavior of persons in interpersonal settings. Ideally, this might be done in the manner suggested throughout this chapter. Rather than merely ranking individuals on dispositional dimensions that describe how they differ from one another on average and correlating these rankings with inter-individual differences in some relationship outcome, one might explore the architecture of the intra-individual personality systems that come into play as people pursue, develop, and reflect upon their relationships with romantic partners. This model of intra-individual personality architecture might then guide assessments of those psychological qualities that are most important to the health of one's relationships with others.

One tool for exploring these aspects of personality architecture is found in research on personality and social cognition. Much work indicates that one way in which persons and relationships are intertwined is that relationship experiences contribute to people's enduring personal knowledge. Specifically, people develop relational representations, that is, knowledge structures that represent the relationship between themselves and significant others. In social interaction, relational representations contribute to people's perceptions of others (Andersen & Miranda, 2000, Andersen et al., chapter this volume), attributions regarding others' intentions (Downey & Feldman, 1996; Downey, Mougios, Ozlem, London, & Shoda, 2004), and thoughts about themselves (Baldwin & Sinclair, 1996; Park, Crocker, & Mikelson, 2004). The self-regulation of action and affective experience is determined, in part, by contextualized representations of relations between oneself and others (Higgins, 1987; Mikulincer, Shaver, & Pereg, 2003; Shah, 2003).

Relational Schemas

Baldwin (1992, 1999) has made particularly significant contributions to the study of relational representations. The basic premise of his work is that, through social interaction, people form complex, integrated mental representations that incorporate beliefs about both self and others. They form, in other words, relational schemas (Baldwin, 1992). These schematic knowledge structures include beliefs about interaction goals and expectations about others' behavior, as well as representations of typical affective responses in the given relationship.

Baldwin's notion of relational schemas exemplifies a central theme of our present chapter, namely, that one can make progress in the understanding of personality and social behavior through analyses in which persons are embedded in situations rather than separated from them. The positing of relational representations immediately moves one beyond a "person versus situation" discourse. It undoes the artificial separation of persons and situations by indicating that a central feature of persons is their enduring mental representations of a key situational context: interpersonal relations. The self, in this view, is not an entity that is isolated from the social world. Instead, it is recognized that the self often is experienced as a self-with-others. Developmentally, self-with-other representations also are situationally embedded in that they stem from past interactions (Baldwin, 1992).

Empirical evidence reveals that the functioning of relational representations is revealed in situationally contingent *if...then...* patterns of the sort highlighted by Mischel and Shoda's (1995) CAPS model of cognitive-affective personality dynamics. Relational schemas do not exert global or trans-situational effects on social outcomes. Instead, the knowledge structures become active *if* the person experiences particular social contexts. Research has demonstrated that information that activates the *if* part of a contingency primes the *then* half. Baldwin & Sinclair (1996) used a sequential priming paradigm to test whether people with low self-esteem hold if...then structured relational schemas in which their self-worth is dependent on how they are perceived by others. To vary the *if* part of the contingency, participants were exposed to a word associated with success (e.g., competent) or failure. To assess the *then* part, participants identified target words associated either with acceptance or rejection. Compared with people who scored high on self-esteem, people who were low in self-esteem were relatively faster at identifying positive relational outcome words (e.g., cherished) when trials were preceded by a success word as well as faster at identifying negative relational outcome words when trials were preceded by a failure word. Results indicate that failure/success feedback is more likely to activate socially contingent aspects of self-concept among individuals classified as low in self-esteem.

The activation of relational representations also has been shown to influence feelings of self-worth. The presentation of rejection- and acceptance-related words activates mental representations of self-with-others and thereby influences feelings of self-esteem (Baldwin & Sinclair, 1996) and self evaluative and affective reactions (Baldwin, 1994; Baldwin & Main, 2001). The study of relational expectancies, then, may inform the emergence of enduring individual differences in perceived self-worth.

The activation of relational schemas can be understood within the framework of general principles of knowledge accessibility (Higgins, 1996). Chronic and cued accessibility influence whether relational expectancies come to mind (Baldwin, Carrell, & Lopez, 1990; Baldwin & Meunier, 1999; Baldwin & Sinclair, 1996). Relational representations can be activated automatically, outside of conscious awareness or without the need for consciously controlled search processes (Baldwin, Baccus, & Fitzsimons, 2004; Glassman & Andersen, 1999; Shah, 2003). These general relational expectancies can be transferred from one context to another via paired association (classical conditioning; Baldwin & Main, 2001; Baldwin & Meunier, 1999).

Applications of the Relational Representations Construct

Advances in the study of relational representations have extended our understanding of the range of cognitive, affective and behavioral patterns elicited by activation of relational representations. One implication of these advances is theoretical; they reconceptualize constructs historically of importance to personality and social psychology, such as expectancies, self-concept, goals, or standards, so that the constructs capture the socially contextualized nature of these representations. A second implication is applied; an exciting application of basic research on relational expectancies is devising ways to modify them.

Changing Interpersonal Expectancies.
Since some relational expectancies (e.g., pinning one's self-worth on others' approval or mistaking others behaviors as acts of rejection) can be deleterious, investigators have developed training procedures to change relational representations. For example, work by Baldwin and colleagues (Baccus, Baldwin, & Packer, 2004) has employed a classical conditioning manipulation in which participant's own self-related information is paired repeatedly with positive social feedback (a smiling face). The manipulation increases implicit self- esteem as assessed by the IAT. In a second study, Dandeneau & Baldwin (2004) successfully trained people to inhibit social rejection information; participants with chronic low self-esteem who were repeatedly asked to identify smiling faces in a matrix of frowning faces were later found to be better at inhibiting rejection words on a Stroop task compared to controls.

Downey and colleagues have developed strategies for helping people to overcome maladaptive interpersonal expectations involving 'rejection sensitivity,' or the tendency to construe ambiguous behavior by close others as rejecting or hostile and to maintain a state of hypervigilance for rejection (e.g., Downey & Feldman, 1996; Downey, Mougios, Ozlem, London, & Shoda, 2004). Self-regulatory skills (assessed via success in a delay of gratification task during childhood) can mitigate the negative interpersonal consequences of rejection sensitivity (Ayduk et al., 2000). Applying this finding, Ayduk, Mischel, and Downey (2002) demonstrated that when people engaged in a delay of gratification task—keeping attention focused on 'cool' features of an imagined rejection interaction rather than how they would have felt ('hot' features)—they felt less angry, expressed less anger and hurt, and were slower to identify hostility-related words in a lexical decision task.

These applications reveal a major advantage to construing personality in terms of interpersonal dynamics rather than inter-individual taxonomies. Unlike work on taxonomic classifications, analyses of intra-individual personality architecture yield information about psychological systems that can be the targets of change in interventions.

Relationships, Self-Regulation, and Health Behavior

Although we generally feel personally responsible for our actions and for our futures, others also play important roles in shaping our goals and determining whether we are able to achieve them. In close relationships, the actions, thoughts, and feelings that are key to self-regulation are shaped by reciprocal interactions with others. Yet until very recently the role of close relationships has received insufficient attention in basic self-regulation research (cf. Baumeister & Vohs, 2004).

There are a number of ways in which understanding the relational context of goals helps detect coherent patterns in goal striving. Relational outcomes can motivate behavior choices. People primed with the goal of being socially accepted are more likely to choose to interact with persons who view them as more likable rather than people who view them as less likeable but competent (Baldwin & Baccus, 2003). Goals that we perceive others to hold for us can influence our behavior (Fitzsimons & Bargh, 2003; Shah, 2003). Participants subliminally exposed to their mothers' names reported increased commitment to goals they perceived as being valued by their mothers, and individuals who were close to their fathers, who perceived that their fathers would want them to succeed on particular tasks, and who were primed with their fathers' names were more persistent and performed better on the tasks than others (Shah, 2003). Importantly, in this work goal accessibility mediated the effects of priming on motivation and behavior.

Future research ought further to explore the real-life implications of relational goals. We know, for example that self-regulatory skills and close, supportive relationships both have a major impact on a person's health. The importance of our capacity to set goals and direct our behavior toward achieving these goals is dramatically illustrated by the gains in health and longevity people can achieve by making health behavior changes (e.g., Knoops et al., 2004; Mokdad, Marks, Stroup, & Gerding, 2004). There is considerable evidence that close emotional ties or lack thereof have profound effects on health (Berkman & Syme, 1979; House, Robbins, & Metzner, 1982; Kiecolt-Glaser & Newton, 2001; Ross, Mirowsky, & Goldsteen, 1990). While no single mechanism has been implicated, evidence suggests that close others, including family members, influence health behavior (e.g., Cohen & Lichtenstein, 1990; DiMatteo, 2004; Franks, Pienta, & Wray, 2002; Gallant, 2003; Umberson, 1987).

Recent research highlights the importance of relational health goals. In one study (Orom, 2006) college-aged smokers who varied in their motivation to quit smoking were asked the extent to which they were motivated to quit smoking for the sake of an important close other and the extent to which they believed this person wanted them to quit. Motivation to quit smoking was correlated, modestly but highly significantly, with both wanting to quit for this person and perceiving this other person as wanting one to quit (Orom, 2006). These correlations may underestimate the potential strength of concordance between wanting to quit and wanting to quit for a close other, given that in this study the close other was also required to be another smoker. An interesting prospect is that relational motives might vary in importance across different points in the quit process. When correlations were computed separately for smokers who were highly motivated to quit smoking (to the least they intended to quit within 30 days) and those who were less motivated (intended to quit within six months or longer), we found that these correlations were even stronger for those who were less motivated, but nonsignificant for those who were already more motivated to quit, suggesting that relational motives might be associated with starting to contemplate quitting but might not have a large impact on motivating actual behavior change.

PERSONALITY ASSESSMENT AND A CASE EXAMPLE: HUMOR

Any approach to the study of personality, such as the one we are advancing here, should provide not only theoretical tools such as a conceptual model of personality architecture. It also should provide practical tools that enable investigators to carry out the variety of jobs taken up by both basic and applied personality psychologists (Cervone & Pervin, in press). One such job is to assess the qualities of individuals and the differences among them.

If one views personality as individual differences in qualities that people exhibit irrespective of social context, then the assessment of personality is relatively straightforward. One identifies major dimensions of between-person variation and locates persons on these dimensions, usually via self-report questionnaires. The task is so straightforward that people's standing on a comprehensive set of personality structures can be assessed by asking them to respond to as few as 10 self-report items (Gosling, Rentfrow, & Swann, 2003).

If one takes an intra-individual approach to personality, the question of assessment changes considerably, as we noted above (see Cervone, 2004b; Cervone, Shadel, & Jencius, 2001). The task no longer is merely to compare people to others in terms of what they do "on average," since the average is no longer the gold standard of personality. One's focus shifts, instead, to the challenge of assessing (a) patterns of overt personality functioning, including meaningful variations in behavior from one context to another, and (b) contextualized personality structures that contribute to these overt patterns. One domain in which this challenge recently has been taken up, and that illustrates the general strategy of assessment embraced by the KAPA model of personality architecture (Cervone, 2004), is the assessment of humor.

Assessing Humor: Global Inter-Individual and Contextualized Intra-Individual Strategies

The study of humor and personality again reveals the contrast between personality psychology in the past and more recent trends. A century ago, the study of personality and humor was grounded in theories of underlying personality structure and dynamics (Freud, 1905/1960). The theoretical formulation of Freud examined the mental life of the individual, and it was expected that the individual's experiences and actions might vary dynamically across time and context. In the recent era, researchers instead have focused their attention on the assessment of surface-level tendencies in humorous behavior, rather than underlying personality structure, and have centered their assessments on average displays of humor-related behavior.

This shift in focus, from the study of dynamic personality structures and processes to the description of overt tendencies, is quite explicit. In constructing a humor response questionnaire (reviewed immediately below), Martin and Lefcourt (1984) explain that a behavioral indicator of humor production, the tendency to smile and laugh in a variety of situations, was chosen "to avoid the debate over the processes involved in humor." The processes that Martin and Lefcourt avoid are exactly those processes to which one's attention is drawn if one adopts an intra-individual approach to personality assessment. The cost of ignoring these processes, and the associated within-person variability, may not be merely a loss of information. The cost may include a loss of validity of the nomothetic assessments themselves, for two reasons. First, people joke *about* things – typically about things that are happening in some but not other situations; in other words, there is intra-individual variability in the use of humor and in its underlying reasons, such that it is not clear exactly what one is assessing by ignoring this source of variation. Second, without some theoretical understanding of what causes individuals to use humor in one versus another situation, there are no criteria by which to validate its measurement (cf. Borsboom, Mellenbergh, & van Heerden, 2004). Such is the case with nomothetic measures of humor, whereby behaviors are treated as transparent indicators of goals. Two prominent humor measures, the SHRQ and the HSQ are discussed below in reference to these issues.

The SHRQ (Martin & Lefcourt, 1984). The SHRQ is a 21-item measure of the tendency to smile and laugh in a variety of situations. For 18 of the items, participants are confronted with a scenario and asked how they would respond to it or how they have responded in the past. For instance, the item, "If a friend gave you a puzzle to solve and you found, much to your friend's surprise, that you were able to solve it very quickly," is followed by five Guttman-style options, ranging from "I wouldn't have found it particularly amusing" to "I would have laughed heartily." Three additional items assess the desirability of a sense of humor in choosing friends, the general likelihood of being amused in a variety of situations, and the tendency to vary from one situation to another in behavior.

This measure asks individuals about their humor across a variety of contexts. To compute an index of an individual's tendency to respond with mirth, one then aggregates across these contexts. In doing so, the item, "You had accidentally hurt yourself and had to spend a few days in bed," is treated as interchangeable with "You were eating in a restaurant with some friends, and the waiter accidentally spilled a drink on you." Though researchers may treat these situations as functionally the same, participants may not if they are individuals who interpret social encounters and act according to those interpretations. If, as in the real world, individuals' use of humor is dependent at least in part on their judgments of the appropriateness of using humor within these contexts, then it is not clear if the SHRQ is assessing *how much* humor people have vs. *what* constellation of events evokes humorous responding. And so this measure of on-average humorous responding is arguably a measure of beliefs about situations. Accordingly, when we add up people's responses and order them on a continuum of low to high humor, it is difficult to make the argument that the clusters of people at either end share a tendency (or lack thereof) for mirth. Rather, their family resemblance may be due to a shared a view that some situations are or are not amenable to humor. Unless respondents are instructed to ignore contextual information when filling out the SHRQ, one can not make the argument that the SHRQ is measuring pure person effects or that they can exist. The resulting confusion concerning what drives these scores has implications for scale validation: Because there is little a priori understanding of what causes individuals' scale responses, by what method can we say it is measuring what we want it to? The scale's validity was assessed by computing correlations between it and observed smiles and laughter during an interview, with peer ratings of humorousness, and with mood disturbance, though there is little theoretical reason why these particular scores should be indicators of the same construct. We do not know what might account for between-persons differences in mirth, yet we knew what it should look like.

The HSQ (Martin et al., 2003). The HSQ is a 32-item measure of two dimensions of humor styles: intraindividual vs. interindividual and adaptive vs. maladaptive. The combination of these two dimensions yield four types of reasons for using humor: self-enhancing, affiliative, self-defeating, and aggressive. Self-enhancing humor refers to the tendency to use humor when one is alone to positively cope with adversity; affiliative humor refers to the tendency to use humor to amuse other and increase group cohesiveness; self-defeating humor refers to the tendency to use self-disparaging humor excessively; and aggressive humor refers to the tendency to use humor to disparage others. The goal of Martin et al. in constructing the HSQ was to come up with a way to assess both adaptive and maladaptive uses of humor, such that one could account for more variance in constructs such as self-esteem and mood disturbance.

The HSQ can be criticized on grounds similar to the SHRQ. Where the SHRQ was faulted for its implicit assumption that individuals do not vary idiosyncratically in the meaning they assign to social situations, the HSQ can be faulted for assuming that individuals do not differ idiosyncratically in the meaning they assign to their own behaviors. This is accomplished by positing some high-level trait or goal for humor (e.g., affiliative humor) and then coming up with behavioral indicators for that trait (e.g., "I enjoy making people laugh") that may not correspond at all to what that behavior means to that individual. This strategy presupposes that any one behavior should correspond one-to-one with intention, when in fact it may not. Two behavioral indicators could have potentially the same meaning to some individuals, yet end up on different subscales. That three of the four subscales of the HSQ overlap suggests that this may in fact be happening. The affiliative subscale correlates .35 with the self-enhancing scale and .26 with the aggressive subscale. The aggressive subscale additionally correlates .23 with the self-defeating subscale. Because goals, intentions, and emotions can be concealed or revealed by behavior, perhaps the only individual who has the ability to decide what those behaviors mean is the individual performing them. Goals that underlie humor should be assessed rather than inferred.

The Need for a Structure and Process Distinction in Humor Assessment

Nomothetic measures such as the HSQ fail to distinguish between various types of structures that may differentially contribute to behavior. This has far-reaching implications for a science of personality and humor. Items from the HSQ, for instance, intermix psychological qualities (preferences, capacities, goals, beliefs) generally recognized to be distinct. Consider the first three items from the Self-Enhancing subscale:

2. If I am feeling depressed, I can usually cheer myself up with humor.
6. Even when I'm by myself, I'm often amused by the absurdities of life.
10. If I am feeling upset or unhappy I usually try to think of something funny about the situation to make myself feel better.

Item number 2 refers to an individual's *ability* to use humor to self-enhance in the face of depression. Item number 6 refers to a behavior the individual might engage in that has self-enhancing consequences, though that may not have been driven by a self-enhancing motivation. Item 10 refers to an individual's active attempt at self-enhancement. Because it is likely that there is a difference in the psychology behind what one *can do* versus what one *does* versus what one *tries to do*, treating these structures as functionally similar indicators of an underlying goal (self-enhancement) is problematic. First, these may not be the indicators for every individual's self-enhancing goals, such that for any particular individual, there is the risk that one is aggregating across indicators of many different constructs. Individuals engage in many of the same behaviors, but for different reasons. Additionally, by limiting itself to the assessment of four pertinent structures, some of which may be irrelevant to some individuals' use of humor, the HSQ runs the additional risk of overlooking other highly relevant structures. The suggested solution is to assess structures (e.g., goals, beliefs, preferences) that are relevant to each individual.

Though the HSQ measures structures that give rise to humorous behavior, it ignores the processes through which these goals shape that type of behavior. In particular, it ignores the possibility that a given structure, such as the individual's goal for using humor, will be activated by only a particular subset of situations – the subset of which may be highly idiosyncratic for each individual. Two individuals may in fact be highly schematic for affiliative humor, but report using humor for affiliative purposes in entirely different settings.

These criticisms of the nomothetic approach to humor assessment suggest that, rather than ignoring the processes involved in the production of humor, there may be value to identifying and assessing them and to using the assessments to predict behavior at the level of the individual. By inquiring about humor and intraindividual personality architecture (Cervone, 2004a), one can model the processes through which humor is used by individuals-in-context.

A Personality-Architecture Strategy for Assessing Humor

The purposes for which humor has previously been assessed (i.e., Martin and colleagues' coping, aggressing, affiliating, and self-defeating humor) represent constructs that should exist at both the level of structure and process. Because these two levels are distinct (cf. Cervone, 2004), the first step of assessment would be to measure individuals' beliefs about how they use humor in their own daily lives. Current humor measures (e.g., the HSQ) consist of experimenter-provided categories of the functions of humor to which individuals are asked to fit themselves. This strategy runs the risk either of asking the wrong questions (i.e., of those to whom these categories are irrelevant) or of being incomplete (i.e., by not assessing *all* of the possible self-beliefs individuals may have about how or why they use humor). An alternative strategy better suited for assessing salient beliefs about humor would employ open-ended assessments of individuals' goals in using humor. A less-structured method would ensure that individuals who use humor for reasons that happen not to be part of an experimenter's nomothetic assessment system are lost in the mix, leading to false conclusions about their use of humor.

Such an alternative recently has been executed by Caldwell (2005). The goal of this work is idiographically to assesses KAPA mechanisms and self-reports of the likelihood of using humor as an interpersonal strategy in social situations. Individuals are found to display substantial within-person, across-situation variability in humor use, as would be anticipated by the CAPS model of Mischel and Shoda (1995). Furthermore, as is anticipated by the KAPA model (Cervone, 2004a), these intra-individual patterns are found to be predictable, at the level of the individual case, by prior idiographic assessments of people's enduring knowledge. Specifically, beliefs about the functions served by humor and the relevance of those functions to particular social situations predict intra-individual variability in humor use. This class of behavior is found to be far less predictable if one relies merely on nomothetic assessment schemes that ignore idiosyncracy at the level of the individual (Caldwell, 2005).

This idiographic strategy provides conceptual and methodological tools that can inform questions about personality and humor that simply are not addressed by traditional nomothetic strategies. One can predict to intra-individual variations in the use of humor across contexts. As in Mischel's reconceptualization of personality, this yields a reconceptualization of "humor styles" in which the style is defined in a person–in–context manner that includes unique clustering of situations in which personal beliefs about humor are likely to be activated. Second, individuals will differ from each other in the number and kind of functions they see humor serving in their daily lives. They may indeed spontaneously report that humor serves self-enhancing, aggressive, affiliative, and self-defeating functions, such that at the level of the population, the 4-factor solution that Martin et al. (2003) found would be replicated. However, this solution may not necessarily fit any one individual. Finally, individuals may report using humor for more than one purpose in a given situation, such that any one situation can have many humor functions assigned to it. For example, one can imagine an individual for whom a particular situation is relevant to humor as a coping strategy, as a tool for aggression, and as a way to affiliate with others.

WHAT IS THE DIFFERENCE BETWEEN PERSONALITY AND SOCIAL PSYCHOLOGY?

The alternative meanings of personality—as inter-individual differences or intra-individual architecture—speak to one last issue of importance to readers of a handbook on personality and social behavior: the relationship between the professional fields of personality and social psychology. Our opening story embodies one conception of their relationship, namely, as competitors in a variance-accounted-for contest. One's phenomenon, one might say, is another's error. Turning this conception to research methods, one might say that "the difference between the fields is that personality psychologists run correlations and social psychologists run experiments," as expressed by a colleague of ours—in earnest, as far as could be discerned—at a recent conference. This conception is very much alive in the contemporary field.

The perspective taken in this chapter suggests an alternative conception that has also been recognized by others (e.g., Baumeister, 1999). Once personality psychologists turn to questions of intra-individual personality dynamics and social psychologists investigate cognitive and affective mental systems, the fields no longer compete. They inform one another. That surely is our position; yet it still leaves a significant point unresolved. If personality is construed as a cognitive–affective system, personality psychology itself might seem to disappear. Cognition, affect, and the social contexts in which cognitions and affects develop are the defining interests of other fields of study. What is left, uniquely, for the personality psychologist to do?

As we and others have stressed (Caprara & Cervone, 2000; Cervone & Mischel, 2002; Mischel, 2004), there is something left, and it is a big something. It is the study of the multifaceted yet psychologically integrated person—the coherent individual (Cervone & Shoda, 1999); Magnusson's (1990) "organized whole"; Stern's (1935) "unitas multiplex." Much of psychology's research activity examines variables rather than whole persons, where those variables represent one psychological attribute that persons possess or one way that persons differ one from another. Yet when we observe a social behavior and ask "whodunit?" the answer cannot be merely a part of a person or a variable representing an average difference between the observed person and some others. Neither the present authors' conscientiousness, nor their perceived self-efficacy, nor even their frontal (or any other) lobes wrote this chapter. The only entity that engages in intentional social actions is the "psychophysical unity" (Bennett & Hacker, 2003, p. 3) that is a person. Whole persons "dun it." Organized, integrated, coherent, socially embedded persons thus must be the target of investigation in the explanation of social behavior.

ACKNOWLEDGMENTS

The authors were supported by grant DA14136 from the National Institute on Drug Abuse. We thank Walter Mischel for his comments on an earlier draft of this manuscript. Correspondence concerning this paper should be addressed to Daniel Cervone at Department of Psychology (MC 285), University of Illinois at Chicago, 1007 W. Harrison St., Chicago, IL 60607-7137; email

NOTES

1. Alternatively, one could ask, "For what psychologically significant aspects of situations can one posit constructs that make no reference to persons?" Scholars outside of personality/social psychology have provided situational analyses that capture the mutuality of persons and situations. Bronfenbrenner's (2005) bioecological theory of development features a person-process-context-time model in which the developing person's situations include "progressively more complex activities" (p. 9) within which the person develops intellectual skills and emotional attachments. "Activities" is a situational construct that is inherently person-rich; if there are no persons, there is no activity. The ecological approach of Kelly and associates (Kelly, 2006; Trickett, 2005) in community psychology includes person-rich principles for characterizing community settings: the community's resources for solving problems; the nature of interdependencies among residents of a given community setting; the opportunities for and constraints on individual development that the community provides; the community's investment in future generations of residents. Investigators who embrace a dramatalurgical metaphor for understanding social behavior similarly employ person-laden constructs for understanding situational settings, for example, "audiences" that observe the performance of "parts" in an interpersonal encounter (Goffman, 1959; also see Scheibe, 2000) .

2. Although the factors that summarize inter-individual differences in the population cannot logically be assumed to correspond to intra-individual psychological structures, as the writers cited in the main text of this chapter explain, it should be noted that some investigators have created theoretical positions in which the factors are reified in this manner. Five-factor theory (McCrae & Costa, 1996) explicitly presumes that the between-person factors are universal within-person structures with causal force. The analyses of Borsboom et al. (2003; also see Harré, 1998) thoroughly undermine the evidentiary and conceptual bases of this position. Others have declared similarly that it is in the nature of trait constructs that they refer simultaneously to two things: the overt pattern of behaviors that constitutes the dispositional tendency that requires explanation, and the psychological structures that provide the causal explanation of those dispositional tendencies (Funder, 1991, p. 32). However, as noted previously (Caprara & Cervone, 2000; Cervone, 1999), that position violates a basic principle of scientific explanation. In scientific explanation, "what requires explanation cannot itself figure in the explanation" (Hanson, 1958, p. 120). As Nozick (1982, p. 632) put it, "A fundamental explanation of [a] property...will not refer to other things with that very same property; the possession and functioning of that property is what is to be explained" (Nozick, 1981, p. 632).

REFERENCES

Allport, G. W. (1937). *Personality: A psychological interpretation*. New York: Holt.
Andersen, S. M., & Miranda, R. (2000). Transference: How past relationships emerge in the present. *The Psychologist, 13*, 608–609.
Asendorpf, J. B., & Wilpers, S. (1998). Personality effects on social relationships. *Journal of Personality and Social Psychology , 74*, 1531–1544.
Ashton, M. C., & Lee, K. (2005a). A defence of the lexical approach to the study of personality structure. *European Journal of Personality, 19*, 5–24.
Ashton, M. C., Lee, K., Perugini, M., Szarota, P., de Vries, R. E., Di Blas, L., Boies, K., & De Raad, B. (2004). A six-factor structure of personality-descriptive adjectives: Solutions from psycholexical studies in seven languages. *Journal of Personality & Social Psychology, 86*, 356–366.
Ayduk, O., Mendoza-Denton, R., Mischel, W., Downey, G., Peake, P., & Rodriguez, M. (in press). Regulating the interpersonal self: Strategic self-regulation for coping with rejection sensitivity. *Journal of Personality and Social Psychology, 79*, 776–792.
Ayduk, O., Mischel, W., & Downey, G. (2002). Attentional mechanisms linking rejection to hostile reactivity: The role of "hot" versus "cool" focus. *Psychological Science, 13*, 443–448.
Baccus, J. R., Baldwin, M. W., & Packer, D. J. (2004). Increasing implicit self-esteem through classical conditioning. *Psychological Science, 15*, 498–502.
Baldwin, M. W. (1992). Relational schemas and the processing of social information. *Psychological Bulletin, 112*, 461–484.
Baldwin, M. W. (1994). Primed relational schemas as a source of self-evaluative reactions. *Journal of Social and Clinical Psychology, 13*, 380–403.
Baldwin, M. W. (1999). Relational schemas: Research into social cognitive aspects of interpersonal experience. In D. Cervone & Y. Shoda (Eds.), *The coherence of personality: Social-cognitive bases of consistency, variability, and organization* (pp. 127–154). New York: Guilford.
Baldwin, M. W., & Baccus, J. R. (2003). An expectancy-value approach to self-esteem. In S. J. Spencer, S. Fein, M. P. Zanna, & J. M. Olson (Eds.), *Motivated social percep-*

tion: *The Ontario symposium, Vol. 9. Ontario symposium on personality and social psychology* (pp. 171–194). Mahwah, NJ: Erlbaum.

Baldwin, M. W., Baccus, J. R., & Fitzsimons, G. M. (2004). Self-esteem and the dual processing of interpersonal contingencies. *Self and Identity, 3*, 81–93.

Baldwin, M. W., Carrel, S. E., & Lopez, D. F. (1990). Priming relationship schemas: My advisor and the Pope are watching me from the back of my mind. *Journal of Experimental Social Psychology, 26*, 435–454.

Baldwin, M. W., & Main, K. J. (2001). The cued activation of relational schemas in social anxiety. *Personality and Social Psychology Bulletin, 27*, 1637–1647.

Baldwin, M. W., & Meunier, J. (1999). The cued activation of attachment relational schemas. *Social Cognition, 17*, 209–227.

Baldwin, M. W., & Sinclair, L. (1996). Self-esteem and "if...then" contingencies of interpersonal acceptance. *Journal of Personality and Social Psychology, 71*, 1130–1141.

Bandura, A. (1978). The self system in reciprocal determination. *American Psychologist, 33*, 344–358.

Bandura, A. (1986). *Social foundations of thought and action.* Englewood Cliffs, NJ: Prentice Hall.

Bandura, A. (1999). Social cognitive theory of personality. In D. Cervone & Y. Shoda (Eds.), *The coherence of personality: Social-cognitive bases of consistency, variability, and organization* (pp. 185–241). New York: Guilford.

Bandura, A. (2006). Toward a psychology of human agency. *Perspectives on Psychological Science, 1*, 164–180.

Bandura, A., & Cervone, D. (1983). Self-evaluative and self-efficacy mechanisms governing the motivational effects of goal systems. *Journal of Personality and Social Psychology, 45*, 1017–1028.

Baumeister, R. (1999). On the interface of personality and social psychology. In L. A. Pervin & O. P. John (Eds.), *Handbook of personality: Theory and research* (2nd ed., pp. 367–377). New York: Guilford.

Baumeister, R. F., & Vohs, K. D. (Eds.) (2004). *Handbook of self-regulation: Research, theory, and applications.* New York: Guilford.

Bem, D. J., & Allen, A. (1974). Predicting some of the people some of the time: The search for cross-situational consistencies in behavior. *Psychological Review, 81*, 506–520.

Bennett, M. R., & Hacker, P. M. S. (2003). *Philosophical foundations of neuroscience.* Malden, MA: Blackwell.

Berkman, L. F., & Syme, S. L. (1979). Social networks, host resistance, and mortality: A nine-year follow-up study of Alameda County residents. *American Journal of Epidemiology, 109*, 186–204.

Berridge, K. C., & Robinson, T. E. (2003). Parsing reward. *Trends in Neuroscience, 26*, 507–513.

Borsboom, D., Mellenbergh, G. J., & van Heerden, J. (2003). The theoretical status of latent variables. *Psychological Review, 110*, 203–219.

Borsboom, D., Mellenbergh, G. J., & van Heerden, J. (2004). The concept of validity. *Psychological Review, 111*, 1061–1071.

Caldwell, T. L. (2005). A social-cognitive assessment of humor. Doctoral dissertation, University of Illinois at Chicago.

Cantor, N., & Kihlstrom, J. F. (1987). *Personality and social intelligence.* Englewood Cliffs, NJ: Prentice Hall.

Caprara, G. V., & Cervone, D. (2000). *Personality: Determinants, dynamics, and potentials.* New York: Cambridge University Press.

Caprara, G. V., & Cervone, D. (2003). A conception of personality for a psychology of human strengths: Personality as an agentic, self-regulating system. In L. G. Aspinwall & U. M. Staudinger (Eds.), *A psychology of human strengths: Fundamental questions and future directions for a positive psychology* (pp. 61–74). Washington, D.C.: American Psychological Association.

Carver, C. S., & Scheier, M. F. (2002). Control processes and self-organization as complementary principles underlying behavior. *Personality and Social Psychology Review, 4*, 304–315.

Cervone, D. (1991). The two disciplines of personality psychology. *Psychological Science, 2*, 371–377.

Cervone, D. (1997). Social-cognitive mechanisms and personality coherence: Self-knowledge, situational beliefs, and cross-situational coherence in perceived self-efficacy. *Psychological Science, 8*, 43–50.

Cervone, D. (2004a). The architecture of personality. *Psychological Review, 111*, 183–204.

Cervone, D. (2004b). Personality assessment: Tapping the social-cognitive architecture of personality. *Behavior Therapy, 35*, 113–130. .

Cervone, D. (2005). Personality architecture: Within-person structures and processes. *Annual Review of Psychology, 56*, 423–452.

Cervone, D. (2006). Aristotelian and Galileian modes of thought in contemporary personality psychology: On the enduring importance of Kurt Lewin. In J. Trempala, A. Pepitone, & B. Raven (Eds.), *Lewinian psychology* (pp. 109–128). Bydgoszcz: Kazimierz Wieki University Press.

Cervone, D., Jiwani, N., & Wood, R. (1991). Goal-setting and the differential influence of self-regulatory processes on complex decision-making performance. *Journal of Personality and Social Psychology, 61*, 257–266.

Cervone, D., & Mischel, W. (Eds.) (2002). *Advances in personality science*. New York: Guilford.

Cervone, D., Orom, H., Artistico, D., Shadel, W. G., & Kassel, J. (2007). Using a knowledge-and-appraisal model of personality architecture to understand consistency and variability in smokers' self-efficacy appraisals in high-risk situations. *Psychology of Addictive Behaviors, 21*, 44–54.

Cervone, D., & Pervin, L. A. (in press). *Personality: Theory and Research* (10th ed.). Hoboken, NJ: Wiley.

Cervone, D., Shadel, W. G., & Jencius, S. (2001). Social-cognitive theory of personality assessment. *Personality and Social Psychology Review. 5*, 33–51.

Cervone, D., Shadel, W. G., Smith, R. E., & Fiori, M. (2006). Self-regulation: Reminders and suggestions from personality science. *Applied Psychology: An International Review, 55*, 333–385.

Cervone, D., & Shoda, Y. (Eds.) (1999). *The coherence of personality: Social-cognitive bases of consistency, variability, and organization*. New York: Guilford.

Cloninger, C. R. (2004). *The science of well-being*. New York: Oxford University Press.

Cohen, S., & Lichtenstein, E. (1990). Partner behaviors that support quitting smoking. *Journal of Consulting and Clinical Psychology, 58*, 304–309.

Costall, A. (2004). From Darwin to Watson (and cognitivism) and back again: The principle of animal-environment mutuality. *Behavior and Philosophy, 32*, 179–195.

Dandeneau, S. D., & Baldwin, M. W. (2004). The inhibition of socially rejecting information among people with high versus low self-esteem: The role of attentional bias and the effects of bias reduction training. *Journal of Social and Clinical Psychology, 23*, 584–602.

de Raad, B. (2005). Situations that matter to personality. In A. Eliasz, S. E. Hampson, & B. De Raad (Eds.), *Advances in personality psychology* (Vol. 2., pp. 179–204). Hove, UK: Routledge.

Digman, J. M. (1990). Personality structure: Emergence of the five-factor model. *Annual Review of Psychology, 41*, 417–440.

Dimaggio, G. & Semerari, A., with Carcione, A., Nicolò, G., & Procacci, M. (2006). *Psychotherapy of personality disorder: Metacognition, states of mind and interpersonal cycles*. London: Routledge.
DiMatteo, M. R. (2004). Social support and patient adherence to medical treatment: A meta-analysis. *Health Psychology, 23*, 207–218.
Dion, K. K., Berscheid, E., & Walster, E. (1972). What is beautiful is good. *Journal of Personality and Social Psychology, 24*, 285–290.
Downey, G., & Feldman, S. (1996). Implications of rejection sensitivity for intimate relationships. *Journal of Personality and Social Psychology, 70*, 1327 1343.
Downey, G., Mougios, V., Ayduk, O., London, B. E., & Shoda, Y. (2004). Rejection sensitivity and the defensive motivational system: Insights from the startle response to rejection cues. *Psychological Science, 15*, 668–673.
Dweck, C., & Leggett, E. (1988). A social-cognitive approach to motivation and personality. *Psychological Review, 95*, 256–273.
Ehrlich, P. (2000). *Human natures: Genes, culture, and the human prospect*. Washington, D. C.: Island Press.
Eid, M., & Langeheine, R. (2004). Separating stable from variable individuals in longitudinal studies by mixture distribution models. *Measurement: Interdisciplinary Research and Perspectives, 1*, 179–206.
Elliott, A. J., & Dweck, C. S. (1988). Goals: An approach to motivation and achievement. *Journal of Personality and Social Psychology, 54*, 5–12.
Fitzsimons, G. M., & Bargh, J. A. (2003). Thinking of you: Nonconscious pursuit of interpersonal goals associated with relationship partners. *Journal of Personality and Social Psychology, 84*, 148–163.
Fleeson, W. (2001). Toward a structure- and process-integrated view of personality: Traits as density distributions of states. *Journal of Personality and Social Psychology, 80*, 1011–1027.
Fleeson, W., & Leicht, C. (2006). On delineating and integrating the study of variability and stability in personality psychology: Interpersonal trust as illustration. *Journal of Research in Personality, 40*, 5–20.
Fox, N. A., Henderson, H. A., Marshall, P. J., Nichols, K. E., & Ghera, M. A. (2005). Behavioral inhibition: linking biology and behavior within a developmental framework. *Annual Review of Psychology, 56*, 235–262.
Fraley, R. C., & Roberts, B. W. (2005). Patterns of continuity: A dynamic model for conceptualizing the stability of individual differences in psychological constructs across the life course. *Psychological Review, 112*, 60–74.
Franks, M. M., Pienta, A. M., & Wray, L. A. (2002). It takes two: Marriage and smoking cessation in the middle years. *Journal of Aging & Health, 14*, 336–354.
Freud, S. (1905/1960). Jokes and their relation to the unconscious. The standard edition of the *Complete psychological works of Sigmund Freud, Vol. VIII*. London: Hogarth Press.
Freud, S. (1923/1961). *The ego and the id*. London: Hogarth Press.
Funder, D. C. (2006). Towards a resolution of the personality triad: Persons, situations, and behaviors. *Journal of Research in Personality, 40*, 21–34.
Funder, D. C., & Ozer, D. J. (1983). Behavior as a function of the situation. *Journal of Personality and Social Psychology, 44*, 107–112.
Gallant, M. P. (2003). The influence of social support on chronic illness self-management: A review and directions for research. *Health Education and Behavior, 30*, 170–195.
Gard, D. E., Gard, M. G., Kring, A. M., & John, O. P. (2006). Anticipatory and consummatory components of the experience of pleasure: A scale development study. *Journal of Research in Personality, 40*, 1086–1102.

Geertz, C. (2000). *Available light: Anthropological reflections on philosophical topics.* Princeton, NJ: Princeton University Press.

Giere, R. N. (1999). *Science without laws: Chapter 5: Science without laws of nature.* Chicago: University of Chicago Press.

Glassman, N. S., & Andersen, S. M. (1999). Activating transference without consciousness: Using significant-other representations to go beyond subliminally given information. *Journal of Personality and Social Psychology, 77,* 1146–1162.

Gosling, S. D., & John, O. P. (1999). Personality dimensions in non-human animals: A cross-species review. *Current Directions in Psychological Science, 8,* 69–75.

Gosling, S. D., Rentfrow, P. J., & Swann, W. B., Jr. (2003). A very brief measure of the big five personality domains. *Journal of Research in Personality, 37,* 504–528.

Goldberg, L. R. (1993). The structure of phenotypic personality traits. *American Psychologist, 48,* 26–34.

Gottlieb, G. (1998). Normally occurring environmental and behavioral influences on gene activity: From central dogma to probabilistic epigenesis. *Psychological Review, 105,* 792–802.

Grant, H., & Dweck, C. (1999). A goal analysis of personality and personality coherence. In D. Cervone & Y. Shoda (Eds.), *The coherence of personality: Social-cognitive bases of consistency, variability, and organization* (pp. 345–371). New York: Guilford.

Grant, H., & Dweck, C. (2003). Clarifying achievement goals and their impact. *Journal of Personality & Social Psychology, 85,* 541–553.

Hacker, P. M. S. (1996). *Wittgenstein, mind and will: Part I: Essays.* Oxford, UK: Cambridge University Press.

Harré, R. (2002). *Cognitive Science: A philosophical introduction.* London: Sage.

Harré, R., & Tissaw, M. A. (2005). *Wittgenstein and psychology: A practical guide.* Basingstoke, UK: Ashgate.

Heller, W., Schmidtke, J. I., Nitschke, J. B., Koven, N. S., & Miller, G. A. (2002). States, traits, and symptoms: Investigating the neural correlates of emotion, personality, and psychopathology. In D. Cervone & W. Mischel (Eds.), *Advances in Personality Science* (106–126). New York: Guilford.

Hermans, H. J. M. (1996). Voicing the self: From information processing to dialogical interchange. *Psychological Bulletin, 119,* 31–50.

Hermans, H. J. M. (2001). The construction of a personal position repertoire: Method and practice. *Culture and Psychology, 7,* 323–365.

Higgins, E. T. (1987). Self-discrepancy: A theory relating self and affect. *Psychological Review, 94,* 319–340.

Higgins, E. T. (1990). Personality, social psychology, and person-situation relations: Standards and knowledge activation as a common language. In L. A. Pervin (Ed.), *Handbook of personality: Theory and research* (pp. 301–338). New York: Guilford.

Higgins, E. T. (1996). Knowledge activation: Accessibility, applicability, and salience. In E. T. Higgins & A. W. Kruglanski (Eds.), *Social psychology: Handbook of basic principles* (133–168). New York: Guilford.

Higgins, E. T. (1999). Persons and situations: Unique explanatory principles or variability in general principles? In D. Cervone & Y. Shoda (Eds.), *The coherence of personality: Social-cognitive bases of consistency, variability, and organization* (pp. 61–93). New York: Guilford.

Hoffman, S. G., Moscovitch, D. A., Litz, B. T., Kim, H., Davis, L. L., & Pizzagalli, D. A. (2005). The worried mind: Autonomic and prefrontal activation during worrying. *Emotion, 5,* 464–475.

House, J. S., Robbins, C., & Metzner, H. L. (1982). The association of social relationships and activities with mortality: Prospective evidence from the Tecumseh community health study. *American Journal of Epidemiology, 116,* 123–140.

John, O. P., & Srivastava, S. (1999). The big-five factor taxonomy: History, measurement, and theoretical perspectives. In L. A. Pervin & O. P. John (Eds.), *Handbook of personality: Theory and research* (2nd ed., pp. 102–138). New York: Guilford.
Kagan, J. (2002). *Surprise, uncertainity, and mental structures.* Cambridge, MA: Harvard University Press.
Kagan, J. (2003). Biology, context, and developmental inquiry. *Annual Review of Psychology, 54,* 1–23.
Kagan, J. (2007). The power of context. In Y. Shoda, D. Cervone, & G. Downey (Eds.), *Persons in context: Constructing a science of the individual* (pp. 43–61). New York: Guilford.
Kiecolt-Glaser J. K., & Newton, T. L. (2001). Marriage and health: His and hers. *Psychological Bulletin, 127,* 472–503.
Knoops, T. B., de Groot, L., Kromhout, D., Perrin, A., Moreiras-Vareka, O., & Menotti, A., et al., (2004). Mediterranean diet, lifestyle factors, and 10-year mortality in elderly European men and women: The HALE project. *Journal of the American Medical Association, 292,* 1433–1439.
Kuhl, J., Kazén, M., & Koole, S. L. (2006). Putting self-regulation theory into practice: A user's manual. *Applied Psychology: An International Review, 55,* 408–418.
Kuhl J., & Koole S. L. (2004). Workings of the will: A functional approach. In J. Greenberg, S. L. Koole, & T. Pyszczynski (Eds.), *Handbook of Experimental Existential Psychology* (pp. 411–430). New York: Guilford
Lazarus, R. S. (1991). *Emotion and adaptation.* New York: Oxford University Press.
LeDoux, J. (1996). *The emotional brain.* New York: Simon & Schuster.
Lerner, J. S., & Keltner, D. (2001). Fear, anger, and risk. *Journal of Personality and Social Psychology, 81,* 146–159.
Lewin, K. (1935). *A dynamic theory of personality: Selected papers.* New York: McGraw-Hill.
Little, B. R. (in press). Prompt and circumstance: The generative contexts of personal projects analysis. In B. R. Little, K. Salmela-Aro, & S. D. Phillips (Eds.), *Personal project pursuit: Goals, action and human flourishing.* Mahwah, NJ: Erlbaum.
Little, B. R. (2004). Personality science and personal projects: Six impossible things before breakfast. *Journal of Research in Personality, 39,* 4–21.
Magnusson, D. (1990). Personality development from an interactional perspective. In L. A. Pervin (Ed.), *Handbook of Personality: Theory and Research* (pp. 193–222). New York: Guilford.
Magnusson, D. (2003). The person approach: Concepts, measurements models, and research strategy. *New Directions for Child and Adolescent Development,* 3–23.
Magnusson, D., & Törestad, B. (1993). A holistic view of personality: A model revisited. *Annual Review of Psychology, 44,* 427–452.
Markus, H. (1977). Self-schemata and processing information about the self. *Journal of Personality and Social Psychology, 35,* 63–78.
Markus, H., & Wurf, E. (1987). The dynamic self-concept: A social psychological perspective. In M. R. Rosenweig & L. W. Porter (Eds.), *Annual Review of Psychology, 38,* 299–337.
Martin, R. A., & Lefcourt, H. M. (1984). Situational humor response questionnaire: Quantitative measure of sense of humor. *Journal of Personality and Social Psychology, 47,* 145–155.
Martin, R. A., Puhlik-Doris, P., Larsen, G., Gray, J., & Weir, K. (2003). Individual differences in uses of humor and their relation to psychological well-being: Development of the Humor Styles Questionnaire. *Journal of Research and Personality, 37,* 48–75.
Matthews, G., Schwean, V. L., Campbell, S. E., Saklofske, D. H., & Mohamed, A. A. R. (2000). Personality, self-regulation and adaptation: A cognitive-social framework. In

M. Boekarts, P. R. Pintrich, & M. Zeidner (Eds.), *Handbook of self-regulation* (pp. 171–207). New York: Academic.

McAdams, D. P. (2006). *The redemptive self: Stories Americans live by*. New York: Oxford University Press.

McAdams, D. P., Diamond, A., St. Aubin, E., & Mansfield, E. (1997). Stories of commitment: The psychosocial construction of generative lives. *Journal of Personality and Social Psychology, 72*, 678–694.

McCrae, R. R., & Costa, P. T. (1996). Toward a new generation of personality theories: theoretical contexts for the five-factor model. In J. S. Wiggins (Ed.), *The five-factor model of personality: Theoretical perspectives* (pp. 51–87). New York: Guilford.

Metcalfe, J., & Mischel, W. (1999). A hot/cool-system analysis of delay of gratification: Dynamics of willpower. *Psychological Review, 106*, 3–19.

Mikulincer, M., Shaver, P. R., & Pereg, D. (2003). Attachment theory and affect regulation: The dynamics, development, and cognitive consequences of attachment-related strategies. *Motivation and Emotion, 27*, 77–102.

Mischel, W. (1968). *Personality and assessment*. New York: Wiley.

Mischel, W. (1973). Toward a cognitive social learning reconceptualization of personality. *Psychological Review, 80*, 252–283.

Mischel, W. (2004). Toward an integrative science of the person. *Annual Review of Psychology, 55*, 1–22.

Mischel, W. (2005). Alternative futures for our science. *APS Observer*. Retrieved March 27, 2006 from http://www.psychologicalscience.org/observer/getArticle.cfm?id=1739.

Mischel, W., & Peake, P. K. (1982). Beyond deja vu in the search for cross-situational consistency. *Psychological Review, 89*, 730–755.

Mischel, W., & Shoda, Y. (1995). A cognitive-affective system theory of personality: Reconceptualizing situations, dispositions, dynamics, and invariance in personality structure. *Psychological Review, 102*, 246–286.

Mishel, W., & Shoda, Y. (1998). Reconciling processing dynamics and personality dispositions. *Annual Review of Psychology, 49*, 229–258.

Mokdad, A. H., Marks, J. S., Stroup, D. F., & Gerberding, J. L. (2004). Actual causes of death in the United States, 2000. *Journal of the American Medical Association, 291*, 1238–1245.

Morf, C. C., & Rhodewalt, F. (2001). Unraveling the paradoxes of narcissism: A dynamic self-regulatory processing model. *Psychological Inquiry, 12*, 177–196.

Morgan, M., & Morrison, M. S. (1999). *Models as mediators: Perspectives on natural and social science*. Cambridge, UK: Cambridge University Press.

Moskowitz, D. S., & Zuroff, D. C. (2005). Robust predictors of flux, pulse, and spin. *Journal of Research in Personality, 39*, 130–147.

Murray, H. A. (1938). *Explorations in personality*. New York: Oxford University Press.

Newcomb, T. M. (1952/1965). Attitude development as a function of reference groups: The Bennington study. In E. Maccoby, T. Newcomb, & E. Hartley (Eds.), *Readings in social psychology* (pp. 265–275). New York: Holt, Rinehart & Winston..

Nowak, A., & Vallacher, R. R. (1998). *Dynamical social psychology*. New York: Guilford.

Orom, H. (2005). *Relational expectancies and abstaining from smoking: Rethinking social support*. Doctoral dissertation, University of Illinois at Chicago.

Ozer, D. J., & Benet-Martinez, V. (2006). Personality and the prediction of consequential outcomes. *Annual Review of Psychology, 57*, 401–421.

Park, L. E., Crocker, J., & Mickelson, K. D. (2004). Attachment styles and contingencies of self-worth. *Personality and Social Psychology Bulletin, 30*, 1243–1254.

Park, R. D. (2004). Development in the family. *Annual Review of Psychology, 55*, 365–399.

Paunonen, S. V., Keinonen, M., Trzebinski, J., Forsterling, F., Grishenkoroze, N., Kouznetsova, L., & Chan, D. W. (1996). The structure of personality in six cultures. *Journal of Cross-Cultural Psychology 27*, 339–353.
Pennisi, E. (2001). Behind the scenes of gene expression. *Science, 293*, 1064–1067.
Phelps, E. A. (2006). Emotion and cognition: Insights from studies of the human amygdala. *Annual Review of Psychology, 57*, 27–53.
Read, S. J., & Miller, L. C. (2002). Virtual personalities: A neural network model of personality. *Personality & Social Psychology Review, 6*, 357–369.
Roberts, B., & Pomerantz, E. (2004). On traits, situations, and their integration: A developmental perspective. *Personality and Social Psychology Review, 8*, 402–416.
Ross, C. E., Mirowsky, J., & Goldsteen, K. (1990). The impact of the family on health: The decade in review. *Journal of Marriage and the Family, 52*, 1059–1078.
Ross, L., & Nisbett, R. E. (1991). *The person and the situation.* Boston: McGraw-Hill.
Russell, J. A. (2003). Core affect and the psycholological construction of emotion. *Psychological Review, 110*, 145–172.
Saucier, G., & Simonds, J. (in press). The structure of personality and temperament. In D. K. Mroczek & T. D. Little (Eds.), *Handbook of personality development* (pp. 109–128). Mahwah, NJ: Erlbaum.
Schwarz, N., & Clore, G. L. (1983). Mood, misattribution, and judgments of well-being: Informative and directive functions of affective states. *Journal of Personality and Social Psychology, 45*, 513–523.
Scott, W. D., & Cervone, D. (2002). The impact of negative affect on performance standards: Evidence for an affect-as-information mechanism. *Cognitive Therapy and Research, 26*, 19–37.
Searle, J. R. (1983). *Intentionality: An essay in the philosophy of mind.* New York: Cambridge University Press.
Searle, J. R. (1998). *Mind, language, and society: Philosophy in the real world.* New York: Basic Books.
Shadel, W. G., & Cervone, D. (in press). Evaluating social cognitive mechanisms that regulate self-efficacy in response to provocative smoking cues: An experimental investigation. *Psychology of Addictive Behaviors.*
Shadel, W. G., Cervone, D., Niaura, R., & Abrams, D. B. (2004). Investigating the Big Five personality factors and smoking: Implications for assessment. *Journal of Psychopathology & Behavioral Assessment, 26*, 185–191.
Shah, J. Y. (2003). Automatic for the people: How representations of others may automatically affect goal pursuit. *Journal of Personality and Social Psychology, 84*, 661–681.
Shoda, Y., Cervone, D., & Downey, G. (Eds.). (in press). *Persons in context: Constructing a science of the individual.* New York: Guilford.
Shweder, R. A. (2007). From persons and situations to preferences and constraints. In Y. Shoda, D. Cervone, & G. Downey (Eds.), *Persons in context: Constructing a science of the individual* (pp. 84–94). New York: Guilford.
Shweder, R. A., & Sullivan, M. (1990). The semiotic subject of cultural psychology. L. A. Pervin (Ed.), *Handbook of Personality: Theory and Research* (pp. 399–416). New York: Guilford.
Smith T. W., & Rhodewalt F. (1986). On states, traits, and processes: A transactional alternative to the individual difference assumptions in type A behavior and physiological reactivity. *Journal of Research in Personality, 20*, 229–251.
Stern, W. (1935). *Allgemeine Psychologie auf personalisticher grundlage.* Dordrecht, The Netherlands: Nijoff.
Sugiyama, L. S., Tooby, J., & Cosmides, L. (2002). Cross-cultural evidence of cognitive adaptations for social exchange among the Shiwiar of Ecuadorian Amazonia. *Proceedings of the National Academy of Sciences, 99*, 11537–11542.

Sullivan, H. S. (1953). *The interpersonal theory of psychiatry*. New York: Norton.

Swann, W. B., Jr., & Seyle, C. (2005). Personality psychology's comeback and its emerging symbiosis with social psychology. *Personality and Social Psychology Bulletin, 31*, 155–165.

Toulmin, S. (1961). *Foresight and understanding: An enquiry into the aims of science*. Bloomington: Indiana University Press.

Toulmin, S. (1985). *The inner life: The outer mind*. Worcester, MA: Clark University Press.

Umberson, D. (1987). Family status and health behaviors: Social control as a dimension of social integration. *Journal of Health and Social Behavior, 28*, 306–319.

Vansteelandt, K., & Van Mechelen, I. (2004). The personality triad in balance: Multidimensional individual differences in situation-behavior profiles. *Journal of Research in Personality, 38*, 367–393.

Wiggins, J. S., & Pincus, A. L. (1992). Personality: Structure and assessment. *Annual Review of Psychology, 43*, 473–504.

Wittgenstein, L. (1953). *Philosophical investigations* (G. E. M. Anscombe, Trans.). Oxford, U.K.: Blackwell.

Wittgenstein, L. (1980). *Remarks on the philosophy of psychology* (G. E. M. Anscombe & G. H. von Wright, Eds., G. E. M. Anscombe, Trans.). Oxford, U.K.: Blackwell.

Wong, R. Y., & Hong, Y. (2005). Dynamic influences of culture on cooperation in the prisoner's dilemma. *Psychological Science, 16*, 429–434.

3

The Self and Social Behavior
The Fragile Self and Interpersonal Self-Regulation

FREDERICK RHODEWALT and BENJAMIN PETERSON
University of Utah

Personality represents those characteristics of individuals that give patterning, meaning, and coherence to their thinking, emotions, and behavior (Pervin, 1996). The *self* is one construct that serves such a role (Leary & Tangney, 2003). A vast amount of psychological research supports the claim that the self provides a principle organizing function in human behavior. Many of the major theoretical perspectives in personality posit units that are variants on the self. From psychodynamic approaches such as Erikson's Ego Psychology to phenomenological views such as Roger's "person centered" theory, the self is a central, coordinating unit involved in cognition, affect, motivation, self-regulation, and, most importantly, interpersonal behavior. This point is made clearly in Rogers' (1951, p. 503) statement that, "as experiences occur in the life of the individual, they are either a) symbolized, perceived, and organized into some relationship to the self, b) ignored because there is not an evident perceived relationship to the self-structure, or c) denied symbolization or given distorted symbolization because the experience is inconsistent with the structure of the self."

A theme running through even the earliest statements about the self is that it serves as a nexus linking the individual to his or her social environment. As is the case with most important ideas in psychology, the interpersonal aspect of the self can be traced back to the influential writings of William James. In his essay "The Self," James (1890/1952, p. 201) described what we would characterize as an interpersonal process model of the self. He depicted the self as being comprised of the "known self" or *Me* (with its material, social, and spiritual selves), self-appreciation (self-esteem), and the behaviors that flow from the first two components, such as self-seeking. The *Social Me* is the interpersonal component in that it is comprised of the recognition a person gets from others. To be exact, James said that we have multiple social selves (see Hogg, this volume, for a more detailed discussion), as many as there are persons (or groups of persons) about whose opinion we care. Not only do people know who they are; they know how they feel about who they are. Self-esteem and other self-relevant emotions such as pride, conceit, and humiliation lead to self-satisfaction or dissatisfaction. Finally, according to James, the self is regulated through the largely interpersonal behaviors of self-seeking and self-preservation. Our self-esteem is tied intimately to what "we back ourselves to be and do" (1890/1952, p. 201), where we place our self-worth. We strive through material possession, social admiration and acceptance, and/or moral superiority to meet our pretensions and, thus, sustain our self-esteem.

The connections among the self, self-esteem, and interpersonal behavior have been the focus of an increasing amount of debate and research attention in recent years. There are a host of issues concerning how self-esteem is related to other elements of the self-concept and how it influences and is influenced by interpersonal relationships and processes (for sense of the breadth of these debates, see Kernis, 2006). In this chapter, we briefly review this research and then develop the proposal that much of our social behavior is in the service of *interpersonal* self-regulation. The term "self-regulation" is employed here more narrowly than it is traditionally used. By self-regulation we mean seeking and interpreting interpersonal feedback that protects and maintains desired self-conceptions. It is the person's self-conceptions that are being "regulated." The key question in this view asks: how does the individual use the interpersonal environment to assist in the process of defining and constructing the self, and affirming important beliefs and goals? We then review research from our laboratory that illustrates the utility of characterizing the self as embedded in interpersonal processes and suggest other personality characteristics that may be profitably studied from this perspective.

We contend, as have others (Higgins, 1996; Leary & Baumeister, 2000), that "regulation" of the self through strategic navigation of the social environment is a general and largely adaptive phenomenon. However, it is also the case that some individuals come to rely too much on others for their self-definition and that others may be drawn to regulate maladaptive beliefs and goals (see also Crocker & Park, 2004). Our main argument is that these general self-regulation processes may be revealed through the comparative study of individuals for whom elements of the process have become exaggerated or out of the ordinary. Such individuals serve as markers moving through the intra- and interpersonal aspects of self-regulation who allow us to clarify and map out the processes underlying the social construction and maintenance of the self.

Although we point to William James' view of the self with its contingencies of self-worth (cf. Crocker & Wolfe, 2001) and interpersonal orientation as a starting point for the model described in this chapter, James is not the only theorist to highlight the interpersonal nature of the self. The self is intimately connected to interpersonal relationships and processes in many influential models of personality. A complete review of this literature is beyond the scope of this chapter; however, we mention a few perspectives here in order to illustrate the point that many theorists share the view that the self is a central organizing element in personality and that it is reciprocally linked to interpersonal contexts.

Representatives of the psychodynamic perspective emphasize the significance of early relationships in the formation of important views of the self that subsequently shape adult self-perceptions and behavior. For example, Alfred Adler (1927) described a set of individual differences that collectively formed what he termed a person's *style of life*. Style of life was synonymous with personality in Adler's scheme and included the person's perceptions of self and the world, activity level, interpersonal orientations and relationships, and approaches to problem-solving. Most relevant to our discussion is Adler's contention that the interpersonal context importantly shaped these characteristics through patterns of interaction with others. Such factors as birth order and associated family roles formed the scaffolding in which the child's style of life developed. Style of life gave organization to the person's life by guiding pursuit of their unique set of interpersonal goals and strategies for achieving those goals.

Similarly, Bowlby (1969, 1973, 1980; see Rholes, Paetzold, & Friedman, this volume) views attachment style as the combination of perceptions of the self as good or bad with perceptions of others as good or bad. These perception-based attachment styles are the product of early interactions with significant caregivers and serve as the basis for expectations, perceptions, emotional responding, and behavior in adult relationships. Like Bowlby, Harry Stack Sullivan (1953) placed major importance in early child-caregiver relationships in the development of the self. In Sullivan's view, the self is constructed of reflected appraisals, or what the child perceives others' reactions to say about who they are. Specifically, self-thoughts and behaviors that are associated with pleasurable, low-anxiety interactions become schematized as the "good me," while self-thoughts and behaviors associated unpleasant, anxiety-producing interactions become encoded as the "bad me." Pleasant, low-anxiety reactions from the mother, and later from peers, become associated with any concurrent thoughts and behaviors of the child and personified into the "good me". Unpleasant, anxiety-producing reactions from others become associated with any concurrent thoughts and behaviors and personified into the "bad me." Finally, Sullivan also included interactions that were so anxiety-producing that concurrent thoughts and behaviors were pushed from consciousness but remained in the "not me" dynamism. The person's self, then, contains a set of interpersonal behaviors that have been associated with negligible anxiety and a set of interpersonal behaviors that have been associated with anxiety. According to Sullivan, people seek to minimize anxiety by interacting in ways that minimize disapproval from others. In this sense, Sullivan's self-system is continually involved with regulating anxiety through interpersonal behavior.

The interpersonal nature of the self is even more explicitly delineated in the object-relations perspective (Greenberg & Mitchell, 1983). Although they differ on a number of conceptual issues, object-relations theorists concur that the self develops as a set of mental representations through early interactions with emotionally significant others. These mental representations are multidimensional and include not only a general self, but also representations of the self in relationship to significant others and representations of others with whom they have had these relationships. The self-representations are emotion-laden and are associated with motivation. People seek to re-experience the self in positive relationships and avoid the self in negative relationships. They also seek to maintain coherence among the various and often contradictory self-representations (Kohut, 1977). Although these characterizations are based largely on clinical observation, recent work employing methods and concepts from social cognition document the importance of mental representations of self, significant others, and self with significant other in channeling perception, affect, and interpersonal behavior (see Andersen, Saribay, & Kooij, this volume; Baldwin, 1992).

In summary, the self by various names has long occupied a central place in personality theory. Moreover, it has been frequently described as a major byproduct of early interpersonal relationships. A theme running through many of these theoretical statements is that self-esteem also arises through these interactions and that people behave in ways that, in the past, have garnered positive, esteem-enhancing responses from others.

THE SELF-SYSTEM AND SELF-ESTEEM

Our goal is to provide a framework for understanding the dynamic interplay between the self and interpersonal behavior. The essence of this model is that when people are ego-involved—that is, when their current outcomes are relevant to their self-concepts—their interpersonal agendas will include enhancing or, at minimum, protecting or maintaining desired self-images. Self-esteem is the lynchpin of this model. Following from Epstein's Cognitive Experiential Self Theory (CEST, 1990), we subscribe to the view that self-esteem enhancement is a basic motive, along with the often countervailing (and self-enhancement constraining) basic motive to accurately assimilate data from reality. People wish to view themselves positively, but they also want to function within a consistent and predictable social environment (Swann, 1983). Self-esteem is central because it provides information about the current state of the self and the need for self-regulation. In a sense, (low) self-esteem is the anxiety of the self-system.

Although the current debates about the nature and varieties of self-esteem are beyond the scope of this chapter, there are several distinctions that are foundational to our current concerns. First, it is important to recognize that self-esteem is a much more complex construct than simple feelings of self-worth, liking, and acceptance that vary from low to high. More critical than whether self-esteem is high or low is whether it is secure, true, or optimal versus insecure, inauthentic, and fragile (see Crocker & Wolfe, 2001; Deci & Ryan, 1995; Kernis, 2003). What does it mean to have fragile self-esteem? According to these views, it means having self-esteem that is contingent on meeting external or introjected standards. These standards can be imposed by others, such as the belief that parental love is conditional on academic performance, or introjected, such as the belief one has worth only when one is academically successful. For example, Crocker, Karpinski, and colleages (Crocker, Karpinski, Quinn, & Chase, 2003) reported that students whose self-worth was contingent on academic success displayed greater fluctuations in state self-esteem upon learning that they had been accepted or rejected by graduate schools than did students whose self-worth was not as contingent on academic success. Individuals with fragile self-esteem strive to possess secure self-esteem by working to meet these external or introjected standards and by creating stability in social interactions and reflected appraisals. Much of this striving is interpersonal, such as attempts to repair self-esteem through defensive and hostile behaviors (Baumeister, Smart, & Boden, 1996; Kernis, Grannemann, & Barclay, 1989; see also Tesser, 1988, 2003), strategic self-presentation (Jones & Pittman, 1982; Jones, Rhodewalt, Berglas, & Skelton, 1981; Schlenker & Weigold, 1992), and other attempts to "shape" the surrounding social environment and the feedback obtained (Snyder & Cantor, 1998; Swann, 1985).

Although fragile and contingent self-esteem clearly intensifies the motive for interpersonal self-regulation, we believe there is more to the story. We contend that self-esteem is a central element in all self-regulation. It is an input and outcome of all goal-directed, self-involved behavior. It is an evaluative tag connected to expectations for performance and social outcomes, as well as a reaction to how well expectations have been realized. In a sense, all self-esteem is contingent in this view because it involves the continuous assessment of how well one is doing compared to some standard of expected competence or social acceptance, as well as an awareness of the implications of those comparisons for the self and future behavior.

SELF-ESTEEM AND THE SELF-REGULATION FRAMEWORK

The model that we are proposing recognizes the difficulty in treating self-knowledge, self-regulation, and self-esteem as independent constructs. Rather, the model that we will outline below (see Figure 3.1) attempts to integrate these three elements into a dynamic process framework that accounts for how individuals deal with self-relevant social information and how this in turn influences how they think and feel about themselves. (See also Rhodewalt & Tragakis, 2003, for earlier thoughts on the importance of self-regulation to self-esteem; and Mischel & Morf, 2003, for a description of the self as a motivated cognitive-affective-action system.) Later, we will discuss how problems at various points in this process can leave the self-system fragile and vulnerable, which will ultimately have important implications not only for how individuals react in particular situations, but also for the quality of their interpersonal relationships, mental and physical health, and well-being in general.

The self-regulation model that is depicted in Figure 3.1 owes much to earlier conceptualizations of the self as both a "theory" (Epstein, 1973) and a "digest" of information that guides and informs self-regulation (Higgins, 1996), as well as to theories of self-esteem that focus more on its importance as information or "monitor" (e.g., sociometer theory; Leary & Baumeister, 2000) rather than simply

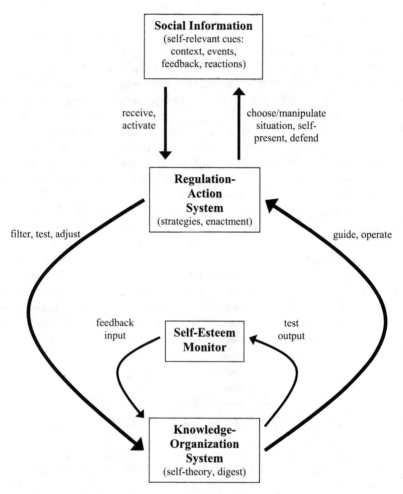

Figure 3.1 A dynamic model of the self and interpersonal self-regulation, emphasizing the role of self-esteem in the process.

something a person possesses. These elements are contained in what we label the *Knowledge-Organization System,* the *Regulation-Action System,* and the input-feedback component *Self-Esteem*. These units interact and operate in a social context that provides *Social Feedback* to the individual. We will describe each element of the model in the following sections but note here that the model is viewed as a complement and extension of existing perspectives on self-esteem rather than an alternative to them.

The self-regulation process starts when a social cue signals that impending events are self-relevant. This may include a variety of situations and events and usually involves the behavior of other people who are more or less important to the individual. The self-system, through its knowledge-organization function, plays an important role in terms of what captures the individual's attention and how it is perceived and interpreted in relation to existing conceptions that may be activated.

Thus, self-knowledge serves as a lens or filter for incoming social information (e.g., the "self-theory" [Epstein, 1973], "personal constructs" [G. Kelly, 1955], or "self-schema" [Markus, 1977]). The specific elements of self-knowledge that are ultimately activated in the situation (and the interpretations that are made) then feed in to plans and strategies for action directed through a process of self-regulation. It is important to acknowledge the self-system's role, through various interpersonal self-regulatory strategies, in choosing and shaping the situations that provide the information to be dealt with. Thus, the self-system is far from a passive entity, and works by actively operating on information received from the environment (reactive regulation), while also actively manipulating the information it is exposed to (proactive regulation). The important dynamic interaction between self-knowledge and self-regulation is linked by a hierarchical structure of motives and goals that give meaning to the specific elements of self-knowledge and direct the situations that are ultimately chosen, the strategies and actions that are pursued, and the standards of progress (success/failure) that are monitored (e.g., Cantor, 1990; Dweck, Higgins, & Grant-Pillow, 2003).

This process sometimes flows smoothly, while at other times it may run into problems. Because of this, the system needs a gauge or "monitor" in the form of (state) self-esteem that indicates the degree of overall effectiveness of the knowledge and regulation components at any given time in response to situational contingencies (most often involving "threats" or challenges to self-construction). This "effectiveness", however, is not judged in an objective sense, but is monitored in accordance with what has been defined as important to the individual, including certain domains, broad motives, and more specific goals, current concerns, life tasks, possible selves, and other standards. Ideally, the level perceived on this monitor will provide important information for potential adjustment to parts of the system, leading to more effective functioning in similar future situations. The effective functioning of the process (as well as the individual's potential for learning and adjusting as a result of indications from self-esteem outcomes) is importantly influenced by the specific content and organization of self-knowledge elements, the adaptiveness of the self-regulatory strategies employed, and the individual's ability (both generally and situation-based) to enact the chosen strategies. Thus, the monitoring function of the self-system (and its relation to self-esteem) is not simply based on the general positivity of one's self-knowledge (what some may refer to as "global" self-esteem), but on one's ability to regulate effectively the self in relation to other people and important goals.

As we will outline later in the chapter, disruptions or vulnerabilities at any point in this system will often produce varying levels of success in goal-directed behavior over time and in different contexts, leading to the fluctuations in (state) self-esteem levels that are seen by many as a hallmark of the "fragile" self (e.g., Kernis, 2003). The nature of these vulnerabilities (and the strategies and behavior patterns they lead to) may allow researchers to differentiate groups of individuals who go about this process of "applying" the self-system to their environment in characteristic ways (e.g., Downey & Feldman, 1996; Morf & Rhodewalt, 2001). The last part of the chapter will apply this framework to additional examples of "fragile" selves and offer future directions for research involving the model.

ELEMENTS OF INTERPERSONAL SELF-REGULATION

In this section, we will give a general overview of the three important parts of the model (self-knowledge, self-regulation, self-esteem) separately, though we once again stress that the process must be viewed as a dynamic whole, with each component both influencing and influenced by the other components. Self-knowledge will be discussed with attention not only to its contents, but also with an eye toward how different ways of conceiving, structuring, and organizing self-knowledge may potentially leave the self-system vulnerable. Next, self-regulation will be discussed in terms of intra- and interpersonal strategies that flow from self-knowledge in the process of negotiating social transactions. Finally, self-esteem will be discussed in terms of its relation to the monitoring function of the self-system, which tracks the effectiveness of the dynamic interaction of the above two components in dealing with information and events from the social environment according to self-defined criteria, such as important goals and standards.

Knowledge-Organization System

Self-knowledge plays a central role in self-regulation and interpersonal behavior—in a sense, the very thing that we are "regulating" in our interactions with the social world is our sense of who we are, or our "self-theory." This more active view of self-knowledge—not only "Who am I?" but also what this means for behavior—has been increasingly emphasized in research on the self in personality and social psychology (Epstein, 1973; Greenwald, 1980; Higgins, 1996; Markus, 1977). The first major function of the self-system, as proposed in the current model, is to organize all self-relevant knowledge into a network of beliefs, expectancies, and goals that allows the person to make sense of their place in the social world. This organizational structure should allow prediction and some sense of control, while importantly enabling action. In describing the self as a *theory*, Epstein (1973) stated that, "like most theories, the self-theory is a conceptual tool for accomplishing a purpose" (p. 407). It not only provides organization to the vast quantities of information already stored in memory, but also (ideally) sets it up as a vehicle for incorporating and integrating new information. In this way, it is not necessarily a static entity; rather, it requires testing and empirical support and is dependent to a certain extent on the latest round of "data" obtained from the social world. This self-theory perspective provides a useful framework for understanding how knowledge about the self is idiographically generated and interpreted, with the potential to be tested and evaluated within one's social environment, garnering "evidence" from reactions of other people as well as other subjective and objective outcomes (i.e., social comparison). The implications of this perspective are many. The most important, however, may be that it puts the individual (as "scientist") in charge of all things "self.". The individual selects what is important and organizes it into an overall theory with testable hypotheses, which ultimately guides action (and reaction) in relation to the social world it depends on for validation.

But, what exactly is important, and what is stored as self-knowledge? While Epstein (1973) certainly emphasized the functionality of the self-theory to a certain point, especially in terms of facilitating problem-solving (and also as being necessary *in order to* function), more recent research and theorizing by Higgins (1996) and others has moved more explicitly forward with the idea that self-knowledge exists only to the extent that it serves important self-regulatory functions for the individual that enable survival in one's social world. Higgins' (1996) idea of the *self-digest*, in particular, fits well with Epstein's conceptualization as a basis for our own model. The digest view of self-knowledge vastly expanded on the notion of self as theory by suggesting which elements of self-knowledge are most functional and important, and in emphasizing the many dimensions on which self-knowledge can be differentiated. In fact, Higgins makes the point that, in order to aid in self-regulation for survival, all self-knowledge is necessarily *contextualized*—that is, it is specific to particular domains and situations that have been personally defined as important. We will first briefly summarize what we see as the main elements of self-knowledge (beliefs, expectancies, evaluations, and goals), as well as the ways in which it can be differentiated and contextualized. Then, we will attempt to integrate the theory and digest perspectives on the self. Finally, we will apply some recent research on the organization and structure of self-knowledge to assess important characteristics that might promote effective self-regulation in the next part of the model. Throughout this discussion, it should once again become clear that an individual's self-knowledge goes far beyond simple self-description (i.e., "Who am I?"). All self-knowledge serves some purpose, both in filtering incoming information and as a guide to action.

Self-Knowledge Content. As part of the self-digest, Higgins (1996) distinguished between three different "actual" selves: the instrumental self, the expectant self, and the monitored self. Whether these are indeed separate selves is open to debate, but we believe that this distinction with its functional framework provides three very important categories of elements that form the bulk of everyone's self-knowledge. These important elements include instrumental beliefs about the contingencies of one's behavior in relation to the social world, expectancies about one's experience with various activities and potential outcomes (including efficacy and ability perceptions), and various needs, motives, and goals that drive behavior and provide standards for ongoing assessment.[1] Self-knowledge content above all is a collection of knowledge, strategies, and decision rules that are idiosyncratic to the individual.

In addition, individuals *evaluate* the contents of their self-knowledge, both in general and in relation to the differentiated aspects, and these evaluations also provide important information for self-regulation, like any element of self-knowledge. Consistent with Kernis and Goldman (2003), we believe that these general and domain-specific self-appraisals should be grouped with the rest of self-knowledge rather than under self-esteem per se. Unlike the outcome-input (state level) self-esteem outlined below, these self-evaluations are relatively stable parts of one's self-construction (though, like other self-knowledge elements, they may be influenced by changes in state-level self-esteem). Also, as part of the (explicitly) constructed self, these relatively stable evaluations are subject to various cognitive distortions employed in the arsenal of intrapersonal self-regulation. Thus, like other parts of self-knowledge, an individual's "global" self-esteem and specific self-appraisals may be more or less in touch with "reality," depending on how the individual construes and interprets it. On the other hand, self-esteem in relation to the self's monitoring function proposed below more accurately reflects reality at any given moment (in terms of one's current effectiveness in goal pursuit), though it is expected to be "calibrated" at the default level of one's general and specific self-appraisals (Leary & Baumeister, 2000).

Self-Knowledge Organization. In the self-regulation view, self-knowledge is highly contextualized and is linked to important domains of potential action and evaluation. At any given moment only a small subset of available self-knowledge is accessible and relevant with regard to goal-directed behavior. Does this mean that it is unnecessary or unimportant to have an integrated, coherent, and overarching sense of self? We suggest that the self-regulation system optimally requires self-knowledge that is de-contextualized to provide an overall, general summary of the individual's beliefs, expectancies, and motives/goals *apart from* any specific domain or situation. This broad, over-arching theory of self serves an integrative function (e.g., Sheldon & Kasser, 1995), while at the same time the different parts of the digest serve to differentiate the contents of the theory into multiple domains and contexts, standpoints, and temporal dimensions. All contents of self-knowledge thus could be organized into a hierarchical web, with higher-order, decontextualized knowledge becoming more differentiated as different domains are identified and combined with standpoints (level of identification, including relational and collective) and temporal dimensions (past, present, and future selves).

The suggestion that adaptive self-knowledge organization requires both differentiation/contextualization along with some degree of higher-level integration bears on the recent debate about self-knowledge structure and adaptive outcomes. In this debate, characteristics that depict "unity" in the self-concept (e.g., self-concept clarity) are often pitted against those that describe "pluralism" (e.g., self-complexity). This research has been reviewed extensively elsewhere (see Campbell, Assinand, & Di Paula, 2003; Showers & Zeigler-Hill, 2003), so we will only address the relevance of these findings to our notion of a Knowledge-Organization System. In short, we argue that research supports the contention that the most "effective" Knowledge-Organization Systems are ones that connect a well-differentiated digest with a clear, coherent, integrated theory of self.

We believe this conclusion is supported by the body of research that has addressed the following questions: Is it good to have a highly differentiated, multi-faceted self-concept (e.g., Linville, 1985)? Or is it best to be clear about who we are (e.g., Campbell, 1990) and be consistent across our different roles (Donahue, Robins, Robers, & John, 1993)? With the exception of Campbell and colleagues (2003), most research on the structure of self-knowledge has addressed either pluralism or unity without looking at both in combination.

Although the results are mixed, we conclude that the tally supports the idea that in most instances integration is more strongly associated with adjustment than is differentiation or compartmentalization (see J. D. Campbell et al., 2003).[2] For example, self-concept clarity (J. D. Campbell, 1990; J. D. Campbell et al., 1996), consistency across experimenter-provided roles (Donahue et al., 1993), and coherence and congruence among goals (Sheldon & Kasser, 1995) all tend to promote positive outcomes, while self-complexity is not necessarily predictive of positive outcomes on its own but tends to serve as a "buffer" against negative outcomes (e.g., depression, anxiety) during times of stress (Linville, 1987). Thus, it would seem from past research that unity in the absence of pluralism is a better state of affairs for self-knowledge organization than pluralism in the absence of unity.

The limitation with this conclusion is that self-clarity research does not also assess how differentiated and contextualized the self is, just as the "self-concept differentiation" research by Donahue and colleagues does not assess how many roles and domains are important to the individual (i.e., idiographically). Similarly, while Sheldon and Kasser's (1995) method directs participants to generate their own important personal strivings for subsequent ratings in terms of coherence and congruence, individual differences in the variety and number of goals generated (a dimension of differentiation or complexity) is not taken into consideration. On the other side, while Linville's (1985) self-complexity technique has participants create multiple categories of attributes that describe themselves, the emphasis is on the extent to which these "self-aspects" are distinct and non-overlapping, not on how they relate and tie together. It is possible that studies assessing unity at a general level in combination with domain specific differentiation would better answer the question of how self-knowledge structure and organization relates to psychological adjustment and resiliency.[3]

Our interpretation of this research area is consistent with analysis by Showers and Zeigler-Hill (2003), who also suggest that self-knowledge organized in such a way as to be optimally differentiated and integrated in a clear, coherent, consistent manner may produce "an exceptionally healthy combination of stability and flexibility" (p. 53). This is also consistent with more general theorizing on the integrative complexity of one's social thinking (e.g., Schroder, 1971; Suedfeld, Tetlock, & Streufert, 1992; Tetlock & Suedfeld, 1988). Applied to thinking about the self, self-knowledge must first be differentiated to a certain extent (complex) before it can be integrated together with a common theme.

In sum, an integratively complex Knowledge-Organization System is sufficiently complex and differentiated so as to provide multiple options when confronted with changing situations, outcomes, and other social information (providing flexibility), yet integrated so that the whole repertoire of "multiple selves" and related goals are connected in some way to a "core self"(providing stability over time).[4]

Regulation-Action System

The regulation action system is the bridge that connects the self to interpersonal behavior and social cognition. More precisely, the analogy of the self as a theory and digest suggests that, like other theories, the self is a guide for what to expect but also requires empirical support. Support is typically in the form of social regard and feedback. People, like scientists, must go about the task of *testing* their theories in their everyday lives. However, the analogy of the self-theorist as scientist is incomplete. If we are scientists, we are zealous scientists who defend our self-views in the face of sometimes (more for some than others) conflicting social data (e.g., Greenwald, 1980). Either way, another important function of the self-system is to test out and apply our beliefs, expectancies, goals, and evaluations in the interpersonal world, and to keep the self in touch with reality.

As we emphasized in the previous section, the actions that are taken in response to self-relevant social information will flow directly from the self-theory and its digest of stored information from past experience (beliefs, expectancies, evaluations), as well as goals and standards that have been set in important domains. Thus, the strategies and actions outlined below (both intrapersonal and interpersonal) will depend on which part of the digest is activated and the goals, beliefs, evaluations, and expectations related to it.

Of course, success in self-regulation will be determined in part by how functional the content of the theory/digest is and how effectively it is structured and organized for use, as well as the ability to choose appropriate strategies and carry them out. Even with a well-organized and functional self-theory and an adequate repertoire of regulatory strategies and potential responses, problems can still arise in the process that prevent the individual from carrying out their theory-directed action. These "implementation" problems may arise from within the person (i.e., individual differences in impulsivity or self-control; e.g., Metcalfe & Mischel, 1999) or as a function of the situation and prior/concurrent behavior (i.e., "ego depletion" or cognitive load; e.g., Muraven, Tice, & Baumeister, 1998).

Once again, the regulation-action system is intertwined with the knowledge-organization system as part of the overall self-system in a dynamic interaction. As mentioned earlier, we have applied the term "self-regulation" in a somewhat selective and idiosyncratic fashion, referring specifically to activities related to self-theory definition and maintenance (Rhodewalt & Sorrow, 2003). The two subsystems interact in a process similar to that described by Carver and Scheier (1981) in the TOTE (test-operate-test-exit) model (see also Baumeister & Vohs, 2003). In this process, the relevant theory-based knowledge is tested by comparing it to incoming social information (comparisons, feedback, behavior from others, etc.) and operating on the information if a discrepancy exists in order to bring it in line with the standard corresponding to the activated goal or motive. The individual may "operate" by performing various cognitive operations on input, often involving selective manipulation of the contents of their own knowledge; these cognitive operations may include selective recall from memory and self-affirmation on unrelated characteristics or defensive distortion of the information itself so that its perceived impact on the self-theory is minimized (intrapersonal self-regulation). Often before these intrapersonal strategies are called upon, the individual may address the information directly through behavioral response, including such varied reactions as withdrawing from a situation, applying more effort to a problem, engaging a self-protective strategy such as self-handicapping, or confronting a threatening person with aggressive behavior (interpersonal self-regulation). Additional tests are then made and further operations are carried out if deemed necessary. Eventually, the system will exit this loop when there is no longer a (perceived) discrepancy and no further operation is needed, or if all possible operations have been exhausted without success.

An important part of the self-system model not explicitly addressed in the TOTE framework is the individual's ability to *adjust* aspects of the self-theory if operations are not successful, either as part of ongoing intrapersonal self-regulation or in response to feedback from the self-esteem monitor described later. A truly "functional" self-system should likely possess the ability to adapt the elements of self-knowledge and goals pursued, as well as the behavioral strategies that serve these, when difficulties are encountered (e.g., Epstein, 1973; Kernis & Goldman, 2003; Paulhus & Martin, 1988). Without the ability to adjust, given the presence of negative feedback from the system as currently constructed, individuals will continue employing the same strategies over and over again with varying levels of success. This idea will be explored more fully later in our discussion of vulnerabilities often seen in "fragile" selves.

Self-Esteem

In the model displayed in Figure 3.1, state self-esteem is an input as well as outcome of the dynamic self-regulation process. In this way, it is intimately tied to the important monitoring function of the self-system, which tracks how well the individual is negotiating the interpersonal environment with regard to the objectives dictated by the self-theory and digest. As an input it informs self-regulation with regard to the current status of the individual, and as an output it informs the individual with regard to the efficacy of self-regulation. Thus, this self-esteem is a "state" feeling or moment-to-moment evaluation of one's worth based on self-regulatory effectiveness, as opposed to more "global" (or general) feelings of self-worth and/or specific self-appraisals in particular domains (though these state feelings certainly have an important influence on the latter evaluations—see our discussion of this point earlier). As stated earlier, we see all of these definitions of self-esteem as related to one another, though general and domain-specific ("typical") self-appraisals are conceptualized as important elements of the individual's self-knowledge (e.g., Kernis & Goldman, 2003) that are relatively stable (in general) on a situation-to-situation basis. Self-esteem as outcome of and subsequent input to the knowledge-regulation process (more "current" appraisals), on the other hand, can be relatively stable or unstable depending on the ongoing effectiveness of one's self-regulatory efforts (and may be influenced by any potential vulnerability within the process that disrupts self-regulation of behavior toward important goals). As such, it may be related not only to Sullivan's earlier conception of anxiety, but also to more recent conceptions of self-related affect (e.g., Tracy & Robins, 2004). The important point is to distinguish this more process-related and "energizing" aspect of self-esteem from the self-appraisals that are more typical and are an important part of our self-knowledge. Both may inform self-regulation (as self-knowledge in general does, for the latter), but at different levels—and only on-line—state is explicitly tied to the contingencies of the current interpersonal environment. This feature, as well as its distinctly affective flavor, give self-esteem its energizing nature that can have important implications for defensive and reactive behavior.

Summary

The components of the self-system described in the preceding sections are dynamically interrelated. The self-system is triggered by any information in the social environment that is deemed self-relevant; this could be certain situations, contextual cues, other people, events, feedback on one's performance or characteristics, and so on. Self-knowledge, with its contents (beliefs, values, expectancies, goals) and organization as theory and digest (e.g., integrative complexity and validity), serves several major purposes for the self-system. First, it gives personal meaning to social information and directs attention toward aspects of the social environment that are defined as important. Second, it serves as a guide for how one should deal with this personally relevant social information. In this way, social information is compared to personal standards and goals to determine what action needs to be taken. Depending on which standards and goals have been activated, as well as what domains they fall under, the system can then employ various self-regulatory strategies in the attempt to bring behavior (interpersonal) and/or cognitions (intrapersonal) in line with the goals and standards that have been set. As self-knowledge and self-regulation interact in this way, there is also a third component of the self-system that is monitoring the action. This monitor provides information in the form of (state) self-esteem that feeds back into self-knowledge and subsequent self-regulation.

The above summary is most applicable in situations where the individual is anticipating or reacting to incoming social information (e.g., ego-involved). One additional part that bears emphasis is the major role the self-system plays in both choosing situations that are most likely to provide feedback congruent with self-conceptions, as well as actively using self-presentational strategies to shape the impressions of other people and their reactions (see Swann, 1985). Thus, some "effective" self-systems can stack the deck in favor of confirming their theory of self by using such proactive self-regulatory strategies, enabling the individual to keep process-level self-esteem at a high level when successful. All in all, this level of state self-esteem should remain stable and relatively high given that individuals are able to negotiate their social environments through proactive interpersonal self-regulatory strategies, while also defending against any discrepant information that makes it through by using reactive interpersonal and intrapersonal self-regulation if need be.

One important point that has not been addressed throughout this discussion of the self-system relates to the recent upsurge in attention to dual-process models in social psychology. While this is not a focus of this chapter, we feel it is important to mention for purposes of the discussion that follows. For example, Epstein's Cognitive-Experiential Self Theory (CEST; 1990) posits that there are two systems in operation as we deal with information from the social world: one that is more rational and controlled, and another that is more affect-driven and automatic (cf., Fazio, 1990; Greenwald & Banaji, 1995; Wilson, Lindsey, & Schooler, 2000). In most descriptions of these two processes, they are seen as relatively separate though mutually influencing, with the experiential/automatic/implicit system possibly residing somewhere in the "preconscious" (Spencer, Jordan, Logel,

& Zanna, 2005). The implications of this perspective for all aspects of the self-system described above are quite obvious. Much of the contents of self-knowledge—including, most importantly, goals, evaluations, and expectancies—could be formulated by the individual at both the explicit and implicit levels. For example, much recent work has been devoted to both self-evaluations (Brown, Bosson, Zeigler-Hill, & Swann, 2003; Greenwald & Farnham, 2000; Jordan et al., 2003) and goals (McClelland, Koestner, & Weinberger, 1989; Thrash & Elliot, 2002) at the implicit level. Additionally, self-regulation of behavior has been shown to proceed at a more automatic level outside of the individual's control (Bargh et al., 2001; Bargh & Williams, 2006). This is most likely to occur when certain goals have been primed below the level of conscious awareness or when the individual is unable to exert conscious control over behavior (i.e., lack of "opportunity"; Fazio, 1990). Thus, it is possible that the self-system as a whole could be engaged either cognitively, with rational thought and an explicit self-theory and digest guiding self-regulation, or experientially, where it is guided in a more automatic manner by an implicit self-theory and digest. As most of this research involving self-evaluations and goals has shown, the extent to which these two routes to engaging the system contain similar elements (are congruent) may play an important role in any discussion of vulnerability within the self-system (e.g., Jordan et al., 2003).

VULNERABILITY IN THE SYSTEM: THE FRAGILE SELF

Most research on the "fragile" self has focused exclusively on the *outcome* aspect of self-esteem in our model; either it is consistently low (e.g., people who are depressed) or it is relatively unstable over time. Very often, this is the manifestation of fragile selves, though it is certainly possible to envision an individual with a vulnerable and fragile self who is able to achieve consistently high outcome-based self-esteem either by effectively self-regulating behavior in relation to important goals or by setting "pretensions" at a low level such that vulnerabilities in the self-system are not enough to pose a problem to self-regulation. But, within the model outlined above, we would emphasize that vulnerabilities can exist within multiple parts of either of the main subsystems (Knowledge-Organization and Regulation-Action) and that these vulnerabilities most likely (but not necessarily) will have an impact on process-level self-esteem that is driven by the system's monitoring function. Thus, anything within the system that makes it difficult for the individual to accomplish important goals within important domains, contexts, and relationships will ultimately leave the individual vulnerable to drops in self-esteem. In turn, a vulnerable self-system must be defended to a greater extent than a system that is more secure, resistant, and/or flexible in the face of threat. Drops in self-esteem, even if temporary, are aversive to most, and much time and effort can be spent on the part of those who may be vulnerable in the maintenance and protection of one's ideal level of self-esteem, as well as in "seeking" it (Crocker & Park, 2004) when the "monitor" is below the ideal level. Thus, it is important to identify some aspects of the self-system that may leave it vulnerable to these temporary drops in self-esteem.

The focus in identifying vulnerabilities, then, is on aspects of the Knowledge-Organization and Regulation-Action Systems (or the surrounding environment) that may make it difficult for the individual to accomplish important goals, and in the process maintain self-esteem as defined in the model. As the two subsystems are reciprocally related in the self's interactions with the social environment, vulnerabilities in one (i.e., unrealistically high evaluation of one's attributes in a certain domain) will often lead to vulnerabilities in the other (strategies involving excessive self-promotion in interpersonal self-regulation). These observations are illustrated in the final section of this chapter.

PUTTING IT ALL TOGETHER: SOME EXAMPLES

If self-esteem is the currency in the exchanges between the self and the person's social environment, it is at a premium when the self is on the line. Are there individuals for whom self-esteem is at a premium more often than it is for other individuals? If so, are there "defensive styles" that provide us insight into the process of interpersonal self-esteem regulation? In this section we attempt to address these questions by briefly describing two lines of research that have attempted to connect specific self concerns to interpersonal behavior for the purposes of self-esteem regulation. These research programs had different starting points. The dynamic, self-regulatory model of narcissism grew out of an interest in understanding the cognitive, affective, and interpersonal processes that underlie a classic personality type (Morf & Rhodewalt, 2001; Rhodewalt, 2001; Rhodewalt & Sorrow, 2003). Self-handicapping, in contrast, was phenomenon driven, and as we expanded our understanding of the social and individual difference parameters of the self-handicapping phenomenon, an interpersonal self-regulation model evolved (Rhodewalt & Tragakis, 2003). These models and supporting research have been extensively reviewed elsewhere (for narcissism, see Morf & Rhodewalt, 2001; Rhodewalt, 2001; and Rhodewalt & Sorrow, 2003; for self-handicapping, see Rhodewalt & Tragakis, 2002), so we will only briefly describe these frameworks here. The discussion will focus on the interpersonal regulation—self-esteem—social feedback elements of these two models and fitting them into the framework described above.

Narcissism and Interpersonal Self-Esteem Regulation

Narcissists possess the characteristics of (a) grandiosity, self-importance, and perceived uniqueness; (b) preoccupations with fantasies of unlimited success, wealth, beauty, and power; (c) exhibitionism and attention seeking; and (d) emotional lability, particularly in response to criticism or threat to self-esteem, manifesting in feelings of rage, shame, or humiliation (*Statistical Manual of Mental Disorder,* American Psychiatric Association, *DSM-IV-TR,* 2000). According to the *DSM-IV-TR,* narcissists are also prone to interpersonal difficulties that likely are attributable to their own interpersonal style. Narcissists convey a sense of entitlement and expect special treatment from others without the need to reciprocate or show empathy. In fact, they exploit others for their own needs. With regard to self-esteem, the *DSM-IV-TR* specifies that "self-esteem is almost invariably very fragile; the person may be preoccupied with how well he or she is doing and how well he or she is regarded by others" (p. 350).

Obviously, narcissism is comprised of a complex set of behaviors that, on the surface, appear contradictory and paradoxical (Morf & Rhodewalt, 2001). However, we contend that a chronic, cognitive/affective preoccupation with the self ties together the surface characteristics into a psychologically coherent pattern (Akhtar & Thompson, 1982; Westen, 1990). Our research has sought to cast narcissism as a set of processes concerned with interpersonal *self*-regulation. Narcissists' selves are always on the line because they possess transient, overblown, and fragile self-images that can only be sustained through social validation. Thus, the selves of narcissists are critically reliant on feedback from others to sustain their senses of self-worth. Narcissistic self-regulation is transactional; narcissists attempt to channel the responses of others so as to receive self-enhancing feedback, and these efforts shape their interpersonal relationships and social contexts. The social context, in turn, makes salient, intensifies, or rechannels current self-concerns. In fact, it can be argued that the narcissist's self is context-bound and that transitions from one social context to another lend to the fragility and vulnerability of their self-views.

The narcissistic self-system described by Morf and Rhodewalt (2001) can be mapped onto Figure 3.1. The narcissist's Knowledge-Organization System incorporates both the cognitive and affective (or evaluative) components of the self. As described above, this Knowledge-Organization System is the mental repository of autobiographical information, reflected appraisals, self-ascribed traits and competencies, and self-schemata, including possible selves, self-with-others, and undesired selves. It also contains the attendant evaluations of what is known about the self or, collectively, "global" self-esteem and domain-specific self-evaluations. A review of research on the narcissistic self-concept is beyond our focus here. In brief, it is highly positive although overblown and inflated (Gabriel, Critelli, & Ee, 1994; John & Robins, 1994; Rhodewalt & Eddings, 2002). Perhaps because it is inflated and unrealistic, narcissists' self-esteem is also fragile in that it is highly reactive to positive and negative feedback from others (Rhodewalt, Madrian, & Cheney, 1998; Rhodewalt & Morf, 1998).

The Knowledge-Organization System is also contextualized according to various domains that are more or less important to the individual, including those on which they base many of their goals that ultimately affect feelings of self-worth. We have recently attempted to take a closer look at the domains of importance to narcissists, as well as their self-evaluations in these domains. Using Pelham and Swann's (1989) Self-Attribute Questionnaire, narcissists tend to rate themselves highly in all possible domains and report that they are highly certain of this, while also reporting that this is very close to their ideal selves in each domain (Rhodewalt & Morf, 1995; Rhodewalt, Tragakis, & Finley, 2002; Rhodewalt, Tragakis, & Peterson, 2003). Additionally, on Crocker and Wolfe's (2001) Contingencies of Self-Worth Scale, the only domain on which narcissists consistently report basing most of their self-worth is the general domain of "competition" (Rhodewalt,

Tragakis, & Peterson, 2003). These results speak to the highly transient nature of the narcissistic self-concept, as well as to their dominant motivation; individuals who believe they are good at everything and base their self-worth on always "winning" are bound to face (and "see") opportunities for both threat and enhancement in most situations they encounter. Again, this type of self-concept contains highly positive self-evaluations but is ultimately extremely vulnerable to discrepant social feedback.

One additional aspect of the narcissistic self-concept bears mention. As we will argue, the narcissistic self-concept is highly dependent on social feedback within specific interpersonal relationships and social contexts. Thus, it is not surprising that the narcissistic self-concept is strongly organized around significant relationships. In a replication of the Hinkley and Andersen (1998) procedure, Rhodewalt, Peterson, and Sorrow (2006) primed positive or negative significant others in participants pre-selected for level of narcissism. Consistent with previous research, the primes produced a shift in the participant's working self-concept in the direction of that participant's self-with-significant-other representations assessed at an earlier session. Participants who were primed with a positive significant other viewed themselves more positively than participants who were primed with another individual's significant other. Likewise, participants who were primed with a negative significant other viewed themselves more negatively than did participants who were primed with another individual's significant other. More important, this effect was significantly greater for narcissists than it was for non-narcissists. Given that narcissism is believed to be a compensation for problematic significant relationships in childhood and adolescence, it is meaningful that in adulthood interaction partners can inadvertently and automatically trigger vulnerable self-conceptions against which the narcissist must defend.

The Regulation-Action System connects the narcissistic self-concept with the social environment through a set of self-regulatory units that include both intra- and interpersonal strategies enacted to protect or enhance positive self-views. Narcissists adopt a number of strategies that allow them to actively manipulate their social relationships both at the point of generation (interpersonal regulation) and at the point of interpretation (intrapersonal regulation). Intrapersonal strategies include distorted interpretations of outcomes and selective recall of past events (Rhodewalt & Eddings, 2002; Rhodewalt & Morf, 1998). Interpersonal regulation covers a multitude of self-presentational ploys and social manipulations executed in the service of engineering positive feedback or blunting negative feedback about the self.

Perhaps the best illustration of narcissists' interpersonal self-regulation can be found in Morf and Rhodewalt (1993). They employed Tesser's Self-Evaluation Maintenance theory (SEM, Tesser, 1988) to demonstrate narcissists' exaggerated and interpersonally destructive responses to perceived threat. SEM involves thinking about and relating to psychologically important others in ways that enhance or maintain positive self-evaluations. Morf and Rhodewalt (1993) sought to examine the extent to which narcissists would engage in self-esteem restorative behavior at the expense of their relationships with others. Participants who were selected based on their responses to the Narcissistic Personality Inventory (NPI, Raskin

& Hall, 1979; Raskin & Terry, 1988) were either slightly or substantially outperformed on an ego-relevant task by a close other. They were then provided with an opportunity to evaluate the outperforming target's personality. Cross-cutting this manipulation was a manipulation of the publicity of the evaluation. Private evaluation participants believed that their evaluations would remain unseen by the target, whereas public evaluation participants believed that they would have to provide their evaluations to the target in a face-to-face interaction. Thus, we pitted the motivation to restore self-esteem against the motivation to be approved of and accepted by others. Narcissists were more negative in their evaluation of threatening targets than they were of non-threatening targets. More important, although threatened narcissists were less negative when their evaluations were public than private, the public, face-to-face feedback provided by threatened narcissists was significantly more negative than the feedback provided by low-threat narcissists and high- and low-threat non-narcissists in other public conditions. In sum, narcissists' interpersonal behavior in the service of self-image protection may often come at the expense of pleasant interactions.

It follows that using others for self-esteem enhancement should ultimately undermine relationships or reduce the likelihood of forming meaningful relationships in the first place. There is support for this expectation. In a study of romantic relationships, W. K. Campbell (1999) reported that narcissists are attracted to romantic partners who possess valued characteristics, such as physical attractiveness, and who are also admiring of the narcissist. They are uninterested in romantic partners who are caring. People also report that their narcissistic acquaintances act to impress others by bragging about themselves and putting others down (Buss & Chiodo, 1991). In addition, other research reveals that narcissists self-promoting interpersonal strategies may have initial short-term gains but long-term negative outcomes. Paulhus (1998) reported that while interaction partners initially found narcissists to be competent and entertaining, after repeated interactions narcissists were viewed as arrogant and hostile (see also Morf, 1994).

Finally, the dynamic, self-regulatory model of narcissism focuses on Self-Esteem as connected to the monitoring function of the self-system, whereby the effectiveness of the Regulation-Action System in meeting the goals and needs of the Knowledge-Organization System is tracked. Evidence for this on-line monitoring function comes from a series of studies that examine the effects of experimental and naturalistic social feedback on narcissists' self-esteem. In the laboratory, Rhodewalt and Morf (1998) provided participants with success and failure feedback on successive tests of intelligence. The impact of this feedback produced greater changes in the self-esteem (and anger) of high NPI participants than it did among low NPI participants.

Similarly, in a series of daily diary studies, we have examined the entrainment of self-esteem to various dimensions of social interaction (Rhodewalt, Madrian, & Cheney, 1998; Rhodewalt, Tragakis, & Hunh, 2000; Rhodewalt, Tragakis, & Finley, 2002). In three of the four studies, NPI-defined narcissism was significantly related to instability of self-esteem, as computed using the standard deviation in daily self-esteem over the span of a week (e.g., Kernis et al., 1989, 1993). Thus, there is some support for the idea that the state self-esteem of narcissists moves around more over time than the state self-esteem of individuals low in narcissism, which we see as a manifestation of narcissists' self-concept vulnerability.

The daily diary studies also provide insight into why narcissists display greater fluctuations in their feelings of self-worth than do less narcissistic individuals. As noted by Kernis (2003), self-esteem will be unstable to the extent that one's self-esteem is contingent on social feedback and the extent to which that feedback varies in its evaluative implications. Narcissism is characterized by disturbances in interpersonal relations. If one's relationships wax and wane from the positive to the conflicted, then self-evaluative social feedback should also be highly varied and inconsistent. The daily diary studies have allowed us to examine the aspects of social feedback with which narcissistic (and non-narcissistic) self-esteem covaries. To illustrate, Rhodewalt et al. (1998, Study 2), had participants describe each significant interaction that transpired during that day and to report their current self-esteem. Respondents evaluated the interactions along dimensions such as intimacy, the amount of disclosure, and the extent to which they felt socially integrated, as well as the overall quality of the interaction. The results revealed that narcissists reported on average that 25% of their interactions were negative, compared to 16% for less narcissistic individuals, supporting the claim that narcissism is characterized by difficult interpersonal relationships (see also McCullough, Emmons, Kilpatrick, & Mooney, 2003, for daily diary evidence that narcissists perceive themselves to more often be the victims of interpersonal transgressions). More critical was the finding that the overall positivity/negativity of their daily social encounters was more strongly related to the daily self-esteem of narcissists than it was to the self-esteem of non-narcissists.

For narcissists, on-line variations in feelings of self-worth are more closely contingent on variations in the quality of their social interactions than is the self-esteem of less narcissistic people. We have pursued this basic finding by trying to uncover the specific qualities of social interactions to which narcissistic self-esteem is entrained (Rhodewalt, Tragakis, & Hunh, 2000). We have learned that for all individuals, self-esteem rises and falls with the extent to which their interactions support their self-concepts, make them feel included, engender a sense of intimacy, and are free of conflict. However, for narcissists, the extent to which they felt socially included and the extent to which the interaction supported their self-concept were more strongly related to their daily self-esteem.

We were somewhat surprised that feelings of social inclusion would so strongly predict the momentary self-esteem of narcissists because other findings indicate that they do not particularly value social acceptance (Raskin, Novachek, & Hogan, 1991). This unexpected finding prompted us to investigate more deeply what narcissists mean by social inclusion. It is possible that social inclusion or integration means something different to narcissists than it does to others. To investigate this, we designed a questionnaire to assess the layperson's understanding of what it means to feel socially included (Rhodewalt, Tragakis, Eddings, & Sorrow, 2001). Based on pilot testing, we asked about six sources of felt inclusion or acceptance by others, and included the possibilities that people could feel more a part of the group or interaction if it made them feel admired or influential, if it validated and respected their opinions, or if it directly bolstered their self-esteem (in addition to making them feel accepted). Our suspicions about narcissists were supported: Narcissists reported that they felt more included when the interaction made them feel like they were admired, supported their self-esteem, and when they felt influential. It is noteworthy and consistent with past research that narcissists reported that social approval was less a source of feelings of inclusion and acceptance than did less narcissistic respondents.

As mentioned previously, there is considerable evidence that narcissists are hyper-responsive to threats to the self, reacting with anger and reductions in self-esteem (Rhodewalt & Morf, 1998). These reactions betray the fact that their positive self-views are confidently held. Recent developments in the assessment of implicit cognition discussed briefly above may offer an alternative way of exploring this issue, and already there are some suggestive findings. For example, Jordan, Spencer, Zanna, Hoshino-Browne, and Correll (2003) administered the NPI to a group of individuals categorized as possessing high or low explicit self-esteem and high or low implicit self-esteem. They report that high explicit/low implicit self-esteem individuals were the most narcissistic as indicated by their NPI scores. Consistent with this finding, Kernis and colleagues (2005) found that high explicit/low implicit individuals were more self-aggrandizing than were people who were high on both measures of self-esteem. Many questions remain to be answered about the assessment and meaning of implicit self-esteem (see Fazio & Olson, 2003), and more research needs to be done, but work in this area may provide important insights into the social motivations of narcissistic individuals.

Self-Handicapping

As introduced by Jones and Berglas (1978), self-handicapping is a defensive strategy in which people erect or claim an impediment to successful performance. The self-handicapper anticipates a threat to the self and, thus, manages the attributional context in which subsequent competency-based performances occur. According to Jones and Berglas (1978), the self-handicapper, by creating an additional explanation for failure that is unrelated to ability, is capitalizing on the attributional principles of discounting and augmentation (Kelley, 1972). Lack of ability is discounted as the cause of failure because of the presence of the handicap, while ability attributions are enhanced or augmented in the event of success because of the presence of the handicap. Decades of research have provided a portrait of the psychology of the self-handicapper (see Rhodewalt & Tragakis, 2002, for a review). Self-handicapping was originally posited to be motivated by the desire to protect a positive but insecurely held competency image (Jones & Berglas, 1978), and experimental inductions such as response-noncontingent success feedback indeed foster self-handicapping responses (Berglas & Jones, 1978; Rhodewalt & Davison, 1986). People who are uncertain about the basis of their competencies are defensive, especially when these competencies are challenged. It is interesting to note that unstable high self-esteem individuals are more likely to self-handicap than are stable high self-esteem individuals (Newman & Wadas, 1997), as too are people who are uncertain about their competencies (Harris & Snyder, 1986).

An irony is that, compared to other responses to challenge such as increased effort or preparation, self-handicapping perpetuates confusion about the self by maintaining attributional ambiguity about one's competencies and capacities. We argue that additional features of the self-handicapper's Knowledge-Organization System justify self-handicapping behavior. Evidence suggests that self-handicapping is most appealing to individuals who hold uncertain but positive competency images and who also believe that those competencies are fixed and immutable, as opposed to incremental and amenable to practice, effort, and improvement (Rhodewalt, 1994; cf., Dweck, 1999; Dweck & Leggett, 1988; Elliot & Dweck, 1988). For these individuals, failure feedback is to be avoided at all costs because failure indicates a lack of ability, attractiveness, or social grace about which nothing can be done. Self-handicapping, then, can be viewed as a strategy in the Regulation-Action System pursued by individuals who hold positive but uncertain and insecure competency images, and who believe that failure feedback in the absence of mitigating circumstances would indicate lack of a competency that cannot be modified by learning, practice, or effort.

Self-esteem plays a monitoring function in the self-handicapping process. In the Rhodewalt and Tragakis (2003) framework, the distal motives to self-handicap clearly involve self-esteem as an input, outcome, and "comparator," Jones and Berglas (1978) suggested that self-handicappers have experienced a pattern of noncontingent success feedback in their past, such as receiving parental praise when the basis of the praise or the cause of the accomplishment itself is unclear. Thus, these individuals possess positive self-conceptions that are fragile and frequently on the line. Research has shown that self-esteem plays an important role in the attributional, motivational, and affective processes that underlie self-handicapping behavior. As noted previously, positive but unstable self-esteem factors into the decision to self-handicap (Harris & Snyder, 1986; Kernis, Grannemann, & Barclay, 1992; Newman & Wadas, 1997), triggers biased processing and attributional strategizing during the threat (Rhodewalt, Morf, Hazlett, & Fairfield, 1991; Tice, 1991), and is an important output of the self-handicapping act (Feick & Rhodewalt, 1998; Rhodewalt & Hill, 1994; Rhodewalt et al., 1991).

Finally, self-handicapping shapes the impressions that others form and impacts their responses to the self-handicapper (Luginbuhl & Palmer, 1991; Rhodewalt, Sanbonmatsu, Tschanz, Feick, & Waller, 1995; Smith & Strube, 1991). Across several studies, there is evidence that perceivers incorporate self-handicapping into an attributional analysis of the actor's performance. Perceivers (like self-handicappers) also discount ability attributions when the target's performance is poor and augment ability attributions when performance is good. However, there are interpersonal costs to self-handicapping. It is clear that perceivers do not like self-handicappers (Luginbuhl & Palmer, 1991; Rhodewalt et al., 1995; Smith & Strube, 1991). In addition, Rhodewalt and colleagues (1995) asked participants to evaluate the performance of confederates who performed equally poorly in an objective sense. They rated the performance of the self-handicapping confederate as significantly worse than they rated the performance of the nonself-handicapping confederate. Thus, although perceivers give self-handicappers the attributional benefit of the doubt, they also provide feedback that is more severe and threatening than the feedback that they would provide to someone who has performed poorly without self-handicapping.

The research described in this section illustrates how the model can organize the study of interpersonal self-regulation. The self is dynamically involved in selecting social settings, eliciting and interpreting social feedback, and affectively monitoring its success in these activities. Perhaps what is most striking about these two illustrations is that among those with fragile selves, narcissists and self-handicappers, the strategies employed to regulate self-esteem and self-knowledge actually undermine the goal of attaining self-certainty.

CONCLUSION AND FUTURE DIRECTIONS

The ideas that the self is a central element in personality and that it is shaped through interpersonal processes are not new. However, in this chapter, we have attempted to expand these ideas by describing the self as being dynamically regulated through social interaction. We suggest that this self-regulation underlies the consistent patterns of behavior that are, in effect, the "hallmarks" of personality (see also Cervone, Caldwell, & Orom, this volume; Mischel & Morf, 2003). The model of interpersonal self-regulation presented in this chapter focuses on the critical role of self-esteem as an input and outcome of the regulation process. In our conception, self-esteem acts in conjunction with the monitoring function of the self-system to provide important information about the state of the system as well as an evaluation of the success of such self-regulatory activities. In its information role, self-esteem directs goal orientation and strategic behavior. In its evaluation role, self-esteem not only affectively tags progress toward goal attainment, but feeds forward into its information and adjustment mode.

We further suggest that because of its role as input to and outcome of self-regulation success, all self-esteem is contingent on the current goal-directed behavior of the individual. This is not to say that self-esteem is not more or less contingent in ways described in other frameworks (Crocker & Wolfe, 2001; Deci & Ryan, 1995). Rather, we suggest that self-esteem may have multiple on-line contingencies. What needs to be considered when judging the effectiveness of the self-esteem system is not whether it is contingent, but what exactly it is contingent on (what is important to the individual? how is this important self-knowledge arranged?) and how these contingencies are pursued (are the strategies used for maintaining/increasing self-esteem adaptive or maladaptive?; cf. Crocker & Park, 2004). Thus, more attention needs to be focused on deeper levels of the process, rather than surface-level contingencies that may or may not be influential.

The self-regulation model of self-esteem is among several perspectives that assign self-esteem a key role in both self understanding and action (e.g., Leary & Baumeister, 2000; Pyszczynski, Greenberg, & Solomon, 2004). Although we acknowledge the importance of an individual's general ("global"), as well as domain-specific, self-appraisals and reports of self-worth, our model emphasizes the self-evaluations that directly flow from the individual's perceived effectiveness in the attainment of important goals ("process-level" or current). That is, self-esteem in our model is intimately tied with goal pursuit, and goal pursuit is intimately tied with self-knowledge content and organization. In this way, to say that it is problematic to be in pursuit of self-esteem or to have contingent self-esteem (e.g., Crocker & Park, 2004) is somewhat rhetorical, as it is difficult to separate these judgments from everyday goal pursuit. Rather, we believe it would be more fruitful to focus on the goals themselves (what exactly is being pursued) as well as the responses enlisted to pursue those goals. Carrying out these recommendations will require a finer-grained analysis and integration of personal goals (e.g., life tasks, current concerns, personal strivings), self-knowledge content and organization, and self-regulatory behaviors. This means more of a reliance on idiographic assessments of goals and other self-knowledge components, as well as diary methods and even more "on-line" assessments of self-evaluation (e.g., Vallacher, Nowak, Froelich, & Rockloff, 2002). Finally, although most of the discussion in this chapter has focused more on the fragile self at the personal/individual level of identification, there remains a need for future research to apply this framework to both the relational (e.g., Andersen & Chen, 2002) and collective (e.g., Hogg, this volume) selves as well.

In the previous section, we applied the model to our research on narcissism and self-handicapping to illustrate examples of one manifestation of a fragile self-system (narcissism) as well as a self-regulatory strategy often employed by fragile self-systems. Future research should also look to other constructs that may be amenable to such a self-regulatory process analysis.

ACKNOWLEDGMENT

We warmly thank Michael Kernis and William Swann for their very careful readings of, and helpful comments and suggestions on, an earlier version of this chapter.

NOTES

1. The contents of self-knowledge are also differentiated in terms of the important *domains* the knowledge will serve ("multiple" selves in context), different *standpoints* on the self (including important others and groups), and *temporal dimensions* (i.e., present actual selves vs. future desired or possible selves).
2. There is a lack of research looking at the effect of self-knowledge organization constructs on the outcome-based state self-esteem proposed as a monitor for the current model (cf. J. D. Campbell, Chew, & Scratchley, 1991).
3. Although not the initial focus of their study, J. D. Campbell and colleagues (2003) report a trend in their data suggestive of the idea that general integration combined with a high level of specific differentiation predicts the best adjustment.
4. This approach is also consistent with several of Epstein's (1973) characteristics of good scientific (and self-) theories, including extensivity, parsimony, and internal consistency. Self-knowledge that incorporates all three of these characteristics would, by definition, display integrative complexity: It would have a wide variety of contents

differentiated across domains and contexts; it would have "both broad, integrative postulates and an efficiently organized set of subpostulates" (p. 409); and it would display consistency both within and between different levels in the hierarchy of its contents.

REFERENCES

Adler, A. (1927). *The practice and theory of individualpPsychology*. New York: Harcourt, Brace, Johanovich.
Akhtar, S., & Thompson, J. A. (1982). Overview: Narcissistic personality disorder. *American Journal of Psychiatry, 139*, 12–20.
American Psychiatric Association. (1980/1987, 1994, 2000). *Diagnostic and statistical manual of mental disorders: DSM-III /III-R/IV/IV-TR*. Washington, DC.
Andersen, S. M., & Chen, S. (2002). The relational self: An interpersonal social-cognitive theory. *Psychological Review, 109*, 619–645.
Baldwin, M. R. (1992). Relational schemas and the processing of social information. *Psychological Bulletin, 112*, 461–484.
Bargh, J. A., Gollwitzer, P. M., Lee-Chai, A., Barndollar, K., & Trotschell, R. (2001). The automated will: Nonconscious activation and pursuit of behavioral goals. *Journal of Personality and Social Psychology, 81*, 1014–1027.
Bargh, J. A., & Williams, E. L. (2006). The automaticity of social life. *Current Directions in Psychological Science, 15*, 1–4.
Baumeister, R. F., Smart, L., & Boden, J. M. (1996). Relation of threatened egotism to violence and aggression: The dark side of high self-esteem. *Psychological Review, 103*, 5–33.
Baumeister, R. F., & Vohs, K .D. (2003). Self-regulation and the executive function of the self. In M. R. Leary & J. P. Tangney (Eds.), *Handbook of self and identity*. (pp. 197–217). New York: Guilford.
Berglas, S., & Jones, E. E. (1978). Drug choice as a self-handicapping strategy in response to non-contingent success. *Journal of Personality and Social Psychology, 36*, 405–417.
Bowlby, J. (1969). *Attachment and loss: Vol. 1. Attachment*. New York: Basic Books.
Bowlby, J. (1973). *Attachment and loss: Vol. 2. Separation: Anxiety and anger*. New York: Basic Books.
Bowlby, J. (1980). *Attachment and loss: Vol. 3. Sadness and depression*. New York: Basic Books.
Brown, R. P., Bosson, J. K., Zeigler-Hill, V., & Swann, W. B. (2003). Self-enhancement tendencies among people with high explicit self-esteem: The moderating role of implicit self-esteem. *Self and Identity, 2*, 169–187.
Buss, D. M., & Chiodo, L. M.(1991). Narcissistic acts in everyday life. *Journal of Personality, 19*, 179–215.
Campbell, J. D. (1990). Self-esteem and clarity of the self-concept. *Journal of Personality and Social Psychology, 59*, 538–549.
Campbell, J. D., Assanand, S., & Di Paula, A. (2003). The structure of the self-concept and its relation to psychological adjustment. *Journal of Personality, 71*, 115–140.
Campbell, J. D., Chew, B., & Scratchley, L. S. (1991). Cognitive and emotional reactions to daily events: The effects of self-esteem and self-complexity. *Journal of Personality, 59*, 473–505.
Campbell, J. D., Trapnell, P. D., Heine, S. J., Katz, I. M., Lavallee, L. F., & Lehman, D. R. (1996). Self-concept clarity: Measurement, personality correlates, and cultural boundaries. *Journal of Personality and Social Psychology, 70*, 141–156.

Campbell, W. K. (1999). Narcissism and romantic attraction. *Journal of Personality and Social Psychology, 77,* 1254–1270.
Cantor, N. (1990). From thought to behavior: "Having" and "doing" in the study of personality and cognition. *American Psychologist, 45,* 735–750.
Carver, C. S., & Scheier, M. F. (1981). *Attention and self-regulation: A control theory approach to human behavior.* New York: Springer-Verlag.
Crocker, J., Karpinski, A., Quinn, D. M., & Chase, S. K. (2003). When grades determine self-worth: Consequences of contingent self-worth for male and female engineering and psychology majors. *Journal of Personality and Social Psychology, 85,* 507–516.
Crocker, J., & Park, L. E. (2004). The costly pursuit of self-esteem. *Psychological Bulletin, 130,* 392–414.
Crocker, J., & Wolfe, C.T. (2001). Contingencies of self-worth. *Psychological Review, 108,* 593–623.
Deci, E. M., & Ryan, R. M. (1995). Human autonomy: The basis of true self-esteem. In M. H. Kernis (Ed.), *Efficacy, agency, and self-esteem* (pp. 31–39). New York: Plenum Press.
Downey, G., & Feldman, S. I. (1996). Implications of rejection sensitivity for intimate relationships. *Journal of Personality and Social Psychology, 70,* 1327–1343.
Donahue, E. M., Robins, R. W., Roberts, B. W., & John, O. P. (1993). The divided self: Concurrent and longitudinal effects of psychological adjustment and social roles on self-concept differentiation. *Journal of Personality and Social Psychology, 64,* 834–846.
Dweck, C. S. (1999). *Self-Theories: Their role in motivation, personality and development.* Philadelphia: Psychology Press.
Dweck, C. S., Higgins, E. T., & Grant-Pillow, H. (2003). Self-systems give unique meaning to self variables. In M. R. Leary & J. P. Tangney (Eds.), *Handbook of self and identity.* (pp. 239–252). New York: Guilfords.
Dweck, C. S., & Leggett, E. L. (1988). A social-cognitive approach to motivation and personality. *Psychological Review, 95,* 256–273.
Elliot, E. S., & Dweck, C. S. (1988). Goals: An approach to motivation and achievement. *Journal of Personality and Social Psychology, 54,* 5–12.
Epstein, S. (1973). The self-concept revisited: Or a theory of a theory. *American Psychologist, 28,* 404–416.
Epstein, S. (1990). Cognitive-experiential self theory. In L. A. Pervin (Ed.), *Handbook of personality: Theory and research* (pp. 165–191). New York: Guilford.
Fazio, R. H. (1990). Multiple processes by which attitudes guide behavior: The MODE model as an integrative framework. In M. P. Zanna (Ed.), *Advances in experimental social psychology* (Vol. 23, pp. 75–109). New York: Academic Press.
Fazio, R. H., & Olson, M. (2003). Implicit measures in social cognition research: Their meaning and use. *Annual Review of Psychology, 54,* 297–327.
Feick, D. L., & Rhodewalt, F. (1998). The double-edged sword of self-handicapping: Discounting, augmentation, and the protection and enhancement of self-esteem. *Motivation and Emotion, 21,* 147–163.
Gabriel, M. T., Critelli, J. W., & Ee, J. S. (1994). Narcissistic illusions in self-evaluations of intelligence and attractiveness. *Journal of Personality, 62,* 143–155.
Greenberg, J. R., & Mitchell, S. (1983). *Object Relations is Psychoanalytic Theory.* Cambridge MA: Harvard University Press.
Greenwald, A. G. (1980). The totalitarian ego: Fabrication and revision of personal history. *American Psychologist, 35,* 603–618.
Greenwald, A. G., & Banaji, M. R. (1995). Implicit social cognition: Attitudes, self-esteem, and stereotypes. *Psychological Review, 102,* 4–27.

Greenwald, A. G., & Farnham, S. D. (2000). Using the Implicit Association Test to measure self-esteem and self-concept. *Journal of Personality and Social Psychology, 79,* 1022–1038.
Harris, R. N., & Snyder, C. R. (1986). The role of uncertain self-esteem in self-handicapping. *Journal of Personality and Social Psychology, 51,* 451–458.
Higgins, E. T. (1996). The "self-digest": Self-knowledge serving self-regulatory functions. *Journal of Personality and Social Psychology, 71,* 1062–1083.
Hinkley, K., & Andersen, S. M. (1996). The working self-concept in transference: Significant other activation and self-change. *Journal of Personality and Social Psychology, 71,* 1279–1295.
James, W. (1890). *Principles of psychology.* New York: Holt.
John, O. P., & Robins, R. (1994). Accuracy and bias in self-perception: individual differences in self-enhancement and the role of narcissism. *Journal of Personality and Social Psychology, 66,* 206–219.
Jones, E. E., & Berglas, S. (1978). Control of attributions about the self through self-handicapping strategies: The appeal of alcohol and the role of underachievement. *Personality and Social Psychology Bulletin, 4,* 200–206.
Jones, E. E., & Pittman, T. S. (1982). Toward a general theory of strategic self-presentation. In J. Suhls (Ed.), *Psychological perspectives on the self* (Vol. 1, pp. 231–262). Hillsdale, NJ: Erlbaum.
Jones, E. E., Rhodewalt, F., Berglas, S. C., & Skelton, A. (1981). Effects of strategic self-presentation on subsequent self-esteem. *Journal of Personality and Social Psychology, 41,* 407–421.
Jordan, C. H., Spencer, S. J., Zanna, M. P., Hoshino-Brown, E., & Correll, J. (2003). Secure and defensive high self-esteem. *Journal of Personality and Social Psychology, 85,* 969–978.
Kelley, H. H. (1972). Attribution in social interaction. In E. E. Jones, D. F. Kanouse, H. H. Kelley, R. E. Nisbett, S. Valins, & B. Weiner (Eds.) *Attribution: Perceiving the causes of behavior* (pp. 1–26). Morristown, NJ: General Learning Press.
Kelly, G. (1955). *The psychology of personal constructs.* New York: Norton.
Kernis, M. H. (2001). Following the trail from narcissism to fragile self-esteem. *Psychological Inquiry, 12,* 223–225.
Kernis, M. H. (2003). Toward a conceptualization of optimal self-esteem. *Psychological Inquiry, 14,* 1–26.
Kernis, M. H. (2006). *Self-Esteem: Issues and answers, a sourcebook of current perspectives.* New York: Psychology Press.
Kernis, M. H., Abend, T. A., Goldman, B. M., Shrira, I., Paradise, A. N., & Hampton, C. (2005). Self-serving responses arising from discrepancies between explicit and implicit self-esteem. *Self and Identity, 4,* 311–330.
Kernis, M. H., Cornell, D. P., Sun, C. R., Berry, A. J., & Harlow, T. (1993). There's more to self-esteem than whether it is high or low: The importance of stability of self-esteem. *Journal of Personality and Social Psychology, 65,* 1190–1204.
Kernis, M. H., & Goldman, B. M. (2003). Authenticity, psychological adjustment, and social motivation. In J. P. Forgas & K. D. Williams (Eds.), *Social motivation: Conscious and unconscious processes.* New York: Psychology Press.
Kernis, M. H., Grannemann, B. D., & Barclay, L. C. (1989). Stability and level of self-esteem as predictors of anger arousal and hostility. *Journal of Personality and Social Psychology, 56,* 1013–1023.
Kohut, H. (1977). *The analysis of the self.* New York: International Universities Press.
Leary, M. R., & Baumeister, R. F. (2000). The nature and function of self-esteem: Sociometer theory. In M. P. Zanna (Ed.), *Advances in experimental social psychology* (Vol. 32, pp. 1–62). New York: Academic Press.

Leary, M. R., & Tangney, J. P. (2003). The self as an organizing construct in the behavioral sciences. In M. R. Leary & J. P. Tangney (Eds.) *Handbook of self and identity* (pp. 3–14). New York: Guilford.
Linville, P. (1985). Self-complexity and affective extremity: Don't put all your eggs in one basket. *Social Cognition, 3,* 94–120.
Linville, P. (1987). Self-complexity as a buffer against stress-related illness and depression. *Journal of Personality and Social Psychology, 52,* 663–676.
Lugenbuhl, J., & Palmer, R. (1991). Impression management aspects of self-handicapping: Positive and negative effects. *Personality and Social Psychology Bulletin, 17,* 65–662.
Markus, H. (1977). Self-schemata and processing information about the self. *Journal of Personality and Social Psychology, 35,* 63–78.
Markus, H., & Nurius, P. (1986). Possible selves. *American Psychologist, 41,* 954–969.
McClelland, D. C., Koestner, R., & Weinberger, J. (1989). How do self-attributed and implicit motives differ? *Psychological Review, 96,* 690–702.
McCullough, M. E., Emmons, R. A., Kilpatrick, S. D., & Mooney, C. N. (2003). Narcissists as 'victims': The role of narcissism in the perception of transgressions. *Personality and Social Psychology Bulletin, 29,* 885–893.
Metcalfe, J., & Mischel, W. (1999). A hot/cool-system analysis of delay of gratification: Dynamics of willpower. *Psychological Review, 106,* 3–19.
Mischel, W., & Morf, C. C. (2003). The self as a psycho-social dynamic processing system: A meta-perspective on a century of the self in psychology. In M. R. Leary & J. P. Tangney (Eds.), *Handbook of self and identity* (pp. 15–43), New York: Guilford.
Morf, C. C. (1994). Interpersonal consequences of narcissists' continual efforts to maintain and bolster self-esteem. (Doctoral dissertation, University of Utah, Salt Lake City, 1994). *Dissertation Abstracts International, 55 (6-B),* 2430.
Morf, C. C., & Rhodewalt, F. (1993). Narcissism and self-evaluation maintenance: Explorations in object relations. *Personality and Social Psychology Bulletin, 19,* 668–676.
Morf, C. C., & Rhodewalt, F. (2001). Unraveling the paradoxes of narcissism: A dynamic self-regulatory processing model. *Psychological Inquiry, 12,* 177–196.
Muraven, M., Tice, D. M., & Baumeister, R. F. (1998). Self-control as limited resource: Regulatory depletion patterns. *Journal of Personality and Social Psychology, 74,* 774–789.
Newman, L. S., & Wadas, R .F. (1997). When stakes are higher: Self-esteem instability and self-handicapping. *Journal of Social Behavior and Personality, 12,* 217–232.
Paulhus, D. L. (1998). Interpersonal and intrapsychic adaptiveness of trait self-enhancement: A mixed blessing? *Journal of Personality and Social Psychology, 74,* 1197–1208.
Paulhus, D. L., & Martin, C. L. (1988). Functional flexibility: A new conceptualization of interpersonal flexibility. *Journal of Personality and Social Psychology, 55,* 88–101.
Pelham, B. W., & Swann, W. B., Jr. (1989). From self-conceptions to self-worth: On the sources and structure of global self-esteem. *Journal of Personality and Social Psychology, 57,* 672–680.
Pervin, L. A. (1996). *The Science of Personality.* New York: Wiley.
Pyszczynski, T., Greenberg, J., & Solomon, S. (2004). Why do people need self-esteem? A theoretical and empirical review. *Psychological Bulletin, 130,* 435–468.
Raskin, R., & Hall, C. S. (1979). A narcissistic personality inventory. *Psychological Reports, 45,* 590.
Raskin, R., Novacek, J., & Hogan, R. (1991). Narcissism, self-esteem, and defensive self-enhancement. *Journal of Personality, 59,* 20–38.
Raskin, R., & Terry, H. (1988). A principal-components analysis of the Narcissistic Personality Inventory and further evidence of its construct validity. *Journal of Personality and Social Psychology, 54,* 890–902.

Rhodewalt, F. (1994). Conceptions of ability, achievement goals and individual differences in self-handicapping behavior: On the application of implicit theories. *Journal of Personality, 62,* 67–85.
Rhodewalt, F. (2001). The social mind of the narcissist: Cognitive and motivational aspects of interpersonal self-construction. In J. P. Forgas, K. Williams, & L. Wheeler (Eds.), *The Social Mind: Cognitive and Motivational Aspects of Interpersonal Behavior.* New York: Cambridge University Press.
Rhodewalt, F., & Davison, J. (1986). Self-handicapping and failure. *Basic and Applied Social Psychology, 7,* (307–322)..
Rhodewalt, F., & Eddings, S. (2002). Narcissus reflects: Memory distortion in response to ego relevant feedback in high and low narcissistic men. *Journal of Research in Personality, 36,* 97–116.
Rhodewalt, F., & Hill, S. K. (1994). Self-handicapping in the classroom: The effects of claimed self-handicaps in responses to academic failure. *Journal of Personality and Social Psychology, 16,* 397–416.
Rhodewalt, F., Madrian, J. C., & Cheney, S. (1998). Narcissism, self-knowledge organization, and emotional reactivity: The effect of daily experiences on self-esteem and affect. *Personality and Social Psychology Bulletin, 24,* 75–87.
Rhodewalt, F. & Morf, C. C. (1995). Self and interpersonal correlates of the Narcissistic Personality Inventory: A review and new findings. *Journal of Research in Personality, 29,* 1–23.
Rhodewalt, F., & Morf, C. C. (1998). On self-aggrandizement and anger: A temporal analysis of narcissism and affective reactions to success and failure. *Journal of Personality and Social Psycholgy, 74,* 672–685.
Rhodewalt, F., Morf, C., Hazlett, S., & Fairfield, M. (1991). Self-handicapping: The role of discounting and augmentation in the preservation of self-esteem. *Journal of Personality and Social Psychology, 61,* 121–131.
Rhodewalt, F., Peterson, B. & Sorrow, D. (2006). Narcisssism and the relational self. Manuscript in preparation. University of Utah.
Rhodewalt, F., Sanbonmatsu, D. M., Tschanz, B., Feick, D. L., & Waller, S. (1995). Self-handicapping and interpersonal trade-offs: The effects of claimed self-handicaps on observers' performance evaluations and feedback. *Personality and Social Psychology Bulletin, 21,* 1042–1050.
Rhodewalt, F., & Sorrow, D. (2003). Interpersonal self-regulation: Lessons from the study of narcissism. In M. Leary & J. P. Tangney (Eds.) *Handbook of self and identity* (pp. 519–535). New York: Guilford.
Rhodewalt, F., & Tragakis, M. (2002). Self-handicapping and the social self: The costs and rewards of interpersonal self-construction. In J. Forgas & Kip Williams (Eds.), *The social self: Cognitive, interpersonal, and intergroup perspectives.* (pp. 121–143). Philadelphia: Psychology Press.
Rhodewalt, F., & Tragakis, M. (2003). Self-esteem and self-regulation: Toward optimal studies of self-esteem. *Psychological Inquiry, 14,* 66–70.
Rhodewalt, F., Tragakis, M., Eddings, S., & Sorrow, D. (2001). Unpublished data, University of Utah.
Rhodewalt, F., Tragakis, M., & Finley, E. (2002). Narcissism, social interaction, and self-esteem II: The meaning of social inclusion. Unpublished data, University of Utah.
Rhodewalt, F., Tragakis, M., & Hunh, S. (2000). Narcissism, social interaction, and self-esteem. Manuscript in preparation, University of Utah.
Rhodewalt, F., Tragakis, M., & Peterson, B. (2003). Narcissism and contingencies of self-worth. Unpublished data, University of Utah.
Rogers, C. (1951). *Client-centered therapy.* Boston: Houghton Mifflin.

Schlenker, B. R., & Weigold, M. F. (1992). Interpersonal processes involving impression regulation and management. *Annual Review of Psychology, 43*, 133–168.

Schroder, H. M. (1971). Conceptual complexity and personality organization. In H. M. Schroder & P. Suedfeld (Eds.), *Personality theory and information processing* (pp. 240–273). New York: Ronald.

Sheldon, K. M., & Kasser, T. (1995). Coherence and congruence: Two aspects of personality integration. *Journal of Personality and Social Psychology, 68*, 531–543.

Showers, C .J., & Zeigler-Hill, V. (2003). Organization of self-knowledge: Features, functions, and flexibility. In M. Leary & J. P. Tangney (Eds.), *Handbook of self and identity* (pp. 47–67). New York: Guilford.

Smith, D. S., & Strube, M. J. (1991). Self-protective tendencies as moderators of self-handicapping impressions. *Basic and Applied Social Psychology, 12*, 63–80.

Snyder, M., & Cantor, N. (1998). Understanding personality and social behavior: A functionalist strategy. In D. T. Gilbert, S. T. Fiske, & G. Lindzey (Eds.), *The handbook of social psychology* (Vol. 1, pp. 635–679. Mahwah, NJ: Erlbaum.

Spencer, S. J., Jordan, C. H., Logel, C. E. R., & Zanna, M. P. (2005). Nagging doubts and a glimmer of hope: The role of implicit self-esteem in self-image maintenance. In A. Tesser, J. V. Wood, & D. A. Stapel (Eds.), *On building, defending, and regulating the self: A psychological perspective* (pp. 153–170). New York: Psychology Press.

Suedfeld, P., Tetlock, P. E., & Streufert, S. (1992). Conceptual/integrative complexity. In C. P. Smith (Ed.), *Motivation and personality: Handbook of thematic content analysis* (pp. 393–400). Cambridge, UK: Cambridge University Press.

Sullivan, H. S. (1953). *The interpersonal theory of psychiatry.* New York: Norton.

Swann, W. B. (1983). Self-verification: Bringing social reality into harmony with the self. In. J Suls & A. Greenwald (Eds.), *Psychological perspectives on the self,* (Vol. 2, pp. 33–66). Hillsdale, NJ: Erlbaum.

Swann, W. B. (1985). The self as architect of social reality. In B. Schlenker (Ed.), *The self and social life* (pp. 100–125). New York: McGraw-Hill.

Tesser, A. (1988). Toward a self-evaluation maintenance model of social behavior. In L. Berkowitz (Ed.), *Advances in experimental social psychology* (Vol. 21, pp. 181–227). New York: Academic Press.

Tesser, A. (2003). Self-evaluation. In M. Leary & J. P. Tangney (Eds.), *Handbook of self and identity* (pp. 275–290). New York: Guilford.

Tetlock, P. E., & Suedfeld, P. (1988). Integrative complexity coding of verbal behavior. In C. Antaki (Ed.), *Lay explanation.* Beverly Hills, CA: Sage.

Thrash, T. M., & Elliot, A. J. (2002). Implicit and self-attributed achievement motives: Concordance and predictive validity. *Journal of Personality, 70*, 729–755.

Tice, D. (1991). Esteem protection or enhancement?: Self-handicapping motives and attributions differ by trait self-esteem. *Journal of Personality and Social Psychology, 60*, 711–725.

Tracy, J. L., & Robins, R. W. (2004). Putting the self into self-conscious emotions: A theoretical model. *Psychological Inquiry, 15*, 103–125.

Vallacher, R. R., Nowak, A., Froehlich, M., & Rockloff, M. (2002). The dynamics of self-evaluation. *Personality and Social Psychology Review, 6*, 370–379.

Westen, D. (1990). Psychoanalytic approaches to personality. In L. A. Pervin (Ed.), *Handbook of personality: Theory and research* (pp. 21–65). New York: Guilford.

Wilson, T. D., Lindsey, S., & Schooler, T. Y. (2000). A model of dual attitudes. *Psychological Review, 107*, 101–126.

4

Contextual Variability in Personality
The Case of the Relational Self and the Process of Transference

SUSAN M. ANDERSEN, S. ADIL SARIBAY,
and CHRISTINA S. KOOIJ

New York University

People's judgments of their own and of others' personality may be embedded in their motivation to navigate close relationships. Personality has long been assumed to be interpersonal (e.g., Carson, 1969; Leary, 1957) and contextually bound in ways relevant to relationships. In this view, attempts to understand personality without reference to interpersonal context are likely to be futile. Likewise, a number of classical theories of personality place emphasis on relationships—with significant persons (e.g., Fairbairn, 1952; Horney, 1939; Sullivan, 1953), and such interpersonal approaches are also of an active interest in clinical theory and research (e.g., Blatt & Zuroff, 1992; Davila, Hammen, Burge, & Paley, 1995; Hammen, 2000; Horowitz, 1991; Safran & Segal, 1990). Relationships are of major importance in social psychology as well—a resurgence of interest has emerged in interpersonal relationships and constructs focused on, for example, mental representations of significant others. Indeed, it has been argued that "[a]ll personality dimensions are apt to have interpersonal aspects or expressions, so purely intrapersonal accounts of them fail to capture essential aspects of personality" (A. P. Fiske & Haslam, 2005, p. 290).

We address interpersonal processes in personality in terms of our model of the relational self and the social-cognitive process of transference (Andersen & Chen, 2002; Andersen, Reznik, & Chen, 1997). Central to both models is the notion that mental representations of significant others are stored in memory and linked to representations of the self. The assumption is that an individual's perceptions and behaviors will vary across situations based on contextual cues (see Higgins & King, 1981). Any concept in memory can be activated and used when triggered by something in the environment, a central social-cognitive insight that is applicable to understanding personality. The cognitive-affective system theory of personality (Mischel & Shoda, 1995) has been substantiated over decades of research, accounting for contextual variability and explaining it in If-Then terms. The particular situation that an individual finds him/herself in will thus evoke a subjective interpretation of cues in that context (i.e., of ifs), which will determine the psychological situation experienced and the individual's resulting behaviors (i.e., thens). We argue for such an If-Then model defined in interpersonal terms, and suggest it predicts the meaning the individual ascribes to people, situations and events when significant-other representations are activated in memory, independently of any elaboration of systematic individual differences in personality.

Indeed, the emphasis on what is idiographic—unique to the person—in terms of what is stored in memory and influences perceptions is predominant in our work, linking it to the classic idiographic-nomothetic distinction (see also Allport, 1937; Kelly, 1955). A conceptual and methodological innovation in our research is its reliance on a *combined idiographic-nomothetic approach*. Although personality theorists long argued for the formulation of a theory sensitive to people's own individual meaning systems and subjective experiences (e.g., Allport, 1937; Kelly, 1955), traditional personality approaches have examined nomothetic differences that index where individuals stand on shared trait dimensions. Defining individual differences generically, in this way, has its value, but we adopt a combined idiographic-nomothetic approach that is sensitive to the unique content of an individual's representations in memory. That is, the content of an individual's significant-other representations is unique, and yet the processes by which these representations are activated and used should be general, and we thus use a standard (and nomothetic) experimental design. Nonetheless, our work also includes nomothetic differences relevant to relationships.

We emphasize the psychological situation in our research (Higgins, 1990; Higgins & King, 1981; Mischel, 1973, 1990; Mischel & Shoda, 1995; Nisbett & Ross, 1980) by focusing on the richly idiographic nature of significant-other representations. When activated in transference, these representations endow newly met individuals with psychological significance. We view these idiographic representations as a primary source of individual differences and suggest that nomothetically defined individual differences may often be traceable to such idiographic constructs (e.g., Higgins, 1987; see also Dodge & Price, 1994).

To address this work, we present our theoretical framework and some basic findings on the transference phenomenon and its influence on everyday interpersonal relations. We then delineate more precisely how both the transference model (Chen & Andersen, 1999) and the theory of the relational self (Andersen & Chen, 2002) characterize interpersonal processes in personality. Finally, we lay out the findings on the relational self and argue that the work is well-suited to conceiving personality processes because it is grounded in part in prominent clinical and personality psychology approaches, and in part in social cognition.

TRANSFERENCE: OUR CONCEPTUALIZATION AND ASSUMPTIONS

Significant-Other Representations

We define significant others as individuals who have had a substantial impact on the self, whom one knows well and cares (or has cared) deeply about. These individuals can be from one's family of origin (i.e., parents, siblings, relatives), or they can be close friends, romantic partners, mentors, and so on. Prior knowledge allows one to subjectively interpret reality (Higgins & King, 1981; Smith, 1998) and significant-other representations are one form of such knowledge.

Representations of significant others are n-of-one representations in memory (exemplars; Linville & Fischer, 1993; Smith & Zarate, 1992), each designating a unique individual. Although distinct from social categories (generic knowledge about members of a social group) in terms of what and whom they refer to, significant-other representations also contain generalized knowledge, including social roles and social category memberships (e.g., Baum & Andersen, 1999; Karylowski, Konarzewski, & Motes, 2000). Individualized significant-other knowledge involves information such as the other's physical characteristics, personality attributes, ways of thinking, styles of interaction, interests, habits, and a variety of internal states that the individual is assumed to have (e.g., Andersen & Cole, 1990; Andersen, Glassman, & Gold, 1998; Chen, 2001, 2003; Johnson & Boyd, 1995; Prentice, 1990). The high level of specificity in significant-other representations differentiates these from knowledge held about generic categories such as stereotypes and even nonsignificant exemplars. Significant-other representations are also heavily laden with affect, and with expectancies and motives to a greater extent—giving them a unique status in social cognition. They also figure prominently in the self and are linked to the self in memory, as noted, which is perhaps less commonly true of generic representations or representations of nonsignificant others.

We assume that a basic need for human connection commonly fuels significant-other relationships, infusing affective and motivational responses based on such prior knowledge—when it is used in relation to new people. For our purposes, significant others have three important features: familiarity (e.g., Andersen, Reznik, & Glassman, 2005; Prentice, 1990), emotional and motivational relevance for the self (Higgins, 1989b), and exigencies of interdependence. These features are naturally confounded with each other, along with the unusual level of richness and distinctiveness of significant-other knowledge, which has been shown (Andersen & Cole, 1990). Beyond this, significant-other representations can and do vary on many dimensions, such as how positively or negatively evaluated the significant other is, and what kinds of standards this other has for the individual. Individual differences are likely, both in the number and quality of significant-other relationships that one has, as well as in the level of "significance" or intimacy in these relationships (Andersen & Chen, 2002). People are unlikely to have limitless significant others, however; the numbers should rarely be huge (see Baumeister & Leary, 1995). There may also be profound differences between various significant others for any given person as well as across individuals in the specific content of their significant-other representations and relationships. Considerable variability in how one experiences the self across different relationships may also exist, a key point we revisit throughout this review. For now, we note that significant-other representations are intertwined with the self via representations of the self-with-other, holding implications for self-experience. Although we have yet to systematically examine all of our assumptions about variability in significant-other representations, research has verified that people not only experience little difficulty when asked to name various kinds of significant others, but they also exhibit considerable variability in describing them (e.g., Andersen, Reznik, & Manzella, 1996; Baum & Andersen, 1999; see also Ashmore & Ogilvie, 1992; Bacon & Ashmore, 1985; Baldwin, Keelan, Fehr, Enns, & Koh-Rangarajoo, 1996). Yet this appears not to matter in the basic process of transference, which seems to generalize across numerous representations.

Historical Roots of Transference in Terms of Our Social-Cognitive Model

Transference has been a central concept in psychoanalysis and psychodynamic theory, as originated by Sigmund Freud (e.g., Ehrenreich, 1989; Greenson, 1965; Luborsky & Crits-Christoph, 1990). Although Freud (1912/1958) viewed transference in terms of the patient-analyst relationship in which the patient experiences childhood fantasies and conflicts with the analyst (see also Andersen & Glassman, 1996), he acknowledged it occurs beyond analysis as well. He also proposed the concept of an "imagoe"—similar to the modern notion of a significant-other representation (Andersen & Cole, 1990; Luborsky & Crits-Christoph, 1990; Schimek, 1983; Singer, 1988; Wachtel, 1981; Westen, 1988), but never fully integrated it into his theory, i.e., the classic drive-structure model (J. R. Greenberg & Mitchell, 1983). For Freud, transference was unconscious, psychosexual, and conflictual. Our model employs only one related assumption, i.e., that the process of transference is unconscious. We also assume it occurs in daily life through "normal" cognitive processes (including a lack of awareness).

Our work has been influenced more directly by Harry Stack Sullivan (1953), a neo-Freudian who abandoned Freud's psychosexual drive (see J. R. Greenberg & Mitchell, 1983). He proposed the existence of "personifications" of the self and significant others, akin to mental representations in contemporary social cognition, and of "dynamisms" or relational dynamics enacted by the self and other. These are central in his theory, not subordinate to other structures. Sullivan termed the transference process *parataxic distortion* and argued that through it, past relational patterns could be re-experienced in illusory ways with new people. This, he argued, should influence interactions in psychotherapy and beyond. He also focused on basic needs, such as that for human connection and integration with others, which he argued is basic to fulfilling needs for satisfaction. The need for satisfaction consists of the urge to express perceptions, thoughts, and feelings, and also the urge to develop talents or capacities and to grow as a person, without having to sacrifice tenderness and connection (i.e., "integrative" experiences) with others. In addition, he posited a need for security—a need to feel safe and protected from literal and symbolic harm. For Sullivan, transference is colored heavily by motivation because it depends on personifications and dynamisms that develop based on these needs. The content of significant-other representations should be learned through experience with these others, driven by these basic needs.

Other conceptions of transference exist, including what is assumed to occur within self-object transferences (Kohut, 1971), in neurotic trends (Horney, 1939), within borderline transferences (Kernberg, 1976), or based on role-relationship configurations (Horowitz, 1989, 1991) or core-conflictual relationship themes (Luborsky & Crits-Christoph, 1990). These tend to differ on which exact factors are to be assumed essential, such as the content that is being transferred, how and when this content is acquired, and the exact mechanism of transference (Ehrenreich, 1989). One statement thought to define transference in this respect—that captures common themes in the psychodynamic literature—suggests that transference is "the experiencing of feelings, drives, attitudes, fantasies, and defenses toward a person in the present which are inappropriate to the person and are a repetition, a displacement of reaction originating in regard to significant persons of early childhood" (Greenson, 1965, p. 156; see also Andersen & Baum, 1994).

Our model fits this general definition and also remains distinctive from earlier frameworks by focusing on what is stored in memory and how it is used. While our model shares much with Sullivan's (1953) interpersonal theory in terms of assumptions about fundamental human motivations, our research also explicitly highlights mental representations (Andersen & Baum, 1994; Andersen & Cole, 1990; see also Singer, 1988; Wachtel, 1981; Westen, 1988) whereas Sullivan presumed the more amorphous concept of "energy transformations." Furthermore, we frame the model such that it can be studied empirically by focusing on mental representations of the significant other, the self, and the self-other relation, which are parallel to personifications and dynamisms. We also examine motivation in transference—again linking this perspective to personality and social behavior.

Our own research suggests that the transference process has broad-based implications for social life and its vicissitudes. The fact that this process can be studied without reference to the drive-based origins of Freudian theory is of theoretical significance, as is the deeply held clinical assumption that transference occurs unconsciously (e.g., Ehrenreich, 1989; Luborsky & Crits-Christoph, 1990), which our evidence validates (Glassman & Andersen, 1999a) bringing this line of empirical work squarely into contact with longstanding clinical theory. The deep-rooted assumption that human suffering may result from experiencing prior relationships in the present (when the significant other is not present) is of obvious relevance to personality and social behavior as well, especially if it is assumed to transpire broadly in everyday social relations.

Cognitive Bases of Transference

The theoretical lineage of our model is also relevant to historical tensions between psychoanalysis and behaviorism and to tensions with cognitive-behavioral and simply cognitive theories (all of which are rooted in learning theory). Behavioral theories have focused on the basic mechanisms by which response patterns are learned, and cognitive theories have examined mental representations and how they function. Neither approach has been influenced by psychoanalytic thought, which developed as an independent field grounded in motivation (whether drive-based and instinctual or more ego-based and/or interpersonal), and in interpersonal suffering and its remediation. In this sense, our model has the advantage of being integrative (see Andersen & Saribay, 2006). It is fundamentally cognitive and comparable with basic processes of learning, and yet is also infused with motivation and emotion in a way that is focused on interpersonal patterns and notions of self.

Most importantly, our approach to transference is social-cognitive and relies heavily on social construct theory (Higgins, 1996a), antecedents for which can be found in Kelly's (1955) personal construct theory. Social construct theory focuses on transient and chronic sources of accessibility of mental constructs and how these bias interpretation, based in part on their applicability to the stimulus at hand. The cognitive bases of transference show that significant-other representations function much as other exemplars and social categories do, except that they are more robust in interpersonal perception (e.g., Andersen & Cole, 1990; Andersen, Glassman, Chen, & Cole, 1995). Transference occurs as an essentially "normal" process not especially associated with pathology (i.e., it reflects a basic aspect of social information processing), and yet also involves "going beyond the information given" (Bruner, 1957) about the new person. To the extent that transference evokes the motivation to be connected, which is relevant to the significant other, the individual may wish to be connected with a new person in transference. Indeed, this may oil the wheels of interpersonal interaction. In psychotherapy, a positive transference may help enable an authentic therapeutic alliance by promoting motives for connection (Miranda & Andersen, 2007). We assume that the outcome of transference will depend on the content and valence of the significant-other representation and of the relational patterns involved.

The Relational Self: Our Theoretical Framework for Understanding Personality and Social Behavior

The model of the relational self (see Andersen & Chen, 2002) is an extension of our research on transference, which proposes that individuals possess separate (though potentially related) relational selves with each significant other in their lives. Each relational self captures ways of relating to a particular other and of expressing and experiencing the self in this other's presence. Through repeated interactions, aspects of the self experienced with the significant other become "entangled" in memory with significant-other knowledge (Andersen & Chen, 2002; Andersen et al., 1997). These representations contain not only idiosyncratic relationship information but also shared realities, such as the respective roles occupied in the relationship (e.g., Andersen & Chen, 2002; Aron, Aron, Tudor, & Nelson, 1991; Baldwin, 1992; Baum & Andersen, 1999; Hardin & Higgins, 1996; Ogilvie & Ashmore, 1991). The relational self is indirectly activated when a significant-other representation is activated, i.e., transference occurs, leading to changes in how the self is experienced and expressed in the immediate context (Hinkley & Andersen, 1996). The notion of relational selves allows us to offer an interpersonal view of personality that simultaneously addresses the regularities of a person and variability in behavior across situations (see also Higgins, 1990).

SELF–OTHER LINKS AND THE IF–THEN MODEL

We adopt a linkage model that posits connections in memory between the self and others, an idea that has existed for over a century in various forms (e.g., Cooley, 1902; Mead, 1934). We assume that typical relational patterns are reflected in each specific link between the self and a significant other. In our view, this is critical to understanding variability in the experience and expression of the self across interpersonal contexts (Andersen & Chen, 2002). Various self-aspects are tightly linked with different significant-other representations and are triggered in transference, influencing what becomes salient in the working self-concept and self-evaluation. The emergence of the relational self in transference has been demonstrated in research on the working self-concept (Hinkley & Andersen, 1996), which we address shortly.

A recent linkage model, the model of relational schemas (Baldwin, 1992), also shares our assumption and emphasizes the contextual cueing of significant others and relationships (e.g., Andersen & Chen, 2002). This research uses incidental priming (e.g., Baldwin, Carrell, & Lopez, 1990) to trigger a significant-other representation *in advance* of encountering a new person and focuses on generic relational patterns (e.g., Baldwin, Fehr, Keedian, Seidel, & Thomson, 1993) rather than idiosyncratic aspects of the self and the relationships we focus on, which involve applicability-based cues—that is, a person's actual characteristics.

An alternative model focused on significant-other relationships assumes the inclusion of the other in the self (Aron et al., 1991). That is, individuals with whom one has a close relationship essentially become incorporated into the self—leading the other's features to become one's own. While this differs from our assumption, the cognitive and affective consequences of emotional bonds between the self and others are central to all three models, and the predictions do not vastly differ. Nonetheless, the incorporation metaphor has spawned an important line of research that has contributed considerably to the field.

The relational self model assumes—converging with the cognitive-affective personality system (CAPS) theory (Mischel & Shoda, 1995)—that what is stable in personality is the overall pattern of responding to specific classes of contextual cues based on the prior knowledge those cues activate. Responses thus necessarily vary across situations (based on the range in the individual's repertoire) and match with cues encountered. This should capture how responses vary from one (set of) situation(s) to another in ways that reflect personality, that is, the individual's personality signature across situations.

To the basic terms of the CAPS theory, we bring a specific focus on interpersonal aspects of personality. We assume that significant-other representations and the relational selves linked to them are relatively temporally stable: They develop in important relationships, deeply impact the person, and take time to change even when they are not healthy or adaptive. Individuals form close relationships that are not simply identical with each other (e.g., Baldwin et al., 1996), and develop relational selves reflecting these differences. The If-Then approach also fits our research on transference more generally because a newly encountered person may trigger a significant-other representation. The Ifs in the sequence are the triggering cues, and the Then is the transference effect—the activated significant-other representation as well as changes in the self-concept, motives, affects, and behaviors that follow. Activation also spreads from the significant-other representation to the relational self with this significant other, triggering the Then of the relational self.

In our If-Then approach to personality, we propose that the transference process underlies both stability and variability in personality and social behavior. The stability is found in the consistency of the relations between triggering cues (Ifs) and interpersonal responses (Thens), and the variability is afforded by the repertoire of relational selves the person possesses and by the different interpersonal contexts that activate these relational selves. When a specific significant-other representation is triggered, the responses that follow are more or less predictable, and the pattern of variability across specific situations should be consistent for the person over time, as is Mischel's personality signature.

Beyond one's primary caretaker, family members, and other individuals known at an early age, new significant-other relationships clearly develop over time. Hence, we assume that relational selves continue to develop as well. Extant relational selves should expand to an extent over time. These new relationships and relational selves may thus be mechanisms by which the self can gradually shake off, for example, the negative impact of unhealthy past relationships, though this presumably requires considerable time and experience.

THE RELEVANCE TO MOTIVATION, SELF-REGULATION, AND EMOTION

Of course, motivation is central to psychodynamic theories that have influenced our model and must be addressed in any adequate model of personality. Many theories have advocated, for example, a fundamental need for human connection—for relatedness, tenderness, attachment, or belonging (see Adler, 1927/1957; Bakan, 1966; Bowlby, 1969; Fairbairn, 1952; J. R. Greenberg & Mitchell, 1983; Guisinger & Blatt, 1994; Helgeson, 1994; Horney, 1939, 1945; McAdams, 1985, 1989; Rogers, 1951; Safran, 1990; Sullivan, 1953). Recent social psychology has also begun to address basic human needs (e.g., Batson, 1990; Deci, 1995; S. T. Fiske, 2003). The need for connection and belonging (Baumeister & Leary, 1995) in particular is reflected in a growing body of work on the cognitive, affective, and behavioral consequences of social bonds. Some of these consequences are known to arise as a function of contingencies for acceptance or rejection that one experiences with significant others as well as with other individuals, such as those representing a group (e.g., Ayduk, Mendoza-Denton, Mischel, Downey, Peake, & Rodriguez, 2000; Bandura, 1986; Baumeister & Leary, 1995; Crocker & Wolfe, 2001; Downey & Feldman, 1996; Higgins, 1989a, 1991; Leary, Tambor, Terdal, & Downs, 1995; Markus & Kitayama, 1991; Smith, Murphy, & Coats, 1999).

We also give the need for human connection a central place in our theory. Without such a need, it is difficult to imagine why an individual would have any significant relationships at all. Without some degree of connection, or when all connection is hampered, it would seem the problematic consequences can be profound. Our model assumes other needs beyond this, such as needs for autonomy or freedom (e.g., Deci & Ryan, 1985); for mastery, competence, or control (e.g., Seligman, 1975); for meaning (e.g., Becker, 1971); and for felt security (e.g., Epstein, 1973). Of course, these needs are also prominent in a wide array of psychological theories (Abramson, Seligman, & Teasdale, 1978; Andersen et al., 1997; Bakan, 1966; Bandura, 1977, 1989; Baumeister, 1991; Becker, 1973; Bruner, 1990; Deci & Ryan, 1991; Dweck & Leggett, 1988; Frankl, 1959; Janoff-Bulman, 1992; Klinger, 1977; Park & Folkman, 1997; Pennebaker, 1997; Silver & Wortman, 1980; Sullivan, 1953; White, 1959).

In conceptualizing the workings of the motivational system in transference, and in empirically investigating it, we adopt the social-cognitive view that motives and goals are stored in memory as mental constructs. This view assumes that goals can be triggered like any other mental construct, shaping cognitive, affective, and behavioral responses (e.g., Bargh, 1990, 1997; Bargh & Gollwitzer, 1994). Goal states and motives, however, are assumed to uniquely energize behavior through the tension between desired end states and also one's proximity to that end state (Carver & Scheier, 1981; Gollwitzer & Moskowitz, 1996; Kruglanski, 1996), suggesting the importance of examining the unique properties of goals and motives separately from other types of representations.

We argue that significant-other representations are linked in memory with goals one typically pursues in relation to the other (Andersen et al., 1996; Berk & Andersen, 2000), as much research now shows (Fitzsimons & Bargh, 2003; Shah, 2003a, 2003b). Motivations toward the significant other, and goals fostered by them (or made salient by their real or imagined presence) should all be key parts of the relational self. Self-regulation should also figure as an essential part of the relational self, due to the emotional-motivational relevance of significant others for the self. Understanding how the motivational system functions in transference and in the relational self may thus provide a key avenue for conceptualizing the link to personality.

Transference: Methodology and Basic Evidence

We turn now to some basic findings that empirically demonstrate the transference process. We begin with a brief characterization of our research paradigm, and then focus on cognitive and evaluative-affective indices of transference, which provide evidence for the idea that when a new person resembles one's significant other, one's representation of this other will be activated and applied to that new person.

Throughout, we indicate how this is relevant to personality and social behavior, about which we say more in the evidence concerned with the relational self.

METHODOLOGY IN BRIEF

In our research on the social-cognitive process of transference, a significant-other representation is typically activated based on triggering cues operationalized as descriptive features about a new person whom participants expect to meet. These features are actually characteristics of the significant other such as attitudes, habits, styles of relating, physical characteristics, and dispositions that are derived from the participant's own descriptions of their significant other. These features are then used to trigger the significant-other representation based on their apparent applicability (see Higgins, 1996a) to the new person. We assume that cues emanating from (or read about) a new person will activate the representation to the extent that they "map onto" the participant's view of the significant other. This activated representation is in turn used to perceive the new person, leading to a number of cognitive, affective, and behavioral responses revealing the occurrence of transference.

More specifically, in a preliminary session participants are led to think of a significant other and are asked to write open-ended descriptions of this individual (or a few, depending on the study). Each sentence is to describe the significant other distinctively, rather than in a way that is descriptive of just anyone. At least two weeks later, participants take part in a supposedly unrelated experiment and are led to believe that another person whom they will meet later on is being interviewed next door. Participants in the significant-other resemblance condition are presented with an equal number of positive and negative descriptions of this "interaction partner," some of which are derived from sentences they generated in the first session to describe their significant other. Following exposure to these features about the new person, participants' memory of the features, their evaluation, affect, motives, and expectancies regarding the new person, and their self-ratings and behavior may be assessed, depending on the particular study. Importantly, for each experimental participant, another participant in the control condition is exposed to the exact same features about the new person. This one-to-one yoking of participants allows stimulus content to be perfectly controlled across conditions, showing that the effects arise not just as a function of the features presented, but based on activation of the significant-other representation.

This combined idiographic-nomothetic design permits us to tap the specific, idiosyncratic aspects of an individual's actual life experience—assuring the meaningfulness of the stimuli—while still allowing for the examination of generalizable mental processes across a range of people. Indeed, although the transference process itself is not idiographic, it is based on idiographic content. Even though we believe that relevant individual differences might facilitate or inhibit transference, we have repeatedly demonstrated its occurrence in fairly diverse samples (in terms of gender and cultural background). Such a method, capturing both idiographic and normative aspects of the self and behavior, is of value in conceptualizing transference as a phenomenon that underlies both variability and stability in the expression and experience of the self. We turn now to the basic evidence.

INFERENCE AND MEMORY EFFECTS

The first research on the cognitive processes of transference examined memory and inferences. When a new person minimally resembles a significant other, it should activate the relevant representation, which should then be applied to the new person in terms of inferences about him or her deriving from the significant other. Indeed, people in such a condition (versus in a no-resemblance control group) report more recognition memory confidence that they had been exposed to features about the new person whom they had not actually seen when these features were derived from their significant-other descriptions (e.g., Andersen & Cole, 1990; Andersen et al., 1995). This has been replicated in numerous studies, independently of the valence of the representation (e.g., Andersen & Baum, 1994; Andersen et al., 1996; Berk & Andersen, 2000), and holds across individual differences such as self-discrepancies from a parent's standpoint, i.e., an ideal or an ought self-discrepancy (research described below, Reznik & Andersen, 2007; see Higgins, 1987). Indeed, the effect is not overturned when one learns that a new person who resembles a significant other is in a contradictory interpersonal role (Baum & Andersen, 1999), and this inference and memory effect is thus often used as a standard index of transference.

An alternative explanation for the inference and memory effect in our studies—that it derives simply from the activation of any social category (e.g., a stereotype) often used by the participant—has been ruled out. When a significant-other representation is activated and used, it is not reducible to what occurs based on the activation of a social stereotype; indeed, the effect is clearly more pronounced for significant-other representations (Andersen et al., 1995; Chen, Andersen, & Hinkley, 1999). Research has shown the power of stereotypes for shaping social perception (e.g., Banaji & Greenwald, 1995; Devine, 1989), suggesting that significant-other representations might pale by comparison. Yet this is not so, and significant-other representations are thus distinguishable from social categories (see also Karylowski et al., 2000). On a related note, one may wonder whether this effect can occur by merely activating a representation of any person, even if that person is not significant. While we believe that people do in fact fill in the blanks about newly-met persons based even on representations of nonsignificant others, the effect is far more pronounced for significant-other representations (e.g., Chen et al., 1999; Glassman & Andersen, 1999b).

Finally, because the new person's features were produced by participants to describe their significant others (for those in transference), it was important to show that the effect is not due to self-generation. No comparable effect occurs when a new person is described by self-generated features reflecting a mixture of various public or historical figures. Moreover, the effect can persist for a week's duration (Glassman & Andersen, 1999b) and tends to be exacerbated with time, suggesting that it has some staying power.

Transient Contextual Cueing. Cues of applicability—that is, minimal significant-other resemblance in a new person—activate a significant-other representation and lead to the transference process, as reflected in inferences and memory about that person. Yet it is not only cues emanating from a new person that lead to this. Priming in advance with content relevant to the significant other before encountering a new person (or with information about a new person to be encountered later) also increases this inference and memory effect (Andersen et al., 1995). Being primed in advance with an incidental cue should transiently activate relevant pre-existing knowledge—particularly, about a significant other. Since both priming and applicability-based cues emanating from the new person are transient sources of activation, this should be true for both, and it is.

Even in the absence of any immediate priming, encountering a new person's features that are similar to a significant other's will evoke the effect. Indeed, the effect occurs regardless of the number of features cueing the significant-other representation (Chen et al., 1999). This is of interest, as we know from research on relational schemas (e.g., Baldwin, 1992) that significant-other representations can be primed, leading to a variety of effects, for example, on self-judgments, motives, and attachment styles (e.g., Baldwin et al., 1990; Fitzsimons & Bargh, 2003; Shah, 2003a, 2003b). This fits well with the If-Then perspective on variability across situations in personality, designated in this case by transference.

Chronic Accessibility. Given the emotional relevance of significant others, it is unsurprising that these mental representations are also chronically accessible—that is, that they are ready to be used in social perception almost willy-nilly. Evidence shows that the recognition memory effect just described is partly due to this chronic accessibility. These representations are used to fill in the blanks about a new individual even when there are no applicable cues in this new person, and no advance priming (Andersen et al., 1995; Chen et al., 1999), providing evidence for some overarching stability across situations, not only in the significant-other representations available in memory, but in those that are used as well.

Of course, applicable cues in the new person (i.e., significant-other resemblance) do activate these representations, as noted, and both transient and chronic activation combine in an additive fashion. This dual influence extends social-cognitive evidence involving trait concepts (Bargh, Bond, Lombardi, & Tota, 1986) into the domain of significant-other representations. In the realm of attachment style, research also indicates that people more readily call to mind relationships that fit their global attachment style than those that do not, suggesting the chronic accessibility of such relationships (Baldwin et al., 1996). At the same time, because people are also shown to have different attachment styles in differing relationships, each can presumably be made transiently accessible by contextual cues, such as priming. Indeed, priming a relationship partner with whom one has a particular attachment style will lead one to prefer dating partners with this same attachment style regardless of chronic attachment style (Baldwin et al., 1996), demonstrating the importance of contextual triggering of significant-other representations.

In short, chronic sources of accessibility provide stability to the self in terms of the significant-other representations and relational knowledge typically activated, while transient sources lead to variability in the particular representation that is triggered and thus in the relational self that is activated.

AUTOMATICITY IN TRANSFERENCE: UNCONSCIOUS ACTIVATION AND EFFICIENCY

Consistent with the social-cognitive assumption that construct activation and use do not depend on consciousness (e.g., Bargh, 1997), we assume that the activation and use of a significant-other representation to interpret a new person does not depend on consciousness (as shown by Baldwin et al., 1990) and is not an effortful process (Andersen et al., 2005). Nothing in our experimental instructions explicitly asks participants to compare a new person to a significant other from their own lives; nonetheless this occurs, often without awareness. Moreover, we instruct participants to be as accurate as possible in their inferences and memory ratings, and such an accuracy goal should act against strategic, intentional bias toward using a significant other to conceptualize the new person. In fact, this recognition memory effect is seen even if participants who became aware of the link between the new person and their significant other are excluded from analyses (e.g., Berenson & Andersen, 2006), suggesting that the transference effect—assessed by our paradigm—occurs with little awareness.

Two studies assessed this in a technically rigorous way. Participants engaged in a computer game, allegedly with another participant (Glassman & Andersen, 1999a). Significant-other features were subliminally presented during this game, which should activate the significant-other representation. As usual, control participants were yoked to participants in the resemblance condition and were thus exposed to the exact same features (also subliminally). An additional control condition controlled for self-generation effects (vis-à-vis features generated in Session 1 and used as stimuli in Session 2). Participants then completed an inference task in which they rated features that were not subliminally presented—but that were derived from the significant other—as more likely to be descriptive of the new person. This did not occur in either of the control conditions.

This evidence supports the hypothesis that unconscious activation of the transference effect occurs, and rules out any necessity of being consciously reminded of a significant other for it to occur, which is relevant to longstanding clinical assumptions (e.g., Freud, 1912/1958; Sullivan, 1953). This evidence was obtained using our inference measure, and we assume that the effect is basically implicit for the phenomenon of transference, and thus for emotional and motivational responses in subsequent sections.

Other evidence complements these findings by showing that these representations are used with particular ease or efficiency. When participants are asked to list various features of a significant other, they retrieve such features much more quickly than those of other exemplars or categories (Andersen & Cole, 1990). Research examining participants' response latencies in making simple judgments has also shown that judgments based on significant-other representations are far faster than comparable judgments about a social category or a nonsignificant-other representation (Andersen, Lambert, & Dick, 1999), providing additional support for automaticity in the use of significant-other representations.

Research has also revealed that judgments about the preferences of significant others (in a priming phase) can also facilitate the ease with which subsequent judgments are made about other individuals, and this occurs more for significant-other representations than for prototypes (Karylowski et al., 2000). In short, significant-other representations enjoy a special processing efficiency compared to other constructs in memory and are employed relatively effortlessly in transference. Indeed, even the affect associated with the significant other is activated and used without effort, in that subliminally priming participants with a relationship partner's face or name can lead to more positive evaluation of Chinese characters that are presented later on (Banse, 1999; see Chen, Fitzsimons, & Andersen, 2007).

Of course, research on relational schemas has shown that representations of important others, such as the Pope (for Catholics) or Bob Zajonc (for doctoral students, when he was their department chair), can also be activated outside of awareness in a way that influences subsequent self-judgments, clearly showing subliminal activation of significant-other representations. Other subliminal priming studies have repeatedly shown significant-other activation based on such cues (Fitzsimons & Bargh, 2003; Shah, 2003a, 2003b), further supporting automaticity in significant-other activation (see also Andersen, Moskowitz, Blair, & Nosek, 2007; Chen et al., 2007).

EVALUATION EFFECTS

We assume that evaluative responses to a new person should be colored by how the significant other is evaluated—if the significant-other representation is applied to that person. That is, when participants learn about a new person who resembles their own significant other (versus a yoked participant's), the new person should be liked or disliked based on whether the significant other is positively or negatively evaluated. Evidence shows that a new person is evaluated more positively when he or she resembles a positive (versus a negative) significant other, which does not occur in the control condition (Andersen & Baum, 1994; Andersen et al., 1996; Berk & Andersen, 2000). Even when only positive significant others are examined, people experience more liking for a new person resembling this significant other versus a yoked participant's positive significant other (Baum & Andersen, 1999). This effect also occurs when the significant other is a parent from whose standpoint one believes one falls short (see Higgins, 1987; Reznik & Andersen, 2007). Because equal numbers of positive and negative features are presented about the new person regardless of evaluation of the significant other (positive vs. negative), in both the transference and control conditions, this evaluation effect cannot simply be an effect of stimulus features (which would wash out the effect), and it is thus considered another standard index of transference.

Of course, it is quite common for people to have mixed feelings about their significant others, suggesting the complexity of evaluation in transference, which we address later. Nonetheless, it remains noteworthy that overall evaluation of a significant other will clearly predict how a new person is regarded in transference. This suggests that a core summary evaluation is linked to significant-other representations in memory, which is then triggered in transference, spilling onto the new person (see also S. T. Fiske & Pavelchak, 1986).

FACIAL AFFECT IN TRANSFERENCE

Relatively immediate emotional responses to a new person should also arise in transference, based on the significant-other representation. That is, participants' facial expressions while reading each feature about a new person in this paradigm should reveal immediate affective responses reflecting the overall affective tone of the significant-other representation, in an extension of the theory of schema-triggered affect (S. T. Fiske & Pavelchak, 1986). The valence (positive or negative) of participants' facial expressions in response to each feature was coded by trained judges and averaged across these features. This showed that when the new person reminds participants of a significant other whom they regard positively (versus negatively), they show more positive (versus negative) facial affect while learning about this person, which does not occur in the control condition. Participants' affective responses are reflected in relatively immediate shifts in facial musculature in the absence of any explicit instruction to evaluate the new person's features. While not conclusive evidence about automaticity, this does suggest that such affect is evoked quickly, thus pervading everyday social encounters.

This process becomes more intriguing when it is problematic. When participants learn about a new person resembling a physically abusive parent, they exhibit considerably more positive facial affect than do comparable participants in a control condition (Berenson & Andersen, 2006). Their responses are indistinguishable from those of participants who were not abused by their parent—that is, regardless of abuse, relatively automatic positive affect occurs. Although this research involves college students and thus involves people who are functional enough to be in a university setting, the evidence nonetheless shows relatively immediate positive affect in response to a new person who resembles a parent—independent of physical and psychological abuse by the parent. This occurs despite the fact that the abused participants also report far more distrust of the new person, more expected rejection, and more indifference to being liked or disliked in transference than nonabused participants do.

This initial evidence on inferences and memory, evaluation, and facial affect shows that transference occurs in interpersonal encounters based on reasonably well-understood social-cognitive processes that are evoked relatively implicitly based on significant-other resemblance in a new person and that can be provoked outside of conscious awareness. The evidence makes clear that the phenomenon is highly laden with affect and that one's overall evaluation of a significant other is readily applied to a new person who is accordingly liked or disliked. Moreover, it speaks to longstanding theory in personality—that stemming from psychoanalysis and its cornerstone assumption of transference. Although we conceptualize the phenomenon differently from Freud, our evidence nonetheless offers the first experimental demonstration of transference, providing an integrative rapprochement between psychodynamic and cognitive (social cognitive) assumptions. Our approach is also ultimately grounded in learning theory and in behavioral approaches to personality and is relevant to personality in this way as well.

EVIDENCE FOR THE RELATIONAL SELF

We now turn to the question of how this and related evidence speak to the nature of the self and how it is manifested across the contexts of each individual's interpersonal life. The way in which the self is experienced and expressed across differing situations has long preoccupied some in personality psychology and, in particular, has been the focus of longstanding research on social-cognitively focused theories of personality (Mischel, 1973; Mischel & Shoda, 1995). Research on transference can be conceptualized in terms of how it systematically varies across situations according to the particular interpersonal cues that are salient. This fits readily within the broader If-Then cognitive-affective theory of personality. In our model, the links between the self and significant-other representations in memory suggest that while the self is rooted in prior close relationships, providing stability, significant-other representations can also be activated, and this spreads to the self and leads to contextual shifts in the relational self experienced and expressed. We thus examine the unfolding of different self-experiences in interpersonal contexts in the pages that follow and explore their relevance to personality.

Expectancies: Interpersonal Acceptance and Rejection

Communication of interpersonal acceptance or rejection in close relationships is crucial to what is stored in memory about any relationship partner (e.g., Andersen et al., 1996; Baldwin & Sinclair, 1996; Downey & Feldman, 1996), perhaps as a result of basic needs for connection or belonging, which presumably have helped individuals survive throughout evolution (see Baumeister & Leary, 1995).

We believe that expectancies of acceptance or rejection with significant others play out in transference (Andersen et al., 1996). When a new person resembles a significant other, one should expect to be accepted (or rejected) by this new person if one feels accepted (versus rejected) by the significant other. Research has examined this hypothesis with simple self-reports, using valence of the significant-other representation (noted in a prior session by the participant) as a proxy for the significant other's "feelings" and self-reported expectancies in transference. On balance, people should perceive that they are accepted, liked, or loved by a positively regarded significant other.

Indeed, the evidence shows that when this person resembles a positive (versus a negative) significant other, people are more likely to expect acceptance from the new person (and not rejection), while no such effect occurs in the control condition (e.g., Andersen et al., 1996). When a new person resembles a loved parent who is associated with a self-discrepancy from the parent's viewpoint, one still expects to be liked and accepted by this new person than in a control condition (Reznik & Andersen, 2007). In this sense, expectancies associated with significant others may be quite stably linked to parental representations. On the other hand, when parents violate trust by psychologically and physically abusing their child, that child may experience a reversal in these "normal" positive expectancies based on a parental transference even though the child claims to love this parent. Indeed, participants expect a new person resembling an abusive parent to be more rejecting of them, as compared to control participants (Berenson & Andersen, 2006). Such a reversal also occurs in transference if one experiences a dreaded (versus desired) self when around the significant other, even when the other is liked or loved, and from one's family (Reznik & Andersen, 2005). Although participants may feel fondly toward this new person, the significant other presumably draws out their worst qualities, and when this significant-other representation is activated, so too are rejection expectancies that are then applied to the new person. These data begin to clarify the complex ways in which acceptance and rejection expectancies may arise in transference, driven not only by the overall tone of the significant-other representation, but also by the relationship.

Although self-reports do not directly tap automaticity in responding, we assume that deliberation is unnecessary for these expectancies to arise in transference. The evidence clearly supports the relatively automatic activation and application of a significant-other representation to a new person (Andersen et al., 2005; Glassman & Andersen, 1999a), as noted. This is of special interest given the growing literature on individual differences in rejection sensitivity (Downey & Feldman, 1996), which shows that the ease with which such expectancies can be contextually triggered is important and that rejection expectancies arise relatively automatically among rejection-sensitive individuals. Once such automatic expectancies are set in motion, only "strategic" attention deployment, emphasizing cues and information *not* signaling rejection, can prevent problematic interpersonal consequences from arising automatically (Ayduk et al., 2000).

Other research has shown that interpersonal acceptance can be perceived as contingent on meeting certain standards that the other holds in the relationship. Some relationships are more unconditional than others, and perceived regularities in conditionality of acceptance should thus be embodied in relational schemas (Baldwin & Sinclair, 1996; see also Baldwin & Meunier, 1999). Supporting this, people with chronically low self-esteem appear to have stronger success-acceptance and failure-rejection associations than do those with high self-esteem. Importantly, thinking of a relationship partner who offers contingent (versus noncontingent) acceptance also activates these same associations (e.g., failure-rejection) regardless of one's chronic self-esteem (Baldwin & Sinclair, 1996).[1]

Rejection sensitivity should develop from repeated rejection experiences in significant relationships (Downey, Khouri, & Feldman, 1997; Feldman & Downey, 1994). Ultimately, individual differences exist in how such sensitivity plays out in situations that are perceived as posing a threat of rejection, and certain individuals are more likely to interpret ambiguous cues in terms of rejection (Downey & Feldman, 1996, Studies 2 & 3; Downey, Lebolt, Rincon, & Freitas, 1998) and to respond with a negative interpersonal script that may jeopardize the relationship and their own well-being (Ayduk, Downey, & Kim, 2001; Downey & Feldman, 1996; Downey, Freitas, Michaelis, & Khouri, 1998). This fits nicely within an If-Then framework of personality: If expectancies are stored with significant-other representations and these representations are chronically accessible, transference may then be a key interpersonal process through which rejection sensitivity becomes especially likely to emerge in new social encounters. In this way, rejection expectancies developed early on in the context of a significant-other relationship may generalize to new relationships. The importance of such expectancies to personality theory is also seen in the numerous assumptions made about them in the cognitive-behavioral literature.

INTERPERSONAL BEHAVIOR

Patterns of responding in a relationship can be persistent and difficult to break, even if one wants to, suggesting the resilience of the mental processes that mediate the transference phenomenon. We assume that the behavioral patterns one engages in with a significant other are stored in memory, and can thus be activated when the significant-other representation is activated in transference. A slight variation of our research paradigm, based on the fundamental social-psychological concept of "behavioral confirmation" (Snyder, Tanke, & Berscheid, 1977), was used to assess the recurrence of behavioral patterns that are associated with a significant other with a new person in transference. In the context of a positive or a negative transference (or no transference), participants had an unstructured telephone conversation with another entirely naïve individual (Berk & Andersen, 2000). Independent blind judges then rated the naïve new person's contribution to the conversation, isolated from the participant's own. In the context of a positive transference, the new person (the participant in the role of "target") appeared to engage in interpersonal (conversational) behavior revealing more positive affect than in a negative transference, which did not occur in the yoked control condition. Transference thus produces behavioral confirmation effects: The participant's own responses somehow provoked affectively congruent behavior from the naïve new person. Presumably this happens without awareness, again suggesting the subtle and powerful role transference can play in coloring everyday encounters and guiding them toward long-established patterns of interaction.

This finding extends transference from intrapersonal processes to real interactions and actual behavior, giving more credence to the idea that variability in interpersonal behavior can be explained using significant-other representations and transference. Indeed, idiosyncrasies in a relationship should play out in behavioral aspects of transference as well, and this remains to be examined.

SHIFTS IN THE SELF-CONCEPT AND IN SELF-EVALUATION

In social psychology in the 80s, monolithic conceptions of the self as a unified entity were dropped in favor of a multi-faceted view, in which the self is thought to vary from moment to moment even while the person's past and his or her identity remain stable (e.g., Markus & Wurf, 1987). The latter notion figures prominently in our work (Andersen & Chen, 2002). Much evidence already described involves the self—e.g., expectations for acceptance or rejection, behavioral patterns in the interaction. Yet it remains important to examine how the self-concept and self-worth are influenced by transference. In transference, the particular self-with-other, or relational self, should be activated, characterizing one's self-relevant thoughts and feelings.

To test this idea, in the first session, participants' baseline self-definition and their self-definition *when with* the significant other are assessed using free-form sentence completions. After learning about the new person, participants' view of themselves at that moment is assessed. The results indicate that the number of features reflecting the self-with-significant-other in participants' self-reports is greater in transference than in a control condition, covarying out baseline self-reports (Hinkley & Andersen, 1996), and this occurs for both positive and negative significant others.

In a still more nuanced approach, we tested this same hypothesis by focusing only on positive significant others with whom participants tended to experience a dreaded (versus desired) sense of self (Reznik & Andersen, 2005), such as by becoming needy or perhaps angry and domineering. Even when the positivity of the significant other is held constant, and only the negative quality of the relational self with the significant other varies, transference still produces a shift in the self relative to the control condition. This occurs both when the relational self is dreaded and when it is desired. The version of the self typically experienced with a significant other is thus clearly stored in memory and is activated based on significant-other activation in transference. This relational self thus comes to characterize the working self-concept in transference.

Transference also influences self-evaluation. Focusing on the evaluation (positive or negative) that participants assigned to the sentences used to describe the self in the pretest session, and controlling for baseline self-evaluation, evidence shows that in a negative transference experience, negative self-features flood into the working self-concept as compared with a positive transference, which yields a positive change in self-evaluation (Hinkley & Andersen, 1996). Indeed, merely thinking about a judgmental relationship partner also impacts self-evaluation based on situationally evoked contingencies (e.g., Baldwin et al., 1990). Interestingly, negative shifts in self-evaluation also occur when a positive significant-other representation is activated in transference, if one experiences a dreaded (vs. desired) self in relation to a new person (Reznik & Andersen, 2005), while no such effect occurs in the absence of transference.

These results clearly show If-Then shifts in the self-concept and self-evaluation as a function of the relational context of transference, providing direct evidence for the relevance of this model to the If-Then model of personality (Mischel & Shoda, 1995). Other evidence shows that cues relevant to contingencies of worth are most evocative in terms of inducing shifts in self-evaluation (Crocker & Wolfe, 2001). Presumably, resemblance to significant-other representations defines a class of stimuli that will indirectly activate contingencies of worth, as this research implies (see also Baldwin et al., 1990; Downey & Feldman, 1996). We argue that transference is a mechanism underlying variability in the experience of the self across different interpersonal contexts. The historical relevance of the self-concept and self-evaluation to personality theory also links this work to personality.

MOTIVATION AND SELF-REGULATION

Activating Approach-Avoidance Motivation

Given our assumption that a fundamental need exists to connect with others and that this need translates into intimate exchange and tenderness in some degree in personal relationships, it makes sense that the desire to be emotionally close should be relevant to significant-other representations and thus that approach-avoidance motivation should emerge in transference. At the most straightforward level, transference involving a positive significant other should evoke the motivation to approach (be emotionally close to) the new person and not avoidance motivation (to withdraw and be emotionally distant). When a significant-other representation is activated in transference, the motivation associated with this other should also be activated and experienced in relation to the new person. Any motivation to approach or avoid this person should be at its peak when expecting to meet a new person. Participants rate their desire to reveal their fears, insecurities, and hopes to the new person, and also their desire to avoid being emotionally intimate with this person, presumed to capture approach/avoidance motivation. The findings indicate that participants are more motivated to approach a new person when he or she resembles a positive (versus a negative) significant other, and this does not occur in the control condition (Andersen et al., 1996; Berk & Andersen, 2000).

This evidence builds on other research showing that goal states are automatically activated (Bargh & Barndollar, 1996; Bargh & Chartrand, 1999; Bargh, Gollwitzer, Lee-Chai, Barndollar, & Trötschel, 2001; see also Aarts & Dijksterhuis, 2000) and extends it into the realm of significant-other representations. Although closeness motivation was assessed through self-report, the relatively implicit activation of the significant-other representation based on significant-other resemblance suggests that automatic goal activation may well occur based on activating a significant-other representation in transference. Indeed, recent research has also shown that subliminally priming a significant-other representation has automatic effects on goal activation, goal commitment (i.e., the value placed on goals), and actual goal-related task performance and persistence, and even on the perceived likelihood of attaining goals (Fitzsimons & Bargh, 2003; Shah, 2003a, 2003b; see

Fitzsimons, Shah, Chartrand, & Bargh, 2005, for a review). Clearly, this shows that interpersonal goals with a significant other can be activated when a significant-other representation is activated (Chen et al., 2007).

Returning to approach motivation in transference, it also seemed relevant to ask when such effects might be disrupted. Hence, we questioned whether the effect would hold when the significant other was a loved parent with whom one held a self-discrepancy. Results in fact show that approach motivation is still evoked in such a case (Reznik & Andersen, 2007), suggesting that the other's problematic expectancies do not interfere with approach motivation. However, when one's need for connection with a significant other is chronically unsatisfied—that is, when the goal to be loved and accepted by the other has long gone unmet—this interferes with emotional approach motivation in transference (Berk & Andersen, 2004).

This work has a unique relevance for understanding the self and personality because it clearly links the transference process with motivation. Motivational dynamics with the significant other (e.g., his or her typical responses to one's needs and motives) are applied to a new person in transference. Differing motives and goals thus appear to arise as a function of interpersonal context, reflecting yet another form of variability in the self and personality.

Activating Self-Regulation

Beyond the simple activation and pursuit of a particular need or goal in transference, we suggest that there are three ways of conceptualizing self-regulation in transference. One is that transference processes may activate a particular self-regulatory focus, i.e., a focus geared toward obtaining positive outcomes or one geared toward avoiding negative outcomes. The other two are linked to threat and protection experienced in transference—that is, protection of the self or protection of the other.

Activating Self-Regulatory Focus. Regulatory focus in transference has been examined as a way of predicting approach and avoidance in transference (Reznik & Andersen, 2007; see Andersen & Chen, 2002) and involves either ideal standards, seeking to attain positive outcomes, and engaging in a promotion focus, or ought standards, trying to avoid negative outcomes, and prevention focus (Higgins, 1996b, 1996c). Each form of regulatory focus should be stored with the relevant significant-other representation if one regulates in the relationship in a way consistent with this regulatory focus. For example, if a discrepancy exists between the other's standards and one's actual self, the relevant discrepancy and regulatory focus should be evoked when the significant-other representation is triggered. Hence, individuals with an ought (versus an ideal) discrepancy should show more avoidance motivation in an imminent encounter with a new person. Indeed, ought-discrepant participants are more motivated to avoid the new person in transference while expecting to meet this new person relative to not expecting to meet him or her, whereas ideal-discrepant participants show a motivation to avoid the new person that is less pronounced while anticipating the meeting than when no longer anticipating it (Reznik & Andersen, 2007). Motivation toward the new person does not shift in the no-transference control condition.

Recent research complements these results by showing that when people are subliminally primed with father-related words and later engage in a problem-solving task, they come to adopt the regulatory focus consistent with their father's standards (Shah, 2003b, Study 3). Beyond the transference paradigm, then, subliminal activation of a significant-other representation can also trigger regulatory focus.

Activating Self-Protective Self-Regulation. Self-regulation should also arise when a threat to the self is experienced. Compensatory self-enhancement or self-inflation protecting the self has been widely documented in other research literatures (e.g., Greenberg & Pyszczynski, 1985; Morf & Rhodewalt, 2001; Showers, 1992; Steele, 1988; Taylor & Brown, 1988). One way to operationalize this kind of a threat to the self is an insult to how positively one views one's self. When the significant other in question is perceived negatively, for example, activation of this significant-other representation should result in an influx of negative elements into the self-concept, as the research shows (Hinkley & Andersen, 1996). This negativity should in turn pose a threat, thus evoking self-protective responses. Indeed, evidence shows that compensatory self-enhancement does occur in a negative transference: Along with the influx of negative self-features into the self-concept comes a flood of especially positive self-views. The self becomes, in fact, markedly positive overall in what appears to be a self-protective process.

In other research, participants learned about a new person resembling a positive significant other (or not) who, participants had previously indicated, was associated with a dreaded or desired self. Even though the positivity of the significant other is held constant, dreaded self-views should flood into the self-concept (in the dreaded-self condition), posing a serious threat to the self and evoking self-regulatory responses. The evidence once again shows an influx of positive aspects of the self—those unrelated to the dreaded self—into the self-concept in the transference involving a dreaded self, and these were especially positive, indicating compensatory self-enhancement (Reznik & Andersen, 2005). Hence, such compensatory self-inflation appears to function as a kind of self-protective self-regulation as a result of a negative or positive transference involving a dreaded self.

Activating Other-Protective Self-Regulation. Significant others are often impossible to replace, and exiting close relationships is not always feasible even when desired. Such relationships are characterized by interdependence and emotional investment, two factors that motivate people to maintain relationships and thus to maintain positive images of positive significant others. People construe significant-other flaws in ways that minimize how threatening these flaws are and maximize the significant other's benevolence. The clumsiness or scatteredness of a spouse, for example, may also be seen as cute (e.g., Murray & Holmes, 1993). Negative aspects of the significant other thus provoke other-protective responses. Hence, in a positive transference, any negative significant-other feature encountered in a new person should activate other-protective self-regulation—reflected in participants' facial affect while learning about the new person. Indeed, participants show especially positive facial affect in response to reading a new person's features in transference when these features reflect negative aspects of their positive significant other (versus positive aspects; Andersen et al., 1996), and no such pattern occurs among control participants. Participants respond affectively to transform the valence of each feature to match the overall valence of the representation, and this occurs relatively immediately and implicitly. Yet, it also appears to be a self-regulatory response—perhaps a relatively automatic one—that protects the view of the other as positive and good.

When one is reminded (consciously or unconsciously) of a positive significant other's negative attributes in transference, this may pose a challenge to needs for connection. Finding a way to positively respond to the other's negative qualities may be essential to maintaining relationships, and a person may be especially likely to regard a loved one positively when reminded of the other's faults (Holmes & Rempel, 1989). If this process is well practiced, it ought to take place relatively automatically, as this evidence suggests.

This kind of automatic response may not always be benign, however—for example, if it occurs in maladaptive relationships. In transference research involving an abusive parent (Berenson & Andersen, 2006), the effects of contextual cues about the new person's frame of mind were also assessed. Based on the idea that anger or frustration in an abusive parent may signal danger to one's well-being, the new person's alleged mood was manipulated. Participants learned about a new person who resembled their abusive parent (or did not), and later that this person was in an increasingly angry mood (or not). More positive facial affect occurs in response to this negative cue in transference than in the control condition, regardless of abuse history. An attempt to protect the image of the other as good may thus be indirectly reflected in affect protecting the other (and the relationship with him or her).

In short, both self-protective and other-protective self-regulatory processes arise in transference in response to threat (Andersen & Chen, 2002). They are experienced in new situations based on activation of a relevant significant-other representation, such that people self-regulate with respect to the significant other. Such self-regulation is dynamic and flexible: While being driven by qualities of the triggered representation, it is also responsive to cues in the present context. Self-regulation, as defined by threats, is comparable to a type of psychological defense—a matter closely relevant to theories of personality.

Emotions. Consistent with recent theorizing in the literature on emotions (Russell, 2003), which suggests that core affect is largely defined on a basic positive versus negative dimension, we have shown, as noted, that generic positive or negative affect arises in transference. Because people are emotionally invested in their significant others, it stands to reason that these others would hold considerable sway in emotions. It is thus curious that research on interpersonal aspects of the self has focused relatively little attention on emotions—although there are some major exceptions, such as self-discrepancy theory (Higgins, 1987) and attachment theory (e.g., Collins, 1996; see also Bersheid, 1994), which we address below.

First, we consider generic positive affect. Although both evaluation and facial affect in transference reflect global regard for the significant other, self-reported mood effects have only occasionally been found (e.g., Andersen & Baum, 1994). There are several reasons why this may be the case. Mood states are diffuse and are influenced by numerous seemingly irrelevant contextual factors, including even the weather (Schwarz & Clore, 1983), and also by various individual differences (e.g., neuroticism; Rusting & Larsen, 1997; negative affectivity; Watson & Clark, 1984).

In the following pages, we consider a number of conditions under which the positive affect otherwise associated with a positive significant other might be discoupled in transference. We then turn to the specific negative emotions that arise in transference, deriving from various individual differences.

Disrupting Positive Affect

One factor that may prevent global positive affect from arising in a positive transference is expectancy violation. There are at least three ways in which the expectancies one has with a positive significant other (that are indirectly activated in transference) may ultimately be violated in transference. We describe each of these effects in turn.

Chronic Need Violation and Chronically Unsatisfied Goals. As noted, a loved or liked other will not necessarily evoke positive mood states when the representation of this person is activated. When a significant-other representation is activated in transference, the goal for love and acceptance should also be activated, along with information about whether or not it has been satisfied. Diminished positive affect or increased frustration and hostility may thus result when such needs go unmet, and this is what the data show. Positive affect is indeed disrupted in a positive transference when one has chronically unsatisfied acceptance goals with this significant other, resulting in heightened hostility. However, when the significant other is from one's family of origin, a paradoxical effect may arise. The more such hostility is evoked in the transference, the more one also engages in overt behaviors designed to solicit acceptance and liking from the new person, pursuing an obsequious strategy that might evoke acceptance, presumably one that did not work in the past (Berk & Andersen, 2004). This is of interest in part because it is the first evidence to examine chronically interrupted goals with a significant other in transference and to show that the same goals may be pursued behaviorally in transference. This evidence is also important because it involves needs for connection with others, which if long unsatisfied, may well have still broader implications for personality (e.g., Downey & Feldman, 1996).

Chronic Self-Induced Violation of Own Standards. If one tends to experience a dreaded self with a liked or loved other (i.e., one responds in ways that one deems unacceptable when around this other), this experience clearly goes against one's own preferred responses. Moreover, this knowledge about the relationship should be stored with the significant-other representation and should thus be activated in transference, disrupting any positive mood that might otherwise result from this positive transference. In fact, when a positive significant other associated with a dreaded self is activated in transference, this diminishes positive mood and increases negative mood, relative to a comparable desired-self-transference condition, which does not occur in the control condition (Reznik & Andersen, 2005).

Contextually-Based Expectancy Violation Through Interpersonal Roles. Even when a relationship becomes quite close and individuating information about the other is at the forefront, norms derived from interpersonal roles continue to guide interactions by prescribing behaviors and expectations. Information about a significant other's role in the relationship should thus be stored in the relational knowledge linked to the significant-other representation and should thus be activated in transference when the representation is activated, leading the individual to hold the same role expectancies in relation to the new person. When contextual cues about the new person indicate that he or she will be in an incongruent role relative to the significant other—a role and expectancy violation that should disrupt positive mood—this indeed results in increased negative mood relative to when the role is congruent. Specifically, when the new person resembles a significant other who is also an authority figure to the participant, and the new person is placed in the position of a novice in the experimental interaction, this leads to depressed affect (Baum & Andersen, 1999).

The complex dynamics of regarding the new person positively but feeling bad personally surely speaks to personality and behavior by tracing the emotional discontinuities that may characterize people's day-to-day experiences and pointing to subtle shifts in perception and emotional responses. As indicated, when one's needs are chronically unsatisfied in relation to a significant other, this is associated with suffering in the relationship that is then evoked in transference. When one chronically violates one's own preferences in the relationship, this too is associated with emotional suffering evoked in transference. Finally, when the violation stems from the immediate context, suggesting that the original role relationship with the significant other (typically satisfied in that relationship) will be reversed, this also disrupts positive affect. A more static approach to personality dispositions or emotional tendencies would neither predict nor be likely to capture this range of contextually provoked responses linked to significant-other representations.

We turn now to work that moves beyond the core positive-negative dimension of affect to make predictions about discrete emotions in transference. One approach to the question of how a positive transference may lead to painful emotions is to examine individual differences that are linked to the self and thus thought to be associated with specific negative emotions. Based on the individual differences that impinge upon significant-other relationships, it should be possible to predict specific negative emotions that will arise in a given transference, even if the other is positive. Independent lines of work examined this by focusing on self-discrepancies from the significant other's perspective and also on attachment style with the significant other. We describe each in turn.

Self-Discrepancies From a Parent's Perspective and Specific Emotional Vulnerabilities

According to self-discrepancy theory, when a discrepancy exists between how one perceives the actual self and how one perceives the ideal self, this results in dejection-related affect, whereas a discrepancy between one's actual and ought selves (e.g., perceived obligations) results in agitation-related affect (Higgins, 1987). Ought and ideal selves can also be held from a significant other's perspective, and either way should lead to these distinct emotional outcomes. The model implies that representations of self and other are intertwined in memory, as we assume in conceptualizing the relational self. The integration of these frameworks suggests that self-discrepancies associated with a significant other should be activated in transference when a significant-other representation is activated, thus evoking the specific emotional reactions associated with these self-discrepancies. In research assessing this, participants classified as having an ideal or ought self-discrepancy (but not both) from a loved parent's perspective took part in a transference experiment (Andersen & Chen, 2002; see Reznik & Andersen, 2007).

Depressed Mood. When a new person resembles a parent who holds an ideal (but not an ought) self-discrepancy, this results in more depressed mood in transference (relative to a control condition; Reznik & Andersen, 2007). That is, the relatively implicit activation of this significant-other representation (based on significant-other resemblance in the new person) is sufficient to evoke the self-discrepancy and the associated affect in transference. Thus, even in this relatively positive transference experience, which includes positive expectancies about the new person, participants' mood is negative, and consistent with the model, they are more depressed.

Hostile Mood (a Lack of Calm). Also consistent with the model, participants with an ought discrepancy from their parent's perspective tend to experience more resentful and hostile mood when a new person resembles this parent relative to a control condition. Hostility is known to be associated with ought discrepancies as part of an agitated response. Again, the implicit activation of the significant-other representation in transference is sufficient to activate the self-discrepancy. That ought-discrepant individuals in transference also report feeling markedly less calm than in the control condition when they no longer expected to interact with the new person—that is, when most other participants are relieved and relatively calm—supports the notion that an agitation-related constellation of affects is associated with the ought self-discrepancy, which is indirectly activated in transference.

These findings are also supported by research in which participants are subliminally primed with father-related words (or not) and later engage in a problem-solving task and then receive positive or negative performance feedback (or none; Shah, 2003b). When the father is primed, this activates the father's standards and thus influences emotional responses to the performance feedback. We argue that to understand affect in transference in precise terms, i.e., in terms of discrete affects, one must understand the aspects of self that are evoked in transference, which are intertwined with the particular significant-other relationship at hand. In this way, individual differences that involve the self and the nature of one's relationships are likely to be meaningfully linked to emotional well-being in these effects, and these differences will arise in a manner that varies as a function of the psychological situation and interpersonal context, thus linking our research to personality.

THE ATTACHMENT SYSTEM AND SPECIFIC ASSOCIATED EMOTIONS

The individual differences just mentioned may also include those that are explicitly interpersonal (e.g., attachment style; Pietromonaco & Feldman Barrett, 1997). Attachment theory addresses both infants and adults and spans clinical, personality, and social psychology. Internal working models of the self and other form the basis of the attachment system, which by definition engages one's needs with a significant other along with a variety of complex affective dynamics. On the simplest level, individuals who are securely attached in a relationship should feel comfortable in it, while insecurely attached individuals should not, and this fact and its emotional sequelae should define the attachment dynamic with the other. Activating a significant-other representation in transference should thus activate the attachment system and the attachment style in that specific relationship.

As noted, recent research clearly shows that people have multiple attachment styles across various relationships and that one's attachment style in each relationship is stored in memory (Baldwin et al., 1996; Pierce & Lydon, 2001). Under certain circumstances, contextual cues can also activate the attachment system (e.g., Mikulincer, Gillath, & Shaver, 2002). It thus makes sense to ask whether or not attachment style with a parent will in fact be activated when a parental representation is activated in transference, and whether the predicted emotional response will arise. Research examining this preselected participants who are securely or insecurely attached to one of their parents (with the latter participants classified as preoccupied, dismissive, or fearful) and led them to take part in transference (Andersen, Bartz, Berenson, & Keczkemethy, 2006).

Global Positive Affect

When a new person resembles a parent and evokes transference, participants who are securely attached to this parent show increases in their overall positive mood relative to the control condition. Triggering transference also yields more positive affect among those securely, versus insecurely, attached (i.e., those classified as avoidant, anxious-ambivalent, or fearful), whereas in the absence of transference this comparison is not significant. This suggests that implicitly activating the significant-other representation activates internal models of the self and other, presumably accounting for these differences in global affect. Hence, the emotional comfort and ease associated with secure attachment are contextually cued by means of significant-other activation in transference. Transference may thus be a mechanism by which the attachment system is set into play across varying interpersonal contexts, and this dovetails with modern, social-cognitive approaches to attachment (e.g., Baldwin et al., 1996).

Beyond changes in global affect, a variety of specific, discrete emotions should also be activated when attachment style with a parent is activated. In particular, individuals with a preoccupied (or anxious-ambivalent) attachment style with a parent should show increased anxiety in transference, while individuals with a dismissive (or avoidant) attachment style should seek to down-regulate their negative emotions with the parent in transference, especially the interpersonal affect of anger.

Evoking Anxious Mood in a Preoccupied Attachment

Individuals whose attachment style with a parent is preoccupied (or anxious-ambivalent) should have a relationship with this parent characterized by constant checking in and worrying, in short, by anxiety. Hence, when the parental representation is activated in transference among individuals with preoccupied attachment, it should lead to increases in anxious mood. In fact the evidence shows that preoccupied individuals become more anxious in transference as compared with the control condition, which does not occur for avoidant, fearful, or secure individuals.

Evoking Suppressed Hostility in Dismissive Attachment

A hallmark of dismissive (or avoidant) attachment style is affective inexpressiveness, particularly a lack of negative emotion. If the attachment system is activated in transference, this should lead individuals who were dismissively attached to this parent to suppress any negative emotion experienced, leading to significant decreases in negative emotion, especially hostility and resentment, relative to the control condition. No such effect should occur for preoccupied, fearful, or secure individuals. Again, the evidence suggests that this occurs. Dismissive individuals appear to suppress their hostility in transference compared with the control condition, in which their hostility is markedly high. Other evidence has also shown that if there is an attachment-related threat, these individuals suppress the accessibility of attachment figures themselves as well, presumably because they are motivated to avoid expressing negative emotions in reference to this (Mikulincer et al., 2002).

In sum, transference involving a loved parent evokes both global positive affect and specific negative moods (anxiety and hostility) as a function of individual differences in the specific attachment dynamics with that parent. Given the long-standing assumption that activating internal working models should evoke the attachment system and the emotional and motivational vicissitudes attendant to it, this evidence addresses a gap in the literature that is of special theoretical relevance, while also linking that literature to research on the activation of significant-other representations in transference.

This research also complements other recent work showing that attachment figures tend to become more accessible after threat-related primes, as do proximity-related thoughts (Mikulincer, Birnbaum, Woddis, & Nachmias, 2000; Mikulincer et al., 2002), which may help to buffer the stressful impact of any threat experienced by means of evoked positive affect occurring in a secure attachment (McGowan, 2002; Mikulincer, Gillath, Halevy, Avihou, Avidan, & Eshkoli, 2001), an effect moderated by individual differences in attachment style. Because people's attachment styles differ across relationships, most individuals may have mental access to a potentially emotionally soothing (secure) relationship representation which they can turn to in times of stress (e.g., Baldwin et al., 1996; Pierce & Lydon, 2001). After half a century of theorizing, significant-other representations have thus been linked empirically to the attachment system, and this research suggests, as noted, that transference may be a mechanism by which the attachment system is activated in interpersonal relations. At the very least, this evidence demonstrates an important sense in which an If-Then model of the relational self can contribute to our understanding of personality and social behavior. Moreover, research in this domain is particularly integrative in that it tests some of the most influential theoretical concepts in clinical and personality theory using social-cognitive tools.

CONCLUSION

We have argued that the interpersonal context of people's lives—both as represented in memory and as reflected in the specific cues encountered in everyday situations—is informative about the kinds of interpretations, expectancies, motivations, and emotions they will experience. If the vicissitudes of affect and motivation bonded to the particular, individualized meanings an individual gives to contextual cues is not informative about personality, we do not know what is. It is the psychological situation the individual perceives at any given moment that shapes his or her responses. In our view, an individual's interpersonal history is encoded in memory and defined largely by significant people in his or her life. The self is thus entangled with significant others in memory such that the individual has a relatively distinctive relational self with each significant other. Hence, contextual cues that activate a significant-other representation will activate the relevant relational self, accompanied by shifts in self-evaluation, self worth, and also self-regulation, all shaping the psychological situation for the individual. Moreover, it is clearly not sufficient to simply know the global evaluation of a significant other (i.e., whether he or she is liked or loved) if one wishes to predict emotional responses in transference. What is crucial is that the precise relationship with the significant other is understood as well, as it is the activation of the relational self that predicts affective responses in transference.

Beyond this, to the degree that various individual difference measures tapping generic differences in personality help more precisely demarcate the psychological situation experienced in a particular context, perhaps by means of tapping differences in significant-other relationships, they are likely to be of considerable value in understanding the person. Moreover, independently of such measures, we argue that If-Then shifts in how people interpret and respond to various interpersonal situations—by virtue of the social-cognitive process of transference—are revealing about personality in part by showing that this century-old empirical concept at last has empirical support. Indeed, the If-Then shifts in the relational knowledge brought to bear on present situations as "baggage" also tell us something important about both stability and variability in the self and personality. Variability in personality and behavior rests on the unique meanings that individuals come to assign (consciously or unconsciously) to the various interpersonal cues they encounter, and this cueing function is what defines which aspects of self will in fact be at play. We argue that this interplay, which the reviewed research demonstrates, captures something essential about the person.

ACKNOWLEDGMENT

This research was funded in part by a grant from the National Institute of Mental Health (#R01-MH48789).

NOTE

1. Research on judgmental and conditional relationships assumes an If-Then contingency is evoked when the representation of a relationship partner who offers contingent acceptance is made accessible. These If-Then contingencies are further paired with neutral stimuli, such as an auditory tone, which becomes associated with the contingency such that these neutral stimuli can evoke the contingency, depending partially on individual differences such as attachment style (Baldwin & Kay, 2003; Baldwin & Meunier, 1999).

REFERENCES

Aarts, H., & Dijksterhuis, A. (2000). Habits as knowledge structures: Automaticity in goal-directed behavior. *Journal of Personality and Social Psychology, 78,* 53-63.

Abramson, L. Y., Seligman, M. E. P., & Teasdale, J. D. (1978). Learned helplessness in humans: Critique and reformation. *Journal of Abnormal Psychology, 87,* 49-74.

Adler, A. (1957). *Understanding human nature.* New York: Fawcett Premier. (Original work published 1927)

Allport, G. (1937). *Personality: A psychology interpretation.* New York: Holt, Rinehart & Winston.

Andersen, S. M., Bartz, J., Berenson, K., & Keczkemethy, C. (2006). *Triggering the attachment system in transference: Evoking specific emotions through transiently activating a parental representation.* Unpublished manuscript, New York University.

Andersen, S. M., & Baum, A. (1994). Transference in interpersonal relations: Inferences and affect based on significant-other representations. *Journal of Personality, 62,* 459-498.

Andersen, S. M., & Chen, S. (2002). The relational self: An interpersonal social-cognitive theory. *Psychological Review, 109,* 619-645.

Andersen, S. M., & Cole, S. W. (1990). "Do I know you?" The role of significant others in general social perception. *Journal of Personality and Social Psychology, 59,* 383-399.

Andersen, S. M., & Glassman, N. S. (1996). Responding to significant others when they are not there: Effects on interpersonal inference, motivation, and affect. In R. M. Sorrentino & E. T. Higgins (Eds.), *Handbook of motivation and cognition* (Vol. 3, pp. 262–321). New York: Guilford.

Andersen, S. M., Glassman, N. S., Chen, S., & Cole, S. W. (1995). Transference in social perception: The role of chronic accessibility in significant-other representations. *Journal of Personality and Social Psychology, 69,* 41–57.

Andersen, S. M., Glassman, N. S., & Gold, D. (1998). Mental representations of the self, significant others, and nonsignificant other: Structure and processing of private and public aspects. *Journal of Personality and Social Psychology, 75,* 845–861.

Andersen, S. M., Lambert, L., & Dick, W. (1999). Significant-other exemplars: Processing efficiency in instance-based judgments. Unpublished manuscript, New York University.

Andersen, S. M., Moskowitz, G. B., Blair, I. B., & Nosek, B. N. (2007). Automatic thought. In E. T. Higgins & A. W. Kruglanski (Eds.), *Social psychology: Handbook of basic principles* (2nd ed., pp. 138–175). New York: Guilford.

Andersen, S. M., Reznik, I., & Chen, S. (1997). The self in relation to others: Motivational and cognitive underpinnings. In J. G. Snodgrass & R. L. Thompson (Eds.), *The self across psychology: Self-recognition, self awareness, and the self-concept* (pp. 233–275). New York: New York Academy of Science.

Andersen, S. M., Reznik, I., & Glassman, N. S. (2005). The unconscious relational self. In R. Hassin, J. S. Uleman, & J. A. Bargh (Eds.), *The new unconscious* (pp. 421–481). New York: Oxford University Press.

Andersen, S. M., Reznik, I., & Manzella, L. M. (1996). Eliciting facial affect, motivation, and expectancies in transference: Significant-other representations in social relations. *Journal of Personality and Social Psychology, 71,* 1108–1129.

Andersen, S. M., & Saribay, S. A. (2006). Thinking integratively about social psychology: The example of the relational self and the social-cognitive process of transference. In P. A. M. Van Lange (Ed.), *Bridging social psychology* (pp. 199–206). Mahwah, NJ: Erlbaum.

Aron, A., Aron, E. N., Tudor, M., & Nelson, G. (1991). Close relationships as including other in the self. *Journal of Personality and Social Psychology, 60,* 241–253.

Ashmore, R. D., & Ogilvie, D. M. (1992). He's such a nice boy . . . when he's with Grandma: Gender and evaluation in self-with-other representations. In T. M. Brinthaupt & R. P. Lipka (Eds.), *The self: Definitional and methodological issues* (pp. 236–290). Albany: State University of New York Press.

Ayduk, O., Downey, G., Kim, M. (2001). Rejection sensitivity and depressive symptoms in women. *Personality and Social Psychology Bulletin, 27,* 868–877.

Ayduk, O., Mendoza-Denton, R., Mischel, W., Downey, G., Peake, P. K., & Rodriguez, M. (2000). Regulating the interpersonal self: Strategic self-regulation for coping with rejection sensitivity. *Journal of Personality and Social Psychology, 79,* 776–792.

Bacon, M. K., & Ashmore, R. D. (1985). How mothers and fathers categorize descriptions of social behavior attributed to daughters and sons. *Social Cognition, 3,* 193–217.

Bakan, D. (1966). *The duality of human existence.* Chicago: Rand McNally.

Baldwin, M. W. (1992). Relational schemas and the processing of information. *Psychological Bulletin, 112,* 461–484.

Baldwin, M. W., Carrell, S. E., & Lopez, D. F. (1990). Priming relationship schemas: My advisor and the Pope are watching me from the back of my mind. *Journal of Experimental Social Psychology, 26,* 435–454.

Baldwin, M. W., Fehr, B., Keedian, E., Seidel, M., & Thompson, D. W. (1993). An exploration of the relational schemata underlying attachment styles: Self-report and lexical decision approaches. *Personality and Social Psychology Bulletin, 19,* 746–754.

Baldwin, M. W., & Kay, A. C. (2003). Adult attachment and the inhibition of rejection. *Journal of Social and Clinical Psychology, 22*, 275–293.

Baldwin, M. W., Keelan, J. P. R., Fehr, B., Enns, V., & Koh-Rangarajoo, E. (1996). Social-cognitive conceptualization of attachment working models: Availability and accessibility effects. *Journal of Personality and Social Psychology, 71*, 94–109.

Baldwin, M. W., & Meunier, J. (1999). The cued activation of attachment relational schemas. *Social Cognition, 17*, 209–227.

Baldwin, M. W., & Sinclair, L. (1996). Self-esteem and "if...then" contingencies of interpersonal acceptance. *Journal of Personality and Social Psychology, 71*, 1130–1141.

Banaji, M. R., & Greenwald, A. G. (1995). Implicit gender stereotyping in judgments of fame. *Journal of Personality and Social Psychology, 68*, 181–198.

Bandura, A. (1977). Self-efficacy: Toward a unifying theory of behavioral change. *Psychological Review, 84*, 191–215.

Bandura, A. (1986). *Social foundations of thought and action: A social cognitive theory.* Englewood Cliffs, NJ: Prentice Hall.

Bandura, A. (1989). Human agency in social-cognitive theory. *American Psychologist, 44*, 1175–1184.

Banse, R. (1999). Automatic evaluation of self and others: Affective priming in close relationships. *Journal of Social and Personal Relationships, 16*, 803–821.

Bargh, J. A. (1990). Auto-motives: Preconscious determinants of social interaction. In E. T. Higgins & R. M. Sorrentino (Eds.), *Handbook of motivation and cognition: Foundations of social behavior* (Vol. 2, pp. 93–130). New York: Guilford.

Bargh, J. A. (1997). The automaticity of everyday life. In R. S. Wyer, Jr. (Ed.), *Advances in social cognition* (Vol. 10, pp. 1–61). Mahwah, NJ: Erlbaum.

Bargh, J. A., & Barndollar, K. (1996). Automaticity in action: The unconscious as repository of chronic goals and motives. In P. M. Gollwitzer & J. A. Bargh (Eds.), *The psychology of action: Linking cognition and motivation to behavior* (pp. 457–481). New York: Guilford.

Bargh, J. A., Bond, R. N., Lombardi, W. L., & Tota, M. E. (1986). The additive nature of chronic and temporary sources of construct accessibility. *Journal of Personality and Social Psychology, 50*, 869–878.

Bargh, J. A., & Chartrand, T. (1999). The unbearable automaticity of being. *American Psychologist, 54*, 462–479.

Bargh, J. A., & Gollwitzer, P. M. (1994). Environmental control of goal-directed action: Automatic and strategic contingencies between situations and behavior. In W. D. Spaulding (Ed.), *Integrative views of motivation, cognition, and emotion* (pp. 71-124). Lincoln: University of Nebraska Press.

Bargh, J. A., Gollwitzer, P. M., Lee-Chai, A., Barndollar, K., & Trötschel, R. (2001). The automated will: Nonconscious activation and pursuit of behavioral goals. *Journal of Personality and Social Psychology, 81*, 1014–1027.

Batson, C. D. (1990). How social an animal? The human capacity for caring. *American Psychologist, 45*, 336–346.

Baum, A., & Andersen, S. M. (1999). Interpersonal roles in transference: Transient mood states under the condition of significant-other activation. *Social Cognition, 17*, 161–185.

Baumeister, R. F. (1991). *Meanings of life.* New York: Guilford.

Baumeister, R. F., & Leary, M. R. (1995). The need to belong: Desire for interpersonal attachments as a fundamental human motivation. *Psychological Bulletin, 117*, 497–529.

Becker, E. (1971). *The birth and death of meaning* (2nd ed.). New York: Free Press.

Becker, E. (1973). *The denial of death.* New York: Free Press.

Berenson, K., & Andersen, S. M. (2006). Childhood physical and emotional abuse by a parent: Transference effects in adult interpersonal relationships. *Personality and Social Psychology Bulletin, 32,* 1509–1527.

Berk, M. S., & Andersen, S. M. (2000). The impact of past relationships on interpersonal behavior: Behavioral confirmation in the social-cognitive process of transference. *Journal of Personality and Social Psychology, 79,* 546–562.

Berk, M. S., & Andersen, S. M. (2004). Chronically unsatisfied goals with significant others: Triggering unfulfilled needs for love and acceptance in transference. Unpublished manuscript, New York University.

Berscheid, E. (1994). Interpersonal relationships. *Annual Review of Psychology, 45,* 79–129.

Blatt, S. J., & Zuroff, D. C. (1992). Interpersonal relatedness and self-definition: Two prototypes for depression. *Clinical Psychology Review, 12,* 527–562.

Bowlby, J. (1969). *Attachment and loss: Vol. 1. Attachment.* New York: Basic Books.

Bruner, J. S. (1990). *Acts of meaning.* Cambridge: Harvard University Press.

Bruner, J. S. (1957). Going beyond the information given. In H. E. Gruber, K. R. Hammond, & R. Jessor (Eds.), *Contemporary approaches to cognition* (pp. 41–69). Cambridge, MA: Harvard University Press.

Carson, R. C. (1969). *Interaction concepts of personality.* Chicago: Aldine Publishing.

Carver, C. S., & Scheier, M. F. (1981). *Attention and self-regulation: A control theory approach to human behavior.* New York: Springer.

Chen, S. (2001). The role of theories in mental representations and their use in social perception: A theory-based approach to significant-other representations and transference. In G. B. Moskowitz (Ed.), *Cognitive social psychology: The Princeton symposium on the legacy and future of social cognition* (pp. 125–142). Mahwah, NJ: Erlbaum.

Chen, S. (2003). Psychological-state theories about significant others: Implications for the content and structure of significant-other representations. *Personality and Social Psychology Bulletin, 29,* 1285–1302.

Chen, S., & Andersen, S. M. (1999). Relationships from the past in the present: Significant-other representations and transference in interpersonal life. In M. P. Zanna (Ed.), *Advances in experimental social psychology* (Vol. 31, pp. 123–190). San Diego, CA: Academic Press.

Chen, S., Andersen, S. M., & Hinkley, K. (1999). Triggering transference: Examining the role of applicability and use of significant-other representations in social perception. *Social Cognition, 17,* 332–365.

Chen, S., Fitzsimons, G. M., & Andersen, S. M. (2007). Automaticity in close relationships. In J. A. Bargh (Ed.), *Automatic processes in social thinking and behavior* (pp. 133–172). New York: Psychology Press.

Collins, N. L. (1996). Working models of attachment: Implications for explanation, emotion, and behavior. *Journal of Personality and Social Psychology, 71,* 810–832.

Cooley, C. H. (1902). *Human nature and social order.* New York: Scribner.

Crocker, J., & Wolfe, C. T. (2001). Contingencies of worth. *Psychological Review, 108,* 593–623.

Davila, J. (2001). Refining the association between excessive reassurance seeking and depressive symptoms: The role of related interpersonal constructs. *Journal of Social and Clinical Psychology, 20,* 538–559.

Davila, J., Hammen, C., Burge, D., & Paley, B. (1995). Poor interpersonal problem-solving as a mechanism of stress generation in depression among adolescent women. *Journal of Abnormal Psychology, 104,* 592–600.

Deci, E. L. (1995). *Why we do what we do.* New York: Putnam.

Deci, E. L., & Ryan, R. M. (1985). *Intrinsic motivation and self-determination in human behavior.* New York: Plenum.

Deci E. L., & Ryan, R. M. (1991). A motivational approach to self: Integration in personality. In R. Dienstbier (Ed.), *Nebraska symposium on motivation: Vol. 38. Perspectives on motivation* (pp. 237–288). Lincoln: University of Nebraska Press.

Devine, P. G. (1989). Stereotypes and prejudice: Their automatic and controlled components. *Journal of Personality and Social Psychology, 56,* 5–18.

Dodge, K., & Price, J. M. (1994). On the relation between social information processing and socially competent behavior in early school-aged children. *Child Development, 65,* 1385–1397.

Downey, G., & Feldman, S. I. (1996). Implications of rejection sensitivity for intimate relationships. *Journal of Personality and Social Psychology, 70,* 1327–1343.

Downey, G., Freitas, A. L., Michaelis, B., & Khouri, H. (1998). The self-fulfilling prophecy in close relationships: Rejection sensitivity and rejection by romantic partners. *Journal of Personality and Social Psychology, 75,* 545–560.

Downey, G., Khouri, H., & Feldman, S. (1997). Early interpersonal trauma and adult adjustment: The mediational role of rejection sensitivity. In D. Cicchetti & S. Toth (Eds.), *Rochester symposium in developmental psychopathology, Volume VIII: The effects of trauma on the developmental process* (pp. 85–114). Rochester, NY: University of Rochester Press.

Downey, G., Lebolt, A., Rincon, C., & Freitas, A. L. (1998). Rejection sensitivity and children's interpersonal difficulties. *Child Development, 69,* 1074–1091.

Dweck, C. S., & Leggett, E. L. (1988). A social–cognitive approach to motivation and personality. *Psychological Review, 95,* 256–273.

Ehrenreich, J. H. (1989). Transference: One concept or many? *The Psychoanalytic Review, 76,* 37–65.

Epstein, S. (1973). The self-concept revisited or a theory of a theory. *American Psychologist, 28,* 405–416.

Fairbairn, W. R. D. (1952). *Psychoanalytic studies of personality.* London: Tavistock.

Feldman, S., & Downey, G. (1994). Rejection sensitivity as a mediator of the impact of childhood exposure to family violence on adult attachment behavior. *Development and Psychopathology, 6,* 231–247.

Fiske, A. P., & Haslam, N. (2005). The four basic social bonds: Structures for coordinating interaction. In M. W. Baldwin (Ed.), *Interpersonal cognition* (pp. 267–298). New York: Guilford.

Fiske, S. T. (2003). *Social beings: A core motives approach to social psychology.* New York: Wiley.

Fiske, S. T., & Pavelchak, M. (1986). Category-based versus piecemeal-based affective responses: Developments in schema-triggered affect. In R. M. Sorrentino & E. T. Higgins (Eds.), *Handbook of motivation and cognition* (pp. 167–203). New York: Guilford.

Fitzsimons, G. M., & Bargh, J. A. (2003). Thinking of you: Nonconscious pursuit of interpersonal goals associated with relationship partners. *Journal of Personality and Social Psychology, 84,* 148–164.

Fitzsimons, G. M., Shah, J. Y., Chartrand, T. L., & Bargh, J. A. (2005). Friends and neighbors, goals and labors: Interpersonal and self regulation. In M. W. Baldwin (Ed.), *Interpersonal cognition* (pp. 130–125). New York: Guilford.

Frankl, V. E. (1959). *Man's search for meaning.* Boston, MA: Beacon Press.

Freud, S. (1958). The dynamics of transference. In J. Strachey (Ed. & Trans.), *The standard edition of the complete psychological works of Sigmund Freud* (Vol. 12, pp. 97–108). London: Hogarth. (Original work published 1912)

Glassman, N. S., & Andersen, S. M. (1999a). Activating transference without consciousness: Using significant-other representations to go beyond what is subliminally given. *Journal of Personality and Social Psychology, 77,* 1146–1162.

Glassman, N. S., & Andersen, S. M. (1999b). Transference in social cognition: Persistence and exacerbation of significant-other based inferences over time. *Cognitive Therapy and Research, 23,* 75–91.
Gollwitzer, P. M., & Moskowitz, G. B. (1996). Goal effects on action and cognition. In E. T. Higgins & A. W. Kruglanski (Eds.), *Social psychology:Handbook of basic principles* (pp. 361–399). New York: Guilford.
Greenberg, J., & Pyszczynski, T. (1985). Compensatory self-inflation: A response to the threat to self-regard of public failure. *Journal of Personality and Social Psychology, 49,* 273–280.
Greenberg, J. R., & Mitchell, S. A. (1983). *Object relations in psychoanalytic theory.* Cambridge: Harvard University Press.
Greenson, R. R. (1965). The working alliance and the transference neurosis. *Psychoanalytic Quarterly, 34,* 155–179.
Guisinger, S., & Blatt, S. J. (1994). Individuality and relatedness: Evolution of a fundamental dialectic. *American Psychologist, 49,* 104–111.
Hammen, C. (2000). Interpersonal factors in an emerging developmental model of depression. In S. L. Johnson & A. M. Hayes (Eds.), *Stress, coping, and depression* (pp. 71–88). Mahwah, NJ: Erlbaum.
Hardin, C. D., & Higgins, E. T. (1996). Shared reality: How social verification makes the subjective objective. In R. M. Sorrentino & E. T. Higgins (Eds.), *Handbook of motivation and cognition* (Vol. 3, pp. 28–84). New York: Guilford.
Helgeson, V. S. (1994). Relation of agency and communion to well-being: Evidence and potential explanations. *Psychological Review, 116,* 412–428.
Higgins, E. T. (1987). Self discrepancy: A theory relating self and affect. *Psychological Review, 94,* 319–340.
Higgins, E. T. (1989a). Knowledge accessibility and activation: Subjectivity and suffering from unconscious sources. In J. S. Uleman & J. A. Bargh (Eds.), *Unintended thought* (pp. 75–123). New York: Guilford.
Higgins, E. T. (1989b). Continuities and discontinuities in self-regulatory and self-evaluative processes: A developmental theory relating self and affect. *Journal of Personality, 57,* 407–444.
Higgins, E. T. (1990). Personality, social psychology, and person–situation relations: Standards and knowledge activation as a common language. In L. A. Pervin (Ed.), *Handbook of personality* (pp. 301–338). New York: Guilford.
Higgins, E. T. (1991). Development of self-regulatory and self-evaluative processes: Costs, benefits, and tradeoffs. In M. R. Gunnar, & L. A. Stroufe (Eds.), *Self processes and development: The Minnesota Symposia on Child Development* (Vol. 23, pp. 125–165). Hillsdale, NJ: Erlbaum.
Higgins, E. T. (1996a). Knowledge: Accessibility, applicability, and salience. In Higgins, E. T., & A. W., Kruglanski (Eds.), *Social psychology: Handbook of basic principles* (pp. 133–168). New York: Guilford.
Higgins, E. T. (1996b). Ideals, oughts, and regulatory focus: Affect and motivation from distinct pains and pleasures. In P. M. Gollwitzer & J. A. Bargh (Eds.), *The psychology of action* (pp. 91–114). New York: Guilford.
Higgins, E. T. (1996c). The self-digest: Self-knowledge serving self-regulatory functions. *Journal of Personality and Social Psychology, 71,* 1062–1083.
Higgins, E. T., & King, G. (1981). Accessibility of social constructs: Information processing consequences of individual and contextual variability. In N. Cantor & J. F. Kihlstrom (Eds.), *Personality, cognition and social interaction* (pp. 69–121). Hillsdale, NJ: Erlbaum
Hinkley, K., & Andersen, S. M. (1996). The working self-concept in transference: Significant-other activation and self change. *Journal of Personality and Social Psychology, 71,* 1279–1295.

Holmes, J. G., & Rempel, J. K. (1989). Trust in close relationships. *Review of Personality and Social Psychology, 10*, 187–219.
Horney, K. (1939). *New ways in psychoanalysis.* New York: Norton.
Horney, K. (1945). *Our inner conflicts.* New York: Norton.
Horowitz, M. J. (1989). Relationship schema formulation: Role-relationship models and intrapsychic conflict. *Psychiatry, 52*, 260–274.
Horowitz, M. J. (Ed.). (1991). *Person schemas and maladaptive interpersonal patterns.* Chicago: The University of Chicago Press.
Janoff-Bulman, R. (1992). *Shattered assumptions: Towards a new psychology of trauma.* New York: Free Press.
Johnson, J. T., & Boyd, K. R. (1995). Dispositional traits versus the content of experience: Actor/observer differences in judgments of the "authentic self." *Personality and Social Psychology Bulletin, 21*, 375–383.
Jung, C. G. (1933). *Modern man in search of a soul.* New York: Harcourt, Brace.
Karylowski, J. J., Konarzewski, K., & Motes, M. (2000). Recruitment of exemplars as reference points in social judgments. *Journal of Experimental Social Psychology, 36*, 275–303.
Kelly, G. A. (1955). *The psychology of personal constructs.* New York: Norton.
Kernberg, O. (1976). *Object relations theory and clinical psychoanalysis.* New York: Aronson.
Klinger, E. (1977). *Meaning and void.* Minneapolis: University of Minnesota Press.
Kohut, H. (1971). *The analysis of the self.* New York: International Universities Press.
Kruglanski, A. W. (1996). Goals as knowledge structures. In P. M. Gollwitzer, & J. A. Bargh (Eds.), *The psychology of action: Linking cognition and motivation to behavior* (pp. 599–618). New York: Guilford.
Leary, M. R., Tambor, E. S., Terdal, S. K., & Downs, D. L. (1995). Self-esteem as an interpersonal monitor: The sociometer hypothesis. *Journal of Personality and Social Psychology, 68*, 518–530.
Leary, T. (1957). *Interpersonal diagnosis of personality: A functional theory and methodology for personality evaluation.* Oxford, England: Ronald Press.
Linville, P. W., & Fischer, G. W. (1993). Exemplar and abstraction models of perceived group variability and stereotypicality. *Social Cognition, 11*, 92–125.
Luborsky, L., & Crits-Christoph, P. (1990). *Understanding transference: The CCRT method.* New York: Basic Books.
Markus, H., & Kitayama, S. (1991). Culture and the self: Implications for cognition, emotion, and motivation. *Psychological Review, 98*, 224–253.
Markus, H., & Wurf, E. (1987). The dynamic self-concept: A social–psychological perspective. *Annual Review of Psychology, 38*, 299–337.
McAdams, D. P. (1985). *Power, intimacy, and the life story: Personological inquiries into identity.* New York: Guilford.
McAdams, D. P. (1989). *Intimacy: The need to be close.* New York: Doubleday.
McGowan, S. (2002). Mental representations in stressful situations: The calming and distressing effects of significant others. *Journal of Experimental Social Psychology, 38*, 152–161.
Mead, G. H. (1934). *Mind, self, and society: From the standpoint of a social behaviorist.* Chicago: University of Chicago Press.
Mikulincer, M., Birnbaum, G., Woddis, D., & Nachmias, O. (2000). Stress and accessibility of proximity-related thoughts: Exploring the normative and intraindividual components of attachment theory. *Journal of Personality and Social Psychology, 78*, 509–523.

Mikulincer, M., Gillath, O., & Shaver, P. R. (2002). Activation of the attachment system in adulthood: Threat-related primes increase the accessibility of mental representations of attachment figures. *Journal of Personality and Social Psychology, 83*, 881–895.

Mikulincer, M., Gillath, O., Halevy, V., Avihou, N., Avidan, S., & Eshkoli, N. (2001). Attachment theory and reactions to others' needs: Evidence that activation of the sense of attachment security promotes empathic responses. *Journal of Personality and Social Psychology, 81*, 1205–1224.

Miranda, R., & Andersen, S. M. (2007). The therapeutic relationship: Implications from social cognition and transference. In P. Gilbert & R. Leahy (Eds.), *The therapeutic relationship in the cognitive behavioural psychotherapies* (pp. 63–89). London: Routledge.

Mischel, W. (1973). Toward a cognitive social learning reconceptualization of personality. *Psychological Review, 80*, 252–283.

Mischel, W. (1990). Personality dispositions revisited and revised: A view after three decades. In L. A. Pervin (Ed.), *Handbook of personality: Theory and research* (pp. 111–134). New York: Guilford.

Mischel, W., & Shoda, Y. (1995). A cognitive-affective system theory of personality: Reconceptualizing situations, dispositions, dynamics, and invariance in personality structure. *Psychological Review, 102*, 246-268.

Morf, C. C., & Rhodewalt, F. (2001). Unraveling the paradoxes of narcissism: A dynamic self-regulatory processing model. *Psychological Inquiry, 12*, 177–196.

Murray, S. L., & Holmes, J. G. (1993). Seeing virtues in faults: Negativity and the transformation of interpersonal narratives in close relationships. *Journal of Personality and Social Psychology, 65*, 707–722.

Nisbett, R. E., & Ross, L. (1980). *Human inference: Strategies and shortcomings of social judgment.* Englewood Cliffs, NJ: Prentice Hall.

Ogilvie, D. M., & Ashmore, R. D. (1991). Self-with-other representation as a unit of analysis in self-concept research. In R. C. Curtis (Ed.), *The relational self: Theoretical convergencies in psychoanalysis and social psychology* (pp. 282–314). New York: Guilford.

Park, C. L., & Folkman, S. (1997). Meaning and the context of stress and coping. *Review of General Psychology, 1*, 115–144.

Pennebaker, J. W. (1997). Writing about emotional experiences as a therapeutic process. *Psychological Science, 8*, 162–166.

Pierce, T., & Lydon, J. E. (2001). Global and specific relational models in the experience of social interactions. *Journal of Personality and Social Psychology, 80*, 613–631.

Pietromonaco, P. R., & Feldman Barrett, L. (1997). Working models of attachment and daily social interactions. *Journal of Personality and Social Psychology, 73*, 1409–1423

Prentice, D. (1990). Familiarity and differences in self- and other-representations. *Journal of Personality and Social Psychology, 59*, 369–383.

Reznik, I., & Andersen, S. M. (2005). Becoming the dreaded self: Diminished self-worth with positive significant others in transference. Unpublished manuscript, New York University.

Reznik, I., & Andersen, S. M. (2007). Agitation and despair in relation to parents: Activating emotional suffering in transference. *European Journal of Personality, 21*, 281–301.

Rogers, C. (1951). *Client-centered therapy.* Boston: Houghton Mifflin.

Russell, J. A. (2003). Core affect and the psychological construction of emotion. *Psychological Review, 110*, 145–172.

Rusting, C. L., & Larsen, R. J. (1997). Extraversion, neuroticism, and susceptibility to positive and negative affect: A test of two theoretical models. *Personality and Individual Differences, 22*, 607–612

Safran, J. D. (1990). Toward a refinement of cognitive therapy in light of interpersonal theory: I. Theory. *Clinical Psychology Review, 10,* 87–105.

Safran, J. D., & Segal, Z. V. (1990). *Interpersonal process in cognitive therapy.* New York: Basic Books.

Schimek, J. (1983). The construction of the transference: The relativity of the "here and now" and the "there and then." *Psychoanalysis and Contemporary Thought, 6,* 435–456.

Schwarz, N., & Clore, G. L. (1983). Mood, misattribution, and judgments of well-being: Informative and directive functions of affective states. *Journal of Personality and Social Psychology, 45,* 513–523.

Seligman, M. E. P. (1975). *Helplessness: On depression, development, and death.* San Francisco: Freeman.

Shah, J. (2003a). Automatic for the people: How representations of significant others implicitly affect goal pursuit. *Journal of Personality and Social Psychology, 84,* 661–681.

Shah, J. (2003b). The motivational looking glass: How significant others implicitly affect goal appraisals. *Journal of Personality and Social Psychology, 85,* 424–439.

Showers, C. (1992). Compartmentalization of positive and negative self-knowledge: Keeping bad apples out of the bunch. *Journal of Personality and Social Psychology, 62,* 1036–1049.

Silver, R. C., & Wortman, C. B. (1980). Coping with undesirable life events. In J. Garber & M. E. P. Seligman (Eds.), *Human helplessness* (pp. 279–340). New York: Academic Press.

Singer, J. L. (1988). Reinterpreting the transference. In D. C. Turk & P. Salovey (Eds.), *Reasoning, interference, and judgment in clinical psychology* (pp. 182–205). New York: Free Press.

Smith, E. R. (1998). Mental representation and memory. In D. Gilbert, S. T. Fiske & G. Lindzey (Eds.), *Handbook of social psychology* (4th ed., Vol. 1, pp. 391–445). New York: McGraw-Hill.

Smith, E. R., Murphy, J., & Coats, S. (1999). Attachment to groups: Theory and management. *Journal of Personality and Social Psychology, 77,* 94–110.

Smith, E. R., & Zarate, M. A. (1992). Exemplar-based model of social judgment. *Psychological Review, 99,* 3–21.

Snyder, M., Tanke, E. D., & Berscheid, E. (1977). Social perception and interpersonal behavior: On the self-fulfilling nature of social stereotypes. *Journal of Personality and Social Psychology, 35,* 656–666.

Steele, C. M. (1988). The psychology of self-affirmation: Sustaining the integrity of the self. In L. Berkowitz (Ed.), *Advances in experimental social psychology* (Vol. 21, pp. 261–302). New York: Academic Press.

Sullivan, H. S. (1953). *The interpersonal theory of psychiatry.* New York: Norton.

Taylor, S. E., & Brown, J. D. (1988). Illusion and well-being: A social psychological perspective on mental health. *Psychological Bulletin, 103,* 193–210.

Wachtel, P. L. (1981). Transference, schema, and assimilation: The relationship of Piaget to the psychoanalytic theory of transference. *Annual of Psychoanalysis, 8,* 59–76.

Watson, D., & Clark, L. A. (1984). Negative affectivity: The disposition to experience aversive emotional states. *Psychological Bulletin, 96,* 465–490.

Westen, D. (1988). Transference and information processing. *Clinical Psychology Review, 8,* 161–179.

White, R. W. (1959). Motivation reconsidered: The concept of competence. *Psychological Review, 66,* 297–333.

5

Ties That Bind
Linking Personality to Interpersonal Behavior Through the Study of Adult Attachment Style and Relationship Satisfaction

W. STEVEN RHOLES, RAMONA L. PAETZOLD,
and MIKE FRIEDMAN
Texas A&M University

Although relationship satisfaction may stem from many causes, one of its important correlates is having a secure attachment style—that is, having an attachment style that represents an appropriate balance between closeness to, and distance from, one's partner, an ability to have one's needs met for both security and autonomy. In this chapter we review the research that links attachment style to relationship satisfaction, primarily via a set of risk factors (some of which may be mediating variables) that have been shown to flow from an analysis of attachment styles and to be important for attaining or maintaining relationship satisfaction.

Since the mid-1980s, research on adult attachment has flourished, with a focus on its association with satisfaction in romantic relationships coming into full swing beginning in the 1990's. According to attachment theory, people develop beliefs about themselves and others (i.e., complex cognitive schema or working models) as a result of childhood and adolescent experiences with attachment figures (Bowlby, 1969, 1973; Ainsworth, Blehar, Waters, & Wall, 1978). Conceptualizations and operationalizations of attachment style may vary across researchers, but three primary attachment styles are relevant for the study of marital and romantic relationships: secure, anxious, and avoidant. We begin this chapter with a general discussion of the attachment system, explaining its evolutionary underpinnings and how it interacts with the other primary behavioral systems (caregiving, sexuality, and exploration). We describe the three basic attachment styles and briefly introduce evidence that they are associated with relationship satisfaction. We then turn to a discussion of the risk factors for relationship satisfaction. To complement this discussion, we also examine the implications for the partners of individuals having either secure or insecure attachment styles. Limitations of the existing literature and directions for future research are presented at the end of the chapter.

In this chapter we do not, and indeed could not, cover all of the literature suggesting connections between attachment style and relationship satisfaction. For example, we do not review the vast literature focusing on cognitive and affective processing as part of the working models of attachment (except for the literature clearly addressing anger, which to us is essential to understanding insecure attachment styles). Also largely absent from our chapter is the literature based on an assessment of attachment style according to the Adult Attachment Interview (AAI; Main & Goldwyn, 1998). This measurement technique originated in the developmental psychology literature and has to date been used much less extensively in the social psychology literature, particularly as it relates to relationship or marital satisfaction. Despite these and other lacunae in coverage, our presentation provides a substantial overview of the nature of adult attachment style and the major risk factors it appears to present for relationship dissatisfaction.

A BRIEF INTRODUCTION TO ATTACHMENT THEORY: EVOLUTION, ATTACHMENT STYLES, AND ITS RELATION TO OTHER BEHAVIORAL SYSTEMS

Among contemporary approaches to personality, attachment theory (Bowlby, 1969, 1973, 1980) may be the most thoroughly interpersonal. It includes the idea that involvement in close relationships is inherently motivated. It also asserts that personality (or attachment style) develops through social interaction with others in close relationships, and that attachment styles, in turn, play a life-long role in shaping behavior in close relationships. Although we briefly discuss inherent social motives and the development of attachment styles, our primary topic is the connection between attachment styles and interpersonal behavior, consistent with the theme of this volume. We argue that a history of insecure attachment relationships in infancy, childhood, and adolescence creates personal insecurities and habitual affective responses in adults that drive their maladaptive perceptions of partners (e.g., as unsupportive) and situations (e.g., as highly conflictual), as well as leading to their own maladaptive behaviors (e.g., resolving conflicts poorly). Insecure adults attribute their resulting dissatisfaction with relationships to aversive conditions (such as unresolved conflict), limited opportunities for intimacy and closeness, and alienation from their relationship partners, leading them to behave in ways that confirm their pessimistic perceptions and expectations and result in even further relationship dissatisfaction. Finally, we provide an overarching framework for understanding the perceptions, expectations, and behaviors of persons with insecure attachment styles, emphasizing how their habitual anger and egoistic concern with meeting their own needs for security and autonomy—to the exclusion of the needs of others—thwarts their ability to obtain higher levels of relationship satisfaction.

According to Bowlby (1969, 1973, 1980), humans have an innate attachment system that motivates infants to remain in close proximity to their caregivers, who serve as attachment figures. This system has evolved as a means of increasing the likelihood of survival and reproduction of a species whose members are relatively helpless at birth. Proximity to an attachment figure provides infants with comfort and security, allowing them to engage in other forms of essential behaviors such as exploration of their environments. While particularly critical during early stages of life, the attachment system remains active over a person's life span, from "the cradle to the grave" (Bowlby, 1973, p. 203), generating thoughts, feelings, and behaviors associated with the maintaining of proximity to attachment figures (Bowlby, 1988).

Although the proximity-seeking motive is posited to be universal as well as innate, not all attachment figures can or will provide the forms of caregiving that lead to feelings of security and safety in their offspring. As a result, different patterns of attachment emerge in infants (Ainsworth et al., 1978). Infants who receive consistent care and support from their primary attachment figure (typically, although not necessarily, their mother) tend to develop a *secure* attachment style. As demonstrated by Ainsworth et al. (1978), using what she called the Strange Situation Paradigm, these infants engage in high levels of exploration while using their mothers as a secure base when they become distressed or anxious. At the other extreme, when mothers are consistently unresponsive to their infants' needs to be comforted, the infants develop *avoidant* attachment styles. Ainsworth et al. (1978) noted that these infants did not seek care or support from their mothers when they were distressed; instead, they actively avoided their mothers and were prematurely self-reliant. Finally, when mothers were inconsistent in their caregiving, sometimes being highly responsive while at other times being inattentive, their infants developed an *anxious* (sometimes referred to as anxious/ambivalent or resistant) attachment style. Infants in this situation appeared to be conflicted, hypervigilant, and angry, engaging in less exploration while making inconsistent attempts to obtain support from their mothers when they became distressed.

Early attachment experiences generate mental working models of the self and others that give rise to attitudes, beliefs, and expectations about relationships, providing a framework for interpreting and influencing relationship experiences (Bowlby, 1973, 1980; Collins & Read, 1994; Simpson & Rholes, 1998). These working models represent complex cognitive and affective schemas that, by predicting the availability and responsiveness of others, allow individuals to generate their own behaviors. Because the attachment system, as an evolutionary device, is concerned with providing safety and security for individuals, each of the attachment styles has come to be characterized as a set of individual differences reflecting patterns of responses to significant threats to safety and security (Kobak & Sceery,

1988; Sroufe & Waters, 1977). Further, although the initial studies of adult attachment styles, including many reviewed in this chapter, assessed styles in terms of a typology or as prototypes (Bartholomew, 1990; Bartholomew & Horowitz, 1991; Hazan & Shaver, 1987), they are today typically assessed in terms of two continuous, orthogonal dimensions: avoidance and anxiety (Brennan, Clark, & Shaver, 1998; Simpson, 1990; Simpson, Rholes, & Nelligan, 1992). The anxiety dimension represents the extent to which the attachment system is activated in times of environmental or relationship threat or stress, whereas the avoidance dimension reflects the degree to which closeness with an attachment figure is desired. Nonetheless, for convenience throughout this chapter, persons who are high on the avoidance dimension are categorically referred to as avoidant, those high on the anxiety dimension are referred to as anxious, and those low on both avoidance and anxiety are referred to as secure.[1] No attempt is made to distinguish the method of assessing attachment style used in the research studies cited; the findings discussed in this chapter appear to be robust across measurement method except as otherwise noted.

In adults, attachment-related anxiety manifests itself in low levels of trust regarding the availability and responsiveness of attachment figures in times of need. Anxious adults hypervigilantly experience anxiety over the possibility of abandonment and having their needs for care and affection left unfulfilled in the future, while, at the same time, they are angry over having been rejected in the past (Bowlby, 1973). They tend to have low self-esteem (Brennan & Morris, 1997; Bylsma, Cozzarelli, & Sumer, 1997) and a negative self-image (Mikulincer, 1995), feeling that they are unworthy of better treatment; yet they may feel that they are entitled to receive higher levels of caregiving and love and engage in coercive attempts to get their needs met (Corcoran & Mallinckrodt, 2000).

Proximity and separation are particularly salient for anxious individuals, who find it difficult to obtain sufficient levels of "felt security" because of their concerns about abandonment (Sroufe & Waters, 1977). They feel insecure upon physical separation from their relationship partner, experiencing the joint needs for closeness and autonomy in a paradoxical manner that tends to favor excessive demands for physical and/or psychological closeness with their relationship partners (Brennan et al., 1998; Fraley & Shaver, 1998; Hazan & Shaver, 1987), yet at the same time report that their desired degree of closeness is not provided (Grabill & Kerns, 2000; Hazan & Shaver, 1987). Their obsessive search for security is associated with negative affect and rumination about the future of their close relationships (Mikulincer & Florian, 1998; Mikulincer & Orbach, 1995; Simpson, 1990). They have low levels of trust in their relationship partners (Levy & Davis, 1988) and are quick to see trust violations, attributing them to stable causes such as their partner's personality (Mikulincer, 1998b).

Attachment-related avoidance manifests itself in the almost certain expectation that attachment figures will not be available or responsive when needed and may be actively rejecting, causing them to be viewed as uncaring and untrustworthy. Particularly in times of stress, avoidant individuals tend to distance themselves from their relationship partners instead of seeking support from them (Collins & Feeney, 2000; Fraley & Shaver, 1998). At the same time, however, avoidant individuals can experience physiological arousal upon separation from their partners (B. C. Feeney & Kirkpatrick, 1996), indicating that distancing strategies for emotions and behaviors are the result of suppression of still intact attachment-related needs. Attachment theory predicts that the anger evident in anxious individuals should also exist in avoidant individuals, but that it is held in check through repressive defense mechanisms (Bowlby, 1988). Avoidant individuals tend to report having high self-esteem and may have a relatively positive view of self in spite of a history of rejection from attachment figures (Bartholomew, 1990; Bartholomew & Horowitz, 1991; Brennan & Morris, 1997; Mikulincer, 1995), but they tend to have low levels of trust and interdependence with their relationship partners (Levy & Davis, 1988).

Independence and autonomy are primary motives for avoidant individuals (Mikulincer, Florian, Cowan, & Cowan, 2002; Mikulincer & Nachson, 1991). They may be unresponsive and insensitive to relationship partners, preferring self-reliance and eschewing neediness, vulnerability, or dependence in their partners (Hazan & Shaver, 1987; Mikulincer & Shaver, 2003). This apparent desire for distancing, particularly during high levels of distress, can be viewed as the result of a need to avoid the re-experiencing of the pain of past rejection, as well as a strategy for avoiding future rejection (Bowlby, 1973, 1980, 1988). It can also be driven by anger, as will be described below. Their underlying need for close, emotional connection simply remains unfulfilled.

Individuals with a secure attachment style are able to manage their distress by accepting it and turning for support in a constructive fashion to close others, who are seen as available, trustworthy, and well-intended (Bowlby, 1988). They may also turn to "internalized" attachment figures as a means of coping with distress or threat (e.g., Mikulincer, Gillath, & Shaver, 2002; Mikulincer & Shaver, 2004). They balance their needs for closeness and autonomy, maintain high levels of self-esteem (Bartholomew & Horowitz, 1991; Bylsma et al., 1997; Mikulincer, 1995), and are generally responsive to their partners (B. C. Feeney & Collins, 2003). Their positivity in cognition (Brennan & Morris, 1997; Mikulincer, 1995), affect (Tucker & Anders, 1998), and orientation toward their partners allows persons with a secure attachment style the cognitive and emotional resources to work on maintaining quality in their relationships (e.g., Collins & Feeney, 2000).

The attachment styles can be further delineated by a more nuanced consideration of anger and hostility. Bowlby (1973) distinguishes functional anger (the anger of hope) from dysfunctional anger (the anger of despair), noting that an individual can use functional anger to maintain attachment bonds by protesting that his or her needs are not being met and by serving to change the partner's negative behaviors. In contrast, dysfunctional anger can be destructive of attachment bonds and, in adults, can result from unresolved anger against earlier attachment figures. It can be manifested as hostility or resentment toward the partner and may incorporate revenge; dysfunctional anger can alienate the partner and may even result in aggression or violence (Bowlby, 1988).

Persons with all three attachment styles experience anger, particularly when their security is threatened or their needs are not met (Feeney, 1995, 1999; Mikulincer, 1998a; Muris, Meesters, Morren, & Moorman, 2004), but their expression of anger differs. As expected, attachment security is associated with functional and adaptive manifestations of anger, coupled with the beliefs that the partner's negative behavior is well-intended and remediable (Feeney, 1999; Mikulincer, 1998a). Further, secure persons tend to acknowledge their angry emotion in a manner that is consistent with their physiological experience of anger (Mikulincer, 1998a).

Insecure attachment is associated with dysfunctional anger in ways that are consistent with the anxiety and avoidance working models. Anxious adults experience intense anger when they believe or fear that their relationship partners are unavailable to meet their needs (Creasey & Hesson-McInnis, 2001; Mikulincer, 1998a), ruminating on threat-related thoughts that may intensify and prolong their anger (Mikulincer, 1998a; Mikulincer & Shaver, 2003, 2005). Their anger may be associated with their tendency to make more negative attributions of their partner's intent, even in ambiguous situations (Mikulincer, 1998a). These negative attributions may be the result of their tendency to project their own assumed negative characteristics onto their partner (Mikulincer & Horesh, 1999), which would include their own anger and hostility. Out of fear of losing their partner, however, they may fail to express their anger outwardly (Feeney, 1995, 1998; Mikulincer, 1998a), dysfunctionally controlling it and turning it inward (Mikulincer, 1998a). These findings have also been apparent in naturalistic interactions in a study by Simpson, Rholes, and Phillips (1996), who found that anxious persons felt greater anger and hostility toward their dating or marital partners during and after stressful, conflictual interactions.

Persons with an avoidant attachment style, consistent with their tendency to distance themselves from attachment-related distress and deactivate the attachment system, tend to experience what has been called "dissociated anger" (Mikulincer, 1998a). In other words, although avoidant persons self-report lower levels of anger than secure persons, physiological signs indicate the presence of intense anger and hostility. This approach to anger begins as an infant, according to Ainsworth et al. (1978), when, although avoidant babies were viewed as behaving angrily toward their rejecting mothers in a home environment, they later (in the Strange Situation, which was highly stressful) were noted as experiencing but suppressing their anger in order to avoid the expected rejection associated with seeking proximity to their attachment figure and thus reduce their angry arousal. Avoidant adults tend to attribute hostility to their partners, even in the presence of information suggesting nonhostile intent (Mikulincer, 1998a), a type of "defensive projection" that may serve the purpose of enhancing their own self-esteem (Mikulincer & Horesh, 1999).

Although in infants, direct expression of anger to the attachment figure can sometimes be a dangerous way of trying to get needs met (Ainsworth et al., 1978), as adults, avoidant persons need not fear distancing their partners by their angry behaviors, and so may be more likely to express strong anger in relationship interactions under circumstances that involve meeting their needs, such as trying to re-attain an optimal sense of distance that has been violated by a partner. They may also be likely to reciprocate anger. For example, Rholes, Simpson, and Oriña (1999) found that highly avoidant women displayed intense anger toward their partners during a stressful situation, particularly when they were highly distressed and their partners were themselves angry. Avoidant men displayed greater anger during the stressful period than did less avoidant men, particularly when their partners were distressed, sought more support from them, or displayed more anger.

To become angry at attachment figures necessarily involves understanding that one's legitimate needs have not been met. Even if socialized as children not to think about their attachment needs or the ways in which they have not been fulfilled (Bowlby, 1988), insecure individuals often still recognize at some level that they make legitimate claims on attachment figures. As a consequence, we suggest that they form a linkage between their anger and the knowledge that their needs can only be met through their own efforts (whether it be through the compulsive pursuit of their attachment figures for anxious persons or the compulsive distancing from their attachment figures for avoidant persons). This combination of anger and knowledge encourages or produces an egoistic stance; that is, insecure persons tend to focus on getting their needs met to the exclusion of the needs of those with whom they are angry, including their attachment figures. The conceptual models shown in Figure 5.1 depict schematically our understanding of attachment anxiety, avoidance, and anger as they pertain to processes linked to relationship satisfaction.

The attachment system is but one of four innate behavioral systems—attachment, caregiving, sexual, and exploration—described by Bowlby (1969). The first three systems are clearly interrelated in that they involve relationships between persons, while exploration is a system that provides for learning and individual growth through curiosity about the environment. Attachment researchers have focused primarily on the attachment system itself, although, as will be seen, some research has been conducted on the interaction between the attachment and caregiving and attachment and sexuality systems in adults. Though not discussed further in this chapter, romantic love has been conceptualized as an integration of the attachment, caregiving, and sexuality systems (Shaver, Hazan, & Bradshaw, 1988). Also not discussed in any detail in this chapter is the relationship between the attachment and exploration systems, except to note that persons having a secure attachment style, as opposed to an anxious or avoidant attachment style, are generally viewed as being best able to explore the social and physical environment (Ainsworth et al., 1978; Mikulincer et al., 2002). The "optimal balance" between dependence and autonomy allows such individuals to participate fully in close relationships while pursuing activities related to their own interests and personal development (Mikulincer et al., 2002).

ATTACHMENT STYLE AND RELATIONSHIP SATISFACTION

Satisfaction in relationships is related to a complex of interpersonal processes (e.g., Bradbury, Fincham, & Beach, 2000). For example, attributions about partner behaviors and intent, negative affect, behavioral interaction patterns, partner affection and support, and relationship violence are all processes that interest relationship and, particularly, marriage researchers (Bradbury et al., 2000). As suggested by the focus of this chapter, there is a vast literature linking attachment style to dating and marital satisfaction. Because high-quality close relationships

124 PERSONALITY AND SOCIAL BEHAVIOR

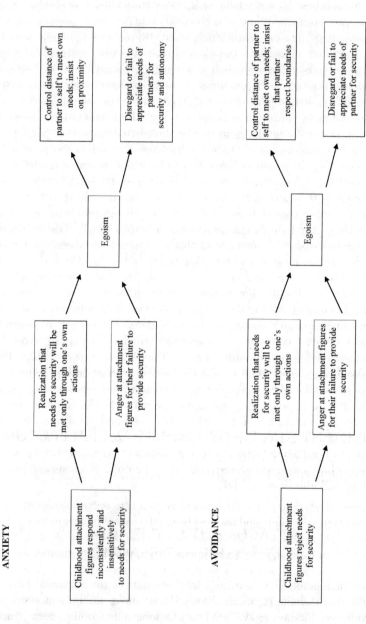

Figure 5.1 Models linking attachment anxiety and avoidance of an individual to nature of interactions with partner.

are essential to happiness and well-being, and because attachment theory provides a framework for understanding closeness and security in relationships in relation to caregiving and sexuality, which are important aspects of adult relationships, attachment researchers have studied a variety of individual characteristics and interpersonal processes that relate attachment style to relationship satisfaction.

The relationship literature investigates satisfaction as a function of individual behavior (e.g., conflict management) and as a function of situations and responses to them (e.g., periods of high stress, transition points in relationships). In this chapter, we discuss attachment research in each of these categories. Our analysis of behaviors focuses on support and caregiving, conflict management, violence, and the establishment of closeness through self-disclosure and sexual relations. Our examination of situations focuses on the transition made when couples first become parents. Finally, we also review the relatively few studies that have investigated individuals' satisfaction as a function of their partner's attachment styles. In each of these domains, our goal is to point out the linkage between attachment styles and risk factors for relationship dissatisfaction.

In general, studies have indicated that persons with secure attachment styles have greater commitment to and greater satisfaction with their (dating or marital) relationship partners than do those individuals who are either anxious or avoidant (e.g., Collins & Read, 1990, Feeney, Noller, & Roberts, 1998; Pistole, 1989; Simpson, 1990; but see Hollist & Miller, 2005, finding no relationship between attachment style and marital satisfaction in midlife marriage). Persons having an anxious attachment style tend to have the lowest levels of relationship satisfaction (e.g., Feeney, 1994; 1996; 1999; Feeney et al., 1998; Kobak & Hazan, 1991; Pistole, 1989; Rholes, Simpson, & Blakely, 1995; Simpson, 1990), although their levels of relationship satisfaction can be affected by factors such as perception of partner support (Campbell, Simpson, Boldry, & Kashy, 2005). Persons with avoidant styles typically fall between anxious and secure individuals (Mikulincer et al., 2002).

ATTACHMENT STYLE AND POTENTIAL RISK FACTORS FOR RELATIONSHIP (DIS)SATISFACTION: GIVING, SEEKING, AND PERCEIVING CARE AND SUPPORT

The fundamental purpose of the attachment system is to encourage infants, children, and adults to seek safety and comfort from attachment figures in times of distress. According to attachment theory, however, it should be relatively uncommon for people high in avoidance to seek support from attachment figures, because acknowledging a need for care from another undermines their desire to maintain psychological independence (Bowlby, 1973). Both self-report (Berant, Mikulincer, & Florian, 2001; Florian, Mikulincer, & Bucholtz, 1995; Mikulincer & Florian, 1995; Mikulincer, Florian, & Weller, 1993; Ognibene & Collins, 1998; Rholes, Simpson, Campbell, & Grich, 2001) and observational studies (Fraley & Shaver, 1998, Simpson, Rholes, & Nelligan, 1992) show that avoidant people are less likely to seek support from close others, thus limiting opportunities for interactions that could promote closeness. Individuals high in avoidance view others who seek their support in pejorative terms, as weak, immature, dependent, and unstable (Wilson, Simpson, & Rholes, 2000); thus, in addition to their desire to maintain independence, their reluctance to seek care may stem from its implications for self-perception. They also may hesitate to seek support because they believe that it will not be forthcoming (Florian et al., 1995; Kobak & Sceery, 1988; Rholes et al., 2001).

Studies of support seeking among anxious individuals yield less consistent results. Retrospective self-report studies suggest that support seeking is positively correlated with anxiety (Florian et al., 1995; Mikulincer et al., 1993; Ognibene & Collins, 1998), but some observational studies and studies in which reports of support seeking are taken during a stressful period do not (Collins & Feeney, 2000; Mikulincer & Florian, 1995; Rholes et al., 2001; Simpson et al., 1992). Rholes et al. (2001) found that during the stressful months shortly before and after the birth of their first child, the more anxious women sought significantly less support than their less anxious counterparts. Anxious women perceive support to be less available, which may partially explain their behavior (cf. Florian et al., 1995). After stress subsides, self-perceptions and social desirability may encourage anxious people to perceive that they have sought support, but in the "heat" of a stressful episode their mistrust of relationships and relationships partners (Wallace & Vaux, 1993) appears to undermine actual support seeking.

Perceptions of the availability of support are strongly linked to attachment anxiety. Rholes et al. (2001) found that more anxious women going through the transition to parenthood were highly satisfied with their marriages if they perceived that their husbands were supportive. Unfortunately, however, most anxious women in this study reported that their husbands were not highly supportive. Several other studies also have found anxiety to be linked to the belief that relationship partners are unsupportive (Bartholomew, Cobb, & Poole, 1997; Florian et al. 1995; Priel & Shamai, 1995; Wallace & Vaux, 1993; Wilson, Rholes, Simpson, & Tran, 2007). Such perceptions can encourage denigration of partners, conflict, and anger and therefore constrain opportunities for relationship satisfaction.

Whether these perceptions accurately reflect at partner's behavior or whether they are constructions of supportiveness that are biased by the anxious working model is unclear. Rholes et al. (2001) found that husbands of more anxious women reported that they provided less support to them during the period surrounding the birth of their first child. Anxious women, however, reported that they received even less support than their husbands reported, but their non-anxious counterparts reported that they received more support than their husbands said they provided. This study thus indicates that support may actually be less available to anxious individuals, but also that the pessimistic working models of anxious individuals may further contribute to the perception that partners are unsupportive. Collins and Feeney's (2004) results strongly implicate perceptual bias. In their study, more anxious individuals who received a moderately unsupportive communication from their dating partners rated it as less supportive than their less anxious counterparts did and, after receiving the communication, remembered the behavior of their partner in a previous interaction as comparatively unsupportive, despite reports of objective raters to the contrary. Apparently, moderately unsupportive behavior by partners activates latent doubts among anxious individuals that impose a negative bias on their construction (or reconstruction) of their partners' behavior.

The primary purpose of the caregiving system is to encourage attachment figures to provide safety and care when sought by infants, children, or adult partners. Effective caregivers, according to attachment theory and research (e.g., Ainsworth et al., 1978), are able to "read" the internal states of others, provide care that is timed contingently on the other's signals and states of need, are warm and accepting of efforts to elicit help, and are consistently available to offer help when needed. Ineffective caregivers are intrusive, controlling, inconsistent, and unaccepting of the needs of others.

Insecure adults are generally ineffective caregivers. Attachment theory (Bowlby, 1988) argues that people with strong avoidant tendencies fear and distrust relationships in part because they do not want to be "trapped into" providing care to a relationship partner. Feeling at some level that no one ever has provided care to them, providing care to others may seem an unfair burden and may generate anger (Rholes et al. 1999). Consistent with the theory, more avoidant husbands indicated that they provided less support to their partners during labor and delivery (Wilson et al., 2007) and in general during the transition to parenthood (Rholes et al., 2001). Several observational studies also have linked avoidance to lower levels of supportive behavior (Rholes et al., 1995; Simpson et al., 1992, 1996; Westmaas & Silver, 2001), but at least one, Collins & Feeney (2000), did not. Avoidant people appear to be least supportive when they or their partners are comparatively distressed (Simpson et al., 1992, 1996). Thus, their behavior may reflect efforts to keep their attachment systems deactivated (Simpson et al., 1992). More proximal causes of their behavior appear to be less empathic and compassionate responses to the distress of others (Mikulincer et al., 2001; Mikulincer, Shaver, Gillath, & Nitzberg, 2005) and believing themselves to be less obligated to provide support and being more uncomfortable when asked to do so (Wilson et al., 2000).

There is little evidence that more anxious people provide less support to their partners overall. There is evidence, however, that they are less effective as caregivers and are motivated to help in part by egoistic concerns (e.g., B. C. Feeney & Collins, 2003; Kunce & Shaver, 1994). Consistent with the ineffective profile, anxious caregivers are described in the literature as providing less effective support overall, as being less emotionally and cognitively responsive to their partners, as being more dismissive and unhelpful to care-seekers, as being less able to perceive partners' needs for support, as being more controlling, and as becoming over-involved in their partners' problems (e.g., Collins & Feeney, 2000; B. C. Feeney & Collins, 2001; Kunce & Shaver, 1994). These differences in behavior may be partially explained by the greater endorsement of self-centered motives for helping partners by anxious caregivers (e.g., to keep their partner tied to them and to receive other benefits; B. C. Feeney & Collins, 2003). They also may result from the greater personal distress and less empathic responses that are characteristic of more anxious caregivers' response to the distress of others (Mikulincer et al., 2001, 2005; Westmaas & Silver, 2001).

Partners who receive more effective, responsive care and those who believe that support is available should they need it report that they feel loved and that they are more satisfied with their relationships (Collins & Feeney, 2000; Feeney, 1996; B. C. Feeney & Collins, 2003). Even highly anxious and avoidant individuals seem to benefit from partner support (Rholes et al., 2001; Simpson et al., 1992). Thus, the relationship dissatisfaction often experienced by insecure individuals and individuals involved in relationships with insecure partners may arise from their own inadequate care-seeking, inadequate caregiving by their partners, or perceptual biases that prevent them from perceiving support that is available to them.

Intimacy

Although the word "intimacy" is used widely in relationship research, often as a synonym for some forms of physical and psychological closeness (e.g., "a feeling of connectedness with another person"; Laurenceau, Troy, & Carver, 2005 , pp. 1123-1124), we prefer to think of intimacy as a strategy based on a capacity for negotiating closeness (cf. Cassidy, 2001). Hence, we do not view "seeking intimacy" as a relationship goal. Closeness (or its avoidance) is the goal, with different attachment styles being related to different processes or capacities for negotiating it. We focus here on two important strategies for negotiating closeness: self-disclosure (Keelan, Dion, & Dion, 1993; Laurenceau, Barrett, & Rovine, 2005; Mikulincer & Nachson, 1991) and sexual behavior (Cassidy, 2001; Feeney & Noller, 2004).

Self-Disclosure. Self-disclosure represents the process by which we reveal ourselves to others and is generally viewed as being critical to the establishment of closeness in relationships. Attachment researchers have studied a variety of aspects of self-disclosure, including its quantity, nature, flexibility, responsiveness, and target, as well as considering it both a trait and state construct. If self-disclosure is a means of attaining greater closeness, then persons with an avoidant attachment style should, because of their desire to maintain a controlled distance—i.e., independence and autonomy—from their partners, be expected to disclose less often, and less personally, than persons having a secure or anxious attachment style. This appears to be a robust finding in the attachment literature, regardless whether the self-disclosure is to relationship partners or strangers (Bartholomew & Horowitz, 1991; Bradford, Feeney, & Campbell, 2002; Mikulincer & Nachson, 1991). Their lack of self-disclosure presents fewer opportunities for their partners to feel close to them, thereby also limiting their partners' opportunities to engage in their own self-disclosure.

In Mikulincer and Nachson's (1991) experimental study using confederates as "partners," avoidant persons did not flexibly reciprocate self-disclosure and appeared insensitive to the nature of the confederate partner's self-disclosure. Further, although avoidant individuals had low levels of liking for self-disclosing partners regardless of the amount of personal information they revealed about themselves, self-disclosing partners who provided more personal details about themselves were liked less by avoidant individuals than by individuals who were secure or anxious. Avoidant individuals also tended to experience more negative emotion when interacting with partners who were high-disclosers than did secure or anxious individuals (Mikulincer & Nachson, 1991; Pistole, 1993). More recent research has found that avoidant persons have less desire to know personal information about their relationship partners than do secure or anxious persons (Rholes, Simpson, Tran, Martin, & Friedman, 2005). Thus, consistent with their working model, persons who are avoidant shun intimate strategies for self-disclosure on their own part and on the part of their partners, presumably as a means of controlling psychological and emotional distance.

Attachment theory would predict that anxious individuals engage in self-disclosure behaviors that are consistent with their desire to feel secure. In other words, they may enjoy self-disclosure from a partner if it signals that they are at low risk for rejection, but they may fail to reciprocate the nature of that self-disclosure if their focus is on their own neediness and fear of rejection instead of on their partner's needs. On the other hand, as a means of establishing security early in a relationship or during times of relationship threat, anxious persons may excessively self-disclose (even to persons who would find such intimate revelations inappropriate) and thus self-disclose more than either persons who are secure or avoidant. Thus, the self-disclosure of anxious persons should be based on contingency. In general, it has been found that in many ways the self-disclosure of anxious persons is like that of secure persons: high-disclosing partners tend to be more liked than low-disclosing partners, and the partner's level of self-disclosure tends to be reciprocated. However, an apparent lack of both flexibility and topical reciprocity on the part of anxious individuals suggests that they may be preoccupied with their own needs as part of their self-disclosure instead of fully attending to the needs of their partner; in other words, their self-disclosure does not represent an intimate strategy for obtaining mutual closeness (Mikulincer & Nachson, 1991).

By contrast, secure persons seek closeness in their close relationships and are more likely to self-disclose, and to disclose to relationship partners more than to others, as a means of obtaining closeness (Keelan et al., 1993; Mikulincer & Nachson, 1991; Pistole, 1993; Simpson, 1990). Additionally, secure individuals are more flexible and responsive in their self-disclosure and tend to engage in more topical reciprocity than persons who are anxious or avoidant, suggesting that they are more intimate in their relationships than the other two attachment styles (Mikulincer & Nachson, 1991).

Sexuality. Sexuality is another important aspect of intimacy in close relationships (Feeney & Noller, 2004). Research indicates that attachment style is associated with the way a person uses sexuality to meet his or her needs. For example, whereas procreation may provide a sexual motive for those who are secure or anxious, the effect is not as strong for avoidants (Davis, Shaver, & Vernon, 2004; Rholes, Simpson, Blakely, Lanigan, & Allen, 1997). For anxious persons, sexual motives are linked to feelings of closeness (for example, feeling loved by one's partner; Schachner & Shaver, 2004) and insecurity (Implett & Peplau, 2002; Schachner & Shaver, 2004). They tend to obsess and feel passionate about their sexual partners (Davis et al., 2004; Feeney & Noller, 1990), experience strong sexual jealousy (Buunk, 1997; Guerrero, 1998), prefer affectionate touching to genital contact (Hazan, Zeifman, & Middleton, 1994, as cited in Davis et al., 2004), and worry about the possibility of losing their partners to others (Schachner & Shaver, 2002). They may engage in sex as a means of pleasing their partner instead of as a way to meet their own needs (Davis et al., 2004; Tracy, Shaver, Albino, & Cooper, 2003).

Anxious women, in particular, may engage (or indicate willingness to engage) in unwanted but consensual sex (Gentzler & Kerns, 2004; Impett & Peplau, 2002). These behaviors may reflect manipulation instead of concern for one's partner; in other words, anxious persons may use sex as a form of self-protection from their partner's anger, to elicit caregiving from their partner, or to exert power over their partner (Davis et al., 2004).

Individuals with an avoidant attachment style have sexual motives that are linked to autonomy and self-enhancement among peers (Schachner & Shaver, 2002, 2004; Tracy et al., 2003). They tend to eschew both the physical and psychological intimacy that accompany sex and thus may avoid sexual intercourse (Cooper, Shaver, & Collins, 1998; Hazan et al., 1994, as cited in Davis et al., 2004; Tracy et al., 2003); in addition, avoidance tends to be negatively related to passion (Davis et al., 2004) and love for one's partner (Tracy et al., 2003). They are more likely to engage in casual sex, including one-night stands (Brennan & Shaver, 1995; Feeney, Noller, & Patty, 1993; Fraley, Davis, & Shaver, 1998; Gentzler & Kerns, 2004; Schachner & Shaver, 2002). Avoidant persons tend to prefer physical genital contact via forms of sexual intercourse (e.g., oral or anal sex) to more emotional expressions of affection such as cuddling or kissing (Hazan et al., 1994, as cited in Davis et al., 2004).

Both insecure attachment styles maintain consistent motivations for sexual intercourse when engaged in sexual activity outside of their primary relationships. In a study of extradyadic sexual involvement, anxious persons reported closeness motives while avoidant persons reported autonomy motives (Allen & Baucom, 2004). Although results are somewhat inconsistent across insecure attachment types, there is evidence that attachment insecurity is associated with having more affairs (Gangestad & Thornhill, 1997; Kirkpatrick, 1998), having sexual intercourse at an earlier age (Bogaert & Sadava, 2002; Gentzler & Kerns, 2004), and engaging in risky sexual behaviors (Bogaert & Sadava, 2002; Feeney, Peterson, Gallois, & Terry, 2000).

In contrast, attachment security is related to having a variety of sexual experiences within committed, long-term relationships (Hazan et al., 1994, as cited in Davis et al., 2004; Tracy et al., 2003) and having fewer partners in total (Brennan & Shaver, 1995; Cooper et al., 1998). Secure individuals also report more positive emotions regarding past sexual experiences than do anxious or avoidant persons (Tracy et al., 2003).

Conflict

Conflict has the potential to interfere with—i.e., reduce or enhance—marital or relationship satisfaction in various ways. For example, the mere presence of conflict could be viewed as either positive or negative, depending on the nature of the conflict, its frequency, how the partners attempt to resolve it, and how partners cope with the conflict; how partners communicate with each other during conflict is relevant as well (e.g., Gottman & Krokoff, 1989; Marchand & Hock, 2000; Noller, Feeney, Bonnell, & Callan, 1994). Attachment style has been demonstrated to be related to at least some of these features of conflict.

If conflict poses a potential threat to a relationship (e.g., Kobak & Duemmler, 1994; Pistole, 2003; Torquati & Vazsonyi, 1999), so that one partner may expect rejection or alienation, then attachment behaviors should be activated, leading to approaches to conflict consistent with attachment style. Persons with an avoidant attachment style would be expected to engage in strategies that would de-emphasize or avoid the conflict and facilitate emotional and psychological distancing from the partner (e.g., compromising to end the conflict, Pistole, 1989; withdrawing, Shi, 2003), while persons with an anxious attachment style would be hypervigilant to both the partner and associated distress during conflict and might be more likely to give in to the partner as a way of pleasing him or her instead of employing a strategy that would risk loss (e.g., Pistole, 1989; Shi, 2003). On the other hand, anxious persons are also concerned about getting their needs met and may therefore tend, at least to some degree, to be confrontational, demanding, and/or dominating and less able to engage in productive conflict resolution strategies (Corcoran & Mallinckrodt, 2000; Feeney, Noller, & Callan, 1994; Shi, 2003; Simpson et al., 1996). Secure persons, because they have expectations that their partners will be available and responsive in times of need, may not even perceive conflict as a threat to the relationship and would be expected to be open and flexible with their partners during conflict (Kobak & Duemmler, 1994; Simpson et al., 1996).

For example, it has been demonstrated that, based on self-reports from college students in romantic relationships, positive conflict management skills such as displaying affection, validating the partner, staying focused on the positive nature of the specific conflict, and using effective arguing and/or a mutually integrating strategy were negatively related to anxiety and avoidance and positively related to being secure (e.g., Creasey & Hesson-McInnis, 2001; Pistole, 1989, 2003). At the same time, nonconstructive management skills involving negativity, escalation, and withdrawal were positively related to anxiety and avoidance (and negatively related to being secure), with persons who were anxious having the most difficulty in managing conflict (e.g., Creasey & Hesson-McInnis, 2001; Pistole, 2003).

Perceptions of and attitudes toward conflict have also been demonstrated to be related to attachment style. For example, although it might normally be expected that conflict would be viewed negatively by individuals having an anxious attachment style (i.e., as a threat to relationship security), Fishtein, Pietromonaco, & Feldman Barrett (1999) demonstrated that such persons may view high-conflict interactions more positively than others because of the overall potential for more responsiveness from their partners. In addition, while all persons in high-conflict relationships (regardless of attachment style) demonstrated more complex knowledge about negative attributes of their relationship, only anxious persons in high-conflict relationships showed greater complexity in knowledge of positive relationship aspects.

In a recent daily diary study of dating partners, persons high in attachment anxiety perceived more daily relationship conflict than others, even higher than would be expected given the level of relationship conflict reported by their partners (Campbell et al., 2005). Further, the perceived conflict was viewed by anxiously attached persons as escalating beyond the original topic of conflict and being more hurtful than persons who were not high in attachment anxiety considered it to be. No significant relationship was found between attachment avoidance and perceptions of conflict and hurtfulness. Further, in an accompanying observational study of conflict resolution for the dating partners, Campbell et al. (2005) found that anxious individuals were seen as escalating existing conflict and reacting too strongly to it, whereas avoidant individuals (and by implication, secure individuals) were not.

In addition to being associated with attachment style, conflict is clearly a risk factor for level of relationship satisfaction, as has been evidenced by several studies. For example, Feeney (1994) demonstrated that mutual understanding during conflict was related to both anxiety (negatively for both husbands and wives) and relationship satisfaction (positively for both husbands and wives), with mutuality fully mediating the relationship between anxiety and satisfaction for wives while only partially mediating the same relationship for husbands. Similarly, Carnelley, Pietromonaco, & Jaffe (1994), in a study of depression and relationship satisfaction, noted that women with insecure attachment styles were less likely than secure women to use constructive approaches to conflict resolution and were more likely to report less relationship satisfaction. Marchand's (2004) study of husbands and wives revealed that husbands who were anxious or avoidant engaged in significantly more attacking behaviors than those who were secure, whereas wives who were anxious or avoidant engaged in both more attacking and fewer compromising behaviors than their secure counterparts. Further, for wives, the negative relationship between their attachment anxiety and level of marital satisfaction was partially mediated by their attacking behaviors.

The study by Campbell et al. (2005) demonstrated that when anxious persons perceive more conflict, they themselves are less optimistic about the future of their relationship, believing that their partners are dissatisfied with the relationship and pessimistic about its future. Further, their work suggests that persons high in attachment anxiety attend carefully to daily events in their relationship when making assessments of relationship quality, thereby possibly perceiving it as less stable.

Violence

Studies of relationship violence can be divided into those that involve individuals whose abusiveness has brought them into the legal system and those that involve community samples of individuals or couples and (typically) less severe forms of violence. Studies in the later group, which include studies of adolescents and adults, routinely find that the anxious attachment style is related to the perpetration of verbal abuse and physical violence (e.g., Bookwala, 2002; Orcutt, Garcia, & Pickett, 2005; Roberts & Noller, 1998). Moreover, it is not the case that people with an anxious attachment style are more violent simply because they are less satisfied with their relationship generally or have more interpersonal problems with their spouse (Bookwala & Zdaniuk, 1998), which suggests that the dynamics of the anxious working model may affect violence regardless of general characteristics of marriage or other close relationships. In a study that focused only on violence perpetrated by women in dating relationships, Orcutt et al. (2005) found that women in relationships in which both partners were violent reported higher levels of attachment anxiety, and women who perpetrate violence in the absence of partner violence reported higher levels of attachment anxiety coupled with lower levels of avoidance. Other studies (e.g., Bookwala & Zdaniuk, 1998), however, report that violence is common among individuals who combine the anxious and avoidant attachment styles. Roberts and Noller (1998) report that men and women with an anxious attachment style are particularly likely to engage in violence if their partners' attachment styles are avoidant. Also highlighting the complexity of the relationship between attachment style and violence, Wekerle and Wolfe (1998) found that attachment styles moderate the relationship of childhood abuse to violence directed at adult partners. Men who were abused in childhood were more likely to act violently if their attachment styles were either anxious or avoidant, and women who were abused were more likely to be violent if their attachment style was anxious.

Studies involving male batterers referred to therapy report findings similar to those above. Pistole and Tarrant (1993) report that male batterers do not differ from controls on attachment style. Several other studies, however, challenge this finding (Dutton, Saunders, Starzomski, & Bartholomew, 1994; Dutton, Starzomski, & Ryan, 1996; Mauricio & Gormley, 2001; Tweed & Dutton, 1998). These studies report that attachment anxiety and a combination of anxiety and avoidance distinguish batterers from controls.

Bowlby (1973) argues that anger and violence toward partners is a response to real or threatened separation from attachment figures. He reports that parents who discipline their children by threatening separation or abandonment arouse both intense fear and intense anger. He further suggests that violence in adult couples is a reaction to separation, whether real, threatened, or imagined (Bowlby, 1988). From this perspective, it is easy to see why attachment anxiety is more broadly associated with violence than attachment avoidance: Anxious individuals' obsession with possible abandonment or with their partner's potential disregard of their needs makes violence and anger high in their hierarchy of responses (cf. Collins, 1996), and their tendency to see threats in many everyday behaviors can provide frequent triggers for such response. Concerns about separation and abandonment are much weaker among avoidant people, and the environmental conditions that may raise such concerns should be few. Avoidant people often are described by those who know them as hostile (Kobak & Sceery, 1988). That this hostility does not often manifest itself in relationship violence seems to attest to the control that avoidant individuals exercise over their behavior. This control may be broken down under very difficult, stressful circumstances (cf. Mayseless, 1991) or when their proclivity toward hostility is enhanced by childhood abuse (Wekerle & Wolfe, 1998).

The Transition to Parenthood

Whereas potentially vulnerable relationships (e.g., those in which one or both partners are insecure) may fare reasonably well during their early stages, the eventual encounter with difficult life circumstances may be an occasion in which destructive behaviors and perceptions are first unleashed. These events may thus mark the beginning of a long-term deterioration of relationship well-being. Simpson and Rholes (1994), however, argue that despite their destructive potential, difficulties that are met successfully through collaborative, mutually supportive and positive interactions may have a long-term "steeling" effect that encourages relationship well-being into the future. In support of their position, they cite research showing that recalling a time in which couple members helped one another through a difficult period encourages constructive problem-solving behavior and benevolent attributions (Holmes, 1991). They also note that friendships are strengthened when friends support each other through difficult times (Woolsey & McBain, 1987). Based on the material reviewed above, however, it seems likely that positive outcomes from encounters with stressors occur primarily among couples in which one or both partners are secure.

Becoming a parent for the first time occasions adaptation to new roles and identities, and for many couples these changes plus the responsibility for providing care to an infant make the transition to parenthood highly stressful (Heinicke, 1995). Because it is one of the most common experiences of marriage and other long-term relationships, the transition to parenthood may provide one of the best opportunities to study an event that may initiate processes that strengthen or weaken relationships over the long term. Given the challenges that the transition poses, it should not be surprising to find that conflict between new parents increases and companionate activities decline or that overall marital satisfaction declines during the transition to parenthood (Belsky & Pensky, 1988; Cowan & Cowan, 2000; see also Twenge, Campbell, & Foster, 2003). Not all couples show these trends, however. Tucker and Aron (1993) found that the variation in the quality of marital relationships increases during the transition, suggesting that although some couples find this period of time troubling, others maintain their equilibrium or even come through the transition with stronger relationships.

Anxious women are particularly vulnerable to declines in marital satisfaction across the transition, especially if they perceive that their partners do not adequately support their needs (Rholes et al., 2001). Support by partners may be particularly important to anxious women because they tend to appraise the threats attendant to pregnancy, motherhood, their health, and their infants as more severe than do other women and cope with these and other stressors less effectively (Alexander, Feeney, Hohaus, & Noller, 2001; Mikulincer & Florian, 1998). In addition to marital satisfaction, the combination of attachment anxiety and either inadequate caregiving by husbands (Feeney, Alexander, Noller, & Hohaus, 2003) or wives' perceptions that husbands were unsupportive (Simpson, Rholes, Campbell, Tran & Wilson, 2003) predicts increases in depressive symptoms across the transition period.

Rholes et al. (2001) found that more avoidant women also were less satisfied with their marriages just before and 6 months after the birth of their infants, but this did not worsen with the passage of time, and it did not interact with perceptions of support, as it did among anxious women. Avoidant women appraise the threats associated with the transition to parenthood as higher than secure women (Mikulincer & Florian, 1998), and both avoidant men and women find child care to be more stressful and less personally meaningful than do others (Rholes, Simpson, & Friedman, 2006). Avoidant men and women also cope with the stressors associated with the transition less effectively than their secure counterparts do (Alexander at al., 2001). Perhaps also contributing to their marital dissatisfaction during this period, avoidant parents engage in less relationship maintenance behavior (Curran, Hazen, Jacobvitz, & Feldman, 2005) and under some circumstances engage in higher levels of escalation of negative affect during problem-solving interactions (Paley et al., 2005). As is the case with anxiety, there are links between avoidance and depression during the transition (Simpson et al., 2003), but not all studies report this outcome (Feeney et al., 2003).

LIVING WITH SECURE AND INSECURE PARTNERS: THE EFFECTS OF PARTNER INSECURITY

Individuals involved in relationships with partners who have anxious attachment styles report themselves to be less satisfied with their relationships (Davila, Bradbury, & Fincham, 1998; Feeney, 1996; 1999; Lussier, Sabourin, & Turgeon, 1997; Rholes et al., 2001; Simpson, 1990). They experience more negative and fewer positive emotions (Davila et al., 1998; Simpson, 1990), including more sadness, depression, and anxiety and less happiness and love (Feeney, 1999). They also experience more distress in conflict-resolving discussions (Campbell et al., 2005) and evaluate everyday interactions with their partners more negatively (Bradford et al., 2002). In addition to dissatisfaction, Marcaurelle, Belanger, Marchand, Katerlos, & Mainguy (2005) report that, in a vulnerable clinical sample, individuals married to more anxious partners display more symptoms of clinical depression. Involvement with an anxious partner, thus, appears to constitute a risk factor similar to those discussed above. These results may easily be seen as responses to the ways in which anxious people either perceive their partners (as unsupportive) or engage in interpersonal behaviors as discussed previously.

The adverse impact of anxiety appears to be most pronounced when anxious partners believe that their needs for support are not being met. In a study of the transition to parenthood, Rholes et al. (2001) found that husbands of anxious wives were dissatisfied with their marriages primarily when their wives believed that they were not receiving adequate emotional support, a common condition among anxious women in this study. In contrast, husbands whose anxious wives felt that their needs were being met reported high levels of satisfaction (as did the anxious wives themselves). This study did not address what anxious wives who felt unsupported might have done, if anything, to alienate their partners, but it does show how their partners behaved toward them. Anxious wives were disparaged as immature, unstable, dependent, and weak, with their husbands providing increasingly less support to them over time. Feeney and Hohaus (2001) also found that husbands provided less support to anxious wives, with Feeney and Collins (2003) indicating that one reason for this may be the belief that anxious partners are too needy. In other words, anxious people appear to generate reactions from partners that confirm the negative perceptions and expectations present in their working models of attachment anxiety.

There also are reports that partners of avoidant persons are less satisfied with their relationships, but they are fewer in number. In general, it appears that partner anxiety is more strongly and consistently linked to one's dissatisfaction than partner avoidance. Simpson (1990) found that female, but not male, college students who were paired with avoidant partners were less satisfied with their relationships; Rholes et al. (2001) found that partners of more avoidant individuals were more dissatisfied during the transition to parenthood; and Davila et al. (1998) found an indirect link between greater partner avoidance and lower marital satisfaction through the experience of negative affect in relationships. Collins, Cooper, Albino, & Allard (2002) measured attachment styles among a group of adolescents and examined their romantic relationships six years later. Partners of avoidant individuals were less satisfied with their relationships and reported their avoidant partners to be less disclosing, more critical and jealous, more likely to withdraw from discussions about problems, and (for male partners) more aggressive, consistent with the findings discussed above. Interestingly, this study also found that the partners of avoidant individuals were lower in agency, higher in negative emotionality, and had insecure attachment models of self. Thus, their dissatisfaction with their avoidant partners may have sources other than their partners' behavior.

CONCLUSIONS: GENERAL THEMES, LIMITATIONS OF EXISTING RESEARCH, AND DIRECTIONS FOR THE FUTURE

The year 2007 marked the fiftieth anniversary of Bowlby's initial presentation on attachment theory to his colleagues in the British psychoanalytic community. Hostility and incredulity best describe the reactions of his fellow psychiatrists to his ideas. Because he had abandoned key psychoanalytic concepts (secondary drives, psychic energy, libidinal phases, and the dependency theory of children's ties to their primary caregiver), his ideas were considered radical. Adding to his colleagues' confusion, he introduced concepts from unfamiliar disciplines (e.g., systems theory and ethology), and he conceptualized the bond between children and their caregivers as a species-general instinct that was not in principle different from those investigated among "lower" species. In short, Bowlby introduced a strikingly new conceptual framework into the conservative, insulated world of British psychoanalysis of the 1950's. Refining and advancing his framework was the central project of his professional life from the 1950's through the publication of his last major book in 1980. During these years, psychoanalytic theories of development changed markedly in response to the accumulation of empirical findings that link relationships with attachment figures to adaptive and maladaptive behavior in children and adults (Westin & Gabbarad, 1999). Attachment theory, however, has not completely turned away from its psychoanalytic roots. The substantial body of attachment research on implicit, uncontrolled cognitive processes, for example, shows its continuing influence (Shaver & Mikulincer, 2002).

One indication of just how far Bowlby's ideas were from those of his contemporaries is the number of connections they make to current trends in personality research. The most obvious link is to evolutionary approaches to personality (Buss, 1999). Like this approach, attachment theory begins by postulating inherent, species-wide behavioral dispositions among humans. An important difference between attachment and evolutionary approaches is the stronger emphasis that attachment research has placed on delineating the ways in which environmental factors alter the expression of innate motives on the formation of personality. The best known of this research is Ainsworth's pioneering study of the impact of maternal care on attachment to mothers (Ainsworth et al., 1978). Another point of difference is that attachment theory addresses only a limited number of inherent motivational systems, whereas contemporary evolutionary psychology has a much broader focus, investigating a wide range of cognitive and behavioral predispositions.

The other link is to "cognitive" approaches to personality (Cantor, 1990; Dweck & Leggett, 1988; Mischel & Shoda, 1995). The connecting concepts are attachment theory's internal working models and personality theory's schema. Schemas and working models have almost identical functions. Like schemas, working models guide the interpretation of complex social events. They also are used to predict the behavior of others and select appropriate responses to these predictions or to observed behaviors, functioning as a set of If-Then rules (Mischel & Shoda, 1995). Working models shape interpersonal goals (e.g., to maintain psychological distance) and influence basic cognitive processes, including attention, perception, and memory (Cantor, 1990; Collins & Feeney, 2004). The centrality of the working model in attachment theory places it, along with most cognitive approaches, in the "doing" rather than the "having" tradition in personality theory and research.

Bowlby himself emphasized the dynamic nature of personality. To summarize his view of the impact of experiences with attachment figures on personality development, he wrote:

> [A]n individual who has been fortunate in having grown up in an ordinarily good home with ordinarily affectionate parents has always known people from whom he [sic] can seek support, comfort, and protection.... So deeply established are his expectations and so repeatedly have they been confirmed that as an adult he finds it difficult to imagine any other kind of world....
>
> For many more, the likelihood that a care-taking figure would respond in a supportive and protective way has been at best hazardous and at worst nil. When such people become adults it is hardly surprising that they have no confidence that a care-taking figure will ever be truly available and dependable. Through their eyes the world is seen as comfortless and unpredictable; and they respond either by shrinking from it or by doing battle with it. (Bowlby, 1973, p. 208)

In this chapter we have pointed out some of the consequences of not having grown up in an ordinarily good home as they pertain to relationship satisfaction—in particular, the realization that one's needs will be met only through one's own efforts and the anger that this realization and the experiences that led to it can engender. Avoidant adults have learned to withdraw from others to protect themselves and, as we suggest, to control their emotions, particularly anger. They find it difficult to leave their zone of comfort even though this means that the needs of others are ignored, and they appear to resent behavior that violates their boundaries or limits their control (e.g., emotions of partners that limit their control by forcing them to respond; appeals for help that have the same effect). Anxious adults, in contrast, have learned to do battle. They attempt to demand that others attend to their needs for security, often to the exclusion of any concern about the needs of others for autonomy and security.

We view egoism and the anger that is associated with it to be the linchpins for understanding attachment anxiety (see Figure 5.1). Although anxious persons can be characterized as having goals of obtaining closeness, these goals may be fueled in part by unresolved anger. Their compulsive focus on getting their needs for security met may make it more accurate to view anxious persons as seeking control over their partners in furtherance of their own egoistic concerns instead of seeking genuine closeness.

Anxious people are given to intense, often dysfunctional anger when partners are perceived to be unavailable, although their expression of anger may sometimes be blocked by a fear of alienating the partner. Presumably because they are more prone to anger, they also are more likely than their secure or avoidant counterparts to perpetrate violence against relationships partners. The way in which anxious people deal with conflicts also shows signs of both anger and egoism. They reveal less understanding of their partners' point of view during episodes of conflict, and they attack more and compromise with their partners less. They escalate conflict, and they perceive more conflict in their relationships than their partners. The literature on support and caregiving also reveals the egoism of anxious individuals. They appear to center their perceptions of their partners around what they receive from their partners, and they appear to be unable to perceive fully the support from their partners that is available to them. They are less empathic and as caregivers are less responsive, more controlling, and more often motivated to help by selfish concerns. As a consequence of their behavior, anxious individuals often find themselves in relationships with others who are dissatisfied. Their partners evaluate everyday interactions with them more negatively, report more negative and fewer positive emotions, and withdraw emotional support over time, which, ironically, anxious people appear to need in abundance to feel satisfied with their relationships.

Anger and egoism can also be seen to characterize avoidance (see Figure 5.1), even though the anger-prone nature of avoidant people appears largely to be kept below the level of consciousness as a result of defense mechanisms developed to accommodate their history of interaction with attachment figures. As noted by both Bowlby (1973) and Ainsworth et al. (1978), avoidant individuals experience anger early on in their lives as a result of rejection or abandonment by attachment figures. Consequently, they learn to experience proximity to an attachment figure as something to be avoided to reduce the risk of further rejection and to help to keep their anger over past rejections in check. Avoidant individuals develop attachment strategies to self-protectively avoid attachment figures in times of threat as a result of this anger; they also develop defense mechanisms to suppress the anger that is associated with closeness to their attachment figures. Thus, although the goal of maintaining distance appears to be the most salient aspect of their close relationships, this goal can be viewed in part as furthering a need to suppress anger.

Avoidant individuals do express anger at their partners under some circumstances, particularly when they are highly distressed or when their boundaries have been violated. Their desire to maintain distance from their partners appears to be the most salient aspect of their relationships. They do not often approach their partners and do not want their partners to approach them. They denigrate people who ask for their help and become angry when their partners seek their support. They engage in little self-disclosure and do not like others who disclose personal information to them. Their sex lives are characterized by less intimacy. They withdraw from problem-solving, presumably to minimize emotion-laden interaction with their partners. They seek less emotional support from partners and give less to them. Although their egoism may appear to be less obvious, avoidant individuals seem to be focused on their own needs and insensitive to the needs of their partners. Their desire to maintain a comfortable distance from others, even to the point of ignoring their needs, is a dominant theme in their relationships, and their ability to satisfy this desire may be the key to their relationship satisfaction.

As indicated earlier, anxious persons tend to report the greatest levels of relationship dissatisfaction, and secure persons report the lowest (Mikulincer et al., 2002). Thus, attachment anxiety appears to provide for a greater level of dysfunctionality than does attachment avoidance, particularly in conjunction with romantic relationships. However, caution must be used in interpreting these findings. First, it could be that avoidant individuals are just as unhappy with their relationships as anxious ones but report less unhappiness due to the defense mechanisms that suppress attachment-related affect. Thus, under sufficient levels of distress or cognitive load, avoidant persons may also reveal high levels of relationship dissatisfaction. Second, the findings may be affected by the nature of the relationships available for study. It could be, for example, that when secure persons become unhappy in their relationships, they are willing to end them sooner and move on to more fulfilling relationships. Avoidant persons, because they do not expect their partners to meet their needs for security and are accustomed to being self-reliant, may also be willing to end relationships that are unsatisfactory relatively quickly. Anxious persons, on the other hand, have needs for security and closeness as paramount and fear losing close relationships. They may tend to stay in relationships longer than either secure or avoidant persons, even though those relationships may not, or may be perceived not, to meet their needs. Thus, at any point in time, there could be a greater probability that an anxious person's relationship is an unhappy one. Further research is needed to investigate these possibilities.

It is also possible that insecure persons, whether anxious or avoidant, lay the groundwork for their own dissatisfaction through partner selection. For example, it is clear that some psychological characteristics of partners (for example, a partner's depression) can adversely affect relationships (Joiner, Coyne, & Blalock, 1999). Most studies do not attempt to determine the mental health or other characteristics of the partners of insecure and secure adults and thus do not examine the extent to which individuals having different attachment styles may select the types of partners who themselves will pose difficulties for the relationship. One exception is Collins et al. (2002), who, as reported earlier, found that partners of avoidant adults were higher in negative emotionality, lower in agency, and had more negative self models. The extent to which insecure persons are engaged in relationships with troubled or otherwise problematic partners is therefore unclear, as are the processes through which such pairings might arise. For example, insecure individuals may select problematic partners because they are unable to perceive their potential partners accurately; they may be attracted to partners who exhibit behaviors that others recognize as signs of future problems; or, due to low self-esteem, they may believe that they do not deserve partners who might treat them better or make them happier. Self-verification theory (Swann & Read, 1981) suggests that insecure individuals, particularly those who are anxious, may select partners who confirm their negative self-views (cf. Brennan & Morris, 1997). They may also engage in behaviors motivated by a desire to create negative partner perceptions of them when the need for self-verification is high and other avenues for verification are unavailable.

Further, partners of anxious persons report more relationship dissatisfaction than do partners of avoidant persons. It is not a priori theoretically clear why this should be true. Both anxiety and avoidance are associated with risk factors that lead to dissatisfaction; from our point of view, both anxiety and avoidance are linked to an egoistic stance that allows the needs of the individual to supersede those of the partner. Part of the explanation may involve need for autonomy and the way in which egoism is manifested. Although neither anxious nor avoidant persons may excel at meeting the attachment needs of their partners, only anxious persons appear to be clingy and needy, sometimes "suffocating" their partners and denying them sufficient personal space. The explanation might also reside in the differential way in which anger is experienced and expressed. In other words, an avoidant individual's ability to suppress anger in most situations may lead to greater overall partner satisfaction. More research is needed to examine the joint role of anger and egoism in attachment style and the ways in which they act to produce relationship dissatisfaction.

Another area where research is needed is in the objective measure of behavioral risk factors. This is illustrated by findings from studies of partner support. Anxious individuals report that their partners do not provide adequate support, and partners of anxious adults report that they provide less support to them. Most studies of satisfaction, whether they focus on support, conflict, or other issues, are unable to determine whether the observed effects are driven by the intra-psychic dynamics of attachment models (i.e., dissatisfaction is linked to perceptions that the partner is behaving badly) or the objective behaviors of partners (dissatisfaction is linked to the fact that the partner is actually behaving badly). Assessing partners' self-reported behaviors can be helpful for providing a gauge against which to measure an individual's perceptions, but it has clear limitations. The partner's self-reported behaviors are subject to the same biases that the individual's reports of the partner's behavior are. Unfortunately, few studies to date have included objective assessments of behavior, so effects due to working models and partner behavior have been confounded.

There is also a need to examine further the kinds of behavior that anxious and avoidant individuals provoke that adversely affect their own satisfaction in relationships. This complex interdependent cycle of behaviors is only beginning to be studied. It could certainly be the case that insecure individuals, by making their partners dissatisfied, end up in a "dissatisfaction spiral." In order to break this cycle, studies of partner behaviors that could mitigate dissatisfaction for insecure persons are needed. For example, some individuals may provide naïve "therapy" to their insecure partners to help reduce their relationship dissatisfaction. Studies of other factors that could encourage relationship satisfaction for insecure persons are also needed.

Finally, since the publication of the initial studies linking attachment style to relationship satisfaction (e.g., Simpson, 1990), a major goal of attachment researchers has been to identify factors that explain or mediate the association between these two variables; studies of conflict management and caregiving typify this effort. Less attention has been devoted to moderating variables. Level of stress is one moderating factor that has been addressed, with results often showing that the expected association between attachment styles and outcomes is stronger when stress levels are elevated. Because moderating factors have not been extensively studied, we do not know the range of conditions under which insecure adults may be satisfied with their relationships. We also do not know when or how processes, such as poor conflict management or the display of dysfunctional anger, that should mediate the effects of attachment style are triggered. Addressing these issues will provide a more nuanced understanding of the association between attachment style and relationship satisfaction.

NOTE

1. Persons who score high on both the anxiety and avoidance dimensions are sometimes referred to as "fearful." Although we do not refer to a "fearful" category, we do indicate when relationship effects are associated with a combination of both high anxiety and avoidance.

REFERENCES

Ainsworth, M. D. S., Blehar, M. C., Waters, E., & Wall, S. (1978). *Patterns of attachment.* Hillsdale, NJ: Erlbaum.

Alexander, R., Feeney, J., Hohaus, L., & Noller, P. (2001). Attachment style and coping resources as predictors of coping strategies in the transition to parenthood. *Personal Relationships, 8,* 137–152.

Allen, E. S., & Baucom, D. H. (2004). Adult attachment and patterns of extradyadic involvement. *Family Process, 43,* 467–488.

Bartholomew, K. (1990). Avoidance of intimacy: An attachment perspective. *Journal of Social and Personal Relationships, 7,* 147–178.

Bartholomew, K., Cobb, R. J., & Poole, J. A. (1997). Adult attachment patterns and social support processes. In G. R. Pierce, B. Lakey, I. G. Sarason, & B. R. Sarason (Eds.), *Sourcebook of social support and personality* (pp. 359–378). New York: Plenum Press.

Bartholomew, K., & Horowitz, L. (1991). Attachment styles among young adults: A test of a four-category model. *Journal of Personality and Social Psychology, 61,* 226–244.

Belsky, J., & Pensky, E. (1988). Marital change across the transition to parenthood. *Marriage and Family Review, 13,* 133–156.

Berant, E., Mikulincer, M., & Florian, V. (2001). Attachment style and mental health: A one-year follow-up study of mothers of infants with congenital heart disease. *Personality and Social Psychology Bulletin, 8,* 956–968.

Bogaert, A. F., & Sadava, S. (2002). Adult attachment and sexual behavior. *Personal Relationships, 9,* 191–204.

Bookwala, J. (2002). The role of own and perceived partner attachment in relationship aggression. *Journal of Interpersonal Violence, 17,* 84–100.

Bookwala, J., & Zdaniuk, B. (1998). Adult attachment styles and aggressive behavior within dating relationships. *Journal of Social and Personal Relationships, 15,* 175–190.

Bowlby, J. (1969). *Attachment and loss: Vol. 1. Attachment.* New York: Basic Books.

Bowlby, J. (1973). *Attachment and loss: Vol. 2. Separation: Anxiety and anger.* New York: Basic Books.

Bowlby, J. (1980). *Attachment and loss: Vol. 3. Sadness and depression.* New York: Basic Books.

Bowlby, J. (1988). *A secure base: Clinical applications of attachment theory.* London: Routledge.

Bradbury, T. N., Fincham, F. D., & Beach, S. R. H. (2000). Research on the nature and determinants of marital satisfaction: A decade in review. *Journal of Marriage and the Family, 62,* 964–980.

Bradford, S. A., Feeney, J.A., & Campbell, L. (2002). Links between attachment orientations and dispositional and diary-based measures of disclosure in dating couples: A study of actor and partner effects. *Personal Relationships, 9,* 491–506.

Brennan, K., Clark, C., & Shaver, P. (1998). Self-report measurement of adult attachment: An integrative overview. In J. A. Simpson & W. S. Rholes (Eds.), *Attachment theory and close relationships* (pp. 46–76). New York: Guilford.

Brennan, K. A., & Morris, K. A. (1997). Attachment styles, self-esteem, and patterns of seeking feedback from romantic partners. *Personality and Social Psychology Bulletin, 23,* 23–31.

Brennan, K. A., & Shaver, P. R. (1995). Dimensions of adult attachment, affect regulation, and romantic relationship functioning. *Personality and Social Psychology Bulletin, 21,* 267–283.

Buunk, B. P. (1997). Personality, birth order, and attachment styles as related to various types of jealousy. *Personality and Individual Differences, 23,* 997–1006.

Buss, D. M. (1999). Human nature and individual differences: The evolution of human personality. In L. Pervin & O. John (Eds.), *Handbook of personality: Theory and research* (pp. 31–57). New York: Guilford.

Bylsma, W. H., Cozzarelli, C., & Sumer, N. (1997). Relation between adult attachment styles and global self-esteem. *Basic and Applied Social Psychology, 19,* 1–16.

Campbell, L., Simpson, J. A., Boldry, J., & Kashy, D. A. (2005). Perceptions of conflict and support in romantic relationships: The role of attachment anxiety. *Journal of Personality and Social Psychology, 88,* 510–531.

Cantor, N. (1990). From thought to behavior: "Having" and "doing" in the study of personality and cognition. *American Psychologist, 45,* 735–750.

Carnelley, K. B., Pietromonaco, P. R., & Jaffe, K. (1994). Depression, working models of others, and relationship functioning. *Journal of Personality and Social Psychology, 66,* 127–140.

Cassidy, J. (2001). Truth, lies, and intimacy: An attachment perspective. *Attachment and Human Development, 3,* 121–155.

Collins, N. L. (1996). Working models of attachment: Implications for explanation, emotion, and behavior. *Journal of Personality and Social Psychology, 71,* 810–832.

Collins, N. L., Cooper, M. L., Albino, A., & Allard, L. (2002). Psychosocial vulnerability from adolescence to adulthood: A prospective study of attachment style differences in relationship functioning and partner choice. *Journal of Personality, 70,* 965–1008.

Collins, N. L., & Feeney, B. C. (2000). A safe haven: An attachment theory perspective on support-seeking and caregiving in adult romantic relationships. *Journal of Personality and Social Psychology, 78,* 1053–1073.

Collins, N. L., & Feeney, B. C. (2004). Working models of attachment shape perceptions of social support: Evidence from experimental and observational studies. *Journal of Personality and Social Psychology, 87,* 363–383.
Collins, N. L., & Read, S. J. (1990). Adult attachment, working models, and relationship quality in dating couples. *Journal of Personality and Social Psychology, 58,* 644–663.
Collins, N. L., & Read, S .J. (1994). Cognitive representations of attachment: The structure and function of working models. In K. Bartholomew & D. Perlman (Eds.), *Advances in personal relationships* (Vol. 5, pp. 53–90). London: Jessica Kingsley.
Cooper, M. L., Shaver, P. R., & Collins, N. L. (1998). Attachment styles, emotion regulation, and adjustment in adolescence. *Journal of Personality and Social Psychology, 74,* 1380–1397.
Corcoran, K., & Mallinckrodt, B. (2000). Adult attachment, self-efficacy, perspective taking, and conflict resolution. *Journal of Counseling & Development, 78,* 473–483.
Cowan, L. P., & Cowan, P. A. (2000). *When partners become parents: The big life change in couples.* Mahwah, NJ: Erlbaum.
Creasey, G., & Hesson-McInnis, M. (2001). Affective responses, cognitive appraisals, and conflict tactics in late adolescent romantic relationships: Associations with attachment orientations. *Journal of Counseling Psychology, 48,* 85–96.
Curran, M., Hazen, N., Jacobvitz, D., & Feldman, A. (2005). Representations of early family relationships predict marital maintenance during the transition to parenthood. *Journal of Family Psychology, 19,* 189–197.
Davila, J., Bradbury, T. N., & Fincham, F. (1998). Negative affectivity as a mediator of the association between adult attachment and marital satisfaction. *Personal Relationships, 5,* 467–484.
Davis, D., Shaver, P. R., & Vernon, M. L. (2004). Attachment style and subjective motivations for sex. *Personality and Social Psychology Bulletin, 30,* 1076–1090.
Dutton, D. G., Saunders, K., Starzomski, A., & Bartholomew, K. (1994). Intimacy-anger and insecure attachment as precursors of abuse in intimate relationships. *Journal of Applied Social Psychology, 24,* 1367–1386.
Dutton, D. G., Starzomski, A., & Ryan, L. (1996). Antecedents of abusive personality and abusive behavior in wife assaulters. *Journal of Family Violence, 11,* 113–132.
Dweck, C. S., & Leggett, E. L. (1988). A social-cognitive approach to motivation and personality. *Psychological Review, 95,* 256–273.
Feeney, B. C., & Collins, N. L. (2001). Predictors of caregiving in adult intimate relationships: An attachment theoretical perspective. *Journal of Personality and Social Psychology, 80,* 972–994.
Feeney, B. C., & Collins, N. L. (2003). Motivations for caregiving in adult intimate relationships: Influences on caregiving behavior and relationship functioning. *Personality and Social Psychology Bulletin, 29,* 950–968.
Feeney, B. C., & Kirkpatrick, L. A. (1996). The effects of adult attachment and presence of romantic partners on physiological responses to stress. *Journal of Personality and Social Psychology, 70,* 255–270.
Feeney, J. A. (1994). Attachment style, communication patterns, and satisfaction across the life cycle of marriage. *Personal Relationships, 1,* 333–348.
Feeney, J. A. (1995). Adult attachment and emotional control. *Personal Relationships, 2,* 143–159.
Feeney, J. A. (1996). Attachment, caregiving, and marital satisfaction. *Personal Relationships, 3,* 401–416.
Feeney, J. A. (1998). Adult attachment and relationship-centered anxiety: Responses to physical and emotional distancing. In J. A. Simpson & W. S. Rholes (Eds.), *Attachment theory and close relationships* (pp. 189–218). New York: Guilford.

Feeney, J. A. (1999). Adult attachment, emotional control, and marital satisfaction. *Personal Relationships, 6,* 169–185.

Feeney, J. A., Alexander, R., Noller, P., & Hohaus, L. (2003). Attachment insecurity, depression, and the transition to parenthood. *Personal Relationships, 10,* 475–493.

Feeney, J. A., & Hohaus, L. (2001). Attachment and spousal caregiving. *Personal Relationships, 8,* 21–39.

Feeney, J. A., & Noller, P. (1990). Attachment style as a predictor of adult romantic relationships. *Journal of Personality and Social Psychology, 58,* 281–291.

Feeney, J. A., & Noller, P. (2004). Attachment and sexuality in close relationships. In J. H. Harvey, A. Wenzel, & S. Sprecher (Eds.), *Handbook of sexuality in close relationships* (pp. 183–201). Mahwah, NJ: Erlbaum.

Feeney, J. A., Noller, P., & Callan, V. J. (1994). Attachment style, communication and satisfaction in the early years of marriage. In K. Bartholomew & D. Perlman (Eds.), *Advances in personal relationships* (Vol. 5, pp. 269–308). London: Jessica Kingsley.

Feeney, J. A., Noller, P., & Patty, J. (1993). Adolescents' interaction with the opposite sex: Influences of attachment style and gender. *Journal of Adolescence, 16,* 169–186.

Feeney, J. A., Noller, P., & Roberts, N. (1998). Emotion, attachment, and satisfaction in close relationships. In P. A. Andersen & L. K. Guerrero (Eds.), *Handbook of communication and emotion: Research, theory, applications, and contexts* (pp. 473–505). San Diego, CA: Academic Press.

Feeney, J. A., Peterson, C., Gallois, C., & Terry, D. J. (2000). Attachment style as a predictor of sexual attitudes and behavior in late adolescence. *Psychology and Health, 14,* 1105–1122.

Fishtein, J., Pietromonaco, P. R., & Feldman Barrett, L. (1999). The contribution of attachment style and relationship conflict to the complexity of relationship knowledge. *Social Cognition, 17,* 228–244.

Florian, V., Mikulincer, M., & Bucholtz, I. (1995). Effects of adult attachment style on the perception and search for social support. *The Journal of Psychology: Interdisciplinary and Applied, 129,* 665–676.

Fraley, R. C., Davis, K. E., & Shaver, P. R. (1998). Dismissing-avoidance and the defensive organization of emotion, cognition, and behavior. In J.A. Simpson & W.S. Rholes (Eds.), *Attachment theory and close relationships* (pp. 249–279). New York: Guilford.

Fraley, R. C., & Shaver, P. R. (1998). Airport separations: A naturalistic study of adult attachment dynamics in separating couples. *Journal of Personality and Social Psychology, 75,* 1198–1212.

Gangestad, S. W., & Thornhill, R. (1997). The evolutionary psychology of extrapair sex: The role of fluctuating asymmetry. *Evolution and Human Behavior, 18,* 69–88.

Gentzler, A. L., & Kerns, K. A. (2004). Associations between insecure attachment and sexual experiences. *Personal Relationships, 11,* 249–265.

Gottman, J. M., & Krokoff, L. J. (1989). Marital interaction and satisfaction: A longitudinal view. *Journal of Consulting and Clinical Psychology, 57,* 47–52.

Grabill, C. M., & Kerns, K. A. (2000). Attachment style and intimacy in friendship. *Personal Relationships, 7,* 363–378.

Guerrero, L. K. (1998). Attachment-style differences in the experience and expression of romantic jealousy. *Personal Relationships, 5,* 273–291.

Hazan, C., & Shaver, P. R. (1987). Romantic love conceptualized as an attachment process. *Journal of Personality and Social Psychology, 52,* 511–524.

Heinicke, C. M. (1995). Determinants of the transition to parenthood. In M. H. Bornstein (Ed.), *Handbook of parenting: Status and social conditions of parenting* (Vol. 3, pp. 277–303). Mahwah, NJ: Erlbaum.

Hollist, C. S., & Miller, R. B. (2005). Perceptions of attachment style and marital quality in midlife marriage. *Family Relations, 54,* 46–57.

Holmes, J. G. (1991). Trust and the appraisal process in close relationships. In W. H. Jones & D. Perlman (Eds.), *Advances in personal relationships* (Vol. 2, pp. 57–104). London: Jessica Kingsley.
Impett, E. A., & Peplau, L. A. (2002). Why some women consent to unwanted sex with a dating partner: Insights from attachment theory. *Psychology of Women Quarterly, 26,* 360–370.
Joiner, T., Coyne, J. C., & Blalock, J. (1999). The interpersonal nature of depression: Overview and synthesis. In T. Joiner & J. C. Coyne (Eds.), *The interactional nature of depression* (pp. 3–20). Washington, D.C.: American Psychological Association.
Keelan, J. P. R., Dion, K. K., & Dion, K. L. (1993). Attachment style and relationship satisfaction: Test of a self-disclosure explanation. *Canadian Journal of Behavioural Sciences, 30,* 24–35.
Kirkpatrick, L. A. (1998). Evolution, pair-bonding, and reproductive strategies: A reconceptualization of adult attachment. In J. A. Simpson & W. S. Rholes (Eds.), *Attachment theory and close relationships* (pp. 353–393). New York: Guilford.
Kobak, R. R., & Duemmler, S. (1994). Attachment and conversation: Toward a discourse analysis of adolescent and adult security. In K. Bartholomew & D. Perlman (Eds.), *Advances in personal relationships* (Vol. 5, pp. 121–149). London: Jessica Kingsley.
Kobak, R. R., & Hazan, C. (1991). Attachment in marriage: The effects of security and accuracy of working models. *Journal of Personality and Social Psychology, 60,* 861–869.
Kobak, R. R., & Sceery, A. (1988). Attachment in late adolescence: Working models, affect regulation, and representation of self and others. *Child Development, 59,* 135–146.
Kunce, L. J., & Shaver, P. R. (1994). An attachment-theoretical approach to caregiving in romantic relationships. In K. Bartholomew & D. Perlman (Eds.), *Advances in personal relationships* (Vol. 5, pp. 205–237). London: Jessica Kingsley.
Laurenceau, J-P., Barrett, L. F., & Rovine, M. J. (2005). The interpersonal process model of intimacy in marriage: A daily-diary and multilevel modeling approach. *Journal of Family Psychology, 19,* 314–323.
Laurenceau, J-P., Troy, A. B., & Carver, C. S. (2005). Two distinct emotional experiences in romantic relationships: Effects of perceptions regarding approach of intimacy and avoidance of conflict. *Personality and Social Psychology Bulletin, 31,* 1123– 1133.
Levy, M. B., & Davis, K. E. (1988). Lovestyles and attachment styles compared: Their relations to each other and to various relationship characteristics. *Journal of Social and Personal Relationships, 5,* 439–471.
Lussier, Y., Sabourin, S., & Turgeon, C. (1997). Coping strategies as moderators of the relationship between attachment and marital adjustment. *Journal of Social and Personal Relationships, 14,* 777–791.
Main, M., & Goldwyn, R. (1998). Adult attachment scoring and classification system. Unpublished manuscript. University of California at Berkeley.
Marcaurelle, R., Belanger,C., Marchand, A., Katerlos, T. E., & Mainguy, N. (2003). Marital predictors of symptom severity in panic disorder with agoraphobia. *Journal of Anxiety Disorders, 19,* 211–232.
Marchand, J. F. (2004). Husbands' and wives' marital quality: The role of adult attachment orientations, depressive symptoms, and conflict resolution behaviors. *Attachment and Human Development, 6,* 99–112.
Marchand, J. F., & Hock, E. (2000). Avoidance and attacking conflict-resolution strategies among married couples: Relations to depressive symptoms and marital satisfaction. *Family Relations, 49,* 201–206.
Mauricio, A. M., & Gormley, B. (2001). Male perpetration of physical violence against female partners. *Journal of Interpersonal Violence, 16,* 1066–1081.
Mayseless, O. (1991). Adult attachment patterns and courtship violence. *Family Relations, 40,* 21–28.

Mikulincer, M. (1995). Attachment style and the mental representation of the self. *Journal of Personality and Social Psychology, 69,* 1203–1215.

Mikulincer, M. (1998a). Adult attachment style and individual differences in functional versus dysfunctional experiences of anger. *Journal of Personality and Social Psychology, 74,* 513–524.

Mikulincer, M. (1998b). Attachment working models and the sense of trust: An exploration of interaction goals and affect regulation. *Journal of Personality and Social Psychology, 74,* 1209–1224.

Mikulincer, M., & Florian, V. (1995). Appraisal of and coping with a real-life stressful situation: The contribution of attachment styles. *Personality and Social Psychology Bulletin, 21,* 406–414.

Mikulincer, M., & Florian, V. (1998). The relationship between adult attachment styles and emotional and cognitive reactions to stressful events. In J. A. Simpson & W. S. Rholes (Eds.), *Attachment theory and close relationships* (pp. 143–165). New York: Guilford.

Mikulincer, M., Florian, V., Cowan, P. A., & Cowan, C. P. (2002). Attachment security in couple relationships: A systemic model and its implications for family dynamics. *Family Process, 341,* 405–434.

Mikulincer, M., Florian, V., & Weller, A. (1993). Attachment styles, coping strategies, and posttraumatic psychological distress: The impact of the Gulf War in Israel. *Journal of Personality and Social Psychology, 64,* 817–826.

Mikulincer, M., Gillath, O., Halevy, V., Avihou, N., Avidan, S., & Eshkoli, N. (2001). Attachment theory and reactions to others' needs: Evidence that activation of the sense of attachment security promotes empathic responses. *Journal of Personality and Social Psychology, 81,* 1205–1224.

Mikulincer, M., Gillath, O., & Shaver, P. R. (2002). Activation of the attachment system in adulthood: Threat-related primes increase the accessibility of mental representations of attachment figures. *Journal of Personality and Social Psychology, 83,* 881–895.

Mikulincer, M., & Horesh, N. (1999). Adult attachment style and the perception of others: The role of projective mechanisms. *Journal of Personality and Social Psychology, 76,* 1022–1034.

Mikulincer, M., & Nachson, O. (1991). Attachment styles and patterns of self-disclosure. *Journal of Personality and Social Psychology, 61,* 321–331.

Mikulincer, M., & Orbach, I. (1995). Attachment styles and repressive defensiveness: The accessibility and architecture of affective memories. *Journal of Personality and Social Psychology, 68,* 917–925.

Mikulincer, M., & Shaver, P. R. (2003). The attachment behavioral system in adulthood: Activation, psychodynamics, and interpersonal processes. In M. P. Zanna (Ed.), *Advances in experimental social psychology* (Vol. 35, pp. 53–152). New York: Academic.

Mikulincer, M., & Shaver, P. R. (2004). Security-based self-representations in adulthood: Contents and processes. In W. S. Rholes & J. A. Simpson (Eds.), *Adult attachment: Theory, research, and clinical implications* (pp. 159–195). New York: Guilford.

Mikulincer, M., & Shaver, P. R. (2005). Attachment theory and emotions in close relationships: Exploring the attachment-related dynamics of emotional reactions to relational events. *Personal Relationships, 12,* 149–168.

Mikulincer, M., Shaver, P. R., Gillath, O., & Nitzberg, R. A. (2005). Attachment, caregiving, and altruism: Boosting attachment security increases compassion and helping. *Journal of Personality and Social Psychology, 84,* 817–839.

Mischel, W., & Shoda, Y. (1995). A cognitive-affective system theory of personality: Reconceptualizing situations, dispositions, dynamics, and invariance in personality structure. *Psychological Review, 102,* 246–268.

Muris, P., Meesters, C., Morren, M., & Moorman, L. (2004). Anger and hostility in adolescents: Relationships with self-reported attachment style and perceived parental rearing styles. *Journal of Psychosomatic Research, 57*, 257–264.
Noller, P., Feeney, J. A., Bonnell, D., & Callan, V. J. (1994). A longitudinal study of conflict in early marriage. *Journal of Social and Personal Relationships, 11*, 233–252.
Ognibene, T. C., & Collins, N. L. (1998). Adult attachment styles, perceived social support and coping strategies. *Journal of Social and Personal Relationships, 15*, 323–345.
Orcutt , H. K., Garcia, M., & Pickett, S. M. (2005). Female-perpetrated intimate partner violence and romantic attachment style in a college student sample. *Violence and Victims, 20*, 287–302.
Paley, B., Cox, M. J., Kanoy, K. W., Harter, K. S. M., Burchinal, M., & Margand, N. A. (2005). Adult attachment and marital interaction as predictors of whole family interactions during the transition to parenthood. *Journal of Family Psychology, 19*, 420–429.
Pistole, M. C. (1989). Attachment in adult romantic relationships: Style of conflict resolution and relationship satisfaction. *Journal of Social and Personal Relationships, 6*, 505–510.
Pistole, M. C. (1993). Attachment relationships: Self-disclosure and trust. *Journal of Mental Health Counseling, 15*, 94–106.
Pistole, M. C. (2003). Understanding attachment: Beliefs about conflict. *Journal of Counseling and Development, 81*, 318–328.
Pistole, M. C., & Tarrant, N. (1993). Attachment style and aggression in male batterers. *Family Therapy, 20*, 165–173.
Priel, B., & Shamai, D. (1995). Attachment style and perceived social support: Effects on affect regulation. *Personality and Individual Differences, 19*, 235–241.
Rholes, W. S., Simpson, J.A., & Blakely, B. S. (1995). Adult attachment styles and mothers' relationships with their young children. *Personal Relationships, 2*, 35–54.
Rholes, W. S., Simpson, J.A., Blakely, B. S., Lanigan, L., & Allen, E. A. (1997). Adult attachment styles, the desire to have children, and working models of parenthood. *Journal of Personality, 65*, 357–385.
Rholes, W. S., Simpson, J.A., Campbell, L., & Grich, J. (2001). Adult attachment and the transition to parenthood. *Journal of Personality and Social Psychology, 81*, 421–435.
Rholes, W. S., Simpson, J. A., & Friedman, M. (2006). Avoidant attachment and the experience of parenting. *Personality and Social Psychology Bulletin, 32*, 275–285.
Rholes, W. S., Simpson, J .A., Trans, S., Martin, A M., & Friedman, M. (2007). *Personality and Social Psychology Bulletin, 33*, 422–438.
Rholes, W. S., Simpson, J. A., & Oriña, M. M. (1999). Attachment and anger in an anxiety-provoking situation. *Journal of Personality and Social Psychology, 76*, 40–957.
Roberts, N., & Noller, P. (1998). The association between adult attachment and couple violence: The role of communication patterns and relationship satisfaction. In J.A. Simpson & W.S. Rholes (Eds.), *Attachment theory and close relationships* (pp. 317–350). New York: Guilford.
Schachner, D. A., & Shaver, P. R. (2002). Attachment style and human mate poaching. *New Review of Social Psychology, 1*, 122–129.
Schachner, D. A., & Shaver, P. R. (2004). Attachment dimensions and sexual motives. *Personal Relationships, 11*, 179–195.
Shaver, P. R., Hazan, C., & Bradshaw, D. (1988). Love as attachment: The integration of three behavioral systems. In R.J. Sternberg & M. Barnes (Eds.), *The anatomy of love* (pp. 68–98). New Haven, CT: Yale University Press.
Shaver, P. R., & Mikulincer, M. (2002). Attachment-related psychodynamics. *Attachment and Human Development, 4*, 133–161.
Shi, L. (2003). The association between adult attachment styles and conflict resolution in romantic relationships. *The American Journal of Family Therapy, 31*, 143–157.

Simpson, J. A. (1990). Influence of attachment styles on romantic relationships. *Journal of Personality and Social Psychology, 59,* 971–980.

Simpson, J. A., & Rholes, W. S. (1994). Stress and secure base relationships in adulthood. In K. Bartholomew & D. Perlman (Eds.), *Advances in personal relationships* (Vol. 5, pp. 181–204). London: Jessica Kingsley.

Simpson, J. A., & Rholes, W. S. (1998). Attachment in adulthood. In J.A. Simpson & W. S. Rholes (Eds.), *Attachment theory and close relationships* (pp. 3–21). New York: Guilford.

Simpson, J. A., Rholes, W. S., Campbell, L., Tran, S., & Wilson, C. L. (2003). Adult attachment, the transition to parenthood, and depressive symptoms. *Journal of Personality and Social Psychology, 84,* 1172–1187.

Simpson, J. A., Rholes, W. S., & Nelligan, J. S. (1992). Support-seeking and support-giving within couples in an anxiety-provoking situation: The role of attachment styles. *Journal of Personality and Social Psychology, 62,* 434–446.

Simpson, J. A., Rholes, W. S., & Phillips, D. (1996). Conflict in close relationships: An attachment perspective. *Journal of Personality and Social Psychology, 71,* 899–914.

Sroufe, L. A., & Waters, E. (1977). Attachment as an organizational construct. *Child Development, 48,* 1184–1199.

Swann, W. B., Jr., & Read, S. J. (1981). Self-verification processes: How we sustain our self-conceptions. *Journal of Experimental Social Psychology, 17,* 351–372.

Torquati, J. C., & Vazsonyi, A. T. (1999). Attachment as an organizational construct for affect, appraisals, and coping of late adolescent females. *Journal of Youth and Adolescence, 28,* 545–562.

Tracy, J. L., Shaver, P. R., Albino, A. W., & Cooper, M. L. (2003). Attachment styles and adolescent sexuality. In P. Florsheim (Ed.), *Adolescent romance and sexual behavior: Theory, research, and practical implications* (pp. 137–159). Mahwah, NJ: Erlbaum.

Tucker, P., & Anders, S. L. (1998). Adult attachment style and nonverbal closeness in dating couples. *Journal of Nonverbal Behavior, 22,* 124–129.

Tucker, P., & Aron, A. (1993). Passionate love and marital satisfaction at key transition points in the family life cycle. *Journal of Social & Clinical Psychology, 12,* 135–147.

Tweed, R. G., & Dutton, D. G. (1998). A comparison of impulsive and instrumental subgroups of batterers. *Violence and Victims, 13,* 217–230.

Twenge, J. M., Campbell, W. K., & Foster, C. A. (2003). Parenthood and marital satisfaction: A meta-analytic review. *Journal of Marriage and Family, 65,* 574–583.

Wallace, J. L., & Vaux, A. (1993). Social support network orientation: The role of adult attachment style. *Journal of Social and Clinical Psychology, 12,* 354–365.

Wekerle, C., & Wolfe, D. A. (1998). The role of child maltreatment and attachment style in adolescent relationship violence. *Development and Psychopathology, 10,* 571–586.

Westin, D., & Gabbard, G. O. (1999). Psychoanalytic approaches to personality. In L. Pervin & O. John (Eds.), *Handbook of personality: Theory and research* (pp. 57–101). New York: Guilford Press.

Westmaas, J. L., & Silver, R. C. (2001). The role of attachment in responses to victims of life crises. *Journal of Personality and Social Psychology, 80,* 425–438.

Wilson, C. L., Rholes, W. S., Simpson, J. A., & Tran, S. (2007). Labor, delivery, and early parenthood: An attachment theory perspective. *Personality and Social Psychology Bulletin, 33,* 505–518.

Wilson, C. L., Simpson, J. A., & Rholes, W. S. (2000). Attachment orientation and support giving. Poster presented at the Midwestern Psychological Association Annual Conference, Chicago, IL.

Woolsey, L. K., & McBain, L. (1987). Women's networks: Strengthening the bonds of friendship between women. In K. Storrie (Ed.), *Women, isolation, and bonding* (pp. 59–76). Toronto: Methuen.

6

Different Toolkits for Different Mind-Readers
A Social-Cognitive Neuroscience Perspective on Personality and Social Relationships

GERALDINE DOWNEY and JAMIL ZAKI
Columbia University
JASON MITCHELL
Harvard University

During an interview, Kurt Vonnegut once advised young writers as follows. "If you describe a landscape, or a cityscape, or a seascape, always be sure to put a human figure somewhere in the scene. Why? Because readers are human beings, mostly interested in human beings" (Vonnegut, 1965). This insight has been shared by both psychologists and (more recently) cognitive neuroscientists, who have remarked on the centrality other people hold in our mental lives. People are astoundingly efficient at gaining information about the contents of other people's thoughts and spend a great deal of their time inferring and responding to them. One group of researchers who recorded, transcribed, and categorized everyday conversations has found that gossip (defined as "anything that has to do with explicit social activities, personal relationships, and personal likes and dislikes") accounts for about two thirds of the time people spend talking to each other, further underscoring the importance of social cognition (Dunbar, 2004).

Our preoccupation with the other people's minds makes sense because thinking about mental states is the easiest, most effective way to predict what other people will do (Reis & Downey, 1999). Daniel Dennett (1987) first pointed out that we can think about people's actions with respect to their physical characteristics and capabilities (*design stance*), or by treating them as rational agents with beliefs and desires and then predicting their actions based on these internal states (*intentional stance*). While the design stance is most efficient in predicting that a person will wince after being kicked in the shins, we gain significantly more insight about complex human behaviors by instead using an intentional stance.

Social psychology research has concerned itself with mental state inference for several decades, usually in the context of stereotyping and attribution theory (Allport, 1954). Much of this work has emphasized the automaticity with which we attribute the actions of another person (target) to stable traits (Uleman & Moskowitz, 1994; Winter, Uleman, & Cunniff, 1985). Correcting these attributions by appealing to information about a target's current mental state, on the other hand, requires more of our attentional resources, and under cognitive load people are unable to make these corrections (Gilbert, Pelham, & Krull, 1989). These data have led social psychologists towards several dual-process models of social cognition, in which automatic attribution heuristics and controlled mentalizing both contribute to a perceiver's ideas about targets. In this way, an observer can use fast, automatic processing of social cues to gain information about a target with relatively little effort, or to gain more detailed information using controlled processes if they have the resources and inclination to do so. This ability to adapt in a flexible and discriminative way to various situations is vital to survival.

We know, however, that people vary in characteristic ways in their responses within and across situations. The essence of the trait or structural approach to personality is that people differ on average from one another on a limited number of dimensions, such as agreeableness, conscientiousness, neuroticism, extraversion and openness. Another way of characterizing individual differences is in terms of the distinctive and consistent ways in which people process and make meaning of particular situations. In this view of personality, people behave in ways that are consistent with the meaning that situations have for them, meanings that reflect their individual biology and their history. Mischel (1973) developed this view of personality to explain why people intuitively describe themselves and others as aggressive, agreeable, neurotic despite evidence that people do not behave in consistent ways across diverse situations. Rejecting the assumption that consistency meant similar behavior across different situations, he proposed that consistency could be found by analyzing behavior in its situational context. He predicted that such an analysis would reveal that people have consistent *if-then* situation-behavior patterns, or contextualized personality signatures. This view locates the essential building blocks of personality in the cognitive and affective processes people use to mentally represent situations and to shape their efforts to behave adaptively and discriminatively. The Cognitive-Affective-Processing System (CAPS) model (Mischel & Shoda, 1995) formalizes Mischel's view of the type of processing system that would allow a person to show both stability in behavior as well as lawful variability with changes in context and/or mental representation.

Mischel's view of personality is highly compatible with the view of how the mind operates that is emerging from cognitive neuroscience as well as experimental social psychological approaches to social cognition. However, as we will see below, cognitive neuroscience research reminds us that people differ not only in the content and ease of accessibility of the expectancies, values, and goals and other cognitive-affective building blocks of personality that they use to make meaning of a particular situation. People also differ, as a result of biology and experiences, in the availability of particular types of processing tools. Thus, problematic social behavior may reflect the absence or compromised development of particular processing tools and the consequent over reliance on other tools that may be situationally inappropriate. Personality researchers are, of course, aware of the possibility that some people may be predisposed to use certain types of processing tools rather than others, and there are several excellent examples of research based on this premise. For example, Metcalfe and Mischel have proposed that individuals who are unable to delay gratification in the face of temptation (e.g., when viewing marshmallows) are cued by desirable stimuli to use "hot" automatic processing streams, whereas people with higher self-regulation ability may employ a more controlled "cool processing stream," allowing them to avoid succumbing to temptation (Metcalfe & Mischel, 1999). However, personality researchers have not paid as much attention to the ways people may differ in their approach to understanding other minds.

COGNITIVE-NEUROSCIENCE APPROACHES TO INDIVIDUAL DIFFERENCES

Cognitive-neuroscience approaches to individual differences have roots in animal models of behavior, which are tested by selectively removing or otherwise manipulating brain structures or neural pathways hypothesized to underlie aspects of behavior. Until the advent of functional neuroimaging, establishing the generalizability of animal findings to humans depended on patients with brain damage. By specifying neural structures that a patient's injury had affected, and matching it to behavioral deficits, neuropsychologists made inferences about the function of those structures. With the development of neuroimaging techniques, scientists were given a window into the functioning of the live, alert human brain. This allowed cognitive neuroscience studies of individual differences to move away from neurological patient studies and, instead, focus on whether patients with specific behavioral disorders (e.g., autism, depression, anxiety disorders, Alzheimer's) under- or overused specific brain structures.

More recently, personality research has begun to use neuroimaging approaches to study normal variation in personality dispositions (e.g., Canli, 2004; Canli, Sivers, Witfield, Gotlib, & Gabrieli, 2002; Kross, Egner, Ochsner, Hirsch, & Downey, under review). The marriage of the traditional logic of cognitive neuroscience with that of the trait and process approach to personality suggests some interesting ways for considering how individuals may differ from one another in the context of social relationships. In particular, new techniques highlight the need to think about dispositional differences as the tendency to use one type of processing tool rather than another and to develop research paradigms that can pinpoint under what circumstances and in whom shifts in the use of particular processing tools will occur.

Distinguishing Cognition That Is Uniquely Social

The purpose of this chapter is to suggest reasons why cognitive neuroscience can help us understand social cognition and especially individual differences in social-cognitive processing and resultant social behavior. First, however, we should be clear about the boundaries that define cognition that is uniquely social as distinct from generic cognition applied to the social world. If we used the same mental processes to understand the internal states and actions of our friends and our computers, then merely pointing those processes towards people does not qualify them as being social cognition. Instead, social cognition must be defined as a type of thought, feeling, or perception that we can *only* have with respect to another intentional agent. As we will see below, neuroimaging data have helped to clarify and classify two core mental processes that fit this description as uniquely person-oriented: *mental state inference* and *empathy*. The first refers to processes by which we use the intentional stance to understand the complex mental states of other people; the second refers to the alignment of our emotional (and perhaps cognitive) states with those of others. These two types of uniquely social mental processes have distinct neural substrates and are uniquely affected by our states and traits. For the purposes of this chapter, social cognition will be the term applied to both empathy and mental state inference.

A third, orthogonal process—*motivation to attend* to social cues—will be included in our analysis of individual differences in social cognition. While not a social cognitive process per se, socially motivated attention critically impacts people's ability to infer mental and emotional states from others. Furthermore, social motivation may be at the root of several types of individual differences in social cognition. For example, while autistic children have difficulty identifying mental states in others, if their attention is explicitly directed at relevant cues (i.e. sincerity or irony in auditory speech), their performance improves. Furthermore, attention-related improvements covary with the social functioning capacity of children with autism (Wang, Lee, Sigman, & Dapretto, 2006), suggesting that the use of motivated attention critically interacts with more reflexive social-cognitive processes to produce social behavior. It has recently been suggested that socially motivated attention is served by the oxytocin neurotransmitter system and that administering oxytocin to autistic individuals increases their attention to social cues, perhaps because the system increases the reward value of these cues (Bartz & Hollander, 2006). Other dispositional differences, such as rejection sensitivity (RS; Downey & Feldman, 1996), and personality disorders such as borderline and avoidant personality disorder (BPD), involve *increased* attention to social cues, especially those involving relationship-threatening information.

Linking Cognitive Neuroscience and Personality Research

Two conceptual bridges are necessary to demonstrate the utility of neuroimaging for personality research: *modularity* and *situational accessibility*. To establish modularity, we need to document that mental state inference and empathy are "special," in that they do not merely represent social expression of more general processes (e.g., attention). To establish situational accessibility, we need to demonstrate that the way perceivers deploy social-cognitive processes can differ across situations. If both of those ideas hold, then we can hypothesize that individual differences could express themselves as chronic tendencies towards using one or another social-cognitive process.

Modular Nature of Social Cognition. One of neuroimaging's great hopes is that by examining the brain's engagement during two or more cognitive processes, experimenters can use differences and overlaps in neural activity to infer that these processes are similar or different from each other (Henson, 2005). For example, a long debate over the difference or similarity of basic vision and visual imagery was resolved when, using positron emission topography (PET) and functional magnetic resonance imagery (fMRI), researchers found that the same brain regions were involved in both imagining and seeing objects (Kosslyn & Ochsner, 1994; Kosslyn, Thompson, & Alpert, 1997). Similarly, neuroimaging has shown that, instead of being unitary, social cognition is made up of a constellation of processes that together shape our interpretation of social cues. Each process is modular, such that it can work with limited input from other systems.

Situational Influences on the Use of Social-Cognitive Processes. The other contribution that neuroimaging has provided to social cognition research is new insight into how the internal and external contexts can alter the deployment of social-cognitive processes. Recent neuroimaging studies have shown that perceivers use different cognitive and neural mechanisms when thinking about the mindsets of different types of people—our parent's, our own, or those of a stranger. When we think about a person's mind, her relationship to us, alliance towards or against us, familiarity, and perceived trustworthiness color the processes we use and the conclusions we draw about her. Similarly, our moods and cognitive busyness or stress level, as well as our expectancy about another person (is he likely to accept or reject us, to view us as higher or lower in status) change the way we employ available social-cognitive processes. In sum, whether and to what extent we employ either mental state inference or empathy or attend to social cues changes in a fluid way to reflect changes in the situation and in our internal states.

GOALS OF THE CHAPTER

The chapter reviews evidence for a model of fluid, situation-dependent deployment of social-cognitive processes and considers how the model can inform personality research. Particular attention is given to personality dispositions and disorders that have a strong impact on social relationships. An example of such a *relational* disposition is rejection sensitivity, the disposition to anxiously expect, readily perceive, and intensely react to rejection. An example of a relational personality disorder is borderline personality disorder characterized by marked instability in relationships, mood and identity, and by impulsive self-destructive behavior typically triggered by real or imagined rejection.

Though several experiments have documented the ways in which our *states* can affect the way we think about other people, little work has attended to dispositional differences in how we use mental state inference and empathy. Thus an under-explored but potentially important question in understanding how personality shapes relationships is: How do individual differences in established personality dispositions emerge in average levels of use of particular social-cognitive modules and in their situational accessibility?

Personality Disorders Characterized by Specific Deficits in Social Cognition

Viewing mental state inference and empathy as separate processes implies that there should be patient populations who lack the ability to infer the mental states of other targets, but who suffer no more general cognitive impairment, including no deficits in empathic processes. Furthermore, another population should have intact mental state inference abilities, but lack normal emotional empathy. Autism and psychopathy provide just such cases (Blair, 2005). Autism spectrum disorder is characterized by lack of interest in social cues and deficits in understanding mental states, but intact sensory and cognitive function (Baron-Cohen, 1994; Dakin & Frith, 2005). From an early age, autistic individuals do not attempt to draw the attention of others, nor are they drawn to human faces and eyes the way other children are. Their inability to use mental state information in understanding the actions of others is even more profound. The classic example of mental state inference deficits in autism is their failure at simple problems such as the *false belief task*. In this task, subjects read vignettes describing social situations. One of the characters in each vignette has the wrong idea about some aspect of the story (for example, "Sally places a ball inside toy box A, but while she turns her back Anne moves it to toy box B"), and subjects are asked to infer what the character's mistaken mental state is ("Where will Sally look for the ball?"). Though normal children can easily infer that Sally will mistakenly look for her ball in box A, autistic children instead project their own knowledge onto Sally, guessing that she will look for her ball in box B, and failing to allow Sally her own, independent mental state.

The continued failure of autistics in the social world underscores the modularity of social cognition (Frith & Happe, 1994), and led to the theory that one core process, called "theory of mind," underlies our social-cognitive abilities. Leslie and his colleagues (1994, 2004) have argued that a single theory of mind mechanism is disrupted in autistics and accounts for most of their difficulties interpreting the social world. Beyond arguing for modularity, however, the case of autistics also suggests that other dispositional differences can uniquely affect social cognition. For example, while not failing at mental state inference, psychopaths cannot easily identify or respond to the emotions of other people. Circumscribed failures in empathy covary with psychopaths' levels of violent behavior, and with volumetric loss in a prefrontal cortex region involved in emotion identification (Raine, Lencz, Bihrle, LaCasse, & Colletti, 2000). Borderline personality disorder is also characterized by difficulty in interpreting others' emotions accurately and researchers are beginning to explore the possibility of altered mental state inference or empathic processes in these populations (Bateman & Fonagy, 2004). The fact that the impulsive behavior characteristic of borderline personality disorder (e.g., self-harm, binge eating, hostility, abruptly terminating relationships) is typically triggered by perceptions of threatened or actual rejection suggests the utility of viewing borderline personality disorder as involving situationally cued changes in mental state inference in an if-then fashion, as used by Mischel and Shoda (1995) to discuss personality more generally.

Using Neuroimaging to Show Modularity in Social Cognition

The first neuroimaging studies of social cognition used paradigms from autism research to search for brain regions uniquely engaged by mental state inference. Most commonly, participants were scanned using fMRI or PET while performing some variant of a false belief task using either vignettes or pictures (Brunet, Sarfati, Hardy-Bayle, & Decety, 2000; Castelli, Happe, Frith, & Frith, 2000; Fletcher, Happe et al., 1995; Gallagher et al., 2000; Saxe & Kanwisher, 2003). Later, these studies expanded to include asking participants to make inferences about targets' *knowledge* (Goel, Grafman, Sadato, & Hallett, 1995), *traits or abilities* (Harris, Todorov, & Fiske, 2005; Mason & Macrae, 2004; Mitchell, Heatherton, & Macrae, 2002; Mitchell, Macrae, & Banaji, 2005), or *affective states* (Baron-Cohen et al., 1999; Hynes, Baird, & Grafton, 2006; Ochsner et al., 2004; Vollm et al., 2006). Studies of *real-time social interactions* most often ask participants to compete in economics games that require attending to their competitor's mental state in order to predict his or her actions (Decety, Jackson, Sommerville, Chaminade, & Meltzoff, 2004; Gallagher, Jack, Roepstorff, & Frith, 2002; McCabe, Houser, Ryan, Smith, & Trouard, 2001; Montague et al., 2002; Rilling, Sanfey, Aronson, Nystrom, & Cohen, 2004a, 2004b; Sanfey, Rilling, Aronson, Nystrom, & Cohen, 2003).

Across different paradigms and experimental tasks, researchers have identified a consistent set of brain regions that is preferentially engaged when thinking about other people's minds (see Figure 6.1). This network includes dorsal and ventral

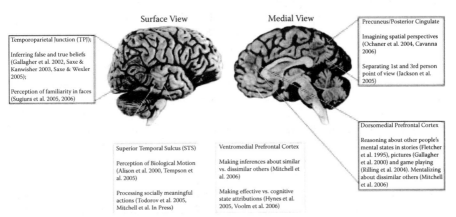

Figure 6.1   Brain regions contributing to Theory of Mind.

medial prefrontal cortex (MPFC), bilateral superior temporal sulci (STS), right temporo-parietal junction (TPJ), posterior cingulate cortex (PCC), and the temporal poles. Although theory of mind was initially thought to be a largely unitary construct, neuroimaging suggests that, instead, several brain regions (and presumably associated cognitive processes) go into social cognition, with each region preferentially engaged for different aspects of social-cognitive processing. For example, while the medial prefrontal cortex and temporo-parietal junction are specifically involved in mental state inference, the superior temporal sulci responds to the presence of people per se in subjects' visual fields. The superior temporal sulci also respond to perceptions of human movement (Allison, Puce, & McCarthy, 2000; Pelphrey, Morris, & McCarthy, 2004; Thompson, Clarke, Stewart, & Puce, 2005) and descriptions of socially significant actions (Mitchell, Cloutier, Banaji, & Macrae, 2006). The posterior cingulate cortex and adjacent parietal cortices are engaged for imagining spatial perspectives and reflecting on the relevance of social information (Cavanna & Trimble, 2006; Fletcher, Frith et al., 1995; Vogt, Vogt, & Laureys, 2006).

Many of the regions involved in social cognition are also engaged when people reflect on their own traits, preferences, or emotions (Mitchell, Banaji, & Macrae, 2005; Ochsner et al., 2004; Vogeley et al., 2001). Some researchers have concluded that people use *shared representations* to understand mental states of others by imagining what they (the observer) would feel or think in a target's position. This is especially the case for more implicit forms of social cognition, such as empathy for pain, disgust, and other emotional states. In support of this view, Singer et al. (2004) has shown an overlap in brain activation between experiencing a state and observing it in others. The study involved scanning participants while they either received a mildly painful electric shock or watched their romantic partner receive an identical shock. The researchers used the overlap in brain regions that were activated by both "self" and "other" pain to made inferences about the extent to which people use shared representations for thinking of themselves and others.

Most experiments on empathy have focused on self/other overlaps for sensory states: these overlaps in the brain have been explored for feeling and perceiving *pain* (Botvinick et al., 2005; Jackson, Brunet, Meltzoff, & Decety, 2006; Jackson, Meltzoff, & Decety, 2005; Morrison, Lloyd, di Pellegrino, & Roberts, 2004; Saarela et al., 2006), *disgust* (Wicker et al., 2003), and *touch* (Keysers et al., 2004), and facial expression of *basic emotions* such as anger, fear, amusement (Carr, Iacoboni, Dubeau, Mazziotta, & Lenzi, 2003; Leslie, Johnson-Frey, & Grafton, 2004). Together, this work has identified a second network of brain regions whose activity tracks overlap at this level (see Figure 6.2). This network, which includes anterior cingulate cortex (ACC), anterior insula (AI), inferior frontal gyrus (IFG), amygdala, and inferior parietal cortex (IPC), is largely non-overlapping with the social-cognitive network described above for mental state inference, suggesting that these networks represent dissociable processing streams.

All of us can remember cringing when we saw someone hurt himself, or how contagious laughter can be. There is evidence that imitating emotional expressions increases our ability to perceive them in targets (Niedenthal & Brauer, 2001) and can make us feel congruent moods (Neumann & Strack, 2000). Furthermore,

DIFFERENT TOOLKITS FOR DIFFERENT MIND-READERS 157

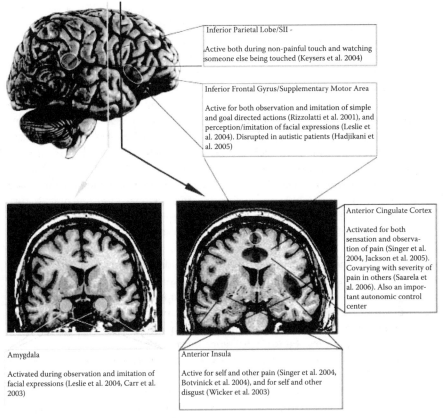

Figure 6.2   Brain regions contributing to "shared representations."

patient evidence suggests that brain lesions to the insula and amygdala (brain regions often associated with processing disgust and fear, respectively) selectively damage patients' abilities both to feel certain emotions and to identify them in others (Adolphs et al., 2005; Calder, Keane, Manes, Antoun, & Young, 2000). Based on these findings, researchers have proposed a "motor theory of social cognition" which posits that observers infer mental and emotional states of targets by covertly imitating the posture, facial expression, and other physical cues they give off,\ and inferring which internal states correspond with those cues (Gallese, 2003b; Gallese, Keysers, & Rizzolatti, 2004). This idea is also supported by studies of so-called "mirror neurons," a group of neurons first found in the inferior frontal gyrus of macaque monkeys. Remarkably, these cells respond not only when a monkey performs an action, but also when they observe another monkey performing the same action (Rizzolatti, Fogassi, & Gallese, 2001). An analogous mirror neuron system exists in humans and becomes engaged during both action and facial expression imitation (Carr, Iacoboni, Dubeau, Mazziotta, & Lenzi, 2003; Iacoboni et al., 1999). Neuroimaging studies have revealed that autistic patients have both structural and functional abnormalities in their mirror neuron system (Dapretto et al., 2006; Hadjikhani, Joseph, Snyder, & Tager-Flusberg, 2005). If one's own behavior and one's observation of other's emotional displays are as intimately connected as these data suggest (cf. Decety & Jackson, 2004), personality researchers could use similar paradigms to explore whether relational personality dispositions and disorders involve abnormalities in automatic mirroring or other aspects of empathic processing.

Researchers studying either shared representations/empathy or mental state inference have tended to draw pictures of social cognition that are overly dependent on one of these processes. That is, motor theorists believe that mental state inference is accomplished through self/other overlap (some low level empathic process), and proponents of theory of mind believe all social cognition is a result of complex inferences (Gallese, 2003a; Saxe, 2005). Such accounts, however, run into trouble both functionally and neuroanatomically. First, neither pure theory nor pure simulation could alone represent the highly varied ways in which humans understand each other. For example, when we read about a natural disaster that has taken the lives of a thousand people in a country we have never been to, we may feel sadness and even despair, but this emotion is driven by abstract representations of what those people are enduring. On the other hand, when significant others accidentally cut themselves a few feet from us, we respond to the visceral and visual cues we receive from them, and not to any rule-based processing. Different situations call for different patterns of deployment of social-cognitive processes (in these cases, mental state inference or empathy).

Furthermore, temporal, spatial, or social distance between people can moderate the extent to which we tend to use each of these processes in a manner similar to that outlined in Trope's levels of construal theory (Fujita, Henderson, Eng, Trope, & Liberman, 2006). Construal theory proposes that temporal distance changes people's responses to future events by changing the way they mentally represent them. The greater the temporal distance, the more likely people are to represent events in terms of a few abstract features rather than in terms of more concrete and nuanced details. In a similar manner, a perceiver unable to pay attention to the sources of someone else's behavior may make simplified, trait level attributions about that other person instead of making a situational correction ofr judgment. Similar changes in construal may be created by other situational factors, such as whether a perceiver likes the other person who is being focused on, or shares group identity with them, or is under stress while making judgments. Elaborating on how and in which cases internal and external context influences use of mental state inference and empathy will help provide an avenue to studying individual differences in the use of social-cognitive processes.

CONTEXTUAL INFLUENCES OF THE USE OF SOCIAL-COGNITIVE PROCESSES

Recent views of how social cognition operates have appealed to the idea of a "toolbox," comprised of multiple component processes that can be engaged flexibly depending on the cognitive and affective state and the relational context of a perceiver (Ames, 2004; Cloutier, Mason, & Macrae, 2005). The toolbox model, unlike single process conceptualizations, does not suffer the woes of that proverbial hammer owner who sees everything as a nail. We may employ different types of social cognition when thinking of our uncles, our spouses, and the British Prime Minister. Additionally, we may use different processes to understand a friend who is upset by their impending divorce and another who is upset about losing a parking space. Finally, our thinking about a friend's divorce may take on a different flavor, depending on whether we have experienced divorce ourselves. These examples represent context-dependent or if-then shifts in mental state inference and empathy based on one's relationship with the observed other, one's available psychological resources and expectations, and interactions between the perceiver and the observed other. In what follows, we will explore a growing literature on these context effects.

Effect of Relationship Between Self and Other on Social Cognition

Effects of In- versus Out-Group Membership of Other. People ascribe more flexibility and subtlety to the mental states of those they consider members of their own group—those they include in "we"—than those they view as members of different groups—those they view as "they." If a member of our family is rude to a waitress one night, while we may be nonplussed, we will probably seek out mitigating factors to explain their behavior (e.g., they just had a stressful day at work). That is, we will make a situational correction. On the other hand, we are more likely to attribute similar actions engaged in by distant or dissimilar others to permanent traits (i.e. ignorance, aggressiveness). We are also less likely to perceive secondary emotions such as embarrassment and pride in outgroup members (Leyens et al., 2000). These attributional distinctions not only apply to members of specific established outgroups, but also to novel groups. Gathering together several strangers and separating them according to their preference for Klee or Kandinsky is enough to create ingroup and outgroup biases. Minimal group paradigms demonstrate just how readily situational factors guide how we make inferences about others' behavior (Brewer, 1997).

One theory about the way in which group membership can affect social cognition is that people may use themselves as a template (hereby referred to as "simulation") to understand *some, but not all* other people. That is, while trying to infer the mental state of similar or close others, observers will spontaneously employ simulation, using themselves as a template to guide their perceptions of that target's state. Ames (2004) gave participants information about a target person's group membership (e.g., business school student) and preferences (e.g., being a fan of the television show South Park, enjoying a particular painting over another). These preferences either matched (similar other) or did not match (dissimilar other) those of the participant. In a subsequent social judgment task, participants read socially meaningful vignettes about the target and attributed mental states and motivations to them. When asked how they themselves would feel in such a situation, and how the stereotypical member of the target's group would feel, participants attributed their own mental states and motivations to similar targets, but used stereotypes to infer the mental states and motives of dissimilar others. The time that participants spent judging similar others was shorter if they made a judgment about themselves immediately beforehand than if they had made a judgment about a stereotypical member of their target's group. This effect was reversed for dissimilar others. Judgments about targets were wholly independent of the dimensions of similarity/difference along which they were primed, suggesting that once the use of simulation or stereotyping is primed, it remains engaged as the dominant method of inferring mental states in that target.

Are the processes we use to mentalize about similar and dissimilar others different in degree, or in kind? Ames' study leaves open the idea that people may be using both simulation and stereotype information for both in- and outgroup others, but using these in different *proportions* depending on the prime. A recent neuroimaging study sought to tease apart the processes underlying such mentalizing differences (Mitchell, et al., 2006). After being primed to believe that targets either did or did not share their political beliefs, participants were scanned while they guessed targets' opinions on various political issues (e.g., "would this person support their roommate if he/she came out as gay?"). Two regions in subjects' medial prefrontal cortex responded preferentially to similar and dissimilar targets, respectively. The more ventral area (vMPFC) engaged during inference about similar others has previously been identified during affective vs. cognitive mentalizing (Vollm et al., 2006). Thus, the findings of Mitchell et al. dovetail with the idea that affective attribution may rely more heavily on simulation than does cognitive attribution, which could also explain the relative infrequency of attributing emotions to outgroup members. This finding also suggests that people typically do not attend to distant others at a depth necessary to feel emotional empathy.

Competitiveness/Cooperativeness. Whether we view the other person as friend or foe, as on our side or against us, will likely affect our mental (and especially affective) representations of, and empathy toward, him or her. After leading subjects to expect cooperation or competition from a confederate, Lanzetta & Englis (1989) examined the subjects' emotional responses to videotapes of the confederate's displays of pleasure and distress. Skin conductance, heart rate and EMG data showed that expectations of cooperation promoted empathy, with subjects tensing when the confederate winced and relaxing when the confederate smiled. By contrast, expectations of competition promoted counterempathy, with subjects relaxing when the confederate winced, and tensing when the confederate smiled.

Neuroimaging experiments suggest similar effects of social stance towards a target on empathy and emotional processing (Singer, Kiebel, Winston, Dolan, & Frith, 2004). When subjects viewed pictures of faces they believed represented their partners in an economics game, activity in bilateral amygdala and insula (as referred to above, brain regions associated with fear and autonomic arousal) increased if the partner associated with that face cheated in the game. This finding dovetailed with studies of economics games in which unfair play by supposedly human confederates (but not by computers) correlated with insula activity (Rilling, Sanfey, Aronson, Nystrom, & Cohen, 2004b; Sanfey, Rilling, Aronson, Nystrom, & Cohen, 2003). In a subsequent study (Singer et al., 2006), subjects watched confederates who had proven to be either fair or unfair receive mild shocks. Brain areas previously seen to engage during "empathic pain" (including the insula and anterior cingulate cortex) were less engaged while subjects watched an unfair other receiving shocks. This finding converges with prior evidence that areas of the brain related to reward may become engaged while punishing unfair others (de Quervain et al. 2004).

These data suggest that our emotional reactions to and empathy towards others are crucially affected by whether they are for or against us. It remains unclear, however, whether mental state inference is affected in the same way. Does social threat make people think more or less deeply and with greater or lesser effort about the mental state of the threat source? Does keeping our enemies at arm's length cognitively, and thus making little effort to individualize them, help us compete with them efficiently? Studies probing whether fairness/unfairness affects the use of effortful mental state inference or stereotyping could explore whether social stance towards a person affects social cognition in the same way as group membership.

Familiarity. Neuroimaging research suggests that personal familiarity with someone else engages special processing steps. Consistently, brain areas in the social-cognitive network described above engage preferentially to pictures of familiar others, such as (female) subjects' children (Leibenluft, Gobbini, Harrison, & Haxby, 2004; Nitschke et al., 2004) or close friends. Seeing personally familiar faces more robustly engages parts of the mental state inference network described above than does viewing famous (known, but not personally familiar) faces (Haxby, Hoffman, & Gobbini, 2002; Hoffman & Haxby, 2000). Some (but not all) of these areas even respond to the acquired familiarity of a face presented repeatedly over the course of a scanning session (Kosaka et al., 2003). Increased engagement in these regions for familiar faces even occur in autistic patients, suggesting autistic patients' well-documented social-cognitive abnormalities may attenuate when they think of people who are familiar, and thus more salient, to them (Pierce, Haist, Sedaghat, & Courchesne, 2004). Perhaps, as Pierce et al. suggest, the need for help and support from familiar others makes their faces more important to autistic people, and this need could drive increased motivation to attend to those faces.

Increased activity for familiar, relative to unfamiliar, faces in the social cognition networks serving mental state inference is compelling. However, it is still unclear precisely what this differential neural activity means. Do we think about familiar others in a fundamentally different way? Or, do we simply pay more attention to them, thereby enhancing processing in the same cognitive and neural networks used to think about less familiar others? Are familiar others simply ingroup exemplars, or do we access information about them (i.e., personal knowledge and episodic memories) to engage in social-cognitive processes only possible with personal familiarity? Work in social psychology suggests that we may see people close to us as similar to us, as indexed by overlapping self-other representations (Mashek, Aron, & Boncimino, 2003). Having shared representations with familiar others may also be what buffers close others from stereotyping or attributional biases. For example, one study found that situational corrections (as described above) occur more for familiar than for non-familiar targets, but that familiarity only caused a difference in attribution patterns if targets were important to subjects (Idson & Mischel, 2001). It is still unclear how a familiar adversary, such as a former close friend who has betrayed one's trust, would affect social cognition. These data suggest that it is not just familiarity, but the motivation that familiarity can create, that makes us think more carefully about people we know well. In addition to influencing mental state inference processes, there is reason to speculate that familiarity may facilitate simulation and empathy.

HOW FEATURES OF THE PERCEIVER AFFECT SOCIAL COGNITION

The use of social-cognitive processes is likely to be influenced by what the perceiver brings to the situation as well as by the nature of his or her relationship with the target. Our expectations about how people should think and feel may cause us difficulties in understanding or empathizing with them if their actions conflict with these expectations. Additionally, our moods, motivations, and available cognitive resources may all affect our ability to, and preference for, employing particular social-cognitive processes.

Perceiver Expectancies. Within neuroimaging, perceiver expectancy effects have only been examined for the detection of distress. Sommerville and colleagues (Sommerville, Kim, Johnstone, Alexander, & Whalen, 2004) demonstrated that anxious observers were more likely to show amygdala engagement while looking at neutral faces and also more likely to attribute fear to these faces. In a complementary study (Kim et al., 2004), subjects were shown pictures of surprised faces, and each was prefaced with either a positive (she just won $500) or negative (she just lost $500) context. Perceivers' expectancies influenced their ratings as to whether the surprised face was positive or negative. Furthermore, amygdala activity was only present for trials in which perceivers rated the faces as negative, suggesting that brain activity was again influenced by the perceiver's expectations.

Kim et al.'s paradigm has a precedent in work on the power of expectancy in affecting the emotions we attribute to others. Carrol and Russell (1996) showed subjects emotionally salient vignettes, followed by faces showing incongruent emotional expressions (such as an anger-invoking story followed by a fearful face), and asked them identify what emotion the target was displaying. Participants' judgments reflected a greater reliance on vignettes that they had heard previously than on the actual facial display of emotion. We do not yet know whether expectancies alter our attention to a target's low-level cues (e.g., facial expressions, prosody) or exert their effect in a top-down fashion, biasing our judgment independent of the actual stimulus presented. Additionally, it is unclear how many facets of social cognition are affected by expectations. As the Lanzetta and Englis (1989) study described above suggests, empathic processes may also be affected by expectancies in that we may be more empathic toward people we expect to be on our side and less empathic, or even counter empathic, to those who pose a threat. Expectancy effects may not only apply to the labeling of affective cues, but also influence other aspects of mental state inference, such as inferences about the other person's motivation or the information to which the person has access. At least some evidence suggests that the ability to infer how much knowledge other people have is affected by how much knowledge perceivers have about a situation. When a target and perceiver's knowledge are incongruent, perceivers have to make effortful adjustments to correctly identify what the other person would know, and they often fail to do this effectively (Epley, Keysar, Van Boven, & Gilovich, 2004). Examining anchoring and adjustment through neuroimaging could provide information as to which components of mental state inference and empathy are affected by perceiver expectancy.

Cognitive Busyness and Stress. How we think about others is influenced by the amount of attention we have available to pay to them. Mental state inference is effortful and slow and cannot occur unless we have the resources to apply to it. One important example of attention-related shifts in social cognition is correction of the fundamental attribution error. When seeing someone behave a certain way, we tend to ascribe his or her behavior to a stable trait. Situational corrections do not occur as quickly or automatically as trait attributions. Gilbert et al. (1989) demonstrated this by showing participants silent films of a woman acting anxiously at an interview. Some were told that she was talking about a recent trip to Disney World (implying trait anxiety). Others were told she had just been asked an awkward and personal question (implying situational factors). The woman was rated was as less anxious in general when the situation explained her behavior, but this effect disappeared when raters were under competing cognitive load, suggesting that corrections require more cognitive resources than initial, trait judgments. Perhaps unsurprisingly, people tend to reserve effortful, situational corrections for similar others, individuating them and affording them dynamic motives and influences. Most of all, however, they use situational corrections when thinking about their own actions. Increased tendencies to simulate ingroup members, as well as to attending more closely to them are likely to underlie more complex judgments of their behavior.

Relational Motivation. Though our brains may be tuned by evolution towards understanding other intentional agents (Cosmides, 1989), the work cited above shows that a large part of social cognition involves controlled processes that are turned on and off as our cognitive foci vary. For example, purposefully attending to the mental states of others can make us think of them as more similar to ourselves (Davis, Conklin, Smith, & Luce, 1996), and make us more likely to engage in prosocial behavior towards them (Batson et al., 1988; Batson et al., 2003) as well as able to attune our emotions and attitudes toward them. We do not give these top-down benefits to all of our interaction partners. We may pay close attention to every postural shift and mannerism of a job interviewer, attempting to mine any relevant cues from their behavior, but ignore such information in the person sitting next to us on the train. We may also ignore the same interviewer's off-color joke, choosing not to form lasting opinions that may conflict with the relationship we are interested in maintaining with him or her. In other words, the social-relational goals we bring to a particular situation can importantly bias the information we choose to process about other people, changing our accuracy and resulting judgments as well as our emotional, attitudinal, and behavioral alignment with the interaction partner.

Here we will focus on two examples of motivated biases in social cognition: motivation to attend more closely to social cues during situations of high rejection threat, and motivation to ignore social cues when they threaten valued relationships. Though these examples may initially seem contradictory, they can be conceived of as different sides of the same general task: motivated cognition aimed at facilitating our social goals.

The need to be accepted and avoid rejection socially is among the strongest forces guiding our actions (Baumeister & Leary, 1995), and it makes sense that this same need should affect mental state inference and empathic processes. The task in social connection is to remain close to a potential source of harm. Those we view as most important to us can best satisfy our need for acceptance but also have the potential for inflict to the most harm if they reject us. Situations in which our social goals are at stake (e.g., job interviews, first dates) provide strong motivation to use all of our social-cognitive skills to accurately infer the mental states of those around us and accommodate our behavior accordingly. Some support for this claim is provided by a series of studies by Pickett and colleagues in which participants were induced to feel a high sense of social risk by being rejected by other players in a game. In subsequent interaction tasks, participants thus threatened were more accurate at decoding mental and emotional cues from facial expressions, and the quality of the interactions improved (Pickett, Gardner, & Knowles, 2004). Memory for what happened during the social interactions also improved (Gardner, Pickett, & Brewer, 2000).

Many high-risk social encounters afford us opportunities to advance goals and as such merit close attention to social cues. On the other hand, accurately perceiving the thoughts of others may sometimes be counterproductive. For example, knowing the negative or relationship-threatening thoughts of a romantic partner may cause negative patterns of thoughts and actions, and ultimately strain the relationship. With this in mind, Simpson and Ickes (1995) explored relationship situations that motivated social-cognitive *inaccuracy*. In one paradigm (Simpson, Orina, & Ickes, 2003), members of a couple were asked to make and discuss attractiveness ratings for opposite sex others in the presence of their partner. Afterwards, they watched videotapes of their session and noted their thoughts and feelings at different points. Their partners then viewed the videotapes and guessed the thoughts and feelings that the first member of the couple had reported. Inaccuracy was highest when the level of threat was *high* (pictures being judged were of very attractive others), the couples were *interdependent*, and the partner's actions were *ambiguous* and thus open to alternative explanations, including explanations that gave the partner the benefit of the doubt. *Inaccuracy* predicted greater satisfaction four months later, implying that under these circumstances inaccuracy was adaptive.

Simpson and Ickes framed motivated inaccuracy in terms of mechanistic social cognition, arguing that inferring relationship threatening information from a partner's behavior in a particular situation could lead perceivers to overattribute negative traits to that partner, or to disengage from situational corrections because of overpowering negative affect. Our previous discussion of the cognitive implications of viewing the target as an in- versus out-group member would suggest accurate identification of the situationally negative mind-set of a partner from threatening cues could reflect a perceiver's shift from viewing the partner as being in the ingroup (us) to the outgroup (them) and thus into stereotyping their behavior and becoming negatively biased in interpreting their subsequent actions. Perhaps motivated inaccuracy is a tool that maintains and is maintained by viewing the self and partner as interdependent components of a single unit versus as separate independent individuals. Accordingly, people who react maladaptively to relationship threat (e.g., women high in rejection sensitivity or with borderline personality disorder) may have trouble viewing others as consistently part of the in-group perhaps because they cannot easily "turn down" their attention to social cues in high-threat situations.

A person's dispositional tendency to attend to negative social information probably interacts with more general regulatory capacities to determine their response to particular social situations. For example, those individuals high in rejection sensitivity (and thus highly attentive to social threat) who could delay gratification as preschoolers demonstrated normal social functioning as teenagers and adults, whereas people high in rejection sensitivity and low in delay of gratification suffered from more social and self-esteem problems and showed features of borderline personality disorder (Ayduk, et al., 2000; Ayduk et al., under review). Furthermore, hostility after rejection has been found to increase when subjects reflect on that rejection in a "hot" vs. "cool" manner, suggesting a mechanism through which emotion regulation can help people overcome negative social outcomes (Ayduk, Mischel, & Downey, 2002). Studies probing the brain activity associated with processing negative social experiences will further guide understanding of how regulatory and social-cognitive mechanisms interact in low and high RS individuals.

INTEGRATING INDIVIDUAL DIFFERENCES: A 3-FACTOR MODEL

Could individual differences in relational dispositions—attachment style, rejection sensitivity, need to belong, self-esteem—involve individual differences in people's tendencies to deploy mental state inference or empathy to understand others or in their motivation to attend to social cues? Could severe abnormalities in one or other of these "uniquely social" cognitive processes underlie the difficulty with relationships suffered by borderline, avoidant, or antisocial personality disorders? Our contention is that research probing individual differences in the use of these social-cognitive processes will provide new insights about mechanisms giving rise to characteristic features of these dispositions and disorders. An especially intriguing idea is that particular contexts (such as social situations where the outcome is both important and uncertain, e.g., meeting a prospective dating partner or employer) could cause people to fail at adaptively deploying social-cognitive mechanisms. High arousal or anxiety, for example, can interfere with mental state inference or empathy in the same way that cognitive busyness does. People who feel threatened during social situations could, by this logic, revert to stereotyping the people around them in an if-then manner. Using neuroimaging and/or social-cognitive paradigms to study theoretically indicated contextual influences on the operation of social-cognitive processes in different personality dispositions and disorders will uncover mechanisms involved in creating and maintaining characteristic relationship patterns.

The focus thus far has been on identifying some ways in which the social and psychological context can influence the three dimensions of uniquely social cognition: simulation or empathy, mental state inference, motivated attention to understand a target. To tie together the effects of relatively stable individual differences and relatively transient context effects on these dimensions, we can think of them as constructing a three dimensional "social-cognitive space" in which we can plot different types of thinking about other people (Figure 6.3). For example, thinking about someone's false belief (as revealed by autism research paradigms) could recruit mental state inference and not empathy, whereas thinking about their pain could recruit empathy but not mental state inference (see Figure 6.3a). Furthermore, contextual factors (related to either the perceiver or target) pull people through this three-dimensional space in an if-then manner, causing the same individual to infer mental states in different ways at different times.

Figure 6.3b shows how we can depict examples from earlier in the chapter in terms of altering the use of different processes within this 3-D space. Rejection can cause people to attend more closely to social cues by increasing the motivation to be socially included (Pickett et al., 2004). Thinking of someone as fair or cooperative makes empathizing with that person's pain reflexive, whereas competitive and unfair others inspire less (or even reversed) empathic responses (Singer et al., 2004, 2006). Thinking about others while under cognitive load lessens our ability to make mental state inferences and increases our reliance on more automatic stereotyping or trait attributions (Gilbert et al., 1989).

Link to Personality Dispositions and Disorders. The forgoing discussion makes the case that the typical person's position on each axis of the social-cognitive space is sensitive to context. However, people vary in how sensitive to context their position in social-cognitive space is. Some people's behavior may be highly responsive to context, whereas others may be much less responsive, being, for example,

DIFFERENT TOOLKITS FOR DIFFERENT MIND-READERS 167

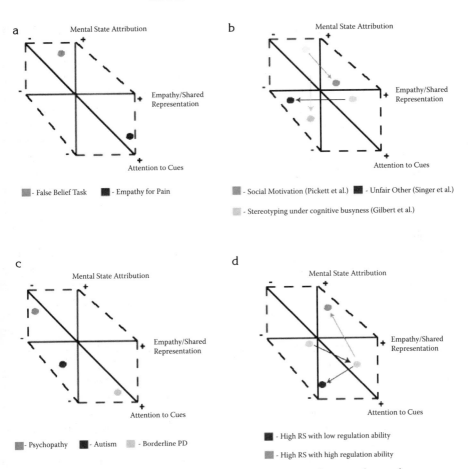

Figure 6.3 "Social-cognitive space" as defined by presence/absence of mental state representation, empathy/shared representations, and attention to social cues. Several levels of state and trait influences over social cognition are overlaid on the space as follows. 3a: Some basic social cognitive phenomena; 3b: state level effects that can alter the expression of these basic phenomena; 3c: clinical disorders that can alter the expression of basic social cognitive processes; 3d: an example of how multiple between trait-level variables can interact to determine the expression of social outcomes.

chronically irritable or chronically calm. People can also differ in the type of cues to which they are sensitive. Whereas narcissists may be highly motivated to attend to whether others are giving them the adulation to which they view themselves as entitled, those high in rejection sensitivity may be particularly motivated to attend to cues about whether others dislike them. Answers to the following questions are also likely to differ across individuals: How similar or familiar does someone have to be for me to empathize with them? How threatening does a social cue have to be for me to increase my attention towards it? Individual differences can shift people along social-cognitive axes in at least two ways: through affecting *set points* and *lability*.

Set Points. Some personality dispositions affect the *chronic* level or set-point of one or another social-cognitive variable. That is, some personality dispositions or disorders may make it more difficult or nearly impossible for people to move away from their social-cognitive set points on some dimensions. Autistic people are chronically poor at mental state inference and attention to social cues, but there is some evidence that their motor empathy (ability to imitate) is less affected. On the other hand, psychopaths, while able to attend to and understand mental states, are chronically unable to understand or react to the emotions of others. Thus dispositional differences in social behavior are likely to reflect differences in the depth and subtlety with which individuals assess other people's mental and emotional states. These dispositional differences in set point are displayed in Figure 6.3c.

Lability. Some personality dispositions involve variability or lability in one or another social-cognitive variable. For example, borderline personality disorder is characterized by unstable mood, identity, and relationships, with shifts in these keys aspects of functioning frequently triggered by social events. It is useful to consider this disorder in terms of Mischel's if..then model of personality with extreme shifts in the deployment of specific social-cognitive processes being triggered by subtle contextual shifts (as plotted in Figure 6.3d).

Link to Combinations of Dispositions. In addition to thinking about how individual relational dispositions can be mapped in social-cognitive space, it is also useful to consider how such dispositions can interact with other non-social forms of individual differences to influence position in social-cognitive space. Adapting the work of Ayduk and colleagues (2000, 2002) to our social-cognitive framework, we can consider high rejection sensitivity as a tendency to increase attention to negative social cues and perceive them more readily and more intensely. Once a rejection has been perceived, rejection sensitive people who are low in self-regulation ability respond "hotly," reducing their empathy towards the rejecting other and stereotyping them while responding with hostility. However, rejection sensitive people who are high in self-regulatory ability are able to avoid this, either by paying less attention to the cues or by considering the mental states/situations of their interaction partner.

A neuroimaging study by Taylor et al. (2006) finds evidence that converges with that of Ayduk et al. (2000). They explored emotion regulation ability as a function of the type of early experiences thought to give rise to rejection sensitivity and to poor self-regulatory competencies. People who had experienced risky childhoods (characterized by neglect and negative emotional patterns; see Repetti, Taylor, & Seeman, 2002) failed to show a previously documented negative correlation between right inferior frontal and amygdala activity during an emotional labeling task. For these individuals, thinking about emotional stimuli intensified rather than dampened their emotional responses to them. That is, they appeared at the neural level to be unable to impose a "cool" framework on "hot" stimuli, consistent with Ayduk et al.'s (2000) characterization of individuals high in rejection sensitivity and low in self-regulatory abilities.

A RESEARCH AGENDA FOR CHARACTERIZING PERSONALITY IN TERMS OF SOCIAL-COGNITIVE PROCESSES

A combination of behavioral and neuroimaging studies is needed to increase our understanding of how personality dispositions reflect the social-cognitive tools we have, as well as the contextualized way in we use these tools to understand and interact with other people. Individual difference measures could track the amount that people stereotype rejecting others, or employ situational corrections. Considering constructs such as rejection sensitivity in terms of the "if...then" use of different social-cognitive processes will inform our understanding of cognition, personality, and context by looking directly at their intersection. Dispositional differences in behavior almost certainly reflect patterned differences in cognition, and exploration of these cognitions is crucial to marrying these two disparate literatures (Bateman & Fonagy, 2004). The data analytic tools needed to capture Person × Context × social-cognitive process are now available in the form of multilevel models (Kenny, Kashy, Bolger, 1998). A richer account of the use of social-cognitive processes as they relate to both context and individual differences could help create assessment and treatment methods more tailored to particular social-cognitive difficulties, which would increase the clinical relevance of social cognition research.

The field reviewed in this chapter is growing explosively. Newer, richer accounts of the cognitive processes evolved to facilitate and manage social interactions are emerging as social-psychological and neuroscientific approaches are integrated more subtly and completely. Our hope is that soon this literature will become relevant not only to studies of general social cognition, but to individual differences in the ways that social-cognitive processes operate across situations. By increasing sensitivity to both the power of the situation and the dispositions that people bring into them, social-cognitive neuroscience can continue enriching its account of the most uniquely human thought processes that we possess—those involved in understanding what is going on in the minds of other humans. These processes are the tools of social relations.

REFERENCES

Adolphs, R., Gosselin, F., Buchanan, T. W., Tranel, D., Schyns, P., & Damasio, A. R. (2005). A mechanism for impaired fear recognition after amygdala damage. *Nature*, 433(7021), 68–72.

Allison, T., Puce, A., & McCarthy, G. (2000). Social perception from visual cues: role of the STS region. *Trends in Cognitive Science*, 4(7), 267–278.

Allport, G. W. (1954). *The nature of prejudice*. Cambridge, MA: Addison Wesley Publishing Co.

Ames, D. R. (2004). Inside the mind reader's tool kit: Projection and stereotyping in mental state inference. *Journal of Personality and Social Psychology*, 87(3), 340–353.

Ayduk, O., Mendoza-Denton, R., Mischel, W., Downey, G., Peake, P. K., & Rodriguez, M. (2000). Regulating the interpersonal self: Strategic self-regulation for coping with rejection sensitivity. *Journal of Personality and Social Psychology, 79*(5), 776–792.

Ayduk, O., Mischel, W., & Downey, G. (2002). Attentional mechanisms linking rejection to hostile reactivity: The role of "hot" versus "cool" focus. *Psychological Science, 13*(5), 443–448.

Baron-Cohen, S. (1994). *Mindblindness.* Cambridge, Mass: MIT Press.

Baron-Cohen, S., Ring, H. A., Wheelwright, S., Bullmore, E. T., Brammer, M. J., Simmons, A., et al. (1999). Social intelligence in the normal and autistic brain: An fMRI study. *European Journal of Neuroscience, 11*(6), 1891–1898.

Bartz, J., & Hollander, E. (2006). The neuroscience of affiliation: Forging links between basic and clinical research on neuropeptides and social behavior. *Hormones and Behavior, 50*(4), 518–528.

Bateman, A. W., & Fonagy, P. (2004). Mentalization-based treatment of BPD. *Journal of Personal Disorder, 18*(1), 36–51.

Batson, C. D., Dyck, J. L., Brandt, J. R., Batson, J. G., Powell, A. L., McMaster, M. R., et al. (1988). Five studies testing two new egoistic alternatives to the empathy-altruism hypothesis. *Journal of Personality and Social Psychology, 55*(1), 52–77.

Batson, C. D., Lishner, D. A., Carpenter, A., Dulin, L., Harjusola-Webb, S., Stocks, E. L., et al. (2003). "...As you would have them do unto you": Does imagining yourself in the other's place stimulate moral action? *Personality and Social Psychology Bulletin, 29*(9), 1190–1201.

Baumeister, R. F., & Leary, M. R. (1995). The need to belong: Desire for interpersonal attachments as a fundamental human motivation. *Psychological Bulletin, 117*(3), 497–529.

Blair, R. J. (2005). Responding to the emotions of others: Dissociating forms of empathy through the study of typical and psychiatric populations. *Conscious and Cognition, 14*(4), 698–718.

Botvinick, M., Jha, A. P., Bylsma, L. M., Fabian, S. A., Solomon, P. E., & Prkachin, K. M. (2005). Viewing facial expressions of pain engages cortical areas involved in the direct experience of pain. *Neuroimage, 25*(1), 312–319.

Brewer, M. (1997). The social psychology of intergroup relations: Can research inform practice? *Journal of Social Issues, 53*(1).

Brunet, E., Sarfati, Y., Hardy-Bayle, M. C., & Decety, J. (2000). A PET investigation of the attribution of intentions with a nonverbal task. *Neuroimage, 11*(2), 157–166.

Calder, A. J., Keane, J., Manes, F., Antoun, N., & Young, A. W. (2000). Impaired recognition and experience of disgust following brain injury. *Nature Neuroscience, 3*(11), 1077–1078.

Canli, T. (2004). Functional brain mapping of extraversion and neuroticism: learning from individual differences in emotion processing. *Journal of Personality, 72*(6), 1105–1132.

Canli, T., Sivers, H., Whitfield, S. L., Gotlib, I. H., & Gabrieli, J. D. (2002). Amygdala response to happy faces as a function of extraversion. *Science, 296*(5576), 2191.

Carr, L., Iacoboni, M., Dubeau, M. C., Mazziotta, J. C., & Lenzi, G. L. (2003). Neural mechanisms of empathy in humans: A relay from neural systems for imitation to limbic areas. *Proceedings of the National Academy of Science, U S A, 100*(9), 5497–5502.

Carroll, J. M., & Russell, J. A. (1996). Do facial expressions signal specific emotions? Judging emotion from the face in context. *Journal of Personality and Social Psychology, 70*(2), 205–218.

Castelli, F., Happe, F., Frith, U., & Frith, C. (2000). Movement and mind: A functional imaging study of perception and interpretation of complex intentional movement patterns. *Neuroimage, 12*(3), 314–325.

Cavanna, A. E., & Trimble, M. R. (2006). The precuneus: A review of its functional anatomy and behavioural correlates. *Brain, 129*(Pt 3), 564–583.
Cloutier, J., Mason, M. F., & Macrae, C. N. (2005). The perceptual determinants of person construal: Reopening the social-cognitive toolbox. *Journal of Personality and Social Psychology, 88*(6), 885–894.
Cosmides, L. (1989). The logic of social exchange: Has natural selection shaped how humans reason? Studies with the Wason selection task. *Cognition, 31*(3), 187–276.
Dakin, S., & Frith, U. (2005). Vagaries of visual perception in autism. *Neuron, 48*(3), 497–507.
Dapretto, M., Davies, M. S., Pfeifer, J. H., Scott, A. A., Sigman, M., Bookheimer, S. Y., et al. (2006). Understanding emotions in others: Mirror neuron dysfunction in children with autism spectrum disorders. *Nature Neuroscience, 9*(1), 28–30.
Davis, M. H., Conklin, L., Smith, A., & Luce, C. (1996). Effect of perspective taking on the cognitive representation of persons: A merging of self and other. *Journal of Personality and Social Psychology, 70*(4), 713–726.
Decety, J., & Jackson, P. L. (2004). The functional architecture of human empathy. *Behavior Cognition Neuroscience Review, 3*(2), 71–100.
Decety, J., Jackson, P. L., Sommerville, J. A., Chaminade, T., & Meltzoff, A. N. (2004). The neural bases of cooperation and competition: An fMRI investigation. *Neuroimage, 23*(2), 744–751.
Dennett, D. (1987). *The Intentional Stance*. Cambridge, MA: MIT Press.
de Quervain, D. J., Fischbacher, U., Treyer, V., Schellhammer, M., Schnyder, U., Buck, A., et al. (2004). The neural basis of altruistic punishment. *Science, 305*(5688), 1254–1258.
Downey, G., & Feldman, S. (1996). The implications of rejection sensitivity for intimate relationships. *Journal of Personality and Social Psychology, 70*, 1327–1343.
Dunbar, R. (2004). Gossip in evolutionary perspective. *Review of General Psychology, 8*, 80–100.
Epley, N., Keysar, B., Van Boven, L., & Gilovich, T. (2004). Perspective taking as egocentric anchoring and adjustment. *Journal of Personality and Social Psychology, 87*(3), 327–339.
Fletcher, P. C., Frith, C. D., Baker, S. C., Shallice, T., Frackowiak, R. S., & Dolan, R. J. (1995). The mind's eye—Precuneus activation in memory-related imagery. *Neuroimage, 2*(3), 195–200.
Fletcher, P. C., Happe, F., Frith, U., Baker, S. C., Dolan, R. J., Frackowiak, R. S., et al. (1995). Other minds in the brain: A functional imaging study of "theory of mind" in story comprehension. *Cognition, 57*(2), 109–128.
Frith, U., & Happe, F. (1994). Autism: Beyond "theory of mind". *Cognition, 50*(1–3), 115–132.
Fujita, K., Henderson, M. D., Eng, J., Trope, Y., & Liberman, N. (2006). Spatial distance and mental construal of social events. *Psychological Science, 17*(4), 278–282.
Gallagher, H. L., Happe, F., Brunswick, N., Fletcher, P. C., Frith, U., & Frith, C. D. (2000). Reading the mind in cartoons and stories: An fMRI study of 'theory of mind' in verbal and nonverbal tasks. *Neuropsychologia, 38*(1), 11–21.
Gallagher, H. L., Jack, A. I., Roepstorff, A., & Frith, C. D. (2002). Imaging the intentional stance in a competitive game. *Neuroimage, 16*(3 Pt 1), 814–821.
Gallese, V. (2003a). The manifold nature of interpersonal relations: The quest for a common mechanism. *Philosophical Transactions of the Royal Society London: B Biological Science, 358*(1431), 517–528.
Gallese, V. (2003b). The roots of empathy: The shared manifold hypothesis and the neural basis of intersubjectivity. *Psychopathology, 36*(4), 171–180.

Gallese, V., Keysers, C., & Rizzolatti, G. (2004). A unifying view of the basis of social cognition. *Trends in Cognitive Science, 8*(9), 396–403.
Gardner, W. L., Pickett, C. L., & Brewer, M. (2000). Social exclusion and selective memory: How the need to belong influences memory for social events. *Personality & Social Psychology Bulletin, 26,* 486–496.
Gilbert, D., Pelham, B., & Krull, D. (1989). On cognitive busyness: When person perceivers meet persons perceived. *Journal of Personality & Social Psychology, 54*(5), 733–740.
Goel, V., Grafman, J., Sadato, N., & Hallett, M. (1995). Modeling other minds. *Neuroreport, 6*(13), 1741–1746.
Hadjikhani, N., Joseph, R. M., Snyder, J., & Tager-Flusberg, H. (2006). Anatomical Differences in the Mirror Neuron System and Social Cognition Network in Autism. *Cerebral Cortex, 16,* 1276–1282.
Harris, L. T., Todorov, A., & Fiske, S. T. (2005). Attributions on the brain: Neuro-imaging dispositional inferences, beyond theory of mind. *Neuroimage, 28*(4), 763–769.
Haxby, J. V., Hoffman, E. A., & Gobbini, M. I. (2002). Human neural systems for face recognition and social communication. *Biological Psychiatry, 51*(1), 59–67.
Henson, R. (2005). What can functional neuroimaging tell the experimental psychologist? *Quarterly Journal of Experimental Psychol A, 58*(2), 193–233.
Hoffman, E. A., & Haxby, J. V. (2000). Distinct representations of eye gaze and identity in the distributed human neural system for face perception. *Nature Neuroscience, 3*(1), 80–84.
Hynes, C. A., Baird, A. A., & Grafton, S. T. (2006). Differential role of the orbital frontal lobe in emotional versus cognitive perspective-taking. *Neuropsychologia, 44*(3), 374–383.
Iacoboni, M., Woods, R. P., Brass, M., Bekkering, H., Mazziotta, J. C., & Rizzolatti, G. (1999). Cortical mechanisms of human imitation. *Science, 286*(5449), 2526–2528.
Idson, L. C., & Mischel, W. (2001). The personality of familiar and significant people: The lay perceiver as a social-cognitive theorist. *Journal of Personality and Social Psychology, 80*(4), 585–596.
Jackson, P. L., Brunet, E., Meltzoff, A. N., & Decety, J. (2006). Empathy examined through the neural mechanisms involved in imagining how I feel versus how you feel pain. *Neuropsychologia, 44*(5), 752–761.
Jackson, P. L., Meltzoff, A. N., & Decety, J. (2005). How do we perceive the pain of others? A window into the neural processes involved in empathy. *Neuroimage, 24*(3), 771–779.
Keysers, C., Wicker, B., Gazzola, V., Anton, J. L., Fogassi, L., & Gallese, V. (2004). A touching sight: SII/PV activation during the observation and experience of touch. *Neuron, 42*(2), 335–346.
Kim, H., Somerville, L. H., Johnstone, T., Polis, S., Alexander, A. L., Shin, L. M., et al. (2004). Contextual modulation of amygdala responsivity to surprised faces. *Journal of Cognitive Neuroscience, 16*(10), 1730–1745.
Kosaka, H., Omori, M., Iidaka, T., Murata, T., Shimoyama, T., Okada, T., et al. (2003). Neural substrates participating in acquisition of facial familiarity: An fMRI study. *Neuroimage, 20*(3), 1734–1742.
Kosslyn, S. M., & Ochsner, K. N. (1994). In search of occipital activation during visual mental imagery. *Trends in Neuroscience, 17*(7), 290–292.
Kosslyn, S. M., Thompson, W. L., & Alpert, N. M. (1997). Neural systems shared by visual imagery and visual perception: A positron emission tomography study. *Neuroimage, 6*(4), 320–334.
Kross, E., Egner, T., Ochsner, K. N., Hirsch, J., & Downey, G. (in press). Neural dynamics of rejection sensitivity. *Journal of Cognitive Neuroscience.*

Lanzetta, J. T., & Englis, B. G. (1989). Expectations of cooperation and competition and their effects on observers vicarious emotional responses. *Journal of Personality and Social Psychology, 56*(4), 543.

Leibenluft, E., Gobbini, M. I., Harrison, T., & Haxby, J. V. (2004). Mothers' neural activation in response to pictures of their children and other children. *Biological Psychiatry, 56*(4), 225–232.

Leslie, A. M. (1994). Pretending and believing: Issues in the theory of ToMM. *Cognition, 50*(1-3), 211–238.

Leslie, A. M., Friedman, O., & German, T. P. (2004). Core mechanisms in "theory of mind." *Trends in Cognitive Science, 8*(12), 528–533.

Leslie, K. R., Johnson-Frey, S. H., & Grafton, S. T. (2004). Functional imaging of face and hand imitation: Towards a motor theory of empathy. *Neuroimage, 21*(2), 601–607.

Leyens, J., Rodriguez-Torres, R., Vaes, J., Demoulin, S., Rodriguez-Perez, A., & Gaunt, R. (2000). The emotional side of prejudice: The attribution of secondary emotions to ingroups and outgroups. *Personality & Social Psychology Review, 4*(2), 186–197.

Mashek, D. J., Aron, A., & Boncimino, M. (2003). Confusions of self with close others. *Personality and Social Psychology Bulletin, 29*(3), 382–392.

Mason, M. F., & Macrae, C. N. (2004). Categorizing and individuating others: The neural substrates of person perception. *Journal of Cognitive Neuroscience, 16*(10), 1785–1795.

McCabe, K., Houser, D., Ryan, L., Smith, V., & Trouard, T. (2001). A functional imaging study of cooperation in two-person reciprocal exchange. *Proceedings of the National Academy of Science U S A, 98*(20), 11832–11835.

Metcalfe, J., & Mischel, W. (1999). A hot/cool-system analysis of delay of gratification: Dynamics of willpower. *Psychological Review, 106*(1), 3–19.

Mischel, W. (1973). Towards a cognitive social learning reconceptualization of personality. *Psychological Review, 8*, 252–283.

Mischel, W., & Shoda, Y. (1995). A cognitive-affective system theory of personality: Reconceptualizing situations, dispositions, dynamics, and invariance in personality structure. *Psychological Review, 102*(2), 246–268.

Mitchell, J. P., Banaji, M. R., & Macrae, C. N. (2005). The link between social cognition and self-referential thought in the medial prefrontal cortex. *Journal of Cognitive Neuroscience, 17*(8), 1306–1315.

Mitchell, J. P., Cloutier, J., Banaji, M. R., & Macrae, C. N. (2006). Medial prefrontal dissociations during processing of trait diagnostic and nondiagnostic person information. *Social Cognitive Affective Neuroscience, 1*, 49–55.

Mitchell, J. P., Heatherton, T. F., & Macrae, C. N. (2002). Distinct neural systems subserve person and object knowledge. *Proceedings of the National Academy of Science U S A, 99*(23), 15238–15243.

Mitchell, J. P., Macrae, C. N., & Banaji, M. R. (2006). Dissociable medial prefrontal contributions to judgments of similar and dissimilar others. *Neuron, 50*, 1–9.

Mitchell, J. P., Macrae, C. N., & Banaji, M. R. (2005). Forming impressions of people versus inanimate objects: Social-cognitive processing in the medial prefrontal cortex. *Neuroimage, 26*(1), 251–257.

Montague, P. R., Berns, G. S., Cohen, J. D., McClure, S. M., Pagnoni, G., Dhamala, M., et al. (2002). Hyperscanning: Simultaneous fMRI during linked social interactions. *Neuroimage, 16*(4), 1159–1164.

Morrison, I., Lloyd, D., di Pellegrino, G., & Roberts, N. (2004). Vicarious responses to pain in anterior cingulate cortex: Is empathy a multisensory issue? *Cognitive Affective Behavioral Neurosci, 4*(2), 270–278.

Neumann, R., & Strack, F. (2000). "Mood contagion": The automatic transfer of mood between persons. *Journal of Personality and Social Psychology, 79*(2), 211–223.

Niedenthal, P., & Brauer, M. (2001). When did her smile drop? Facial mimicry and the influences of emotional state on the detection of change in emotional expression. *Cognition & Emotion, 15*(6), 853–864.

Nitschke, J. B., Nelson, E. E., Rusch, B. D., Fox, A. S., Oakes, T. R., & Davidson, R. J. (2004). Orbitofrontal cortex tracks positive mood in mothers viewing pictures of their newborn infants. *Neuroimage, 21*(2), 583–592.

Ochsner, K. N., Knierim, K., Ludlow, D. H., Hanelin, J., Ramachandran, T., Glover, G., et al. (2004). Reflecting upon feelings: An fMRI study of neural systems supporting the attribution of emotion to self and other. *Journal of Cognitive Neuroscience, 16*(10), 1746–1772.

Pelphrey, K. A., Morris, J. P., & McCarthy, G. (2004). Grasping the intentions of others: The perceived intentionality of an action influences activity in the superior temporal sulcus during social perception. *Journal of Cognitive Neuroscience, 16*(10), 1706–1716.

Pickett, C. L., Gardner, W. L., & Knowles, M. (2004). Getting a cue: The need to belong and enhanced sensitivity to social cues. *Personality and Social Psychology Bulletin, 30*(9), 1095–1107.

Pierce, K., Haist, F., Sedaghat, F., & Courchesne, E. (2004). The brain response to personally familiar faces in autism: Findings of fusiform activity and beyond. *Brain, 127*(Pt 12), 2703–2716.

Raine, A., Lencz, T., Bihrle, S., LaCasse, L., & Colletti, P. (2000). Reduced prefrontal gray matter volume and reduced autonomic activity in antisocial personality disorder. *Archives of General Psychiatry, 57*(2), 119–127; discussion 128–119.

Reis, H., & Downey, G. (1999). Social cognition in relationships: Building bridges between two literatures. *Social Cognition, 17*, 97–117.

Repetti, R. L., Taylor, S. E., & Seeman, T. E. (2002). Risky families: Family social environments and the mental and physical health of offspring. *Psychological Bulletin, 128*(2), 330–366.

Rilling, J. K., Sanfey, A. G., Aronson, J. A., Nystrom, L. E., & Cohen, J. D. (2004a). Opposing BOLD responses to reciprocated and unreciprocated altruism in putative reward pathways. *Neuroreport, 15*(16), 2539–2543.

Rilling, J. K., Sanfey, A. G., Aronson, J. A., Nystrom, L. E., & Cohen, J. D. (2004b). The neural correlates of theory of mind within interpersonal interactions. *Neuroimage, 22*(4), 1694–1703.

Rizzolatti, G., Fogassi, L., & Gallese, V. (2001). Neurophysiological mechanisms underlying the understanding and imitation of action. *Nature Reviews Neuroscience, 2*(9), 661–670.

Saarela, M. V., Hlushchuk, Y., Williams, A. C., Schurmann, M., Kalso, E., & Hari, R. (2007). The compassionate brain: Humans detect intensity of pain from another's face. *Cerebral Cortex, 17*(1), 230–237.

Sanfey, A. G., Rilling, J. K., Aronson, J. A., Nystrom, L. E., & Cohen, J. D. (2003). The neural basis of economic decision-making in the Ultimatum Game. *Science, 300*(5626), 1755–1758.

Saxe, R. (2005). Against simulation: The argument from error. *Trends in Cognitive Science, 9*(4), 174–179.

Saxe, R., & Kanwisher, N. (2003). People thinking about thinking people. The role of the temporo-parietal junction in "theory of mind". *Neuroimage, 19*(4), 1835–1842.

Simpson, J. A. (1995). When the head protects the heart: Empathic accuracy in dating relationships. *Journal of Personality and Social Psychology, 69*(4), 629–641.

Simpson, J. A., Orina, M. M., & Ickes, W. (2003). When accuracy hurts, and when it helps: A test of the empathic accuracy model in marital interactions. *Journal of Personality and Social Psychology, 85*(5), 881–893.

Singer, T., Kiebel, S. J., Winston, J. S., Dolan, R. J., & Frith, C. D. (2004). Brain responses to the acquired moral status of faces. *Neuron, 41*(4), 653–662.
Singer, T., Seymour, B., O'Doherty, J., Kaube, H., Dolan, R. J., & Frith, C. D. (2004). Empathy for pain involves the affective but not sensory components of pain. *Science, 303*(5661), 1157–1162.
Singer, T., Seymour, B., O'Doherty, J. P., Stephan, K. E., Dolan, R. J., & Frith, C. D. (2006). Empathic neural responses are modulated by the perceived fairness of others. *Nature, 439*(7075), 466–469.
Somerville, L. H., Kim, H., Johnstone, T., Alexander, A. L., & Whalen, P. J. (2004). Human amygdala responses during presentation of happy and neutral faces: Correlations with state anxiety. *Biological Psychiatry, 55*(9), 897–903.
Taylor, S. E., Eisenberger, N. I., Saxbe, D., Lehman, B. J., & Lieberman, M. D. (2006). Neural responses to emotional stimuli are associated with childhood family stress. *Biological Psychiatry.*
Thompson, J. C., Clarke, M., Stewart, T., & Puce, A. (2005). Configural processing of biological motion in human superior temporal sulcus. *Journal of Neuroscience, 25*(39), 9059–9066.
Uleman, J. S., & Moskowitz, G. B. (1994). Unintended effects of goals on unintended inferences. *Journal of Personality and Social Psychology, 66*(3), 490–501.
Vogeley, K., Bussfeld, P., Newen, A., Herrmann, S., Happe, F., Falkai, P., et al. (2001). Mind reading: Neural mechanisms of theory of mind and self-perspective. *Neuroimage, 14*(1 Pt 1), 170–181.
Vogt, B. A., Vogt, L., & Laureys, S. (2006). Cytology and functionally correlated circuits of human posterior cingulate areas. *Neuroimage, 29*(2), 452–466.
Vollm, B. A., Taylor, A. N., Richardson, P., Corcoran, R., Stirling, J., McKie, S., et al. (2006). Neuronal correlates of theory of mind and empathy: A functional magnetic resonance imaging study in a nonverbal task. *Neuroimage, 29*(1), 90–98.
Vonnegut, K. (1965). *Wampeters, foma, & granfalloons (Opinions).* New York: Dell Publishing.
Wang, A. T., Lee, S. S., Sigman, M., & Dapretto, M. (2006). Neural basis of irony comprehension in children with autism: The role of prosody and context. *Brain, 129*(Pt 4), 932–943.
Wicker, B., Keysers, C., Plailly, J., Royet, J. P., Gallese, V., & Rizzolatti, G. (2003). Both of us disgusted in my insula: The common neural basis of seeing and feeling disgust. *Neuron, 40*(3), 655–664.
Winter, L., Uleman, J. S., & Cunniff, C. (1985). How automatic are social judgments? *Journal of Personality and Social Psychology, 49*(4), 904–917.

# 7

Personality, Individuality, and Social Identity

MICHAEL HOGG

Claremont Graduate University

The study of collective behavior has a long and illustrious history in social psychology. It was the study of collective behavior that very much defined the new discipline of social psychology at its inception in the late 19th and early 20th century, and collective phenomena such as crowds, riots, deindividuation, and particularly group processes and intergroup relations have maintained a high profile ever since. However, at the same time social psychology has also focused on the self-contained individual person who processes and represents information, has feelings, engages in behavior, and interacts with individual others, an approach that often treats people as being fundamentally different from one another and having unique biographies and enduring personalities.

Because these latter individual and interpersonal concerns appear more focused on what happens in the head of the individual, they have come to characterize social psychology and are often invoked as the basic unit of analysis and level of explanation to make sense of collective and group behaviors. As a result, there is an ongoing tension, and often a metatheoretical disagreement, between social psychologists who feel you can explain collective behavior in terms of individual personality and those who believe you cannot. Over the past 40 years or so the most systematic, enduring, and sometimes strident, critique of personality explanations of collective and group phenomena has come from European social psychology—a critique that has framed the development of a number of key European social psychological theories, in particular minority influence (e.g., Moscovici, 1976; see Martin & Hewstone, 2003), social representations (e.g., Moscovici, 1988; see Lorenzi-Cioldi & Clémence, 2001), and social identity theory (e.g., Tajfel & Turner, 1979; see Hogg 2006).

In this chapter I focus only on social identity theory, broadly conceived, adopting its characterization of personality and individuality and describing how it views the relationship between personality/individuality and collective behavior. To do this, I first give some historical background as to how the study of collective and group behavior has been positioned in social psychology, with a particular emphasis on the European critique of personality explanations (also see Hogg, 2001a; Hogg & Williams, 2000; Turner, Reynolds, Haslam, & Veenstra, 2006). I feel this is important because it gives some insight into the way that social identity has conceived of personality.

I then describe how social identity theory has developed in this metatheoretical context and give a very brief overview of relevant aspects of the theory. The rest of the chapter textures the social identity perspective on the relationship between individuality/personality and the group, building in recent developments, clarifying misunderstandings, and identifying issues and directions for current and future research. In recent years there has been renewed interest among intergroup and social identity researchers in re-examining the relationship between individuality and the group—see Postmes and Jetten (2006) for a recent collection of chapters on this topic.

In this chapter I use the terms *personality* and *individuality* largely interchangeably, which is consistent with broad contemporary definitions of personality; for example Snyder and Cantor write "personality (loosely defined in terms of regularities in feeling, thought, and action that are characteristic of an individual)" (Snyder & Cantor, 1998, p. 635). Snyder & Ickes (1985) take this notion of regularities one step further by drawing a distinction between dispositional, interactional, and situational perspectives on personality.

Dispositional perspectives trace regularities to invariant properties of the individual person; this is very much the traditional perspective on personality (e.g., McCrae & John, 1992). *Interactional* perspectives acknowledge that situations unlock dispositions and allow them to be expressed (e.g., Baron & Boudreau, 1987); regularities arise because a situation prevails that enables the expression of a particular disposition. *Situational* perspectives attribute regularities in behavior to the fact that a person seeks out and remains in the same setting (e.g., Buss, 1987); people and their dispositions shape the settings that they find themselves in. Adopting the language of motivation, Snyder and Cantor characterize these three perspectives in terms of "individuals 'moved' by dispositions and 'moved' by situations, individuals 'moving' their social worlds" (Snyder & Cantor, 1998, p. 666).

From the perspective of the present chapter, although interactional and situational perspectives on personality view the social context as having an important influence on behavior, these perspectives share with the more traditional dispositional perspective a conception of the person as a largely idiosyncratic constellation of personal attributes and dispositions. As I hope to show below, it is this view of the person that some believe is problematic for explanations of group, intergroup, and collective behaviors as well as the collective nature of self.

INDIVIDUAL VERSUS COLLECTIVE IN SOCIAL PSYCHOLOGY

Wundt is generally viewed as the founder of modern psychology as an extension of the natural sciences; he established a psychological laboratory in Leipzig in 1879 and launched a journal, *Philosophische Studien*, in 1881(for historical overviews of social psychology see Farr, 1996; Jones, 1998). However, between 1900 and 1920 he also wrote ten volumes of social psychology, which he called *Völkerpsychologie*, the psychology of a community or group of individuals (a *Volk*). For Wundt, social psychology was the study of "those mental products which are created by a community of human life and are, therefore, inexplicable in terms merely of individual consciousness since they presuppose the reciprocal action of many" (Wundt, 1916, p.3). Wundt's social psychology dealt with collective phenomena, such as language, religion, customs, and myth, that could not, according to Wundt, be understood in terms of the psychology of the isolated individual, the latter being his experimental psychology.

Wundt's collectivist approach to social psychology is evident in early nonexperimental social psychology's analysis of the crowd, for example, LeBon's (1908) notion that the crowd caused a collective "racial unconscious"—containing primitive, aggressive, and antisocial instincts—to take hold, and McDougall's (1921) notion that out of the interaction of individuals there arose a "group mind" that had a reality and existence that was qualitatively distinct from the isolated individuals making up the group. Subsequent experimental social psychological research has indeed confirmed that human interaction produces emergent properties that cannot be properly understood by focusing on the psychology of the isolated individual; for example, Sherif's (1936) research on the emergence of norms, some of Asch's (1952) research on conformity to norms, and research on the emergence of social representations (see Lorenzi-Cioldi & Clémence, 2001).

Durkheim (1898), who was influenced by Wundt, agreed that collective phenomena could not be explained in terms of individual psychology. However, he also believed that such phenomena were not the province of psychology at all, but of the new discipline of sociology, which he sometimes called "collective psychology." Durkheim separated sociology from psychology, placing the psychology of collective phenomena in sociology and the psychology of the individual in psychology—an early disciplinary separation that, according to Farr (1996), helped create a psychological social psychology that prioritized the individual as the level of explanation of collective and group phenomena. The separation of sociology from psychology was complete by about 1925 (Manicas, 1987), separating social psychology and in particular the study of groups from its collectivist past.

Psychology's version of social psychology quickly had an uphill battle to promote collective behavior and the group as a separate level of analysis to personality and the individual. For example, although McDougall's "group mind" was not intended to refer to an extra-psychological entity, critics interpreted it in this way and were successfully able to discredit McDougall's approach and, by association, all collectivist perspectives in social psychology. Many consider the battle to have been lost with Floyd Allport's, authoritative and far reaching dictum that "There is no psychology of groups which is not essentially and entirely a psychology of individuals" (Allport, 1924, p. 4; see Graumann, 1986).

This metatheoretical framework has ensured that most subsequent social psychology of collective phenomena such as groups and intergroup relations has actually been a psychology of the individual person or of interpersonal interaction in dyads or small face-to-face aggregates (see Billig, 1976; Hogg, 1993; Taylor & Brown, 1979; Turner, 1982). For example, the substantial topic of group dynamics, which was dominant from the 1940s into the 1960s (see Shaw, 1981) and had its roots in Lewin's potentially collectivist field theory (e.g., Lewin, 1952), is essentially a study of interpersonal interaction in small face-to-face groups; and two of the major theories of prejudice and discrimination, the authoritarian personality (Adorno, Frenkel-Brunswick, Levinson, & Sanford, 1950) and the frustration-aggression hypothesis (Dollard, Doob, Miller, Mowrer, & Sears, 1939), were explanations in terms of dispositions and personality dynamics (see Billig, 1976). This agenda and emphasis has made it difficult to study large scale social categories, intergroup relations, or the collective self without resorting to personality, the individual, or largely dyadic interaction as the level of explanation.

THE PROBLEM OF REDUCTIONISM

The principal problem that some social psychologists see with this kind of approach to the explanation of group and collective phenomena is one of level of explanation (e.g., Doise, 1986; also see Abrams & Hogg, 2004; Tajfel, 1972a; Turner & Oakes, 1986): It is a reductionist metatheory. The feeling is that if one tries to explain group and collective phenomena in terms exclusively of the individual, individual personality, or interpersonal interaction, many aspects of group behavior are left inadequately explained. It is a bit like asking why drivers stop at stop lights and being given an explanation solely in terms of nerve impulses from the brain to the hand: The level of explanation does not adequately answer the question. Nerve impulses are involved, but a full answer would probably also need some reference to conventions, norms, and the law. Doise (1986) argues that full social psychological explanations of collective and group phenomena require the *articulation* of different levels of explanation into an integrated conceptual framework; referring to individual level processes and structures alone is inadequate.

Concerns about reductionism have always been a part of social psychology, coming to the fore from time to time. For instance, the late 1960s and early 1970s witnessed a well-publicized crisis of confidence in social psychology (e.g., Elms, 1975; Strickland, Aboud, & Gergen, 1976). One major concern was that the psychology of groups had been reduced to interpersonal or individual psychology, in which collective phenomena were merely an aggregate of individual or interpersonal behaviors (e.g., Cartwright, 1979; Festinger, 1980; Steiner, 1974, 1986; Taylor & Brown, 1979; Turner & Oakes, 1986). It was felt that this approach underemphasized the influence of groups and categories on self-conceptualization and social behavior and also provided at best only partial explanations of group phenomena, making it very difficult properly to theorize large scale group phenomena such as prejudice, intergroup conflict, social protest, social structure, social change, and crowd events.

One example of the limitations of reductionist theorizing comes from the group dynamics literature. The group dynamics concept of group cohesiveness captured both the essence of groupness and the psychology of group formation in terms of the development of bonds of interpersonal attraction among group members (e.g., Festinger, Schachter & Back, 1950). Although members of small face-to-face groups may like one another, interpersonal attraction is a very limited explanation of group formation and group cohesion and solidarity (Hogg, 1993). For example, it is implausible as an explanation of processes in large groups like organizations or even larger groups such as a religion; attraction may be a correlate or consequence rather than cause of group formation; and attraction among group members may be produced in a different way than interpersonal attraction, such that you might like someone as a group member but despise her as an individual. Other processes may be involved in group formation and solidarity, specifically—as proposed by social identity theory—ones having to do with people's cognitive representations of a collective and their sense of self-definition in terms of that collective, and their knowledge about the social status of their group and the nature of its relations to other groups.

The critique of reductionism resonated well with the emerging metatheoretical agenda of European social psychology. World War II destroyed social psychology in Europe, and it was not until the 1960s that it began to find its feet again. This resurrection—culturally contextualized by Europe's recent history of wars, revolutions, and ideological conflicts—was self-consciously and single-mindedly framed by a strong metatheoretical conviction and mission. As part of a reconstruction of the infrastructure of European social psychology (for example establishment of the European Association of Experimental Social Psychology in 1966 and the launching of the *European Journal of Social Psychology* in 1971), European social psychologists deliberately developed a European perspective on and agenda for social psychology that set itself up in contradistinction to what they believed was the individualism, reductionism, and asocial nature of mainstream, largely American, social psychology (see Jaspars, 1980, 1986; Tajfel, 1972b).

The European perspective was one that privileged the "social dimension" (e.g., Tajfel, 1984) and in so doing served to provide a distinctive scientific identity around which European social psychologists could organize themselves. The "social dimension" was defined as a

> view that social psychology can and must include in its theoretical and research preoccupations a direct concern with the relationship between human psychological functioning and the large-scale social processes and events which shape this functioning and are shaped by it. (Tajfel, Jaspars, & Fraser, 1984, p. 3)

In practice what this has meant is that many European social psychologists have placed a strong emphasis on research into society, intergroup relations, collective behavior, and the collective self and on theories that articulate concepts from different levels of explanation (e.g., Doise, 1986). There has also generally been a preference to view people as a product of society, rather than vice versa; a top-down analysis has prevailed. From this perspective personality and individuality alone do not adequately explain group phenomena; separate group level constructs are also required. People's sense of who they are, their sense of self, is not based in some form of fixed personality that is prior to society and the groups that make up society; on the contrary, self is constructed from the nexus of groups in society that have specific historical social relations to one another. It is not just that the self is socially constructed, which of course it must be (e.g., Simon, 1997), but that collective self-definition provides the context for more individual and interpersonal self-construal.

Because this metatheoretical orientation was central to the development of a distinct identity for European social psychology, it was particularly vigorously pursued, much like a scientific *jihad*, from the 1960s through 1980s (e.g., *European Journal of Social Psychology*, 1974, p. 4). It remains a distinct theme in European social psychology (e.g., Turner & Bourhis, 1996) but is less identity-defining for European social psychologists, who are now much more diverse in terms of their research foci and orientations.

However, what is important for this chapter is that social identity theory was explicitly developed and has been sustained by this European metatheory (e.g., Abrams & Hogg, 2004; Hogg, 2001a; Hogg & Williams, 2000), which is not surprising, given that it is a European theory, originally developed in Britain in the late 1960s and early 1970s by European social psychologists, key among whom was Tajfel, who was also a leader in the development of the infrastructure of postwar European social psychology.

PERSONALITY, INDIVIDUALITY, AND SOCIAL IDENTITY

Framed by the European metatheory, social identity theory was originally developed as a theory of intergroup relations—an explanation of prejudice, discrimination, and conflict and cooperation between groups (e.g., Tajfel, 1972c, 1974; Tajfel & Turner, 1979). Its development was predicated on a critique (e.g., Billig, 1976) of other dominant explanations of intergroup and group phenomena that relied on personality, such as the authoritarian personality theory (Adorno et al., 1950) and the frustration-aggression hypothesis (Dollarde, 1939), or on the psychology of the individual or of interpersonal interactions, for example small group dynamics (e.g., Shaw, 1981). Although Sherif's (e.g., 1966) realistic conflict theory of group behavior was more in keeping with the emerging social identity theory, it was considered to underemphasize the fundamental role of the socially defined self in group behavior.

Tajfel introduced the term social identity in 1972 to describe how self is conceptualized in intergroup contexts—how a system of social categorizations "... creates and defines an individual's *own* place in society" (Tajfel, 1972c, p. 293). He defined social identity as "... the individual's knowledge that he belongs to certain social groups together with some emotional and value significance to him of this group membership" (Tajfel, 1972c, p. 292). Social identity, the self-concept defined in terms of specific group memberships, was clearly distinguished from personal identity, the self-concept defined in terms of personal idiosyncrasies, personality attributes, and close personal relationships (e.g., Turner, 1982). Behavior, however, was always considered to vary on a continuum from being totally influenced by social identity to being totally influenced by personal identity; most situations were somewhere in the middle, but social identity theory was mostly, if not exclusively, interested in those group and intergroup behaviors located at the social identity end of the continuum.

Social identity theory had little further to say about personal identity; it was considered to play no significant role in group phenomena. Instead, the theory focused on social identity and its generative role in group behavior and the articulation of social cognitive processes associated with social identity and people's socially constructed beliefs about the nature of their group and its relations to other groups (Tajfel & Turner, 1979; also see Ellemers, 1993; Hogg & Abrams, 1988). The social identity and personal identity systems were separate, and within each the self was structured into discrete social and personal identities—constructions of self tied to specific group memberships, specific close relationships, and specific personality attributes (Turner, 1982).

However, people do generally feel they have an integrated and enduring sense of unique individuality, of an overall personality that differentiates them from all other people and provides them with a unique autobiography and a stable sense of who they are (Baumeister, 1998; Cantor & Kihlstrom, 1987; Markus, 1977). Social identity theory did not deny this. It maintained that, all things being equal, we probably never experience ourselves in this holistic manner; rather, we subjectively experience different facets of self in different contexts and situations (see discussion of salience, below). The social context brings into play different experiences of self. For example, in one context you may experience yourself as a psychologist (a social identity), in another as Italian (a social identity), in another as Mary's best friend (a personal identity), in another as a driven and ambitious individual (a personal identity), and so forth.

From a social identity perspective, it is social identity and collective self—not personal identity, individuality or personality—that is related to collective and group behaviors.

SELF-CATEGORIZATION THEORY AND THE INDIVIDUAL

Social identity theory has a number of integrated conceptual foci (for contemporary overviews of social identity theory see Hogg, 2003, 2006; Turner, 1999a). Thus far I have largely discussed the original social identity theory of intergroup relations (e.g., Turner & Tajfel, 1979). A crucial development in the early 1980s was the social identity theory of the group, self-categorization theory (Turner, 1985;

Turner, Hogg, Oakes, Reicher, & Wetherell, 1987), which focused on the role of the categorization process in group identification and group behavior. The main feature of this theory is its explanation of the way that social categorization depersonalizes perception so that people are viewed in terms of group prototypes rather than their individual attributes, and the way that categorization of self, self-categorization, depersonalizes self-construal, self-perception, and people's attitudes, feelings and behaviors.

Depersonalization is not the same as dehumanization or deindividuation (contrast Zimbardo, 1970, with Reicher, Spears, & Postmes, 1995). It does not refer to behavior in which people behave impulsively, antisocially or aggressively; rather it refers to a phenomenon where we represent and experience ourselves and others as relatively "interchangeable" members of a collective, rather than as unique separate individuals.

As with the earlier social identity research, most self-categorization research focused on group and collective phenomena such as stereotyping (e.g., Oakes, Haslam, & Turner, 1994), group cohesion and solidarity (e.g., Hogg, 1993), crowd behavior (e.g., Reicher, 1984), deindividuation phenomena (e.g., Reicher, Spears, & Postmes, 1995), and conformity and normative behavior (e.g., Abrams & Hogg, 1990). However, self-categorization theory left the door open for more serious attention to be paid to the study of individuality in the context of group life.

There were a number of reasons for this, all hinging on the new, more inclusive focus on group behavior as a whole rather than just intergroup behavior between large social categories. For example, when you study social identity processes in small interactive groups, you immediately confront the fact that although social identity processes play out in the usual way, individuality, personality, and interpersonal processes are also very obvious (Hogg, 1996; Hogg, Abrams, Otten, & Hinkle, 2004). The family is a good example—clearly a group, but also very clearly a context for personality and interpersonal processes.

Another example is the study of group norms and social influence in groups (Turner, 1991; also see Hogg & Smith, 2007). Although norms emerge to characterize a group as a whole in distinction to specific outgroups, there is absolutely no doubt that some individuals are more influential than others in shaping the group's norm. This suggested that social identity theory needed to properly consider the role of individual differences in the context of group life. As we shall see below, the problematic of relative influence was addressed, not in terms of idiosyncratic personality or individuality, but in terms of relative group prototypicality (e.g., Abrams & Hogg, 1990; Hogg, 2005; Turner & Oakes, 1989). This was the foundation of the social identity theory of leadership (Hogg, 2001b; Hogg & van Knippenberg, 2003) and social identity analyses of deviance (e.g., Marques, Abrams, Páez, & Hogg, 2001; Marques, Abrams, & Serôdio, 2001).

Some key elements of a self-categorization perspective on personality and individuality have recently been described by Turner and his colleagues (Turner, Reynolds, Haslam, & Veenstra, 2006). There are two key points to this perspective. The first is that all self-definitions and self-conceptions are based on self-categories defined by category prototypes. Self categories vary in size (inclusiveness); large, highly inclusive categories are social groups that define social identity, whereas small exclusive categories, which effectively only have one member, clearly define personal identity or individuality. Most categories are in the middle.

The second key point is that self categories are not stored in mind to be carried from one context to another;they are constructed in situ to define self in that particular context. In this way self-categories and attendant perceptions and behaviors are tied into contexts rather than invariant properties of individuals: If people's lives are circumscribed by a limited number of contexts, their behaviors will appear routinized, with the inference that it reflects invariant personality attributes; if their lives are in greater flux, then their behavior will appear more varied and less easily construed as personality.

Put this way, this second point veers towards social constructionism, appearing on the surface to argue that aspects of self are entirely *determined* by the immediate social context and are not stored in memory for the individual to bring into play to define self in a particular context. However, most social identity researchers do not take this stance, and a close reading of social identity theory, particularly its description of the process of salience (below), shows it to be quite consistent with Kurt Lewin's far reaching "person-situation" view that "every psychological event depends on the state of the person and at the same time on the environment, although their relative importance is different in different cases (Lewin, 1936, p. 12)

Psychological Salience

Context influences self-conception and behavior via a process of psychological salience (e.g., Oakes, Haslam, & Turner, 1994; Turner, Oakes, Haslam, & McGarty, 1994). People draw on accessible social categorizations—ones that are valued, important, and frequently employed aspects of self-conception and social perception (they are chronically accessible in one's memory) and/or because they are self-evident and perceptually salient in the immediate situation (they are situationally accessible). People are very ready to use accessible categories to make sense of their social context, investigating how well the categorization accounts for similarities and differences among people (structural or comparative fit) and how well the stereotypical properties of the categorization account for why people behave as they do (normative fit).

If the fit of a particular categorization is poor, people cycle through other accessible categorizations until an optimal level of fit is obtained. This process is primarily fast and automatic; people strive to reduce feelings of uncertainty about self-conception, social interaction, and people's behavior (e.g., Hogg, 2000, 2007). However, it is also more deliberatively strategic because people strive to make psychologically salient those social categorizations that mediate a more evaluatively positive social identity and self-concept (cf. Tajfel & Turner, 1979). The categorization that has optimal fit becomes psychologically salient in that context as the basis of self-categorization, group identification, and prototype-based depersonalization. It triggers social identity related perceptions, cognitions, affect, and behavior.

The process of salience explains how self-construal and associated behavior are generated and configured by an interaction between, on the one hand, social categorizations and self-knowledge brought by the person to the situation and, on the other hand, information in the situation that points to certain social categorizations and situation-specific configurations of such categorizations.

However, salience is not entirely mechanical; it is influenced by chronically accessible categories and by people's motivations and goals and so forth (e.g., Hogg, 2003, 2006; Simon, 2004). Turner and colleagues write: "Self-categorization is not free to vary in any which way, but is always constrained by the motives, goals, values, experiences, theories and knowledge the perceiver brings to the situation, as well as by the psychological nature of the categorization process and the social situation within which the perceiver defines himself or herself" (Turner, Reynolds, Haslam, & Veenstra, 2006, p. 25).

Personality and individuality certainly play a role here, in so far as people differ in terms of chronic category accessibility and the subjective importance of particular identities, motives, goals, and life experiences; in any given context some of us may be more ready to use one social categorization than another to make sense of the situation and socially locate and define ourselves and others in that situation.

It is also worth noting that the social identity model of salience is not entirely inconsistent with contemporary perspectives on personality, discussed above, in which contexts evoke preexisting dispositions (the interactional perspective) and people are disposed to place themselves in particular situations (the situational perspective; Snyder & Cantor, 1998; Snyder & Ickes, 1985). However, it differs from and goes beyond personality treatments in its focus on a highly differentiated self that structures, and is structured by, the world in terms of social categories.

Personality and Individuality

Personality and individuality may also be a product of the particular level of social comparison that one employs: Where intergroup comparisons are made, then self is clearly defined in collective terms as a group member, but where self-other comparisons are made within a group, individuality may come to the fore (Turner et al., 1987). In this formulation the group is primary because it is the frame of reference that allows individuality and personality to emerge (Hogg, 2001a; Hogg & Williams, 2000). However, it is not clear whether self-other comparisons within a group are truly interpersonal comparisons resting on emergent individuality and personality or actually intragroup comparisons resting on appraisals of self and other as more or less prototypical members of the group (see below).

Another take on individuality within the context of social identity is provided by the notion of "relational self." Drawing on cross-cultural research showing that people in different cultures construe the relationship between individual and group in different ways (Markus & Kitayama, 1991; Oyserman, Coon, & Kemmelmeier, 2002), Brewer has described the relational self as a form of collective self-construal where social identity is defined in terms of networks of interpersonal relationships (Brewer & Gardner, 1996; Yuki, 2003). This form of social identity may be more prevalent in non-Western cultures, but it may also characterize friendship cliques and the family in Western societies.

This analysis does seem to suggest that the network of relations that defines the group is constructed from the bottom up, and thus individuality and personality are primary (e.g., Sedikides & Strube, 1997). However, this does not have to be the case; one can readily see how relational identity and selves can be constructed top down, as described by self-categorization theory.

The notion of relational identity raises the question of roles: Are they personal or social identities? The notion of role identities is important in more sociological social psychology (e.g., Ridgeway, 2001; Thoits & Virshup, 1997). From a social identity point of view, roles describe relationships between people and so can define social or personal identities, depending on whether the role relationship is constructed as being between individuals or between groups (Hogg, Terry, & White, 1995). So, for example, airline pilot vs. cabin crew and professor vs. undergraduate reflect intergroup relations and social identities, and "mother" is more a personal identity when played out between mother and daughter and more a social identity when configured as "soccer mom" vs. working woman.

Finally, Brewer's optimal distinctiveness theory opposes individuality to the group, much as does social identity theory, but argues that people strive for a balance between standing out as a unique individual within the group and being totally immersed in the group (Brewer, 1991; Pickett & Brewer, 2001; Pickett, Silver, & Brewer, 2002). There is a dynamic relationship between individual and group.

Overall, social identity perspectives on the self reject what Turner and Onorato (1999) have recently called the "personality model of self" (also see Hogg 2001a; Onorato & Turner, 2002, 2004) in which the self is a unique, idiosyncratic, enduring, fixed and bounded entity—the view that "I" and "me" rule supreme. Instead, the self is experienced differently depending on context, and individuality and personality are less likely to be behavioral and experiential progenitors than more transitory emergent properties of an interplay of contextual factors and motives, goals and experiences brought to the context. A subjective sense of self and personality does exist, but it is more context-dependent, less enduring and stable, and more group membership-based than allowed by most personality and individual differences research. And of course we habitually construct stable underlying personalities for other people through processes of attribution (e.g., Gilbert & Malone, 1995) and essentialism (e.g., Haslam, Rothschild, & Ernst, 1998).

PROTOTYPICALITY, INDIVIDUALITY, AND INFLUENCE

A key feature of the social identity analysis of self and group, as described above, is that when social identity is salient, people define themselves and others in terms of relevant ingroup and outgroup prototypes. In group contexts people are very attentive to prototype relevant information and to the relative prototypicality of self and fellow ingroup members (Haslam, Oakes, McGarty, Turner, & Onorato, 1995; Hogg, 2005). The fact that groups are subjectively differentiated in terms of the ingroup prototypicality of members means that within groups there is a degree of paradoxical individuality—"paradoxical" because it is based upon perceived group prototypicality.

One consequence of this is that prototypical members are more influential over the life of the group than are less prototypical/marginal members. This idea underpins the social identity theory of leadership (Hogg, 2001b; Hogg & van Knippenberg, 2003; also see van Knippenberg & Hogg, 2003; van Knippenberg, van Knippenberg, De Cremer, & Hogg, 2004), which argues that prototypical members are better able to lead the group; they are more effective leaders who are better able to gain compliance and be innovative. They differ from other members in their ability to manipulate prototypicality (e.g., Reicher & Hopkins, 1996, 2003; Reicher, Hopkins, & Condor, 1997; Reid & Ng, 2000, 2003). Furthermore, group members go through an attribution process in which they construct a charismatic personality for prototypical leaders (e.g., Haslam & Platow, 2001; Platow & van Knippenberg, 2001). Unlike traditional treatments of charisma as a cause of leadership (e.g., Bryman, 1992; Conger & Kanungo, 1998), the social identity analysis sees it as an emergent property of group life.

Group members who are only marginally prototypical have a very different experience within the group. Typically they find it difficult to be influential. They are treated with suspicion, dislike, and sometimes hostility as norm violators and "black sheep" (e.g., Marques, Abrams, Páez, & Hogg, 2001; Marques, Abrams, & Serôdio, 2001; Marques & Páez, 1994) and can be attributed with deviant personality attributes and labeled as deviants (cf. Becker, 1963).

By focusing on differential prototypicality within a salient group, social identity theory can theorize personality as an emergent product of social identity-based perceptions and interactions, in this case focusing on the "construction" of charismatic and deviant personalities.

PERSONALITY AND PREJUDICE

As discussed at the beginning of this chapter, an important aspect of the socio-scientific context in which social identity theory originally developed was the critique of personality and individual differences explanations of prejudice, discrimination, and intergroup behavior (e.g., Billig, 1976). In recent years this critique has been reinvigorated (e.g., Reynolds, Turner, Haslam, & Ryan, 2001; Turner, 1999b; Verkuyten & Hagendoorn, 1998) and focused not only on the theory of the authoritarian personality (Adorno et al., 1950) but also on the newer social dominance theory (e.g., Sidanius & Pratto, 1999) and the theory of right wing authoritarianism (e.g., Altemeyer, 1988).

Predicated on research showing that F-scale, social dominance orientation and right wing authoritarianism scores can all change rather quickly and as a result of influence attempts (e.g., Schmitt, Branscombe, & Kappen, 2003), the key point is that personality, as individual disposition, may, at very least, not be such a monolithic determinant of prejudice. At most, behaviors usually associated with prejudiced personality syndromes may be contextually malleable as a consequence of the social identity salience processes discussed above. Prejudiced personalities may reflect intergroup relations rather than create them.

In their social dominance theory, Sidanius and Pratto (1999) concede that although there are individual differences in social dominance orientation, the extent to which someone has a hierarchy-enhancing or hierarchy-attenuating social dominance orientation will be strongly influenced by whether one is actually a member of a dominant or subordinate group. Nevertheless, critics of social dominance theory argue that it is actually primarily a personality and individual differences theory of prejudice, discrimination, and conflict (e.g., Kreindler, 2005; Schmitt et al., 2003; Turner & Reynolds, 2003), although Sidanius and colleagues disagree with this characterization (Pratto, Sidanius, & Levin, 2006; Sidanius & Pratto, 2003).

CONCLUDING COMMENTS

Social identity theory developed within a metatheoretical tradition in social psychology that sought to explain group and intergroup phenomena in terms of processes associated with the construction and expression of self in collective terms. The idiosyncratic individual self, the classic self of personality theorists, was not seen to play a significant role in group behavior, and explanations of collective phenomena in terms of stable personality dispositions were seen at best to be only partial explanations.

Because social identity theory was initially devised as a theory of intergroup relations, once it had conceptually separated social identity (self defined in collective terms) from personal identity (self defined idiosyncratically), it focused only on the former. Developments in the early 1980s, specifically self-categorization theory, which broadened social identity theory into a general theory of group processes and self-conception, expanded the agenda to facilitate the study of intragroup phenomena. This re-acquainted social identity researchers with the fact that groups are patterned in terms of relative influence, role relations, and interpersonal dynamics. The issue of how social identity and collective self relate to individuality and personality was once more on the table. Specifically, there was a focus on variation in prototypicality within a group and its consequences for relative influence, leadership, and processes of marginalization and deviance.

In this chapter I have described social identity theory's metatheoretical roots, a grounding in the wider critique of explanations of group and intergroup phenomena in terms of individual personality or interpersonal relations. This metatheoretical background has meant that social identity theory has largely ignored literature on personality and individual differences, or has mainly engaged with a rather one-dimensional characterization of personality, what Snyder and Ickes (1985) have called the dispositional perspective on personality, where stable personality determines behavior. Interactional and situational perspectives on personality allow the social context a greater role in human behavior, but from a social identity perspective they nevertheless talk about dispositions being contextually-elicited or people being disposed to "choose" certain situations. This still underplays the notion of a multifaceted self and the role played by group membership and collective self-conception in behavior.

Overall, contemporary social identity research tends to view personality less as a cause of behavior than as a social construct in which people make inferences about stable underlying dispositions or human essences (e.g., Haslam, Rothschild, & Ernst, 1998), for example, in the construction of a charismatic personality for a group's leader or stereotype-consistent racial essences. In a similar vein individual differences are not so much viewed as idiosyncratic attributes that are brought to the group as socially constructed positions within the group based on perceived group prototypicality, positions that nevertheless have far reaching consequences for the group and the individual in terms of relative impact on group life and on how one is treated by the group (the psychology of social influence, persuasion, leadership, deviance, and marginalization).

One feature of individuality that remains relatively unexplored by social identity researchers is how close interpersonal relationships articulate with group life and social identity processes. There is little doubt that friendships are more likely to form and persist within than between groups, but do such friendships reinforce or undermine social identity? And how do such friendships impact the rest of the group? What about intergroup friendships? Wright and his colleagues have reported some intriguing data showing that hostile outgroup stereotypes can be reduced among people who know fellow ingroup members who have close and rewarding friendships with members of the outgroup (Wright, Aron, McLaughlin-Volpe, & Ropp, 1997). Another line of research focuses on the role of the relational self in group life (e.g., Brewer & Gardner, 1996): When do interpersonal relationships define or configure group membership and how do group membership configure relationships?

In conclusion, because social identity theory adopts a collectivist metatheory to focus on group behavior, intergroup relations, and the collective self, it has generally found the concept of personality, as a stable deterministic disposition, to be problematic in the highly context-responsive world of group behavior and social identity. Although in the past this has been a significant hurdle to engagement with research on personality and individual differences, developments in both social identity theory and the way that personality is now conceptualized may be lowering some of these hurdles and laying the groundwork for future dialogue.

REFERENCES

Abrams, D., & Hogg, M. A. (1990). Social identification, self-categorization and social influence. *European Review of Social Psychology, 1,* 195–228.

Abrams, D., & Hogg, M. A. (2004). Metatheory: Lessons from social identity research. *Personality and Social Psychology Review, 8,* 98–106.

Adorno, T. W., Frenkel-Brunswick, E., Levinson, D. J., & Sanford, R. M. (1950). *The authoritarian personality.* New York: Harper.

Allport, F. H. (1924). *Social psychology.* Boston: Houghton Mifflin.

Altemeyer, B. (1998). The other "authoritarian personality." In M. P. Zanna (Ed.), *Advances in experimental social psychology* (Vol. 30, pp. 47–92). Orlando, FL: Academic Press.
Asch, S. E. (1952). *Social psychology*. Englewood Cliffs, NJ: Prentice Hall.
Baron, R. M., & Boudreau, L. A. (1987). An ecological perspective on integrating personality and social psychology. *Journal of Personality and Social Psychology, 53*, 1222–1228.
Baumeister, R. F. (1998). The self. In D. T. Gilbert, S. T. Fiske, & G. Lindzey (Eds.), *Handbook of social psychology* (4th ed., Vol. 1, pp. 680–740). New York: McGraw-Hill.
Becker, H. (1963). *Outsiders: Studies in the sociology of deviance*. New York: The Free Press
Billig, M. (1976). *Social psychology and intergroup relations*. London: Academic Press.
Brewer, M. B. (1991). The social self: On being the same and different at the same time. *Personality and Social Psychology Bulletin, 17*, 475–482.
Brewer, M. B., & Gardner, W. (1996). Who is this 'We'? Levels of collective identity and self representation. *Journal of Personality and Social Psychology, 71*, 83–93.
Bryman, A. (1992). *Charisma and leadership*. London: Sage.
Buss, D. M. (1987). Selection, evocation, and manipulation. *Journal of Personality and Social Psychology, 53*, 1214–1221.
Cantor, N., & Kihlstrom, J. F. (1987). *Personality and social intelligence*. Englewood Cliffs, NJ: Prentice Hall.
Cartwright, D. (1979). Contemporary social psychology in historical perspective. *Social Psychology Quarterly, 42*, 82–93.
Conger, J. A., & Kanungo, R. N. (1998). *Charismatic leadership in organizations*. Thousand Oaks, CA: Sage.
Doise, W. (1986). *Levels of explanation in social psychology*. Cambridge, UK: Cambridge University Press.
Dollard, J., Doob, L. W., Miller, N. E., Mowrer, O. H., & Sears, R. R. (1939). *Frustration and aggression*. New Haven, CT: Yale University Press.
Durkheim, E. (1898). Représentations individuelles et représentations collectives. *Revue de Metaphysique et de Morale, 6*, 273–302.
Ellemers, N. (1993). The influence of socio-structural variables on identity enhancement strategies. *European Review of Social Psychology, 4*, 27–57.
Elms, A. C. (1975). The crisis of confidence in social psychology. *American Psychologist, 30*, 967–976.
Farr, R. M. (1996). *The roots of modern social psychology: 1872–1954*. Oxford: Blackwell.
Festinger, L. (1980). Looking backwards. In L. Festinger (Ed.), *Retrospection on social psychology* (pp. 236–254). New York: Oxford University Press.
Festinger, L., Schachter, S., & Back, K. (1950). *Social pressures in informal groups: A study of human factors in housing*. New York: Harper.
Gilbert, D. T., & Malone, P. S. (1995). The correspondence bias. *Psychological Bulletin, 117*, 21–38.
Graumann, C. F. (1986). The individualization of the social and the desocialization of the individual: Floyd H. Allport's contribution to social psychology. In C. F. Graumann & S. Moscovici (Eds.), *Changing conceptions of crowd mind and behavior* (pp. 97–116). New York: Springer-Verlag.
Haslam, S. A., Oakes, P. J., McGarty, C., Turner, J. C., & Onorato, S. (1995). Contextual changes in the prototypicality of extreme and moderate outgroup members. *European Journal of Social Psychology, 25*, 509–530.
Haslam, S. A., & Platow, M. J. (2001). Your wish is our command: The role of shared social identity in translating a leader's vision into followers' action. In M. A. Hogg & D.

J. Terry (Eds.), *Social identity processes in organizational contexts* (pp. 213–228). Philadelphia: Psychology Press.

Haslam, N., Rothschild, L., & Ernst, D. (1998). Essentialist beliefs about social categories. *British Journal of Social Psychology, 39,* 113–127.

Hogg, M. A. (1993). Group cohesiveness: A critical review and some new directions. *European Review of Social Psychology, 4,* 85–111.

Hogg, M. A. (1996). Social identity, self-categorization, and the small group. In E. H. Witte & J. H. Davis (Eds), *Understanding group behavior (Vol. 2): Small group processes and interpersonal relations* (pp. 227–253). Mahwah, NJ: Erlbaum.

Hogg, M. A. (2000). Subjective uncertainty reduction through self-categorization: A motivational theory of social identity processes. *European Review of Social Psychology, 11,* 223–255.

Hogg, M. A. (2001a). Social identity and the sovereignty of the group: A psychology of belonging. In C. Sedikides & M. B. Brewer (Eds.), *Individual self, relational self, collective self* (pp. 123–143). Philadelphia: Psychology Press.

Hogg, M. A. (2001b). A social identity theory of leadership. *Personality and Social Psychology Review, 5,* 184–200.

Hogg, M. A. (2003). Social identity. In M. R. Leary & J. P. Tangney (Eds.), *Handbook of self and identity* (pp. 462–479). New York: Guilford.

Hogg, M. A. (2005). All animals are equal but some animals are more equal than others: Social identity and marginal membership. In K. D. Williams, J. P. Forgas, & W. von Hippel (Eds.), *The social outcast: Ostracism, social exclusion, rejection, and bullying* (pp. 243–261). New York: Psychology Press.

Hogg, M. A. (2006). Social identity theory. In P. J. Burke (Ed.), *Contemporary social psychological theories* (pp. 111–136). Palo Alto, CA: Stanford University Press.

Hogg, M. A. (2007). Uncertainty-identity theory. In M. P. Zanna (Ed.), *Advances in experimental social psychology* (Vol. 39, pp. 69–126). San Diego, CA: Academic Press.

Hogg, M. A., & Abrams, D. (1988). *Social identifications: A social psychology of intergroup relations and group processes.* London: Routledge

Hogg, M. A., Abrams, D., Otten, S., & Hinkle, S. (2004). The social identity perspective: Intergroup relations, self-conception, and small groups. *Small Group Research, 35,* 246–276.

Hogg, M. A., & Smith, J. R. (2007). Attitudes in social context: A social identity perspective. *European Review of Social Psychology, 18,* 1–43.

Hogg, M. A., Terry, D. J., & White, K. M. (1995). A tale of two theories: A critical comparison of identity theory with social identity theory. *Social Psychology Quarterly, 58,* 255–269.

Hogg, M. A., & van Knippenberg, D. (2003). Social identity and leadership processes in groups. In M. P. Zanna (Ed.), *Advances in experimental social psychology* (Vol. 35, pp. 1–52). San Diego, CA: Academic Press.

Hogg, M. A., & Williams, K. D. (2000). From I to we: Social identity and the collective self. *Group Dynamics: Theory, Research, and Practice, 4,* 81–97.

Jaspars, J. M. F. (1980). The coming of age of social psychology in Europe. *European Journal of Social Psychology, 10,* 421–428.

Jaspars, J. M. F. (1986). Forum and focus: A personal view of European social psychology. *European Journal of Social Psychology, 16,* 3–15.

Jones, E. E. (1998). Major developments in five decades of social psychology. In D. T. Gilbert, S. T. Fiske, & G. Lindzey (Eds.), *The handbook of social psychology* (Vol. 1, pp. 3–57). New York: McGraw-Hill.

Kreindler, S. A. (2005). A dual processes model of individual differences in prejudice. *Personality and Social Psychology Review, 9,* 90–107.

LeBon, G. (1908). *The crowd: A study of the popular mind*. London: Unwin. (French original 1896)
Lewin, K. (1936). *A dynamic theory of personality*. New York: McGraw-Hill.
Lewin, K. (1952). *Field theory in social science*. London: Tavistock.
Lorenzi-Cioldi, F., & Clémence, A. (2001). Group processes and the construction of social representations. In M. A. Hogg & R. S. Tindale (Eds.), *Blackwell handbook of social psychology: Group processes* (pp. 311–333). Oxford: Blackwell.
Manicas, P. T. (1987). *A history and philosophy of the social sciences*. Oxford: Blackwell.
Markus, H. (1977). Self-schemata and processing information about the self. *Journal of Personality and Social Psychology, 35*, 63–78.
Markus, H. R., & Kitayama, S. (1991). Culture and the self: Implications for cognition, emotion, and motivation. *Psychological Review, 98*, 224–253.
Marques, J. M., Abrams, D., Páez, D., & Hogg, M. A. (2001). Social categorization, social identification, and rejection of deviant group members. In M. A. Hogg & R. S. Tindale, (Eds.), *Blackwell handbook of social psychology: Group processes* (pp. 400–424). Oxford: Blackwell.
Marques, J. M., Abrams, D., & Serôdio, R. (2001). Being better by being right: Subjective group dynamics and derogation of in-group deviants when generic norms are undermined. *Journal of Personality and Social Psychology, 81*, 436–447.
Marques, J. M., & Páez, D. (1994). The 'black sheep effect': Social categorization, rejection of ingroup deviates and perception of group variability. *European Review of Social Psychology, 5*, 37–68.
Martin, R., & Hewstone, M. (2003). Social influence processes of control and change: Conformity, obedience to authority, and innovation. In M. A. Hogg & J. Cooper (Eds.), *The Sage handbook of social psychology* (pp. 347–366). London: Sage.
McCrae, R. R., & John, O. P. (1992). An introduction of the five-factor model and its applications. *Journal of Personality and Social Psychology, 60*, 175–215.
McDougall, W. (1921). *The group mind*. London: Cambridge University Press.
Moscovici, S. (1976). *Social influence and social change*. London: Academic Press.
Moscovici, S. (1988). Notes towards a description of social representations. *European Journal of Social Psychology, 18*, 211–250.
Oakes, P. J., Haslam, S. A., & Turner, J. C. (1994). *Stereotyping and social reality*. Oxford: Blackwell.
Onorato, R. S., & Turner, J. C. (2002). Challenging the primacy of the personal self: The case for depersonalized self-conception. In Y. Kashima, M. Foddy, & M. J. Platow (Eds.), *Self and identity: Personal, social, and symbolic* (pp. 145–178). Mahwah, NJ: Erlbaum.
Onorato, R. S., & Turner, J. C. (2004). Fluidity in the self-concept: The shift from personal to social identity. *European Journal of Social Psychology, 34*, 257–278.
Oyserman, D., Coon, H. M., & Kemmelmeier, M. (2002). Rethinking individualism and collectivism: Evaluation of theoretical assumptions and meta-analyses. *Psychological Bulletin, 128*, 3–72.
Pickett, C. L., & Brewer, M. B. (2001). Assimilation and differentiation needs as motivational determinants of perceived ingroup and outgroup homogeneity. *Journal of Experimental Social Psychology, 37*, 341–348.
Pickett, C. L., Silver, M. D., & Brewer, M. B. (2002). The impact of assimilation and differentiation needs on perceived group importance and judgments of ingroup size. *Personality and Social Psychology Bulletin, 28*, 546–558.
Platow, M. J., & van Knippenberg, D. (2001). A social identity analysis of leadership endorsement: The effects of leader ingroup prototypicality and distributive intergroup fairness. *Personality and Social Psychology Bulletin, 27*, 1508–1519.

Postmes, T, & Jetten, J. (Eds.) (2006). *Individuality and the group: Advances in social identity*. London: Sage.

Pratto, F., Sidanius, J., & Levin, S. (2006) Social dominance theory and the dynamics of intergroup relations: Taking stock and looking forward. *European Review of Social Psychology, 17*, 271–320.

Reicher, S. D. (1984). The St Pauls' riot: An explanation of the limits of crowd action in terms of a social identity model. *European Journal of Social Psychology, 14*, 1–21.

Reicher, S. D., & Hopkins, N. (1996). Self-category constructions in political rhetoric: An analysis of Thatcher's and Kinnock's speeches concerning the British miners' strike (1984–5). *European Journal of Social Psychology, 26*, 353–371.

Reicher, S. D., & Hopkins, N. (2003). On the science of the art of leadership. In D. van Knippenberg & M. A. Hogg (Eds.), *Leadership and power: Identity processes in groups and organizations* (pp. 197–209). London: Sage.

Reicher, S. D., Hopkins, N., & Condor, S. (1997). Stereotype construction as a strategy of social influence. In R. Spears, P. J. Oakes, N. Ellemers & S. A. Haslam (Eds.), *The social psychology of stereotyping and group life* (pp. 94–118). Oxford: Blackwell.

Reicher, S. D., Spears, R., & Postmes, T. (1995). A social identity model of deindividuation phenomena. *European Review of Social Psychology, 6*, 161–198.

Reid, S. A., & Ng, S. H. (2000). Conversation as a resource for influence: Evidence for prototypical arguments and social identification processes. *European Journal of Social Psychology, 30*, 83–100.

Reid, S. A., & Ng, S. H. (2003). Identity, power, and strategic social categorizations: Theorizing the language of leadership (pp. 210–223). In D. van Knippenberg & M. A. Hogg (Eds.), *Leadership and Power: Identity Processes in Groups and Organizations*. London: Sage.

Reynolds, K. J., Turner, J. C., Haslam, S. A., & Ryan, M. K. (2001). The role of personality and group factors in explaining prejudice. *Journal of Experimental Social Psychology, 37*, 427–434.

Ridgeway, C. L. (2001). Social status and group structure. In M. A. Hogg & R. S. Tindale (Eds.), *Blackwell handbook of social psychology: Group processes* (pp. 352–375). Oxford: Blackwell.

Schmitt, M. T., Branscombe, N. R., & Kappen, D. M. (2003). Attitudes to group-based inequality: Social dominance or social identity. *British Journal of Social Psychology, 42*, 161–186.

Sedikides, C., & Strube, M. J. (1997). Self-evaluation: To thine own self be good, to thine own self be sure, to thine own self be true, and to thine own self be better. In M. P. Zanna (Ed.), *Advances in experimental social psychology* (Vol. 29, pp. 209–296). New York: Academic Press.

Shaw, M. E. (1981). *Group dynamics: The psychology of small group behavior* (2nd ed.). New York: McGraw-Hill.

Sherif, M. (1936). *The psychology of social norms*. New York: Harper & Bros.

Sherif, M. (1966). *In common predicament: Social psychology of intergroup conflict and cooperation*. Boston, MA: Houghton Mifflin.

Sidanius, J., & Pratto, F. (1999). *Social dominance: An intergroup theory of social hierarchy and oppression*. New York: Cambridge University Press.

Sidanius, J., & Pratto, F. (2003). Social dominance theory and the dynamics of inequality: A reply to Schmitt, Banscombe, & Kappen, and Wilson & Liu. *British Journal of Social Psychology, 42*, 207–213.

Simon, B. (1997). Self and group in modern society: Ten theses on the individual self and the collective self. In R. Spears, P. J. Oakes, N. Ellemers, & S. A. Haslam (Eds.), *The social psychology of stereotyping and group life* (pp. 318–335). Oxford: Blackwell.

Simon, B. (2004). *Identity in modern society: A social psychological perspective.* Oxford: Blackwell.

Snyder, M., & Cantor, N. (1988). Understanding personality and social behavior: A functionalist strategy. In D. T. Gilbert, S. T. Fiske & G. Lindzey (Eds.), *Handbook of social psychology* (4th ed., Vol. 1, pp. 635–679). New York: McGraw-Hill.

Snyder M., & Ickes W. (1985). Personality and social behavior. In G. Lindzey & E. Aronson (Eds.), *Handbook of social psychology* (3rd ed., pp. 883–948). New York: Random House.

Steiner, I. D. (1974). Whatever happened to the group in social psychology? *Journal of Experimental Social Psychology, 10,* 94–108.

Steiner, I. D. (1986). Paradigms and groups. *Advances in Experimental Social Psychology, 19,* 251–289.

Strickland, L. H., Aboud, F. E., & Gergen, K. J. (Eds.) (1976). *Social psychology in transition.* New York: Plenum Press.

Tajfel, H. (1972a). Experiments in a vacuum. In J. Israel & H. Tajfel (Eds.), *The context of social psychology: A critical assessment.* London: Academic Press.

Tajfel, H. (1972b). Some developments in European social psychology. *European Journal of Social Psychology, 2,* 307–322.

Tajfel, H. (1972c). Social categorization. English manuscript of 'La catégorisation sociale'. In S. Moscovici (Ed.), *Introduction à la psychologie sociale* (Vol. 1, pp. 272–302). Paris: Larousse.

Tajfel, H. (1974). *Intergroup behaviour, social comparison and social change.* Unpublished Katz-Newcomb lectures. University of Michigan, Ann Arbor.

Tajfel, H. (Ed.) (1984). *The social dimension: European developments in social psychology.* Cambridge: Cambridge University Press.

Tajfel, H., Jaspars, J. M. F., & Fraser, C. (1984). The social dimension in European social psychology. In H. Tajfel (Ed.) (1984), *The social dimension: European developments in social psychology* (Vol. 1, pp. 1–5). Cambridge: Cambridge University Press.

Tajfel, H., & Turner, J. C. (1979). An integrative theory of intergroup conflict. In W. G. Austin & S. Worchel (Eds.), *The social psychology of intergroup relations* (pp. 33–47). Monterey, CA: Brooks/Cole.

Taylor, D. M., & Brown, R. J. (1979). Towards a more social social psychology? *British Journal of Social and Clinical Psychology, 18,* 173–179.

Thoits, P. A., & Virshup, L. K. (1997). Me's and we's: Forms and functions of social identities. In R. D. Ashmore & L. J. Jussim (Eds.), *Self and identity: Fundamental issues.* Rutgers series on self and social identity (Vol. 1, pp. 106–133). New York: Oxford University Press.

Turner, J. C. (1982). Towards a cognitive redefinition of the social group. In H. Tajfel (Ed.), *Social identity and intergroup relations* (pp. 15–40). Cambridge: Cambridge University Press.

Turner, J. C. (1985). Social categorization and the self-concept: A social cognitive theory of group behavior. In E. J. Lawler (Ed.), *Advances in group processes: Theory and research* (Vol. 2, pp. 77–122). Greenwich, CT: JAI Press.

Turner, J. C. (1991). *Social influence.* Milton Keynes: Open University Press.

Turner, J. C. (1999a). Some current issues in research on social identity and self-categorization theories. In N. Ellemers, R. Spears, & B. Doosje (Eds.), *Social identity* (pp. 6–34). Oxford: Blackwell.

Turner, J. C. (1999b). *The prejudiced personality and social change: A self-categorization perspective.* The Tajfel memorial lecture, invited keynote at the 12th general meeting of the European Association of Experimental Social Psychology. Oxford, UK,. July 6–11, 1999.

Turner, J. C., & Bourhis, R. Y. (1996). Social identity, interdependence and the social group. A reply to Rabbie et al. In W. P. Robinson (Ed.) *Social groups and identities: Developing the legacy of Henri Tajfel* (pp. 25–63). Oxford: Butterworth-Heinemann.

Turner, J. C., Hogg, M. A., Oakes, P. J., Reicher, S. D., & Wetherell, M. S. (1987). *Rediscovering the social group: A self-categorization theory*. Oxford: Blackwell.

Turner, J. C., & Oakes, P. J. (1986). The significance of the social identity concept for social psychology with reference to individualism, interactionism and social influence. *British Journal of Social Psychology, 25*, 237–252.

Turner, J. C., & Oakes, P. J. (1989). Self-categorization and social influence. In P. B. Paulus (Ed.), *The psychology of group influence* (2nd ed., pp. 233–275). Hillsdale, NJ: Erlbaum.

Turner, J. C., Oakes, P. J., Haslam, S. A., & McGarty, C. A. (1994). Self and collective: Cognition and social context. *Personality and Social Psychology Bulletin, 20*, 454–463.

Turner, J. C., & Onorato, R. (1999). Social identity, personality and the self-concept: A self-categorization perspective. In T. R. Tyler, R. M. Kramer, & O. Johns (Eds.), *The psychology of the social self* (pp. 11–46). Mahwah, NJ: Erlbaum.

Turner, J. C., & Reynolds, K. J. (2003). Why social dominance theory has been falsified. *British Journal of Social Psychology, 42*, 199–206.

Turner, J. C., Reynolds, K. J., Haslam, S. A., & Veenstra, K. E. (2006). Reconceptualizing personality: Producing individuality by defining the personal self. In T. Postmes & J. Jetten (Eds.), *Individuality and the group: Advances in social identity* (pp. 11–36). London: Sage.

van Knippenberg, D., & Hogg, M. A. (2003). A social identity model of leadership in organizations. In R. M. Kramer & B. M. Staw (Eds.), *Research in organizational behavior* (Vol. 25, pp. 243–295). Greenwich, CT: JAI Press.

van Knippenberg, D., van Knippenberg, B., De Cremer, D., & Hogg, M. A. (2004). Leadership, self, and identity: A review and research agenda. *The Leadership Quarterly, 15*, 825–856.

Verkuyten, M., & Hagendoorn, L. (1998). Prejudice and self-categorization: The variable role of authoritarianism and ingroup stereotypes. *Personality and Social Psychology Bulletin, 24*, 99–110.

Wright, S. C., Aron, A., McLaughlin-Volpe, T., & Ropp, S. A. (1997). The extended contact effect: Knowledge of cross-group friendships and prejudice. *Journal of Personality and Social Psychology, 73*, 73–90.

Wundt, W. (1916). *Elements of folk psychology: Outlines of a psychological history of the development of mankind*. London: Allen & Unwin. (German original 1912.)

Yuki, M. (2003). Intergroup comparison versus intragroup relationships: A cross-cultural examination of social identity theory in North American and East Asian cultural contexts. *Social Psychology Quarterly, 66*, 166–183.

Zimbardo, P. G. (1970). The human choice: Individuation, reason, and order versus deindividuation, impulse, and chaos. In W. J. Arnold & D. Levine (Eds.), *Nebraska symposium on motivation 1969* (Vol. 17, pp. 237–307). Lincoln: University of Nebraska Press.

to # 8

Leadership as Dynamic Social Process

MARTIN M. CHEMERS

University of California, Santa Cruz

Leadership study might reasonably be described as a field with a long history and a short memory. Each generation of leadership researchers seems prone to the errors of the past. I believe that the most significant of these errors is the tendency to treat leadership as an individual phenomenon and to seek to explain the phenomenon with individually focused research techniques and explanatory models. In this chapter, I will try to make the case that a productive study of leadership must be rooted in the recognition that leadership occurs within a dynamic social process.

FAILURES OF THE "CONVENTIONAL WISDOM"

The "conventional wisdom" has been a poor guide to understanding leadership processes. In the nineteenth century, the dominant view (among people who concerned themselves with the question) was that leadership status was the result of some stable aspect of a person (assumedly a man) that gave him the "right stuff." Philospher Thomas Carlyle (1841/1907) proposed a "great man" theory of leadership that held that great leaders possessed some special characteristic that allowed them to rise to positions of prominence regardless of setting or situation. A genetic explanation was suggested by Galton's (1879) study of the hereditary background of great men. Dubious support for the hereditary thesis was offered by Woods' (1913) inane observation that the brothers of kings also turned out to be men of power and achievement.

The explanatory appeal of the great man theory for people in positions of power and privilege seems obvious, but person-oriented explanations have broader appeal. Such theories are quite consistent with the Western European

197

and American emphasis on individualism. We favor explanations for events that emphasize the role of individuals (Ross, 1978). This tendency is especially strong in perceptions of the personal role of leaders in group or organizational outcomes (Meindl & Ehrlich, 1987; Meindl, Ehrlich, & Dukerich; 1985). We are comfortable with the idea that leadership effects are caused by leaders and their characteristics. However, the real boost to person-oriented approaches in the scientific study of leadership came from the growing utility and popularity of individual difference measurement.

The empirical study of leadership began in earnest in the first and second decade of the twentieth century at a time when the development of intelligence tests promised both explanation and predictability in human behavior (Goddard, 1911; Terman, 1916). If leadership effectiveness does, indeed, arise from internal, stable attributes of the leader, then it should be possible to measure such stable attributes—and to use such measures to select excellent leaders. Thus was born an era of leadership research that can be characterized as the "search for the leadership trait" (Stogdill, 1948).

Early personality research on leadership employed many approaches designed to compare the personal characteristics of leaders and followers. Methods included observations of small groups, nominations or votes by group members, nominations by qualified observers, and analysis of biographical or case history data. The most common approach, however, was to find a group or institution with leaders and followers and to test for differences on characteristics such as personality (e.g., originality, introversion-extroversion, dominance, etc.), physical characteristics (e.g., height, weight, appearance, etc.), intellect (e.g., intelligence, scholarship, judgment, etc.) and other categories. A disorganized literature of such single-trait studies proliferated until a comprehensive review called the endeavor into question (Stogdill, 1948).

The patterns of results in these studies were often weak or contradictory, and Stodgill concluded that, although a few personal characteristics were associated with leadership status at a level greater than would be expected by chance (e.g., intelligence, scholarship, dependability, and—interestingly—socio-economic status), no strong argument could be made for a "leadership trait" or group of such traits. Other reviews (e.g., Mann, 1959) appeared with similar conclusions, and a strong view developed among leadership researchers that personality research was a dead end. In rejecting the notion that "individual characteristics are everything," researchers seemed to have embraced the view that "individual characteristics are nothing."

Both the initial uncritical acceptance of trait determinants of leadership and the later overwhelming rejection of trait approaches were overly simplistic and unwarranted. It is illuminating to delve a bit deeper. Stogdill's (1948) conclusions were more nuanced and complex than the conventional wisdom recognized at the time. I will quote at some length not only to provide a more complete picture of his ideas, but also because his conclusions are, in retrospect, quite prescient for the directions that the field of leadership would take over the next fifty years. The following two points foreshadow future developments:

A person does not become a leader by virtue of the possession of some combination of traits, but the pattern of personal characteristics of the leader must bear some relevant relationship to the characteristics, activities, and goals of the followers. (p. 64)

The findings suggest that leadership is not a matter of passive status, or of the mere possession of some combination of traits. It appears rather to be a working relationship among members of a group, in which the leader acquires status through active participation and demonstration of his capacities for carrying cooperative tasks through to completion. (p. 65)

Stogdill wasn't telling us that personal characteristics play no role in leadership status or success, but rather that the relationship of personal characteristics to leadership outcomes is more complex than a simple trait main effect on leadership performance. He argued for an "interaction" perspective, in the statistical sense that the relationship of a predictor variable to an outcome might strongly vary depending on the followers and the situation, setting, or context.

Zaccaro, Kemp, and Bader's (2004) analysis of the "rise and fall and rise" of leadership trait research reveals that not only were the conclusions based on available data too simplistic, but often the data were also inadequately analyzed. For example, follow-up research by Lord, Devader, and Alliger (1986) used more sophisticated techniques to correct correlation effects reported by Mann (1959) and found that the actual trait effects, including evidence from more recent studies, were in the moderate to fairly strong range (e.g., .50 for the relationships with intelligence, .26 for extraversion, and .24 for adjustment).

A number of studies, including re-analyses (e.g., Kenny & Zaccaro, 1983) and new studies (Ferentinos, 1996; Zaccaro, Foti, & Kenny, 1991), examined evidence from "rotational designs." Rotational designs are studies in which individuals rotate across groups or across tasks to determine if the same individuals emerge as leaders. Early studies found that some individuals did, indeed, repeatedly attain leadership status across groups or tasks, but the methodologies in the early studies were not tight. Some studies (e.g., Bell & French, 1950; Borgatta, Bales, & Crouch, 1954) changed group membership but failed to change tasks, while others (e.g., Carter & Nixon, 1949; Gibb, 1949) changed tasks but left group composition stable. One study, which varied both composition and tasks (Barnlund, 1962), found only nonsignificant associations of individual leadership status across groups and tasks.

However, Kenny and Zaccaro (1983) employed Kenny's "Social Relations" model to conduct a sophisticated reanalysis of Barnlund's (1962) results, in which they decomposed the variance in leader ratings, and they report that 49%-82% of the variance in those ratings was attributable to the individuals being rated, i.e., attributable to some unidentified characteristics of the emergent leaders, possibly flexibility.

New studies have employed more careful and theoretically driven rotational designs (Ferentinos, 1996; Zaccaro et al., 1991). For example, Zaccaro et al. (1991) followed directly on the 1983 Kenny and Zaccaro analysis and hypothesis that flexibility might be involved in repeated instances of emergent leadership. Their experimental design rotated participants through four quite different tasks, with different co-workers for each task. The tasks were chosen to reflect demands for specific, but different, leader behavioral emphases (e.g., for structuring, consultation, persuasion, or production stress). These behaviors are, of course, drawn from the factors of the classic Leader Behavior Description Questionnaire (Halpin & Winer, 1957), which provided appropriate leader behavior rating measures. In analysis, they used the Social Relations model to decompose the overall variance into contributions of rater, ratee, rater-ratee relationship, and group effects. They found that about 40% of the variance in ratings of leadership were attributable to characteristics of the ratees, i.e., to individual differences. The results were, however, weaker when trying to tie specific leader behaviors or leader traits to emergence.

Why did the common knowledge fail? I believe the major contributor was the desire for simple answers to complex problems. Leadership and personality researchers were trying to identify individual differences with a direct impact on leadership outcomes, but they failed to specify what they meant by leadership, which outcomes were important, and what were the processes that underlay those effects.

How Do We Study Leadership?

A significant problem in leadership research in general, and leadership personality research in particular, arises from the failure to specify clearly what is meant by the term leadership. Three broad specifications of leadership are found in the leadership literature: leadership status (focusing on the distinction between leaders, either emergent or appointed) and non-leaders; leadership effectiveness or performance (measured in a multitude of ways); and leadership advancement or managerial career success. Failure to account for differences among these specifications of leadership and the functions and processes that underlie each one has created major opportunities for misunderstanding.

Leadership Status. In the early leadership trait studies, leaders were compared with non-leaders. A variety of testy problems arise from that approach. In some studies the formally appointed leaders in existent organizations were compared with people without leadership status or authority working in those same organizations. Embedded in that operational definition are a number of dubious assumptions and overlooked issues. First, it assumes or implies that people who hold positions of authority in organizations do so on the basis of leadership accomplishment. That assumption confuses managerial status with leadership performance. It also assumes that previous leadership performance is responsible for individuals being chosen for leadership or advanced on the managerial hierarchy. In fact, individuals promoted into the first level of organizational supervision are rarely chosen because of their leadership skills, but are more often selected for technical competence and professional reliability in a non-leadership position. This designation of leadership status also fails to differentiate effective from ineffective performers.

Another approach in leadership status research was to construct ad hoc laboratory groups, composed of college sophomores, in which no individual was initially designated as holding leadership status. Leaders were subsequently identified through observation (e.g., which individual talked the most) or by sociometric means (e.g., ratings by other group members), or other methods. Again, in most of these studies, no attempt is made to assess the quality of the emergent leader's performance. Clearly, a definitional category of leadership that includes both formally appointed corporate managers and emergent student leaders in ad hoc groups (with no history and no future) is too broad.

A more recent form of leadership status research examines the role of personality traits in the prediction of "leadership" career success. These studies use attained managerial level as the measure of leadership. Higher levels managers are compared with lower level managers or non-managers on selected traits. Equating managerial status with leadership success ignores all the non-leadership factors that contribute to career success (e.g., reliability, good health, preferred ethnic or racial status, etc.), and assumes that only successful leaders ascend the managerial hierarchy. While the ability to predict who is likely to attain high-level managerial status might be very valuable, it does not illuminate or even address the processes that underlie leadership performance.

The conclusion that I wish to draw from this line of argument is that if we want to understand the phenomenon of leadership effectiveness, we should study leadership effectiveness. We should employ research designs—whether laboratory or field, whether quantitative or qualitative—that focus on the leadership process and allow us to identify the characteristic traits or behaviors that are associated with leadership effectiveness.

What Do We Mean by "Leadership Effectiveness?"

A single definition of effectiveness cannot be imposed on all groups because groups differ in mission and objectives. A gourmet cooking club might have a very different definition of effectiveness from a professional basketball team or a military combat platoon. Nonetheless, some common measures of effectiveness include productivity, efficiency, and follower reactions.

Groups with tasks that result in a measurable output can be assessed on the dimension of productivity. The number of anagrams solved by a laboratory group, the tons of steel produced on an eight-hour shift by an open hearth steel crew, or the number of games won by a basketball team can be useful measures of productivity. At their best, productivity measures are clearly tied to the group's mission or *raison d'etre* and are objective and quantifiable.

In the pursuit of high productivity, however, a group might act in ways that are actually detrimental to the group or the organization of which it is a part. One example is the use of the group's resources in a profligate manner to achieve short term productivity gains. So, measuring *productivity relative to costs* (i.e., efficiency) provides a better measure of performance for the long run.

When objective measures of performance are not available, ratings by knowledgeable observers (e.g., superiors) can provide measures of productivity or efficiency. One common source of ratings in leadership is other members of the group or team, i.e., followers. Leadership research has used follower ratings of satisfaction, motivation, and commitment to assess leadership performance. Here the leader is judged on the basis of impact on followers. In addition to follower self-ratings, knowledgeable others (e.g., superiors) can provide information relevant to impact on followers. Such information might be objective, as in turnover or absenteeism data, but might also be estimates of follower development in terms of work-relevant capacity or promotion.

There are some who argue that ratings by followers are inappropriate measures of leadership effectiveness because leaders are empowered to perform on the group's assigned task, not to make followers happy. This is a very short-sighted view because follower capacity, motivation, and commitment are usually important contributors to the long-run viability of a group or organization.

A reasonable case can be made that productivity, efficiency, and team development should be combined into an overall measure of mission accomplishment because, at bottom, mission accomplishment is the goal of any group or organization (even if the mission is to have a good time cooking a delicious meal). The most important characteristic of a good dependent measure is that it bears a clear relationship to the goals and objectives of the group and thus provides a vehicle for assessing the effects of leadership.

In summary, research on the role of individual differences in leadership or any other aspect of the leadership phenomenon must focus its attention on the process of leadership and the measurable and appropriate outcomes of that process.

Leadership Effectiveness: Function and Process

Organizational and Leadership Functions. What is the function of leadership in groups and organizations? First, it is important to remember that groups are, by their nature, inefficient (Steiner, 1972). If a task can be accomplished by one individual working alone, there is no need for a group with all the complexities of roles, status distinctions, and communication problems. However, most of the tasks that a society needs to accomplish cannot be done by a single person, working alone. Groups and organizations are developed as vehicles for organizing human effort to address necessary tasks or missions. As the size of a group or an organizations grows, issues of direction and coordination of effort become increasingly important.

At the organizational level, we can identify two major functions that address internal integrity and external reactivity (Schein, 1992; Chemers, 1997). Much of any organization's activity deals with routine and recurrent events that require the organization to develop orderly systems that provide for stability and efficiency. Orderly and efficient systems are characterized by reliability, predictability, and accountability. Reactions to recurrent and expected events should be standardized to provide reliability. Reliable systems allow members of the organization to predict by whom, when, and how events will be managed. A stable and reliable system makes it possible to know who is responsible and accountable for success or failure.

Organizations develop rules, standard operating procedures, and social norms that encourage adherence to expected patterns of behavior.

The conundrum of organizational life, however, is that most organizations do not always deal with stable and routine events. Organizations exist in dynamic environments that create changing demands for success. Changing environments are often characterized by equivocal information (Lawrence & Lorsch, 1967). To deal with external change, organizations must be reactive and adaptive. External adaptability depends on sensitivity, flexibility, and responsiveness. The organization must be sensitive enough to its external environment to detect changing conditions (e.g., new markets, new competitors, changing regulatory environment, etc.). Their internal systems must be flexible enough to respond to change, and the organization must be responsive in developing appropriate new systems.

Organizational systems that build reliability and predictability can be antithetical to change and adaptation. Successful organizational functioning requires a balance between internal stability and external responsiveness. That balancing act is the responsibility of leadership.

The leaders of teams or departments at all levels of an organization must address functions parallel to those at the organizational level. When a group is confronted with a task or mission that is routine and well understood, the leader's primary functions are the motivation and guidance of team members. Group members must be given assignments and guided, trained, and supported in their accomplishment.

When teams are confronted with tasks that are not well understood, that require creativity or problem-solving and decision-making, the leader's functions are different. In less predictable situations, leaders must establish an atmosphere and process that encourage creativity and involvement. Giving orders and expecting compliance is not a viable leadership strategy when neither leader nor follower is sure what orders should be given.

A good analogy for the leadership function in groups is to think of leadership as the group's collective intelligence (Chemers, 2002). Sternberg's (1988) triarchic model of intelligence defines intelligence as the employment of an individual's internal resources to attain desired goals. The individual engages the environment in order both to bring to bear existing knowledge and skills as well as to sample the environment to determine what new skills and knowledge must be developed to meet changing demands. The individual relies on existing capacities to deal with recurrent problems and builds on those resources to develop new capabilities for dealing with change. The hallmark of this process is the capability to turn novel and unpredictable features of the environment into well understood and routinely manageable ones.

The analogy to the function of leadership in groups is apt. In well understood and structured tasks or situations, the leader works to assemble the existing knowledge, expertise, and skills of group members and apply them to the group's task. When confronted with unstructured, unpredictable, or novel situations, the leader helps the group to draw on its existing resources to develop new strategies, i.e., to gather information, make decisions, and solve problems.

Leadership Processes. Turning from what it is that leaders must accomplish, we can ask how they accomplish those functions: That is, what are the processes that underlie effective leadership?

An Historical Overview. After leadership trait research became less popular, empirical research and theorizing proceeded through a number of identifiable phases. In the 1950s, research focused on leadership behavior. Studies with varying methodologies—e.g., interviews with industrial production supervisors and workers (Katz & Kahn, 1966); observations and categorical ratings of groups processes in laboratory groups (Bales & Slater, 1955); and leader behavior surveys (Halpin & Winer, 1957)—came to the common conclusion that leadership behavior fell into two major categories: Structuring or task-relevant behaviors included assigning tasks and evaluating performance, integrating group efforts, and encouraging high performance. Consideration or relationship-oriented behaviors included maintaining high morale, providing advice and support to subordinates, and smoothing intra-group conflict.

During the same time period and into the early 1960s, attention was paid to the impact of situational characteristics on leadership emergence behavior. Studies found that holding a central or focal position in a communication network increased the probability of emergent leadership (Leavitt, 1951). Task characteristics were found to have a strong effect on leadership behavior (Hackman & Morris, 1975). Although these studies did not reach any unified consensus, they helped to establish the importance of situational characteristics in leadership and set the table for the emergence of "contingency theories."

During the late '60s and '70s, leadership researchers developed and tested models that integrated leader characteristics or behaviors with situational parameters. The extensive and groundbreaking work by Fred Fiedler (1967) indicated that leadership motivation or style (i.e., focus on task versus relationship) interacted with situational factors related to the degree of follower support and task clarity. The discovery that the success of each leader type was contingent (i.e., dependent) on the situation led to the coining of the term "contingency model" and revolutionized thinking about leadership. Contingency theories of leader decision-making (Vroom & Yetton, 1973) and follower motivation (House & Mitchell, 1974) followed.

The prominence of theories of social cognition and attribution in the late '70s and '80s influenced leadership research. Perceptions of leaders by followers and observers (Lord, 1985) and perceptions of followers by leaders (Green &Mitchell, 1979) revealed that pre-existing cognitive structures and various information processing biases had significant effects on how leaders and followers were seen, which, in turn, had strong effects on leader-follower interactions.

Following seminal work by Burns (1978) and House (1977) addressing charismatic and exceptional leadership, a strong body of research developed around "transformational leadership." Transformational leadership, in contrast to transactional or "quid pro quo" relationships, changed followers from self-interested negotiators into unselfish, committed, mission-oriented contributors. An extensive body of research by Bass and his associates (Bass, 1985; Bass & Avolio, 1988) identified the leadership characteristics and behaviors associated with transformational leadership. Such leaders were seen as having exceptional abilities and character ("idealized influence"); an appealing and inspiring vision ("inspirational motivation"); the ability to encourage and support follower risk-taking, development, and growth ("intellectual stimulation"); and supportive, sympathetic, and sincere relationships with followers ("individualized consideration"). This work stimulated an intense period of research on exceptional leadership that continues to the present day.

Each of these periods of leadership theorizing and empirical work resulted in some consistent findings, but the failure to integrate the findings into a broader approach resulted in a fragmented and apparently contradictory body of knowledge.

An Integrative Approach. In other work (Chemers, 1997; 2005), I have presented an "integrative" theory of leadership that draws broadly on this research literature and attempts to integrate the most well established findings. In this section, I will introduce the integrative theory's three elements of effective leadership. In later sections, I will expand the discussion by citing the relevant findings, with a focus on how individual differences might fit into the equation.

A common definition of leadership is "a process of social influence in which one person is able to enlist the aid and support of others in the accomplishment of a common task" (Chemers, 1997). This definition recognizes the central and crucial role of influence in leadership. A voluminous literature in social psychology makes it clear that influence is built on credibility (Hovland & Weiss, 1952). The first step in the effective leadership process is the establishment of the leader's credibility with significant others—primarily followers. The integrative theory refers to this element of effective leadership as *image management*.

The second part of the definition highlights the need to enlist aid and support. For followers to aid and support a leader, both capacity and motivation are necessary. The second critical aspect of leadership is the development of that capacity and motivation. Leaders must build relationships with followers that encourage followers to give maximum effort to mission accomplishment and empower and develop the followers' capacity to contribute. This element is referred to as *relationship development*.

Finally, the resources that a motivated group of capable individuals possess must be appropriately applied to the group's task or mission. This element of leadership matches the resources of the group to the problem at hand. Information must be analyzed and digested and decisions made in a manner that uses available capacity most effectively. This element is called *resource deployment*.

In summary, effective leadership depends on the leader developing enough credibility with the group to make influence possible. Then influence must be used to develop and encourage subordinate contribution. Finally, group resources must be successfully deployed for mission accomplishment.

INDIVIDUAL DIFFERENCE MODELS AND LEADERSHIP

In the early part of this chapter, I made the argument that individual differences are an important contributor to effective leadership behavior, but I rejected simple one-to-one correlations of those individual characteristics and broad leadership outcomes. Before turning to a more in-depth description of leadership process, we need to find a more appropriate conceptualization for the individual differences component.

Individual Differences

Some personality theorists have long recognized that no personality trait—regardless of its breadth or stability—can be linked to behavioral outcomes in the absence of some consideration of situational or contextual variables. Rotter (1954) made the case that personality traits influence behavioral choices after consideration of situations and possible rewards and punishments. Kelly's (1955) theory of personal constructs likewise viewed personality as affecting alternative interpretations of similar situations.

Among social psychologists, Allport (1966) recognized that internal characteristics, such as traits or disposition, only manifest themselves in situations that are conducive to their expression. A beacon for social psychological theorizing has long been Lewin's (1935) dictum that behavior is a function of the person in interaction with the situation.

Personality and Cognition. Attempts to find a middle ground between intrapersonal traits and behavior were given momentum by Cantor's (1990) analysis of the role of cognition in the behavioral expression of dispositional tendencies. Cantor presented an analysis of the ways that cognition links intrapersonal factors to behavior in context. She argued that the expression of traits was determined by "the most accessible schema for envisaging future selves and devising strategies to guide behavior in relevant situations" (p. 735). Schemas are organized structures of knowledge about the self and one's life goals. Schemas provide consistency with personal dispositions by channeling perception in support of those goals and self concepts, thus providing some continuity across situations and time. Schemas act in the service of life-tasks or personal agendas and give rise to and shape strategies to direct behavior in a social context of opportunities and constraints.

McCrae and Costa (1996) adopted an ambitious approach to understanding the expression of traits by offering a new model of personality theory built around the five-factor model of personality (i.e., Big 5 personality traits, discussed in detail a bit later). In an approach that is compatible with Cantor's (1990) analysis, McCrae and Costa (1996) argue that to be useful, personality theories need to recognize that the expression of a trait is not universal and unchanging but must take into account the interaction of the trait with the social environment. The models of Cantor and McCrae and Costa provide some suggestions for personality research in leadership.

More recently, personality theorists have made arguments that are very compatible with my own emphasis on function, process, and situation. Wiggins and Trapnell (1996) have synthesized much of the five-factor model of leadership to a focus on "agency" and "communion" as the two most inclusive and important traits in societal perspective. Agency is related to individualism and task-relevant success, while communion parallels interpersonal consideration and collectivism and is the basis for group solidarity. Constructs in leadership theory (i.e., structuring versus consideration; task versus relationship orientation) are treated very similarly.

A particularly strong situationist perspective is taken by Marshall and Brown (2006) in the presentation of the Traits As Situational Sensitivities (TASS) model. Here traits are seen as propensities for action that are elicited or provoked by situational factors. Thus, a person who might be thought of as aggressive might need less provocation to act aggressively but wouldn't necessarily be more aggressive than others in every situation. Hypothesizing such a critical role for situations in the understanding of the effects of individual differences is very consistent with leadership theorizing.

Leadership is, after all, an extremely social phenomenon. Leadership is not an aspect of a person but can only be manifest in social situations. Productive avenues for personality research in leadership need to begin by asking what are the dynamic processes of leadership and how can we identify the characteristic adaptations and self-concepts that relate to those processes. First, let's look at the current state of knowledge.

Individual Differences and Leadership. Zaccaro et al. (2004) recently presented an extensive and perceptive analysis of personality trait research and theory on leadership. After offering a brief history of what they call the "rise and fall and rise of leader trait research," they offer a detailed and comprehensive review of individual difference research on leadership for the period 1990-2003, as well as some propositions delineating the role of individual differences in leadership processes.

Zaccaro et al. group stable individual differences into five broad categories: (1) cognitive abilities; (2) personality; (3) motivation; (4) social appraisal skills; and (5) problem-solving skills, expertise, and tacit knowledge.

Cognitive Abilities. General intelligence has been one of the most widely studied variables in leadership research. Measures of general cognitive ability have been consistently associated with leadership status (e.g., emergence in ad hoc laboratory groups) and career advancement (e.g., attained organizational level of management) and sometimes with leadership effectiveness as well.

Measures of creative or divergent thinking have been associated with differences between leaders and followers and with career achievement. However, delving just a bit deeper reveals significant complexity. For example, in a study of team decision making (LePine, Hollenbeck, Ilgen, & Hedlund, 1997) a measure of the leader's cognitive ability was associated with the decision accuracy of group solutions, but that relationship was moderated by the cognitive abilities of the team members. In an extensive analysis of the effects of leadership intelligence on group performance, Fiedler and Garcia (1987) report extremely complex relationships among leader intelligence, experience, and stress engendered by boss, co-workers, or task. Intelligence tends to be correlated with group performance in low stress situations, while experience predicts performance under high stress situations. The impact of leader abilities and knowledge on performance is also mediated by the leader's willingness to take charge in both high and low stress situations.

A reasonable summary of the role of cognitive abilities in leadership is that smart people are more likely to be rated as having high leadership potential than less intelligent people. People in positions of great authority and responsibility are likely to be smarter, on average, than people in less demanding situations and to have greater career success. The relationship of leader cognitive ability to group performance is far more complex, involving interactions with a host of follower and situational variables.

Personality. Here I will focus on the most prominent and inclusive personality approach—the Big 5.

The Big 5 personality categories (Neuroticism, Extraversion, Conscientiousness, Openness to Experience, and Agreeableness) have been widely studied in support of their growing contribution to managerial selection. The results are complex, but generally supportive of the conclusion that these personality variables are consistently associated with some aspects of leadership. A meta-analysis by Judge, Bono, Ilies, and Gerhardt (2002) included 78 Big 5 studies. They concluded that extraversion has the strongest association with leadership, followed by conscientiousness, neuroticism, and openness, with agreeableness being the weakest. With studies of leadership status (either emergence or career success), all the categories except agreeableness are significant predictors. In studies of leadership effectiveness, all five categories yield reliable results. For all studies included, the multiple R is .48. The Big 5 seem most consistently predictive for career success, and less so for leadership effectiveness in a specific context.

There seems to be little question that deep-seated, endogenous tendencies are related to some specifications of leadership outcomes in some situations and contexts. The challenge seems to be for the development of a conceptual model or strategy to identify or predict which outcomes in which situations.

Motivation. For some time, leadership researchers have been interested in the classic motivational measures of need for power (or dominance), need for achievement, and need for affiliation. A body of research outside the scope of this review uses qualitative historical data (e.g., biographical writings, speeches, etc.) to establish motivational scores for historical figures and relate those scores to variously defined leadership achievements (House, Spangler, & Woycke, 1991; Deluga, 1998).

Turning to research on contemporary leaders, we find that very little evidence supports the association of the need for affiliation with any of the leadership outcomes. The needs for power and achievement, however, do seem to be associated with leadership measures, but not consistently. For example, Connelly, Gilbert, Zaccaro, Threlfall, Marks, and Mumford (2001) reported no effects for needs for dominance or achievement on measures of leader career achievement or leadership problem solution quality. However, Zaccaro, White, et al. (1997) reported effects for both need for achievement and need for dominance on career achievement indices and rated leadership potential for army civilian managers. Illustrating the complexity involved in this type of research, Smith and Foti (1998) found that dominance motivation was associated with leadership emergence, but only in combination with general intelligence and self-efficacy.

Chan and Drasgow (2001) have embarked on a promising line of conceptually driven research around the construct of "motivation to lead." Motivation to lead is conceptualized as a proximal mediator for leadership effects of personality (Big 5), cognitive ability, efficacy, and socio-cultural values. Chan and Drasgow (2001) report results for three samples (Singaporean students, military recruits, and U.S. college students) that support the model. Motivation to lead was positively associated with leadership potential ratings after controlling for all other predictors. The effects on leadership ratings of variables like leader experience, leader efficacy, personality, and values were at least partially mediated by the motivation-to-lead measure. Here again, we see an approach that argues that deep-seated, general personality and ability measures are mediated by a more context relevant, individual difference—in this case a motivational construct.

Social Appraisal Skills. Zaccaro and his colleagues (Zaccaro, 1999, 2001, 2002; Zaccaro, Foti, et al., 1991; Zaccaro, Gilbert, Thor, & Mumford, 1991) have paid considerable attention to the role of social appraisal skills (social intelligence) in leadership outcomes, assigning this variable a central role. The focus is on the "leader's understanding of the feelings, thoughts, and behaviors of others in a social domain and his or her selection of the responses that best fit the contingencies and dynamics of that domain" (Zaccaro, 2004; in Antonakis, p. 115).

One such skill, self-monitoring, has been associated with leadership emergence ratings and rankings and with perceived behavioral responsiveness to situational factors (Zaccaro, Foti, et al., 1991). A meta-analysis of 23 samples found that self-monitoring was strongly associated with leadership (Day, Schleicher, Unckless, & Hiller, 2002).

Social intelligence (various measures) have been associated with leader emergence (Ferentinos, 1996), leadership ranking in a military sample (Zaccaro, Zazanis, Diana, & Gilbert, 1994), and career achievement of military officers (Gilbert & Zaccaro, 1995).

Emotional intelligence is another potential contributor to leadership effectiveness. Caruso, Mayer, and Salovey (2002) enumerate the ways in which a leader would greatly benefit from high levels of emotional intelligence. The ability to *identify* emotions that others are feeling allows a leader to react in appropriate ways when trying to motivate or direct followers. *Understanding* emotions (i.e., the meaning of emotions and the relationships of particular emotions to other feelings and behavior) provides a leader with an ability to navigate the difficult terrain of communication and cooperation in groups. The ability to *use* emotions provides the leader with a powerful tool, i.e., a means for establishing or changing the emotional mood of a group, for example, to enhance motivation or buffer against threat. Finally, the ability to *manage one's own* emotions provides calmness and resilience during the inevitable ups and downs of organizational life.

Problem-Solving, Expertise, and Tacit Knowledge. As noted earlier, uncertain and equivocal situations frequently call on leaders to be problem solvers, i.e., to process available information and make decisions that provide order and direction. Mumford, Zaccaro, et al. (2000) also argued that problem-solving skills are critical to effective leadership. Several studies support that argument, indicating that problem definition and solution predict career achievement (Connelly, et al., 2000; Zaccaro, White, et al., 1997).

Building on Sternberg's triarchic model of intelligence (1988; 2002), Zaccaro et al. (2004) propose that the development of broad tacit knowledge as a result of leadership experience provides leaders with the ability to respond and adapt to changing conditions.

The review by Zaccaro et al. leads to cautious optimism. Although the literature on leadership traits tends to be somewhat scattergun (i.e., many different traits are related to many different outcomes without much theoretical integration or order), many studies do provide compelling evidence that personal traits, dispositions, and knowledge are an important component of the leadership equation.

ELEMENTS OF EFFECTIVE LEADERSHIP IN DYNAMIC PROCESS

I will turn now to a fuller explication of the elements of effective leadership (i.e, image management and relationship development) to suggest how the current leader trait literature might be integrated with a process-oriented leadership model. I will focus on the elements of image management and relationship development because they are the elements most driven by interpersonal process. The literature chosen for inclusion here is not meant to be exhaustive, but rather to provide some examples for consideration. (See Chemers, 1997; 2005 for a fuller exposition.)

Image Management

Prototypical Characteristics of Effective Leaders. As noted earlier, image management is the establishment of the credibility that creates the basis for a leader's informal authority. Early studies of communicator credibility in attitude change research (e.g., Hovland & Weiss, 1952) found that perceptions of competence and trustworthiness were the primary determinants of credibility. In seminal studies on leadership status and influence, Hollander (1958; 1960) found that individuals who were seen as helping a group make progress toward a goal were seen as competent and those who acted in conformity with group norms were seen as trustworthy. Those individuals were accorded greater influence and opportunity for innovation (i.e., *idiosyncrasy credit*).

Hollander's experimental methodology provided opportunities to demonstrate competency and trustworthiness in clear and compelling ways. In life outside the laboratory (e.g., in organizations), group members are rarely offered such clear information, and judgments of leaders are made on diffuse impressions and inferences that arise from a leader's behavior and demeanor. Lord and his associates (Lord, 1985; Lord, Binning, Rush, & Thomas, 1978; Lord & Maher, 1991) have amply demonstrated that such judgments are heavily influenced by implicit theories and stereotypical expectations (prototypes). Observers of a leader, holding prototypes influenced by experience or culture, look for a match between a leader's characteristics and their prototype for the role. Although prototypes vary somewhat for different categories of leadership (e.g., business, military, political, religious, etc.), the common theme across categories encompasses characteristics (e.g., decisiveness, intelligence, honesty, etc.) that suggest a leader's ability to move the group towards mission accomplishment. This extensive literature suggests that along with honesty, task-relevant competency is the most important element in establishing a credible image.

In-Group Salience as a Moderator of the Desirable Leadership Prototype. However, Hogg and his associates (Hogg, 2001; Hogg, Hains, & Mason, 1998; van Knippenberg & Hogg, 2003) offer theory and evidence for a different perspective. From the perspective of *social identity theory* (Tajfel & Turner, 1979), groups are seen as vehicles for individuals to establish and maintain positive personal identities. That identity is based, in part, on the properties of the groups to which a person belongs. This leads individuals to concentrate on the ways in which their group is different from and better than other groups. This categorization encourages clear distinctions between the in-group and other out-groups. Membership and *status* in the in-group are determined by the degree to which an individual's behavior is in agreement with the representative characteristics of the group, i.e., the group prototype. Leadership then, which is very much a question of status, is awarded and maintained on the basis of in-group prototypicality rather than task-relevant competence. In this case, prototypicality is quite similar to the concept of conformity in Hollander's interpretation.

The more salient group identity becomes, the more important prototypicality is as the determinant of status and leadership. Hogg (2005) details the way in which leaders can highlight or even manipulate group identity salience to enhance their hold on leadership status. However, there are also circumstances in which other factors might become more salient than prototypicality (Chemers, 2005). One such circumstance relevant to this discussion is when the group's objective performance on its task or mission is highly salient. Such might be the case, for example, for a sports team in a crucial game or a military combat unit under attack. Thus, the nature of the group and its long-term or short-term situational demands would influence when competence would override prototypicality as a determinant of leadership judgments.

Observer Bias in Prototype Perception. Even when leaders possess and display characteristics consistent with the prototype for a leader, ethnic or gender biases may make a person less likely to be seen as credible leader. Lord and Maher (1991) report that in the early stages of impression formation and evaluation, women are less likely to be seen as good leaders, but the effect of this bias fades as group members have more opportunity to observe the person in action.

Expectation states theory (Berger & Zelditch, 1998) illuminates the ways in which biased expectations influence leadership emergence and evaluation. Members of a group bring with them expectations about others. These expectations, which are often based on the ethnic or gender group to which the other belongs, accord status consistent with the standing of the ethnic or gender group in surrounding society.

However, it is also the case that individual differences may moderate the impact of observer bias on the image of non-traditional leaders. Chemers, Watson, and May (2000) developed a measure of "leadership efficacy" based on Bandura's (1997) concept of self-efficacy. In a longitudinal study of military cadets undergoing instruction and training, Chemers et al. found that leadership efficacy was a strong positive predictor of leadership evaluations by instructors, superior officers, peers, and trained observers. Hoyt and Blascovich (2005) found in a laboratory experiment that women leaders with high leadership efficacy maintained high motivation and exhibited active leadership, even after being reminded of negative stereotypes about female leader, while women low in leadership efficacy showed a dramatic decline in leadership activity.

It is easy to see the problem that these complexities create in any effort to tie particular traits or dispositions to leadership status and image, but the complexity doesn't end with characteristics and processes of observers.

Person/Situation Fit and Prototype Expression. Various situational factors affect the display of valued behavior by a leadership aspirant. For example, the Contingency Model of Leadership Effectiveness (Fiedler, 1972; Fiedler & Chemers, 1974) predicts that a leader will be effective to the degree to which his/her leadership motivational pattern is well suited or "matched" to the situation. Leaders who highly value task success and concentrate on building an orderly structure to achieve success perform most effectively (i.e., are matched) either when the situation is very clear and supportive (which provides a basis for clear structure) or when the situation is extremely uncertain and difficult (which necessitates the need for structure). On the other hand, leaders who value and are motivated by the fellowship and respect of others and who favor more participative and considerate leader behavior are matched when the situation is of moderate complexity. Moderately complex situations are characterized by unclear and unstructured tasks or weak support from followers. These ambiguous and equivocal conditions yield the best performance when all group members are encouraged to contribute to problem solving and decision making (i.e., participative leadership). Fiedler and Garcia (1987) report that leaders who are matched to their situation are seen as more active and more effective. We have now added another level of complexity by including the interaction of a trait and the situation. Sometimes, more than a single trait enters such an interaction.

Moderators of Person/Situation Fit. Ayman and Chemers (1991) reported a Contingency Model study that added the trait of *self-monitoring* (Snyder, 1974). Ayman and Chemers found that, although out-of-match managers were seen as less effective by their subordinates and superiors, the effect didn't hold for leaders high on the self-monitoring construct. Those leaders, even when out of their element, were able to read social cues and behave in ways that were rated highly.

These few studies, from among many that could be cited, reveal that attempts to make direct connections between leadership performance and unitary traits are extremely difficult. Although characteristics like extraversion, honesty, confidence, experience, and knowledge might be good candidates for inclusion in a predictive model of leadership effects, their predictive power and pervasiveness are moderated by the dynamic process in which leader and follower traits and contextual factors interact in complex patterns. How might we use an understanding of process to take a different direction on individual differences?

We might begin by acknowledging the soundness of the suggestion by Zaccaro et al. (2004) that task-relevant skills and tacit knowledge should contribute to follower perceptions of leader competence. To provide a more nuanced version of that hypothesis we might acknowledge that tacit knowledge is the result of experience mediated by intelligence, i.e., smart people learn more from their experience than less intelligent counterparts (Fiedler & Garcia, 1987). We would also recognize that for knowledge to manifest itself, active attempts at leadership must occur, so the knowledge-perceived competency link might be mediated by the motivation to lead (Chan & Drasgow, 2001). Motivation to lead might be more or less affected by leadership efficacy depending on the nature of the leader (i.e., personal characteristics such as personality, gender, etc.) in interaction with contextual or situational variables (e.g., stress, task clarity, follower attitudes; Hoyt & Blascovich, 2005). These moderators and mediators might yield a pattern like the one shown below:

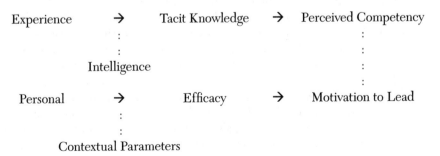

This hypothesis is but one of many possible. Other theoretical frameworks would make different predictions. The important point is that predictions are embedded in a theoretical framework that recognizes social process in context.

RELATIONSHIP DEVELOPMENT

Leaders are able to build supportive and enabling relationships with followers when a sensitive appreciation of followers' abilities, needs, and desires provides the basis for effective coaching in an atmosphere of fairness.

Coaching

Leader Behavior and Situational Moderators. The literature on the relationship of leader behavior to follower satisfaction and performance is extensive. For illustrative purposes, I will focus on the balance between structuring, directive behavior versus considerate and emotionally supportive behavior. Early attempts to determine which set of behaviors was most effective led nowhere. (See Bass, [1981], or Chemers, [1997] for fuller expositions on this work.)

A promising step at resolving this issue was made by *Path-Goal Theory* (House & Mitchell, 1972). This model argues that the nature of a subordinate's work environment—particularly the degree of clarity and structure in assigned tasks—moderates the effectiveness of structuring, versus considerate behavior. Structuring behavior will enhance subordinate motivation and performance when there is a lack of inherent structure in the tasks. Considerate, supportive behavior has its best effects when a subordinate's tasks are boring or aversive. However, structure in terms of characteristics of the task may also be affected by the knowledge, experience, and ability of the subordinate, i.e., a task that seems unstructured for one subordinate may not seem so to another.

An additional complexity is added to the equation when we take into account traits of followers. Griffin (1981) reports an organizational study of Path-Goal predictions in which the "growth need strength" (Hackman & Oldham, 1976) of followers was included. Growth need strength is a measure of the degree to which an individual values opportunities for personal growth and development on the job. Such individuals tend to be energized rather than debilitated by unstructured tasks, because they provide an opportunity for learning and development. Griffin found that subordinates who were high in growth need strength did not react positively to a superior's structuring and directive behavior, even when their task was unstructured and ambiguous. Followers low in growth need strength (i.e., individuals who do not seek challenge in their work) did not react negatively to boring tasks and didn't respond positively to leaders' supportive behavior in those conditions.

These findings make it very clear that to make effective interventions leaders need to know how much structuring or consideration might be suggested by task characteristics, but they must also judge followers' abilities and personal needs. Effective judgments are the necessary conditions for good leader-follower relationships, and a voluminous literature in social psychology attests to the traps and pitfalls inherent in the attribution processes that underlie interpersonal judgments.

Attribution and Judgment. Mitchell and his colleagues (Green & Mitchell, 1979; Mitchell & Wood, 1980) have detailed the problematic nature of leaders' attributions for the causes of subordinate success and failure. They report that leaders choose what course of action to take in the case of subordinate poor performance on the basis of attributions to internal factors (subordinate ability or motivation) or external factors (poorly structured tasks or uncontrollable circumstances). Internal attributions for subordinate failure lead to more punitive actions by a leader. Unfortunately, the attributions to internal or external factors were clouded by considerations, such as outcome severity (i.e., how bad the results of the behavior turned out to be) even when severity was unrelated and irrelevant to the locus of cause in manipulated scenarios.

Biases in attributions by leaders are, in part, generated by the "reciprocal causality" (Weick, 1969) inherent in the leadership relationship, i.e., that the behaviors and performance of leader and follower have important implications for both parties. Subordinate poor performance usually results in poor group performance on which the leader is evaluated. Furthermore, if the causes of subordinate poor performance are external, as in the case of a poorly structured or poorly supported task, the fault probably lies with failures on the leader's part. Brown (1984) noted that leaders are especially prone to ego-defensive attributions (blaming subordinates for their own failures) when poor performance is a characteristic of the whole group, not just a single subordinate, because of the increased repercussions associated with group level failure. Perversely enough, failure at the group level is usually a pretty good indication that the fault lies with the leader rather than every subordinate in the group. Inaccurate attributions (i.e., blaming a subordinate when the leader is at fault) can engender ill-advised (e.g., punitive) actions that may result in follower resentment and disengagement.

Leadership status and the attendant power may be broadly problematic for judgment accuracy. Kipnis (1972; 1976) found in a role-playing exercise that leaders with accentuated power tended to exert more influence tactics, felt more control over subordinates' efforts, and valued them less. Magee, Gruenfeld, Keltner, and Galinsky (2005) present compelling arguments that high levels of power can actually change a leader's focus. Powerful leaders become increasingly self-focused, leading to a tendency towards precipitous action, disinhibition of social constraints, objectification of subordinates, and a focus on personal goals at the expense of the common good. These tendencies can be reduced if powerful leaders are also subject to accountability through surveillance and democratic processes that may weaken the hold on power. The negative effects of power on judgment and action can contribute to leader behavior that is seen as unfair in an organizational context, and fairness is one of the key determinants of successful leader-follower relationships.

Fairness and Justice. The social exchange between leaders and followers is at the very core of the leadership relationship. In an extremely insightful analysis, Messick (2005) puts a human face on the leader-follower relationship and details five important exchanges: Leaders provide (a) vision and direction in exchange for follower focus and self-direction; (b) protection and security for gratitude and loyalty; (c) achievement and effectiveness for commitment and effort; (d) inclusion and belongingness for cooperation and sacrifice; and (e) pride and self-respect for respect and obedience. Based on a large and carefully executed program of research, Tyler (2005) argues that respect is at the core of relationships that are seen as fair and equitable. Respectful relationships are exemplified by leaders who listen to follower opinions when contemplating a decision and who explain the bases for the decisions that are made. Follower voice and leader justification are the essential features of relational fairness.

Thus, leaders who by personality, experience, or training are good at sensing what others need and who can control the pernicious consequences of power are highly effective in the interpersonal exchanges that empower and enable followers and teams. Research that flows from this view of social process might posit that a leader's social and emotional intelligence, moderated by self awareness and ethical values, should enhance the quality of leader judgments and attendant behavior to yield higher levels of follower satisfaction and commitment.

CONCLUSIONS

From Stogdill to Zaccaro, careful analyses have revealed that while individual differences (i.e., traits, dispositions, skills, motivation, etc.) are an extremely important part of effective leadership, the relationship between individual differences and group outcomes is not simple or linear. Leadership involves establishing the validity of influence that allows for relationship building for follower motivation and capacity. The effective utilization of group resources applied to mission accomplishment depends on the leader and the group's environmental sensitivity and strategic flexibility. To bring together individual differences and leadership process requires a research strategy that is empirical, theory driven, and tested in the crucible of actual leadership activities in the pursuit of validly measured outcomes and that recognizes that leadership and followership are part of a dynamic social process.

REFERENCES

Allport, G. W. (1966). Traits revisited. *American Psychologist, 21*, 1–10.
Ayman, R., & Chemers, M. M. (1991). The effect of leadership match on subordinate satisfaction in Mexican organizations: Some moderating influences of self-monitoring. *International Review of Applied Psychology, 40*, 299–314.
Bales, R. F. (1950). *Interaction process analysis.* Reading, MA: Addison-Wesley.
Bales, R. F., & Slater, P. E. (1955). Role differentiation in small decision-making groups. In T. Parsons (Ed.), *Family, socialization, and interaction process.* Glencoe, IL: Free Press.
Bandura, A. (1997). *Self-efficacy: The exercise of the self.* New York: W. H. Freeman.
Barnlund, D. C. (1962). Consistency of emergent leadership in groups with changing tasks and members. *Speech Monographs, 29*, 45–52.
Bass, B. M. (1981). *Stogdill's handbook of leadership* (2nd ed.). New York: Free Press.
Bass, B. M. (1985). *Leadership and performance beyond expectations.* New York: Free Press.

Bass, B. M. (1990). *Bass and Stogdill's handbook of leadership* (3rd ed.). New York: Free Press.
Bass, B. M., & Avolio, B. J. (1990). Transformational leadership, charisma, and beyond. In J. G. Hunt, B. R. Baliga, H. P. Dachler, & C. A. Shriesheim (Eds.), *Emerging leadership vistas* (pp. 29–49). Lexington, MA: Lexington Books.
Bell, G. B., & French, R. L. (1950). Consistency of individual leadership position in small groups of varying membership. *Journal of Abnormal and Social Psychology, 45,* 764–767.
Berger, J., & Zelditch, M. (1998). *Status, power, and legitimacy: Strategies and theories.* New Brunswick, NJ: Transaction Press.
Borgatta, E. F., Bales, R. F., & Crouch, A. S. (1954). Some findings relevant to the great man theory of leadership. *American Sociological Review, 19,* 755–759.
Brown, K. A. (1984). Explaining group poor performance: An attributional analysis. *Academy of Management Review, 9,* 54–63.
Burns, J. M. (1978). *Leadership.* New York: Harper & Row.
Cantor, N. (1990). From thought to behavior: "Having" and "doing" in the study of personality and cognition. *American Psychologist, 45,* 735–750.
Carlyle, T. (1907). *Heroes and hero worship.* Boston: Adams. (Original work published in 1841)
Carter, L. F., & Nixon, M. (1949). An investigation of the relationship between four criteria of leadership ability for three different tasks. *Journal of Psychology, 27,* 245–261.
Caruso, D. R., Mayer, J. D., & Salovey, P. (2002). Emotional intelligence and emotional leadership. In R. E. Riggio, S. E. Murphy, & F. J. Pirozzolo (Eds.), *Multiple intelligences and leadership* (pp. 139–160). Mahwah, NJ: Erlbaum.
Chan, K., & Drasgow, F. (2001). Toward a theory of individual differences and leadership: Understanding the motivation to lead. *Journal of Applied Psychology, 86*(3), 481–498.
Chemers, M. M. (1997). *An integrative theory of leadership.* Mahwah, NJ: Erlbaum.
Chemers, M. M. (2002). Efficacy and effectiveness: Integrating models of leadership and intelligence. In R. E. Riggio, S. E. Murphy, & F. J. Pirozzolo (Eds.), *Multiple intelligences and leadership* (pp. 139–160). Mahwah, NJ: Erlbaum.
Chemers, M. M. (2005). Leadership effectiveness: Functionalist, contructivist, and empirical perspectives. In D. v. Knippenberg & M. A. Hogg (Eds.), *Leadership and power: Identity processes in groups and organizations.* London: Sage.
Chemers, M. M., Watson, C. B., & May, S. (2000) Dispositional affect and leadership effectiveness: A comparison of self-esteem, optimism, and efficacy. In *Personality and Social Psychology Bulletin, 26*(3), 267–277.
Connelly, M. S., Gilbert, J. A., Threlfall, K. V., Marks, M. A., & Mumford. M. D. (2000). Exploring the relationship of leadership skills and knowledge to leadership performance. *Leadership Quarterly, 11,* 65–86.
Connelly, M. S., Gilbert, J. A., Zaccaro, S. J., Threlfall, K. V., Marks, M. A. & Mumford, M. D. (2001). Exploring the relationship of leadership skills and knowledge to leadership performance. *Leadership Quarterly, 11,* 65–86.
Day, D., Schleicher, D., Unckless, A., & N. Hiller (2002). Self-monitoring personality at work: A meta-analytic investigation of construct validity. *Journal of Applied Psychology, 87*(2), 390–401.
Deluga, R. J. (1998). American presidential proactivity, charismatic leadership, and rated performance. *Leadership Quarterly, 12,* 339–363.
Ferentinos, C. H. (1996). Linking social intelligence and leadership: An investigation of leaders' situational responsiveness under conditions of changing group tasks and membership. *Dissertation Abstracts International: Section B: The Sciences & Engineering, 57,* (UMI No. 9625606).

Fiedler, F. E. (1967). *A theory of leadership effectiveness.* New York: McGraw-Hill.
Fiedler, F. E., & Chemers, M.M. (1974). Leadership and management. In J. W. McGuire, (Ed.), *Contemporary management: Issues and viewpoints.* New York: McGraw-Hill.
Fiedler, F. E., & Garcia, J. E. (1987). *New approaches to effective leadership: Cognitive resources and organizational performance.* New York: Wiley.
Galton, F. (1879). *Hereditary genius.* New York: Appleton.
Gibb, C. A. (1949). Some tentative comments concerning group Rorschach pointers to personality traits of leaders. *Journal of Social Psychology, 30,* 251–263.
Gilbert, J. A., & Zaccaro, S. J. (1995, August). *Social intelligence and organizational leadership.* Presented at the 103rd annual meeting of the American Psychological Association, New York.
Goddard, H. H. (1911). Two thousand normal children measured by the Binet measuring scale of intelligence. *Pedagogical Seminary, 18,* 232–259.
Graen, G. (1976). Role making processes with complex organizations. In M. D. Dunnette (Ed.), *Handbook of industrial and organizational psychology* (pp. 1202–1245). Chicago: Rand McNally.
Green, S. G., & Mitchell, T. R. (1979). Attributional processes of leaders in leader-follower interactions. *Organizational Behavior and Human Performance, 23,* 429–458.
Griffin, R. N. (1981). Relationships among individual, task design, and leader behavior variables. *Academy of Management Journal, 23,* 665–683.
Hackman, J. R., & Morris, C. G. (1975). Group tasks, group interaction process, and group performance effectiveness: A review and proposed integration. In L. Berkowitz (Ed.), *Advances in experimental social psychology.* New York: Academic Press.
Hackman, J. R., & Oldham, G. R. (1976). Motivation through the design of work: Test of a theory. *Organizational Behavior and Human Performance, 16,* 250–279.
Halpin, A. W., & Winer, B. J. (1957). A factorial study of the leader behavior descriptions. In R. M. Stogdill & A. E. Coons (Eds.), *Leader behavior: Its description and measurement.* Columbus, OH: Ohio State University Bureau of Business Research.
Hogg, M. A. (2001). A social identity theory of leadership. *Personality and Social Psychology Review, 5,* 184–200.
Hogg, M. A. (2005). Social identity and leadership. In D. M. Messick & R. M. Kramer (Eds.), *The psychology of leadership: New perspectives and research.* Mahwah, NJ: Erlbaum.
Hogg, M. A., Hains, S. C., & Mason, I. (1998). Identification and leadership in small groups: Salience, frame of reference, and leader stereotypicality effects on leader evaluations. *Journal of Personality and Social Psychology, 75,* 1248–1263.
Hollander, E. P. (1958). Conformity, status, and idiosyncrasy credit. *Psychological Review, 65,* 117–127.
Hollander, E. P. (1960). Competence and conformity in the acceptance of influence. *Journal of Abnormal and Social Psychology, 63,* 365–369.
House, R. J. (1977). A 1976 theory of charismatic leadership. In J. G. Hunt & L. L. Larson (Eds.), *Leadership: The cutting edge* (pp. 189–207). Carbondale: Southern Illinois University Press.
House, R. J., & Mitchell, T. R. (1974). Path-goal theory of leadership. *Journal of Contemporary Business, 3,* 81–97.
House, R. J., Spangler, W. D., & Woycke, J. (1991). Personality and charisma in the U. S. Presidency: A psychological theory of effectiveness. *Administrative Science Quarterly, 36,* 334–396.
Hovland, C., & Weiss, W. (1952). The influence of source credibility on communication effectiveness. *Public Opinion Quarterly, 15,* 635–650.
Hoyt, C., & Blascovich, J. J. (2005). Leadership efficacy and women leaders' response to stereotype activation. *Group Processes and Intergroup Relations, 10,* 585–616.

Judge, T. A., Bono, J. E., Ilies, R., & Gerhardt, M. W. (2002). Personality and leadership: A qualitative and quantitative review. *Journal of Applied Psychology, 87,* 765–780.
Katz, D., & Kahn, R. L. (1966). *The social psychology of organizing.* New York: Wiley.
Kelly, G. (1955). *The psychology of personal constructs.* New York: Newton.
Kenny, D. A., & Zaccaro, S. J. (1983). An estimate of the variance due to traits in leadership. *Journal of Applied Psychology, 68,* 678–685.
Kipnis, D. (1972). Does power corrupt? *Journal of Personality and Social Psychology, 24,* 33–41.
Kipnis, D. (1976). *The powerholders.* Chicago, IL: University of Chicago Press.
Lawrence, P. R., & Lorsch, J. W. (1968). *Organization and environment.* Irwin, IL: Homewood.
Leavitt, H. J. (1951). Some effects of certain communication patterns on group performance. *Journal of Abnormal and Social Psychology, 46,* 38–50.
LePine, J. A., Hollenbeck, J. R., Ilgen, D. R., & Hedlund, J. (1997). Effects of individual differences on the performance of hierarchical decision-making teams: Much more than g. *Journal of Applied Psychology, 82,* 803–811.
Lewin, K. (1935). *Dynamic theory of personality.* New York: McGraw-Hill.
Lord, R. G. (1985). An information processing approach to social perceptions, leadership perceptions, and behavioral measurement in organizational settings. In B. M. Staw & L. Cummings (Eds.), *Research in organizational behavior* (pp. 87–128). Greenwich, CT: JAI.
Lord, R. G., Binning, J. F., Rush, M. C., & Thomas, J. C. (1978). The effect of performance cues and leader behavior on questionnaire ratings of leadership behavior. *Organizational Behavior and Human Performance, 21,* 27–39.
Lord, R. G., De Vader, C. L., & Alliger, G. M. (1986). A meta-analysis of the relation between personality traits and leadership perceptions: An application of validity generalization procedures. *Journal of Applied Psychology, 71,* 402–410.
Lord, R. G., & Maher, K. J. (1991). *Leadership and information processing: Linking perceptions and performance.* Boston: Unwin Hyman.
Magee, J. C., Gruenfeld, D. H., Keltner, D. J., & Galinsky, A. D. (2005). Leadership and the psychology of power. In D. M. Messick & R. M. Kramer (Eds.), *The psychology of leadership: New perspectives and research.* Mahwah, NJ: Erlbaum.
Mann, R. D. (1959). A review of the relationship between personality and performance in small groups. *Psychological Bulletin, 56,* 241–270.
Marshall, M. A., & Brown, J. D. (2006). Trait aggressiveness and situational provocation: A test of the Traits as Situational Sensitivities (TASS) model. *Personality and Social Psychology Bulletin, 32*(8), 1100–1113.
McCrae, R. R., & Costa, P. T., Jr. (1996). Toward a new generation of personality theories: Theoretical contexts for the five-factor model. In J. S. Wiggins (Ed.), *The five-factor model of personality: Theoretical perspectives* (pp. 51–87). New York: Guilford.
Meindl, J. R., & Ehrlich, S. B. (1987). The romance of leadership and the evaluation of organizational performance. *Academy of Management Journal, 30,* 91–109
Meindl, J. R., Ehrlich, S. B., & Dukerich, J. M. (1985). The romance of leadership. *Administrative Science Quarterly, 30,* 78–102.
Messick, D. M. (2005). On the psychological exchange between leaders and followers. In D. M. Messick & R. M. Kramer (Eds.), *The psychology of leadership: New perspectives and research.* Mahwah, NJ: Erlbaum.
Mitchell, T. R., & Wood, R. E. (1980). Supervisors' responses to subordinate poor performance: A test of an attributional model. *Organizational Behavior and Human Decision Processes, 25,* 123–138.

Mumford, M. D., Zaccaro, S. J., Harding, F. D., Jacobs, T. O., & Fleischman, E. A. (2000). Leadership skills for a changing world: Solving complex social problems. *Leadership Quarterly, 11,* 11–35.

Ross, L. (1978). The intuitive psychologist and his shortcomings. In L. Berkowitz (Ed.), *Cognitive theories in social psychology.* (pp. 218–241). New York: Academic Press.

Rotter, J. B. (1954). *Social learning and clinical psychology.* Englewood Cliffs, NJ: Prentice Hall.

Schein, E. H. (1992). *Organizational culture and leadership* (2nd ed.). San Francisco: Jossey-Bass.

Smith, J. A., & Foti, R. J. (1998). A pattern approach to the study of leader emergence. *Leadership Quarterly, 9,* 147–160.

Snyder, M. (1974). Self-monitoring of expressive behavior. *Journal of Personality and Social Psychology, 30,* 526–537.

Steiner, I. D. (1972). *Group process and productivity.* New York: Academic Press.

Sternberg, R. J. (1988). *The triarchic mind: A new theory of human intelligence.* New York: Penguin Books.

Sternberg, R. J. (2002). Successful intelligence: A new approach to leadership. In R. E. Riggio, S. E. Murphy, & F. J. Pirozzolo (Eds.), *Multiple intelligences and leadership* (pp. 139–160). Mahwah, NJ: Erlbaum.

Stogdill, R. M. (1948). Personal factors associated with leadership: A survey of the literature. *Journal of Psychology, 25,* 35–71.

Tajfel, H., & Turner, J. C. (1979). An integrative theory of intergroup conflict. In W. G. Austin & S. Worchel (Eds.), *The social psychology of intergroup relations* (pp. 33–47). Monterey, CA: Brooks/Cole.

Terman, L. M. (1916). *The measurement of intelligence.* Boston: Houghton Mifflin.

Tyler, T. R. (2005). Process-based leadership: How do leaders lead? In D. M. Messick & R. M. Kramer (Eds.), *The psychology of leadership: New perspectives and research.* Mahwah, NJ: Erlbaum.

van Knippenberg, D., & Hogg, M. A. (2003). *Leadership and power: Identity processes in groups and organizations.* London: Sage.

Vroom, V. H., & Yetton, P. W. (1973). *Leadership and decision-making.* Pittsburgh, PA: University of Pittsburgh Press.

Weick, K. (1969). *The social psychology of organizations.* Reading, MA: Addison-Wesley.

Wiggins, J. S., & Trapnell, P. D. (1996). A dyadic-interactional perspective on the five-factor model. In J. S. Wiggins (Ed.), *The five-factor model of personality: Theoretical perspectives* (pp. 87–162). New York: Guilford.

Woods, F. A. (1913). *The influence of monarchs.* New York: Macmillan.

Zaccaro, S. J. (1999). Social complexity and the competencies required for effective military leadership. In J. G. Hunt, G. E. Dodge, & L. Wong (Eds.), *Out of the box leadership: Transforming the twenty-first century army and other top-performing organizations* (pp. 131–151). Stamford, CT: JAI.

Zaccaro, S. J. (2001). *The nature of executive leadership: A conceptual and empirical analysis of success.* Washington, DC: American Psychological Association.

Zaccaro, S. J. (2002). Organizational leadership and social intelligence. In R. E. Riggio, S. E. Murphy, & F. J. Pirozzolo (Eds.), *Multiple intelligences and leadership* (pp. 29–54). Mahwah: NJ: Erlbaum.

Zaccaro, S. J., Foti, R. J., & Kenny, D. A. (1991). Self-monitoring and trait-based variance in leadership: An investigation of leader flexibility across multiple group situations. *Journal of Applied Psychology, 76,* 308–315.

Zaccaro, S. J., Kemp, C., & Bader, P. (2004). Leader traits and attributes. In J. Antonakis, A. T. Cianciolo, & R. J. Sternberg (Eds.), *The nature of leadership* (pp. 101–124). Thousand Oaks, CA: Sage.

Zaccaro, S. J., Gilbert, J., Thor, K., & Mumford, M. (1991). Social perceptiveness and behavioral flexibility as characterological bases for leader role acquisition. *Leadership Quarterly, 2,* 317–342.

Zaccaro, S. J., Mumford, M. D. Connelly, M. S., Marks, M. A., & Gilbert, J. A. (2000). Assessment of leader problem-solving capabilities. *Leadership Quarterly, 11,* 37–64.

Zaccaro, S. J., White, L., Kilcullen, R., Parker, C. W., Williams, D., & O'Connor-Boes, J. (1997). *Cognitive and temperament predictors of Army civilian leadership.* (Final Report MRI 97-1 for U. S. Army Research Institute for Social and Behavioral Science). Bethesda, MD: Management Research Institute.

Zaccaro, S. J., Zazanis, M. M., Diana, M., & Gilbert, J. A. (1994 [not 2004]). *Investigation of a background measure of social intelligence* (Technical Report No. ADA298832). Alexandria, VA: U.S. Army Institute for the Behavioral and Social Sciences.

9

Personality and Prejudice in Interracial Interactions

PATRICIA G. DEVINE
University of Wisconsin–Madison

FREDERICK RHODEWALT and MATTHEW SIEMIONKO
University of Utah

In a now classic study, Word, Zanna, and Cooper (1974) demonstrated the subtle but compelling effects of prejudice in the interpersonal interaction sequence. Naïve White interviewers displayed less immediacy, took less time, and made more errors in speech when interviewing a Black interviewee than when interviewing a White interviewee. Then, in a second study, confederate interviewers were trained to exhibit immediate or nonimmediate interview styles for use in interviewing White subject-applicants. Applicant interview performances were judged to be poorer when responding to a nonimmediate interview style than when responding to an immediate interview style. In this example the (unmeasured but assumed) negative stereotypes of Blacks guided the interpersonal behavior of Whites, which, in turn, produced a self-fulfilling prophecy in Black interaction partners.

More generally, these experiments presume a set of psychological elements and processes that have been the focus of personality and social psychological approaches to the study of stereotyping, prejudice, and discrimination. People categorize other individuals and when these categories are negative, behave towards targets in prejudiced and biased ways, which impacts the target's behavior and his or her perceptions of the actor and of the self (Darley & Fazio, 1980; Devine & Vasquez, 1998). Although personality and social psychologists both have long held interests in stereotyping and prejudice, they have pursued these interests along somewhat separate paths. Personality psychology has typically sought to understand the attributes and motivations that make up the prejudiced personality. In contrast, social psychology has attempted to understand the nature of prejudiced attitudes and the situational factors that promote or constrain their use in the social interaction sequence.

Over the past several decades however, personality psychology has shifted its emphasis from descriptions of individual differences to a focus on personality process. During the same time, social psychology, with its increased emphasis on social cognition, has also become more process oriented. The convergence of the two disciplines on questions of how things work affords opportunities to study stereotyping, prejudice, and discrimination from intra- and interpersonal process perspectives that provide a more complete understanding of the transactional nature of these phenomena. In this chapter we briefly discuss traditional personality and social psychology approaches to stereotyping and prejudice. Then, we describe a personality/interpersonal behavior process view of prejudice and social interactions. This approach is illustrated with work on self-regulation and motivation to respond without prejudice in interracial interactions (Devine, 1989; Devine, Brodish & Vance, 2005; Plant & Devine, 2007).[1] We conclude by placing these findings within the context of ongoing interactions and highlight future questions suggested by this approach.

THE "PREJUDICED PERSONALITY" AND EARLY SOCIAL PSYCHOLOGICAL APPROACHES TO STEREOTYPING AND PREJUDICE

Traditional personality research on prejudice has sought to isolate a set or sets of attributes that characterize a "prejudiced personality." A representative example of this approach is Adorno, Frenkel-Brunswick, Levenson and Sanford's (1950) research on the authoritarian personality type. Adorno et al. (1950) reported that authoritarian personalities display tendencies to derogate out-group members and exhibit thought processes characterized by rigid adherence to stereotypes and conventionalism. Indeed, higher authoritarianism is associated with a higher incidence of negative prejudice toward out-group members (Haddock, Zanna, & Esses, 1993). It was theorized that these characteristics were the product of a particularly controlling or disciplinarian child-rearing style.

Martin and Westie's intolerant personality (1959) was an expansion of Adorno et al's. (1950) authoritarian personality, in that it attempted to categorize people as ranging from extreme in negative prejudice to neutrality to extreme in positive prejudice. They then examined the personal and social characteristics of prejudiced and "tolerant" individuals. Intolerant or prejudiced people were more likely to be more nationalistic, competitive, and superstitious, and they thought in more categorical black-and-white terms. Westie and DeFleur (1959) further linked specific physiological responses to these tolerant versus intolerant personality types and proposed that some "deep-seated emotional orientations" lay outside of consciousness, suggesting an implicit or unconscious dimension to prejudice and cognition. In yet another reworking of the authoritarianism construct, Altemeyer (1981) sought to revise and replace Adorno et al.'s (1950) original measure of authoritarianism (i.e., the F-scale) with the Right Wing Authoritarianism Scale (RWA) and reported that higher levels of RWA were related to greater submission, aggression, and conventionalism. Unlike Adorno et al.'s explanation of the roots of authoritarianism (i.e., child-rearing practices), Altemeyer (1981) argued that RWA developed via insecure attachment to one's social group and that extreme out-group prejudice resulted from perceived value conflicts with the out-group (Esses, Haddock, & Zanna, 1993). RWA has been associated with religious fundamentalism (Altemeyer & Hunsberger, 1992) as well as political and ethical ideology (e.g., more conservative standpoint) and enforcing a more universal moral code (McHoskey, 1996).

One characterization of these early personality approaches to individual differences in prejudice is that they attempted to describe those who were blatantly prejudiced. However, as shifting cultural norms made blatant racism less socially acceptable (Crosby, Bromley, & Saxe, 1980), personality and social psychologists shifted their focus toward exploring more symbolic, modern, or ambivalent forms of prejudice (see Dovidio & Gaertner, 1986). Symbolic or modern racism (Kinder & Sears, 1981; McConahay, 1986) occurs when a person sees a legitimate reason or excuse for their personal biases; for example, ideological or political beliefs are used to justify disadvantaging minority group members. In this form of racism, prejudice still exists but is expressed in a way that is less blatant. In ambivalent racism (Katz & Hass, 1988), a person holds simultaneously positive and negative attitudes towards a specific other minority or out-group member. Similarly, aversive racism (Gaertner & Dovidio, 1986) occurs when a person is motivated to reject racism but unconsciously holds racist attitudes. In symbolic, ambivalent, and aversive racism, then, a person has negative racial attitudes about another person or group of people, but the expression of these attitudes is masked or altered so that the person is not necessarily labeled a "racist" or "prejudiced"(at least by the self). Others have argued that some forms of prejudice reflect motivations other than, or in addition to, a bias against particular groups. For example, those high in social dominance orientation (Sidanius & Pratto, 1999) are motivated to view their group as more powerful and dominant than others. It is this motivation to perceive one's own group as dominant that underlies negative views of members of out-groups (Guimand, Damburn, Michinov, & Duarte, 2003). Even arbitrary assignment to a dominant group can increase a person's assertions that those who are more socially dominant deserve more than those who are less dominant. Thus, being a member of a majority group affects one's social dominance orientation and leads to the idea that personality characteristics are shaped by the social context in which one finds him/herself. The general assumption shared by these modern views of racism is that there is motivation on the part of a prejudiced person to conceal his or her racist attitudes, though the strategy differs depending on what form of racism is to be concealed.

Traditionally, social psychology has eschewed a focus on individual differences in attitudes and motivation and instead has concentrated on the content and attitudinal properties of prejudiced beliefs (see Devine & Elliot, 1995) and the effects of these beliefs on inter-group relations. Katz and Braly (1933) defined stereotypes as fixed impressions that do not necessarily map onto the reality of a situation; that is, stereotypes result "from our defining first and observing second" (p. 181). Stereotypes are thus partially overgeneralizations about group members based on group membership. Allport (1954) paved the way for contemporary social cognitive approaches to the study of prejudice by arguing that people naturally categorize others into different groups in order to make sense of the world; this allows for judgment of a particular person based on his or her group category. Although categorization is a fundamental way by which we simplify our social environment (Macrae & Bodenhausen, 2000), it also leads people to view others as members of in-groups or out-groups. As a result, perceivers tend to view out-group members as more homogeneous or similar than members of an in-group, who are seen as more heterogeneous or different from each other (Sedikides, 1997; Ostrom & Sedikides, 1992). Such categorization leads us to perceive our own in-groups more favorably (Rokeach & Mezei, 1966; Tajfel & Turner, 1986), thus setting the stage for intergroup prejudice and conflict. All of this is exacerbated when the content of the stereotype is negative.

Stereotyping need not be effortful or conscious and, in fact, can be activated through implicit priming (Devine, 1989; Fazio, Jackson, Dunton, & Williams, 1995). Given that the content of ethnic, racial, and gender stereotypes is consensually shared (Devine & Elliot, 1995) and automatically activated in appropriate contexts, it is surprising there are not greater incidences of prejudice and discrimination. Clearly at least some people are motivated for a variety of reasons to control prejudice or, at minimum, not appear prejudiced. It is also clear that the control of prejudice takes effort. For example, research suggests that increases in cognitive load reduce one's ability to control the application of stereotypes to targets and to view them not as individuals, but as members of their group (Kruglanski & Freund, 1983; Stangor & Duan, 1991). In addition, values such as egalitarianism and discrepancies between one's ideals of fairness and their actual responses can motivate people to reduce prejudicial biases (Devine & Monteith, 1993; Monteith, 1993; Monteith, Ashburn-Nardo, Voils, & Czopp, 2002; Monteith, Sherman, & Devine, 1998). Empathizing with stigmatized groups and seeing things from the perspective of a different group can also aid in reducing prejudice (Galinsky & Moskowitz, 2000; McGregor, 1993).

The key questions currently occupying social psychologists studying these issues are not whether stereotypes and their pernicious relationship to prejudice and discrimination continue to exist, but rather what intra- and interpersonal processes mediate and moderate stereotyping and the expression of prejudice. In order to answer these questions, social psychology has begun to embrace individual difference approaches to study the cognitive and motivational processes underlying prejudice (Devine, Montieth, Zuwerink, & Elliot, 1991; Dovidio, Kawakami, Johnson, Johnson, & Howard, 1997; Dunton & Fazio, 1997; Plant & Devine, 1998). In the next section we describe one such line of research, the study of self-regulatory processes and intergroup relations (Amodio, Devine, & Harmon-Jones, in press; Devine, Brodish, & Vance, 2005; Plant & Devine, 1998, 2003), specifically interracial interactions, as an exemplar of linking personality and interpersonal behavior in the arena of stereotyping and prejudice.

THE ROLE OF INTERNAL AND EXTERNAL MOTIVATION TO RESPOND WITHOUT PREJUDICE IN INTERRACIAL INTERACTIONS

In recent years, a major set of issues in the study of prejudice has been organized around the challenges involved in interracial interactions. This research has asked what are the effects of individual cognitions and motivations such as expectations, perceptions, and impression management concerns on these intergroup interactions? Contemporary social norms proscribe against the overt expressions of prejudice; thus, the interaction agenda often is shaped by fears of appearing prejudiced. These fears are not atypical in that recent research suggests that majority group members expect to be viewed as prejudiced by out-group members and that these expectations are easily activated in situations that contain a high likelihood for evaluation by an out-group member (Vorauer, Hunter, Main, & Roy, 2000; Vorauer & Kumhyr, 2001; Vorauer, Main, & O'Connell, 1998). Several researchers (Devine & Vasquez, 1998; Shelton, 2003; Vorauer and colleagues) have speculated that majority group members' evaluative concerns may play a role in the unfolding dynamics of intergroup interactions, affecting for example people's strategies for interaction and how people feel about intergroup interactions.

One consequence of concern about appearing prejudiced in intergroup interactions is the experience of intergroup anxiety—feelings of tension and distress experienced in intergroup settings. Specifically, intergroup anxiety arises when people's concerns about appearing prejudiced motivate them to present a nonprejudiced image to their interaction partner, but they have concerns that their efforts will fail (i.e., they expect to be viewed as prejudiced). These concerns or negative outcome expectancies can arise because people do not believe they possess the skills to make the desired, nonprejudiced impression or because they expect the impression will not be received as intended by the interaction partner (see Britt, Boniecki, Vesio, Biernat, & Brown, 1996; Plant & Devine, 2003; Stephan & Stephan, 1985, 1989). Such anxiety may have a number of effects on intergroup interactions. For example, those who report anxiety in intergroup settings expect such interactions to be difficult (Britt et al., 1996) and, when possible, avoid such interactions altogether (Plant & Devine, 2003).

Although there is clear evidence that many people are concerned about appearing prejudiced in interracial situations, and that such concerns can have adverse implications for intergroup interactions, to date it has generally been assumed that a single motive underlies this concern. Despite this research oversight, several scholars have suggested that people may have multiple motivations to present a nonprejudiced impression and, consequently, experience anxiety in intergroup settings for different reasons. For example, Britt et al. (1996) speculated that due to pervasive social norms discouraging the expression of prejudice, the "dominant tendency may be for individuals to avoid making a bad impression (e.g., appearing prejudiced) rather than creating a desired impression" (p. 1185). From this perspective, not being sure how to avoid making a prejudiced impression leads to anxiety. Alternatively, they suggested that for others, intergroup anxiety may reflect uncertainty about how to translate their nonprejudiced personal attitudes into behavior consistent with those attitudes. Echoing these alternative motivational orientations, Fazio and colleagues (Fazio et al., 1995) suggested that concern with making a nonprejudiced impression may "vary from a sincere distaste for the negative reaction ... to a more strategic self-presentation dictated by perceptions of the social norms" (p. 1025). Together, these observations suggest that, indeed, people may be motivated to make a nonprejudiced impression to achieve distinct self-presentational goals. Specifically, whereas for some people the goal of presenting a nonprejudiced identity in intergroup interactions reflects an effort to reveal one's personally accepted nonprejudiced identity, for others this goal reflects strategic efforts to conceal one's personally accepted prejudice from others.

The foregoing discussion suggests that one should be able to distinguish between those individuals who are likely to pursue these alternative goals in intergroup interactions and, then, to investigate the effects of these different individual goals on various aspects of interracial interactions. Plant and Devine (1998) argued that in examining the regulation of prejudice, it is important to consider not only *whether* people are motivated, but also the reasons *why* they are motivated to respond without prejudice.

For example, some people are strongly motivated to respond without prejudice in interracial interactions because they posses personally important nonprejudiced beliefs (Devine, 1989; Devine & Monteith, 1993; Devine et al., 1991; Plant & Devine, 1998). It is also possible to be strongly influenced by social norms discouraging the expression of bias in interracial interactions and to be motivated to control the expression of prejudice to avoid negative reactions from others (Crandall, Eshleman, & O'Brien, 2002; Dunton & Fazio, 1997; Plant & Devine, 1998).

Recently, Devine et al. (2005) suggested that to fully understand the implications of these distinct self-presentational goals in intergroup interactions requires discussing them in terms of the specific self-regulatory challenges involved in intergroup contact settings. To this end, they offered a model of the self-regulatory processes involved in interracial interactions, in which it was argued that intergroup anxiety arises in response to people's concerns that they will fail to meet specific self-presentational goals. Specifically, the model addresses the origins of the alternative self-presentational goals adopted in intergroup interactions, the qualitatively distinct pathways to anxiety in such interactions, the strategies pursued in regulating one's behavior toward the distinct goals, and the implications of these processes for behavior and outcomes in interracial settings.

In a series of studies, Plant and Devine (1998) developed and validated separate scales of internal motivation to respond without prejudice (IMS) and external motivation to respond without prejudice (EMS) toward Blacks. The crucial difference between internal and external motivation is the evaluative audience who imposes the standards proscribing prejudice (i.e., self versus others, respectively). Internal motivation to respond without prejudice arises from internalized, personally important nonprejudiced beliefs. Sample IMS items include "I attempt to act in nonprejudiced ways because it is personally important to me" and "Being nonprejudiced toward Black people is important to my self-concept." In contrast, external motivation to respond without prejudice arises from a desire to avoid negative reactions from others. Sample EMS items include "I attempt to appear nonprejudiced toward Black people in order to avoid disapproval from others" and "I try to act nonprejudiced toward Blacks because of pressure from others."

Plant and Devine (1998) demonstrated that the IMS and EMS are reliable and provided evidence regarding the scales' convergent, discriminant, and predictive validity. The IMS, for example, is highly correlated with self-report measures of prejudice, including the Attitudes Towards Blacks scale (Brigham, 1993) and the Modern Racism Scale (McConahay, Hardee, & Batts, 1981) such that high IMS scores are associated with lower prejudice scores. The EMS, in contrast, is only modestly correlated with traditional prejudice measures, such that high EMS scores are associated with higher prejudice scores. In addition, the EMS is only slightly correlated with measures of general social evaluation, including the Interaction Anxiousness Scale (Leary, 1983), the Social Desirability Scale (Crowne & Marlow, 1960), the Self-Monitoring Scale (Snyder & Gangested, 1986) and the Fear of Negative Evaluation scale (Watson & Friend, 1969). These rather small correlations suggest that the EMS assesses something distinct from generalized fear and anxiety in social situations. Across many samples, the IMS and EMS are largely independent (average $r = -.09$). Thus, individuals can be motivated to respond without prejudice primarily for internal reasons, primarily for external reasons, for both reasons, or they may not be motivated for either reason.

INTERNAL AND EXTERNAL MOTIVATIONS FOR RESPONDING WITHOUT PREJUDICE AS PERSONALITY PROCESS AND SELF-REGULATION

Given evidence for the reliability and validity of the IMS and EMS reviewed in the previous section, we now turn to research which links these "personality" variables to interpersonal behavior. Specifically, we will review evidence that suggests internal and external motivations to respond without prejudice produce different self-regulatory action patterns that have implications for interracial interactions. Our intention here is to place motivations to respond without prejudice into contemporary self-regulatory, dynamic models of personality (Carver & Scheier, 1981, 1998; Cervone, 2004; Cervone, Caldwell, & Orom, this volume; Mischel & Shoda, 1995, 1998). For example, according to Carver and Scheier (1998) human behavior is produced by self-regulatory systems consisting of negative and positive feedback loops. These feedback loops function at all levels of behavior, regulating the pursuit of higher-order goals (e.g., being a thoughtful person) as well as the pursuit of specific strategies that will help to achieve the goals (e.g., opening the door for someone carrying groceries). In Mischel and Shoda's Cognitive-Affective-Personality-Systems (CAPS) framework, IMS and EMS would be dispositional constructs represented by a social context category and a behavioral category connected by "if-then" rules. For example, a particular EMS individual may have the if-then dispositional construct "if interacting with Blacks (social context category), then act nonchalant and conceal anxiety (behavioral category)."

In Carver and Scheier's (1998) self-regulation framework, self-regulation is a continuous process in which one's current behavior is compared to some internal standard. Research has demonstrated that the standards that get activated and serve as reference values are a function of the circumstances in which people find themselves. For example, these self-evaluative processes are activated when a person is self-aware. Accordingly, the public nature of interracial interactions should increase an individual's self-awareness, which results in attention being drawn to standards of behavior that are relevant for the situation (Duval & Wicklund, 1972).

Conceptualizing motivations to respond without prejudice within a self-regulation framework allows one to examine the implications of (1) the standards or reference values against which behavior is regulated; (2) the likelihood of meeting the standards to respond without prejudice and outcome expectancies in interracial interactions; (3) who is most likely to experience anxiety in interracial interactions; and (4) the approach or avoidance goals set and the strategies pursued in interracial interactions. The cumulative implications of this program of research suggest who is most likely to have concerns about appearing prejudiced in interracial interactions and the distinct self-presentational goals set for interracial interactions, as well as the strategies pursued to regulate behavior toward these goals. Conceptualizing internal and external motivations to respond without prejudice as intra individual personality process allows one to map the ongoing dynamical transactions between the person and others in interracial interactions.

Regulatory Significance of Self- Versus Other-Imposed Standards Proscribing Prejudice

Plant and Devine (1998) reasoned that possessing internal and external sources of motivation to respond without prejudice would make particular evaluative audiences salient and that these audiences would define the standards against which individuals would evaluate their behavior. They further reasoned that, to the extent that these standards were important self-regulatory reference values, violations of them would lead to distinct patterns of affective distress (e.g., Higgins, 1987). Higgins' self-discrepancy theory, for example, posits that when people's actual self-characteristics are discrepant from ought (should) standards, agitation-related emotions result, the specific form of which depends on whether the standard violated is one's own (i.e., internal) or imposed on one by others (i.e., external). According to the theory, discrepancies between people's actual responses and their *personal standards* for who they think they *should* be (i.e., ought/own discrepancies) lead to feelings of guilt, uneasiness, and self-contempt (i.e., the feelings associated with self-punishment that result from violating a personally accepted moral standard). When others *prescribe the should standard* against which the appropriateness of responses is evaluated, however, discrepancies (i.e., ought/other discrepancies) are associated with feeling fearful and threatened (i.e., the feelings associated with impending punishments from others).

To explore these issues, Plant and Devine (1998) adapted the method developed by Devine and her colleagues (e.g., Devine et al., 1991) to assess the affective consequences of discrepancies between how one *should* respond and how one reports he or she actually *would* respond across a variety of interracial scenarios. Specifically, Plant and Devine measured participants' self-imposed (personal) standards for how they should treat Blacks and, in a separate sample, measured participants' perceptions of other-imposed (normative) standards for how they should treat Blacks. Plant and Devine also measured how participants reported they actually would respond in the interpersonal setting as an indicator of their current performance. Using Mischel and Shoda's (1995, 1998) approach, Plant and Devine found that among high IMS people, if their actual responses revealed more prejudice than their personal standards permitted, then participants held themselves personally accountable and felt guilty. Among the high EMS people, they found that if their actual responses revealed more prejudice than normative standards permitted, then participants feared punishment from others and felt threatened. In both cases, the larger the discrepancy between the standards proscribing prejudice and the actual responses, the greater the amount of the specific form of affective distress participants reported. These findings suggest that self- and other-imposed nonprejudiced standards serve as important and distinct reference values against which people evaluate their behavior. Moreover, participants' levels of IMS and EMS determine the reference values that possess regulatory significance.

In this study, Plant and Devine also found that when violations were assessed against other-imposed standards, high EMS people who also reported being personally motivated to respond without prejudice (i.e., high IMS) felt not only threat-related affect, but also guilt and self-criticism. Plant and Devine (1998) argued that for those high in both internal and external motivation to respond without prejudice, thinking about other-imposed standards also brings to mind their self-imposed standards. That is, violating other-imposed standards also reflects the violation of a self-imposed standard for individuals high in both EMS and IMS. In sum, it appears that when other-imposed standards are activated, participants who are high in both EMS and IMS also activate their personal, self-imposed standards. Taken together these findings suggest that in interracial interactions, such self- and other-imposed standards are likely to be activated and serve as the reference value(s) against which people are likely evaluate their behavior.

Likelihood of Meeting the Standards and Outcome Expectancies

Recent research examining the magnitude of implicit bias and people's self-reported likelihood of responding with bias suggests that responding with prejudice (i.e., violating self or other imposed standards) is more likely to be a problem for some people than for others. Implicit responses are likely to be particularly problematic in interracial interactions because they occur without intention and are difficult to control. As a result, they may create the need to engage self-regulatory processes to mitigate their effects for those whose standards (whether self- or other-imposed) proscribe prejudice. Using two different measures of implicit bias (i.e., sequential priming measure, Fazio et al., 1995 and the IAT, Greenwald, McGhee, & Schwartz, 1998), across three studies, Devine, Plant, Amodio, Harmon-Jones, and Vance (2002; see also Amodio et al., 2003) found that the likelihood of responding with implicit race bias varied as a function of IMS and EMS. Specifically, high IMS, low EMS participants reported much lower levels of implicit bias than participants with all other combinations of IMS and EMS—and the level of implicit bias was equally high for these latter participants.

As noted previously, several recent studies have shown that in interracial interactions, many White people have negative outcome expectancies (i.e., beliefs that they will be viewed as prejudiced by their interaction partner) for interracial interactions. Such concerns cue the need to draw upon regulatory resources to prevent the expression of bias (Richeson & Shelton, 2003), leaving those who regulated prejudice depleted. Further, Britt et al. (1996) and Plant and Devine (2003) showed that negative outcome expectancies in interracial interactions were related to negative outcomes (i.e., anxiety and avoidance) for such interactions. They did not, however, identify who among their research participants were most likely to report negative, compared with more positive, outcome expectancies.

To explore this issue, in a recent study using measures developed by Plant and Devine (2003), Devine et al. (2005) examined participants' outcome expectancies for an interracial interaction as a function of IMS and EMS. In a mass testing session, participants completed the IMS and EMS and a questionnaire assessing their outcome expectancies for an interaction with a Black student (e.g., "When interacting with a Black person, he or she would see me as prejudiced no matter what I do"; "Even if we hadn't met before, a Black person would expect me to be prejudiced"; "If I were interacting with a Black person, regardless of my behavior he or she would see me as prejudiced"). Participants indicated their agreement with the statements and their responses were averaged to create an outcome expectancy index. The key finding from this study was an IMS X EMS interaction. The form of this interaction suggests that whereas high IMS, low EMS participants reported positive outcome expectancies, all other participants reported fairly negative outcome expectancies. These data are consistent with the implicit race bias findings reported above and suggest that outcome expectancies are systematically associated with the source of people's motivation to respond without prejudice. We next consider implications for intergroup anxiety.

Anxiety in Interracial Interactions. Among those who are likely to be concerned about responding with prejudice in interracial interactions (e.g., those high in IMS and/or EMS), possessing negative outcome expectancies may make them vulnerable to intergroup anxiety (Britt et al., 1996; Plant & Devine, 2003). To explore this possibility, Devine et al. (2005) reported a study in which they tested the hypothesis that if people were motivated to respond without prejudice for any reason and had negative outcome expectancies (the two high EMS groups), they should experience anxiety in the context of an interracial interaction. None of the low EMS participants were expected to report elevated anxiety prior to the intergroup interaction. That is, high IMS, low EMS individuals have positive outcome expectancies, and low IMS, low EMS individuals are not motivated to respond without prejudice; as such each low EMS group lacks one of the necessary ingredients to experience intergroup anxiety (i.e., negative outcome expectancies and motivation to respond without prejudice, respectively). In this study, White participants were led to believe that they would interact with a Black student about a topic relevant to student life on campus. At that point, their interaction partner, a Black confederate, entered the room. Before the interaction, participants reported their affect about the upcoming interaction. Embedded in the affect questionnaire were items designed to assess intergroup anxiety (e.g., anxious, tense, nervous, uneasy). As expected, high EMS participants reported higher levels of anxiety in anticipation of the interracial interaction than their low EMS counterparts. Although the amount of intergroup anxiety reported among high EMS participants did not vary as a function of their level of IMS, Devine et al. (2005) argued that their anxiety stems from concerns about failing to accomplish distinct self-presentational goals. In what follows, we consider what the existing research suggests about the goals set and strategies pursued by such individuals in interracial interactions.

Goals and Strategies for Interracial Interactions. Any analysis of self-regulation would be incomplete without an understanding of the types of overarching goals people set for behavior and the strategies they pursue to meet these goals. Further, these goals need to be translated into specific intentions that guide people's regulatory efforts in particular contexts. Building on classic models of achievement motivation and self-regulation, Plant and Devine (in press) developed an analysis of the types of objectives (end-states) White people pursue in interracial interactions and the general approach vs. avoidance orientations guiding their efforts.

The distinction between the motive to achieve success (a desired end-state) and the motive to avoid failure (an undesired end-state) features prominently in both classic and contemporary achievement motivation work (e.g., Atkinson, 1964; Atkinson & Litwin, 1960; Elliot & Church, 1997; Elliot & Harackiewicz, 1996; Feather, 1967; Hembree, 1988; Mahone, 1960). In this work, for example, the motivation to achieve success leads to active pursuit of the end-state, whereas the motivation to avoid failure results in the tendency to avoid performing actions that are expected to produce the undesired end-state. Similarly, in their cybernetic theory of self-regulation, Carver and Scheier (1981, 1990, 1998) also distinguished between two types of motivational systems, those that focus on approaching desired end-states and those that focus on avoiding undesired end-states. In systems focused on approaching a desired end-state, current behavior is compared to a positive (i.e., desired) reference value. If a discrepancy is detected between the current behavior and the desired end-state, behavior is adjusted in order to diminish the discrepancy (i.e., to approach the desired end-state). In contrast, discrepancy-amplifying systems compare current behavior to a negative (i.e., undesired) reference value. If current behavior is too close to the reference value, behavior is adjusted in order to amplify the discrepancy (i.e., avoid undesired end-state).

In considering whether White people possess an approach or avoidance motivation when regulating behavior in interracial interactions, it is important to reflect upon what they are likely trying to accomplish in interracial interactions. To the extent that White people are primarily focused on having a positive interaction, they may pursue the goal of treating their interaction partner in a pleasant, egalitarian manner (i.e., approach a desired end-state). In contrast, to the extent that White people are primarily concerned with preventing a negative interaction and, therefore, may be focused on the potential for a negative interaction, responding with racial bias is likely to be a highly salient undesired end-state. As a result, they may pursue the goal of avoiding negative outcomes and prejudiced behavior during the interaction (i.e., avoid an undesired end-state).

Plant and Devine (in press) suggested that in interracial interactions, whether White people are primarily concerned with approaching a desired end-state of a pleasant interaction or avoiding an undesired end-state of overt bias in the interaction depends on the reasons underlying their motivation to respond without prejudice. Plant and Devine (in press) proposed that internal motivation to respond without prejudice results in a general approach orientation in interracial interactions, whereas external motivation to respond without prejudice results in a general avoidance orientation. Consider that highly internally motivated people want to respond without prejudice in order to respond consistently with personally important nonprejudiced values. That is, they want to approach a desired end-state of pleasant, egalitarian responding. Supporting this reasoning, Monteith and colleagues (Monteith, 1993; Monteith et al., 2002; Devine & Monteith, 1993) found that guilt resulting from violations of personal nonprejudiced standards activates a self-regulatory cycle that facilitates bringing responses closer to egalitarian, nonprejudiced standards (i.e., a desired end-state). Externally motivated people, in contrast, want to respond without prejudice in order to avoid negative reactions from others. Their primary concern is with avoiding an undesired end-state of overt biased responding that would make them vulnerable to threat-related affect and negative reactions from others. Unlike guilt, threat-related affect motivates moving responses away from the unwanted outcome (i.e., overt bias resulting in social disapproval) (Carver, 2001).

Plant and Devine suggested that distinct approach and avoidance motivational tendencies should have implications for White people's goals in interracial interactions (Carver & Scheier, 1998; Elliot, Gable, & Mapes, 2006; Higgins, 1987). To test these ideas, Plant and Devine (in press) examined the extent to which internal and external sources of motivation to respond without prejudice are associated with distinct approach and avoidance goals. In another set of studies, Plant and Devine (2007) explored the specific regulatory intentions guiding efforts to respond without prejudice. We consider these two lines of research in turn.

In one study designed to explore the link between the source of people's motivation to respond without prejudice and their self-reported goals in interracial interactions, participants were asked to generate their goals for an upcoming interaction in an open-ended format. Participants' responses were coded for approach goals (e.g., "Be friendly," "Treat the person like I would anyone else," "Act normal") and avoidance goals (e.g., "Avoid acting prejudiced," "Don't make racial jokes (or ethnic slurs)," "Try not to think about the stereotype"). High IMS participants were more likely than low IMS participants to generate goals that focused on approaching egalitarian responding. In contrast, high EMS participants were more likely than low EMS participants to generate goals that focused on avoiding biased responding. Further, the high IMS, high EMS participants reported both types of goals. These findings suggest that high IMS, high EMS individuals are concerned with approaching the desired end-state of egalitarianism, but ever mindful of their potential failures in interracial interactions (i.e., negative outcome expectancies, implicit forms of bias), they are also concerned with avoiding the undesired end-state of biased responding.

In a second study, participants anticipating an interaction with a Black student were asked to indicate their goals for the upcoming interaction (Plant and Devine, in press). Embedded in the list were items assessing the extent to which they endorsed a goal of approaching egalitarianism (e.g., to be open, friendly, and unbiased) or a goal of avoiding overt bias (e.g., avoid using stereotypes, avoid coming across as prejudiced, keep the interaction short) during the interaction. The pattern of goal endorsement replicated the self-reported goals. That is, as expected, high IMS participants were more likely to endorse a goal of approaching a pleasant, egalitarian interaction compared to low IMS participants. In addition, high EMS participants were more likely to endorse a goal of avoiding overt bias in the interaction than their low EMS counterparts.

The findings from Plant and Devine's (in press) first study suggest that whether White people's self-reported goals for interactions with Black people focus on approaching egalitarianism or avoiding overt bias is influenced by their motivation to respond without prejudice. To the extent that participants' reports of their goals for interracial interactions reflect chronic regulatory tendencies, then these concerns are likely to become automatically activated upon exposure to relevant cues (Bargh, 1990; Bargh & Barndollar, 1996). To the extent that people who are highly internally motivated to respond without prejudice are chronically concerned with approaching egalitarianism in interracial interactions, we would expect that general approach-related concepts would be highly accessible when exposed to Black people. Further, to the extent that people who are highly externally motivated are chronically concerned with avoiding overt bias for interracial interactions, we would expect that general avoidance-related concepts would be highly accessible when they are exposed to Black people. To explore this possibility, Plant and Devine (in press) examined whether concepts theoretically related to approach and avoidance goals are automatically activated upon exposure to Black people as a function of the source of participants' motivation to respond without prejudice. Specifically, the accessibility of approach- and avoidance-related goals was examined by assessing the speed of response to these concepts following exposure to Black versus White faces. The analysis of response latencies in a lexical decision task revealed that high IMS participants responded more quickly to the approach-related words following Black faces than low IMS participants. High EMS participants, however, responded more quickly to the avoidance-related words following Black faces than low EMS participants.

Taken together, the findings from Plant and Devine's (in press) work demonstrate that highly internally motivated White people are more likely to anticipate pursuing goals that focus on approaching egalitarianism during an interaction with a Black person and to have their approach-related goals automatically activated upon exposure to a Black person than are less internally motivated White people. In addition, highly externally motivated White people are more likely to anticipate pursing goals that focus on avoiding overt bias during such interactions and to have their avoidance-related goals automatically activated upon exposure to a Black person than are less externally motivated White people.

Continuing the development of a self-regulatory analysis of interracial interactions, Plant and Devine (in press) argured that people should be drawn to strategies for interracial interactions that would facilitate achieving their goals (Elliot, 2006; Shah, Higgins, & Friedman, 1998). Specifically, they argued that external motivation, following from an avoidance orientation, gives rise to the intention to conceal prejudice from others. That is, externally motivated individuals' efforts to control prejudice are initiated only in the presence of others and are guided by the intention to hide prejudice in order to avoid public censure. In contrast, they suggested that internal motivation gives rise to the intention to be free of prejudice altogether. Unlike the desire to hide prejudice, this intention is experienced as a moral responsibility that cuts across situations, initiating efforts to control even the subtlest forms of bias and even in the absence of external pressure to be nonprejudiced. These overarching intentions should determine not only why people actively regulate prejudice, but also when and how they pursue such self-regulation.

Plant and Devine (2007) reasoned that any given strategy should be pursued only to the extent that it facilitates effective goal pursuit. In considering the pursuit of strategies to eliminate bias, Plant and Devine argued that it is important to take into account both whether one believes a biased response is likely in interracial interactions and whether one cares about responding with bias. That is, regulatory strategies to reduce bias should only be of interest to the extent that people anticipate that they are likely to respond with bias in interracial situations and would be concerned if they responded with such bias. Previous research indicates that one subset of individuals, those who are primarily internally motivated, do not expect to be viewed as prejudiced during interracial interactions (Devine, Brodish & Vance, 2005; Plant & Devine, 2004). Moreover, across several studies and a variety of measures, including implicit, physiological, and neural measures that are difficult to control, these people consistently exhibit less race bias than others (e.g., Amodio et al., in press; Amodio et al., 2003; Devine et al., 2002).

In contrast, highly externally motivated people, whether they are high or low in internal motivation to respond without prejudice, believe they are likely to respond with bias and are concerned about responding with bias. Thus, they are likely to be interested in pursuing bias reduction strategies; however, their interest is likely to vary as a function of how they believe the strategy will help them. People who are high in external motivation but low in internal motivation to respond without prejudice are concerned with concealing bias from others in order to avoid social disapproval, but they are not personally motivated to overcome prejudice. For these people, strategies that enable one to avoid overt forms of bias should be especially appealing; in contrast, overcoming subtle bias that is not detectable by others would not facilitate their goal pursuit and should be of little interest. Plant and Devine (2007) reasoned that for people high in both internal and external motivation to respond without prejudice, any strategy that facilitates becoming free of bias should be appealing (i.e., whether or not the bias is observable to others).

In one study designed to explore these issues, participants with varying levels of internal and external motivation to respond without prejudice were led to believe that they would be interacting with a Black person (Plant & Devine, 2007). Prior to the interaction, they were given the opportunity to complete a computer program that they were told would decrease racial prejudice. Plant and Devine (2007) manipulated the description of the type of prejudice the program would ostensibly decrease. For example, some participants were led to believe that the computer program decreased *detectable* prejudice (i.e., prejudice that would be perceptible to others). Others learned that the program was designed to decrease *undetectable* prejudice (i.e., prejudice that others would be unable to perceive). Plant and Devine suggested that the objectives of the alternative framing conditions would be differentially appealing to those whose intention is to hide prejudice and those whose intention is to be free of bias. Further, they argued that the amount time spent on the program across the framing conditions provided an indicator of the extent to which their active efforts to regulate prejudice reflected the hide vs. be free of prejudice intentions.

Results indicated that participants' pursuit of the alternative strategies was determined jointly by the source of their motivation to respond without prejudice and how the strategy was framed. As expected, participants low in external motivation to respond without prejudice spent relatively little time on the program in either condition, presumably because the program was not viewed as needed (i.e., for high IMS, low EMS who do not expect to respond with prejudice) or useful (i.e., for low IMS, low EMS who lack motivation to respond without prejudice). The findings for participants high in external motivation to respond without prejudice were also consistent with expectations. Specifically, when the program was framed as reducing undetectable bias, but had no positive benefits for the upcoming interaction, high IMS, high EMS participants spent more time on the program than did all other participants. When the program was framed as reducing overt bias that would be apparent to their Black interaction partner in the upcoming interaction, high EMS participants, regardless of their level of IMS, spent extensive time on the program compared with low EMS participants.

These findings are consistent with the general argument that internal motivation reflects the intention to be free of prejudice and external motivation (in the absence of internal motivation) reflects the intention to hide prejudice. To buttress the case, and address potential ambiguities the findings from the previous study, Plant and Devine (2007) conducted two additional studies. Consider that in the previous study those internally motivated people who were not externally motivated did not pursue strategies that they were told would help reduce bias. Their lack of interest in reducing bias could call into question their intention to be free of bias. Is it the case that they do not intend to be free of bias, or as Plant and Devine argued, that they do not perceive the need for an external aid to respond without prejudice?

To answer this question, Plant and Devine confronted participants with evidence of their own implicit race bias prior to providing them with the opportunity to work on a bias reduction program. Specifically, participants completed either a Black-White or Flower-Insect version of the Implicit Attitude Test (IAT; Greenwald, McGhee, & Schwartz, 1998). It is important to note that Monteith, Voils, and Ashburn-Nardo (2001) demonstrated that the majority of White participants who completed the Black-White IAT were aware that their responses revealed bias against Blacks and that, although high IMS/low EMS individuals tend to respond with less implicit race bias than others, their responses typically reveal *some* level of race bias on the IAT (see Devine et al., 2002). As such, completing the Black-White IAT was expected to challenge these participants' perceptions of themselves as invulnerable to prejudice. In the control condition, participants completed a race-unrelated version of the IAT, which was unlikely to affect participants' perceptions of the need to control prejudice.

After completing the implicit bias measure but prior to the ostensible interaction, participants were given the opportunity to complete the undetectable bias reduction program from the previous study. The findings revealed that, when confronted with evidence of regulatory failure (i.e., their own implicit bias), high IMS individuals, regardless of EMS level, actively pursued the program. Moreover, following the Black-White IAT, high IMS/low EMS participants' interest in the program was related to their level of implicit bias; the more IAT bias they exhibited, the more time they spent on the program. We suggest that these participants viewed their IAT performance as a failure to meet their intention to be free of bias, and they therefore were eager to take advantage of the assistance provided by the program. Taken together these findings provide compelling evidence that internal motivation to respond without prejudice gives rise to active efforts to control prejudice with the intention of being free of prejudice.

Plant and Devine's (2007) final study addressed the potential ambiguity associated with the fact that high IMS/high EMS participants showed equal and high levels of interest in the program in both detectable and undetectable bias conditions. Although Plant and Devine argued that their interest in both bias reduction programs is driven primarily by their intention to be free of bias, an alternative possibility is that these individuals desire both to hide *and* to be free of prejudice. To test this hypothesis, Plant and Devine replicated their first study (i.e., reduce detectable and reduce undetectable conditions) and added a new condition, the goal of which was to pit the intention to hide prejudice against the intention to be free of prejudice. Specifically, in this critical condition, participants learned that decreasing detectable prejudice came at the cost of increasing undetectable prejudice. In this condition, participants learned that the program would *decrease* detectable bias in the upcoming interaction, but that over the long term it would *increase* undetectable bias. Plant and Devine anticipated that the high IMS/high EMS individuals would eschew the opportunity to appear less prejudiced in the upcoming interaction (i.e., by decreasing detectable bias) because the long-term costs of the program (i.e., increasing undetectable bias) would be incompatible with the intention to be free of bias. In contrast, they suggested that increasing detectable bias in the future should not be of concern to low IMS/high EMS individuals if their intention is to hide prejudice.

Consistent with expectations, the findings suggested that individuals possessing both internal and external motivation to respond without prejudice prioritize being free of prejudice over hiding prejudice. Consistent with this notion, and replicating their first study, high IMS/high EMS participants showed interest in the program when it was described as decreasing undetectable and/or detectable bias. Importantly however, when decreasing detectable prejudice came at the cost of increasing undetectable prejudice over the long term, these participants spent little time on the program. Plant and Devine argued that this finding provides strong evidence high IMS/high EMS individuals prioritize being free of prejudice over hiding prejudice. The low IMS/high EMS participants showed high levels of interest in the program when it would lead to decreases in detectable prejudice, even if this outcome led to long-term increases in undetectable prejudice. The increase in prejudice was not troubling to these participants because they did not possess the personal motivation to reduce prejudice.

In a related line of research, Brodish and Devine (2005) demonstrated that among individuals who are externally motivated, those who were also internally motivated were more likely to endorse, activate, and pursue the goal to reveal their nonprejudiced identity in interracial interactions. Thus, they seemed to be focused on approaching an impression in the interaction consistent with their egalitarian self-concept. In contrast, participants who were primarily externally motivated to respond without prejudice were more focused on pursuing the goal of concealing their prejudice, that is, avoiding a prejudiced impression.

MODELING PERSONALITY AND SELF-REGULATION PROCESSES IN INTERRACIAL INTERACTIONS

Synthesizing Plant and Devine's work on the sources of motivation to respond without prejudice with the extant literature addressing intergroup anxiety and interpersonal concerns in interracial interactions, Devine et al. (2005) developed a model of the self-regulatory processes in interracial interactions (e.g., Britt et al., 1996; Plant & Devine, 2003). The model addresses the self-regulatory processes of those most likely to report being concerned about appearing prejudiced in interracial interactions and who, as a result, have the need to regulate their responses in such interactions. As such, the model focuses on high EMS individuals, arguing that the core self-regulatory challenges (i.e., goals and strategies) differ for those who are low, compared to high, in IMS. For example, high EMS/low IMS individuals seem to be primarily concerned with strategically concealing prejudice from others as the way to meet their other-imposed standard proscribing prejudice; these individuals are referred to as *Strategics*. In contrast, high EMS, high IMS individuals appear to be striving to overcome prejudice in any form as the way to meet both their other-imposed and self-imposed nonprejudiced standards;

as such, they are referred to as *Strivers*. Low EMS individuals are not of concern in this model because they either lack motivation to respond without prejudice (i.e., low EMS, low IMS) or lack concern over appearing prejudiced in interracial interactions because they have positive outcome expectancies (i.e., low EMS, high IMS).

According to the model (see Figure 9.1), there are individual differences in the extent to which people are chronically motivated to respond without prejudice for internal or external reasons. When people enter interracial contact situations, self-focus increases and the relevant standards against which behavior will be evaluated are activated. However, the relevant standards vary for Strategics compared with Strivers. For Strategics, other-imposed standards are activated. For Strivers, both other-imposed and self-imposed standards are activated. It is these standards against which Strivers and Strategics will monitor their performance in the interaction. The activation of relevant standards is linked to distinct self-presentational goals in interracial interactions. The self-presentational goal activated for Strategics focuses on the need to conceal their self-accepted prejudice from others (e.g.,

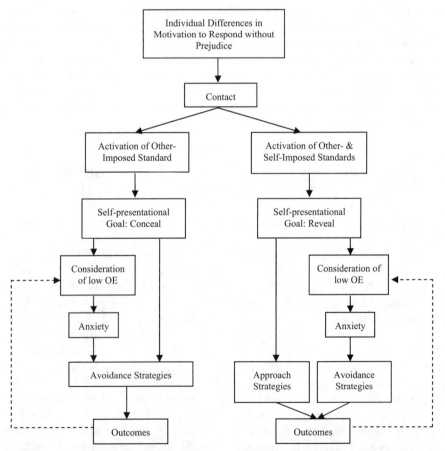

Figure 9.1 Model of self-regulatory processes in interracial interactions.

interaction partner or other observers). In contrast, the self-presentational goal activated for Strivers focuses on their desire to accurately communicate or reveal their personally accepted nonprejudiced identity in the interaction. It is at this point that people consider the likelihood of achieving their self-presentational goal (i.e., consider their outcome expectancies). As previously noted, both Strategics and Strivers report negative outcome expectancies, specifically, concern over the likely failure to meet their distinct conceal or reveal self-presentational goals. The combination of their specific self-presentational goal and their negative outcome expectancies leads both Strategics and Strivers to experience anxiety in the intergroup setting.

According to the model, the strategies pursued in the interaction follow from both the specific self-presentational goal and from intergroup anxiety. Specifically, whereas Strategics' conceal goal leads to the activation and pursuit of avoidance-related strategies, Strivers' reveal goal leads to the activation and pursuit of approach-related strategies. For both Strivers and Strategics, intergroup anxiety is associated with activation and pursuit of avoidance strategies. The various strategies pursued will lead to outcomes that can be evaluated against one's standards and goals to determine the extent to which adjustments in behavior are needed to bring behavior in line with the standards and goals. Finally, it is important to note that the model is dynamic in that outcomes or feedback about one's performance in the interaction can influence one's affective reactions as well as one's outcome expectancies (e.g., success can lead to the development of more positive outcome expectancies). According to the model, altering outcome expectancies will affect actual performance in interracial interactions.

PERSONALITY AND PREJUDICE REVISITED

We began this chapter with a brief review of the history of theory and research on personality and prejudice. The early work can best be characterized as interindividual personality research (Cervone et al., this volume) because it attempted to describe differences between people who were high or low in prejudice. The program of research described in the following sections derives from a more contemporary intra-individual approach that seeks to understand the prejudiced personality in terms of complex dynamic, cognitive affective systems within the person (see Mischel & Shoda, 1995, 1998). We have described Devine and colleague's (Devine, Brodish, & Vance, 2005; Devine & Vasquez, 1998) model of individual differences in motivation to control prejudice in the language of classic models of self-regulation (e.g., Carver & Scheier, 1998). However, we believe it is worthwhile to consider connections between Devine's model and other contemporary intraindividual approaches to personality. Most notably, one could conceptualize IMS and EMS as dispositional constructs represented by a social context category and a behavioral category connected by "if-then" rules (Mischel & Shoda, 1995, 1998). Indeed, recently there has been a great deal of interest in the personality field in thinking of dispositions as categories of knowledge (e.g., self, social contexts, other people, behaviors, and linking rules). Framing the issues in this way may offer novel insights for linking personality and prejudice literatures.

Mischel and Shoda's (1995) concept of dispositional constructs has been applied productively to interpersonal relationships and interactions (Andersen, Saribay, & Kooij, this volume; Baldwin, 1992; 1997; Chen, Boucher, & Tapias, 2006), and, thus, may be particularly useful in charactering personality process in interracial interactions. The core idea is that one way in which the self is represented in memory is in terms of self-with-others schemata. For example, Baldwin describes relational schema containing information about who one is in relation to significant others and contends that relational schemas are cognitive structures that represent regularities in interpersonal relatedness (Baldwin, 1992, 1997; see also Chen, Boucher, & Tapias, 2006). One can have a relational self with regard to one's spouse, boss, sibling, or any significant other. The relational self with, say, one's boss is the cognitive representation one has of "me when interacting with my boss." The relational schema provides a set of expectancies for the interaction with significant others, including affective reactions as well as scripts for how to behave in the interaction, a self-schema for how the self is experienced in specific interpersonal situations, and a schema for what to expect from the other person in the interaction. Through experience, then, the individual develops patterns of behavior that elicit praise from one's boss and avoid behaviors that elicit the boss's disapproval. A core assumption of such models is that the different components of relational schemas are highly interdependent and they are updated and changed based on experience in a reciprocal and dynamic way (e.g., knowing my behavior affects my boss's behavior and how I feel about the exchange). Through repeated experience with others, people essentially develop cognitive maps that help them make sense of and negotiate interactions with others.

Although relational schemas have historically been conceptualized in the context of interpersonal relationships and the social context category is most often target-based (i.e., self in relation to a specific other), we would like to suggest that this type of analysis applies when the social context category is group-based. That is, relational schema may be more generalized. From this perspective, many interactions with people of different races or ethnicities unfold more as intergroup (i.e., me, a person of Group X, in relation to member of Group Y) rather than interpersonal interactions (i.e., me in relation to a specific other). The elements of the relational schema may, as a result, not be grounded in personal direct experience with others but may be tied to indirect experience and stereotypic expectations. What is particularly interesting about this analysis is that absent direct experience, people's generalized expectations about the other may be incorrect (i.e., the other expects people like me to be prejudiced), and people are unlikely to have well-defined scripts for how to interact with others or clear schemas for what to expect from the other in specific interaction situations. Indeed, one's self-schemas are likely to be unfamiliar in this context and their behavior influenced by feared selves (e.g., appearing more prejudiced than desired). At the same time, although the schemas are not based on direct experience, they provide expectations, albeit untested, about the ensuing interaction and serve as a guide to behavior. Behavior, in turn, influences interaction partner behavior, which provides the "direct experience" that consolidates the interracial relational schema.

Returning to the self-regulatory analysis summarized previously, IMS and EMS when considered in conjunction may suggest distinct relational schemas that affect White people's construal of interracial interactions and guide their behaviors. For example, a high EMS/low IMS individual may have the if-then dispositional construct "if interacting with Blacks (social context category), then make a nonprejudiced impression by concealing signs of prejudice bias and acting nonchalant (behavioral category)." In contrast, a high EMS/high IMS individual may have the if-then dispositional construct, "if interacting with Blacks, then make a nonprejudiced impression by revealing my nonprejudiced self and acting normal." We suspect that for the low EMS/high IMS person, the if-then rule takes the form "if interacting with a new person, then try to get to know the person." For this type of person, the race of the other does not feature strongly into the relational schema applied. That is, the relational schema may be "me when I interact with a new person." For low IMS/low EMS person, the nature of the if-then rule is not all that clear. These individuals are not inclined to approach interracial interactions and they do not appear to try and regulate their behavior in such situations. They may, however, adopt the if-then rule to get out of the situation as soon as possible (Word et al., 1974; Devine & Vasquez, 1998).

Even when if-then rules are clear, challenges remain for White individuals motivated to respond without prejudice in interracial interactions. That is, the if-then rules specify the overarching goal and the general objective. Translating the objectives into specific behavioral scripts to achieve the goals may require experience and feedback from the other concerning whether one has been successful (i.e., knowing what behaviors allow one to conceal prejudice or the behaviors that communicate a nonprejudiced identity). Consider, for example, the low IMS/high EMS person who enters an interracial interaction with an interracial relational schema (i.e., if interacting with Blacks, then conceal prejudice). The person must select a strategy for concealing prejudice. Zinner and Devine (2007) recently observed that in efforts to conceal prejudice, White people spontaneously attempt to suppress their prejudice. Although participants believed this to be an effective behavioral strategy, their interaction partners rated their partners as prejudiced. This example serves to highlight the complexities of relational schemas in interracial interactions specifically and interpersonal interactions more generally. Although one can intend to communicate a particular identity, success ultimately depends on whether the other "accepts" the identity and how the other responds. Thus, success and failure can be defined only in a relational sense.

Moreover, when entering interracial interactions, interaction partners' expectations for what the other expects may or may not be accurate and, hence, the schema one has for the other may interfere with successful implementation of the intended behavioral script. These challenges are compounded when one considers that interactions are reciprocal and dynamic and that both interaction partners have their own sets of expectations and objectives. As the interaction unfolds, they interpret each other's behavior in light of those expectancies, update their expectancies, and adjust their behavior in accordance with expectations. Indeed, dynamic interactions are extremely complex. They are made all the more difficult because neither party in the interaction is typically explicit about his or her goals, intentions, or concerns. As a result, the interactants make assumptions about the others' goals and expectations. Much of the updating of one's interpersonal script occurs silently within the minds of the respective interaction partners.

When these expectancies and objectives match (e.g., Whites expect to be viewed as prejudiced and Blacks expect the White to be prejudiced), interactions may unfold with ease and little tension (even though the interaction may not be positive). However, when there is a mismatch in expectancies and objectives, the stage is set for interpersonal difficulties, miscommunication, and intergroup tension (Devine & Vasquez, 1998). The mismatch may also engender self-verification needs (Swann, 1983; 1985) that can affect the course of the interaction.

Finally, the interracial relational schema perspective can account for coherent patterns of *variability* in behavior across interracial interactions. For example, a high EMS/low IMS person may possess the interracial relational schema "if with Blacks, then conceal anxiety" but may have a different interracial relational schema for Blacks in specific roles such that the "if-then" contingencies would predict a different interaction style (c.f., Bardin, Maddux, Petty, & Brewer, 2004). Or, the same high EMS/low IMS person may have target-based relational schema that, when salient, supersede category-based relational schema.

These are but a few of the potentially important questions generated by an intra-individual approach to personality and prejudice. Swann and Selye (2005) have commented on the potential theoretical bounty from the recent symbiosis of personality psychology with social psychology. We suggest that the program of research described in this chapter nicely illustrates one realization of this promise.

NOTE

1. The focus of this work is on Black and White interracial interactions. This focus reflects the fact that a majority of prior theory and research on prejudice and stereotyping has examined Whites' prejudice towards Blacks. This does not imply that interactions with other groups are not important or amenable to study within this framework.

REFERENCES

Adorno, T. W., Frenkel-Brunswick, E., Levinson, D. J., & Sanford, R. N. (1950). *The authoritarian personality*. New York: Harper & Row.

Allport, G. W. (1954). *The nature of prejudice*. Reading, MA: Addison-Wesley.

Altemeyer, B. (1981). *Right-wing authoritarianism*. Winnipeg: University of Manitoba Press.

Altemeyer, B. (1988). *Enemies of freedom: Understanding right-wing authoritarianism.* San Francisco: Jossey-Bass.

Altemeyer, B., & Hunsberger, (1992). Authoritarianism, religious fundamentalism, quest, and prejudice. *International Journal for the Psychology of Religion, 2,* 113–133.
Amodio, D. M., Devine, P. G., & Harmon-Jones, E. (in press). Neural signals for the detection of race bias: Implications for individual differences in regulatory ability. *Journal of Personality and Social Psychology.*
Amodio, D. M., Harmon-Jones, E., & Devine, P. G. (2003). Individual differences in the activation and control of affective race bias as assessed by startle eyeblink responses and self-report. *Journal of Personality and Social Psychology, 84,* 738–753.
Atkinson, J. W. (1964). *An introduction to achievement motivation.* Princeton, NJ: Van Nostrand.
Atkinson, J. W., & Litwin, G. H., (1960). Achievement motive and test anxiety conceived as motive to approach success and motive to avoid failure. *Journal of Abnormal and Social Psychology, 60,* 52–63.
Baldwin, M. W. (1992). Relational schemas and the processing of social information. *Psychological Bulletin, 112,* 461–484.
Baldwin, M. W. (1997). Relational schemas as a source of if-then self-inference procedures. *Review of General Psychology, 1,* 326–335.
Barden, J., Maddux, W. W., Petty, R. E., & Brewer, M. B. (2004). Contextual moderation of racial bias: The impact of social roles on controlled and automatically activated attitudes. *Journal of Personality and Social Psychology, 87,* 5–22.
Bargh, J. A. (1990). Auto-motives: Pre-conscious determinants of social interaction. In E. T. Higgins & R. M. Sorrento (Eds.) *Handbook of motivation and cognition: Foundations of social behavior, Vol. 2* (pp. 93–130). New York: Guilford.
Bargh, J. A., & Barndollar, K. (1996). Automaticity in action: The unconscious as repository of chronic goals and motivates. In P. M. Gollwitzer & J. A. Bargh (Eds.), *The psychology of action* (pp. 457–481). New York: Guilford Press.
Britt, T. W., Boniecki, K. A., Vescio, T. K., Biernat, M. & Brown, L. M. (1996). Intergroup anxiety: A person X situation approach. *Personality and Social Psychology Bulletin, 22,* 1177–1188.
Brodish, A. B., & Devine, P. G. (2005). The dynamics of prejudice, stereotyping, and intergroup relations: Intrapersonal and interpersonal processes. *Social Psychological Review, 7,* 54–70.
Carver, C. S. (2001). Affect and the functional bases of behavior: On the dimensional structure of affective experience. *Personality and Social Psychology Review, 5,* 345–356.
Carver, C. S., & Scheier, M. F. (1981). The self-attention-induced feedback loop and social facilitation. *Journal of Experimental Social Psychology, 17,* 545–568.
Carver, C. S., & Scheier, M. F. (1990). Origins and functions of positive and negative affect: A control-process view. *Psychological Review, 97,* 19–35.
Carver, C. S., & Scheier, M. F. (1998). *On the self-regulation of behavior.* New York: Cambridge.
Cervone, D. (2004). The architecture of personality. *Psychological Review, 111,* 183–204.
Chen, S. Boucher, H. C., & Tapias, M. P. (2006). The relational self revealed: Integrative conceptualization and implications for interpersonal life. *Psychological Bulletin, 132,* 151–179.
Crandall, C. S., Eshleman, A., & O'Brien, L. (2002). Social norms and the expression and suppression of prejudice: The struggle for internalization. *Journal of Personality and Social Psychology, 82,* 359–378.
Crosby, F., Bromley, S., & Saxe, L. (1980). Recent unobtrusive studies of black and white discrimination and prejudice: A literature review. *Psychological Bulletin, 87,* 546–563.
Crowne, D. P., & Marlow, D. (1960). A new scale of social desirability independent of psychopathology. *Journal of Consulting Psychology, 24,* 349–354.

Darley, J., & Fazio, R. H. (1980). Expectancy confirmation processes arising in the social interaction sequence. *American Psychologist, 35,* 867–881.

Devine, P.G. (1989). Stereotypes and prejudice: Their automatic and controlled processes. *Journal of Personality and Social Psychology, 56,* 5–18.

Devine, P. G., Brodish, A. B., & Vance, S. L. (2005). Self-regulatory processes in interracial interactions: The role of internal and external motivation to respond without prejudice. In J. P. Forgas, K. D. Williams, & S. M. Laham (Eds.) *Social motivation: Conscious and unconscious processes* (pp. 249–273). New York: Psychology Press.

Devine. P. G., & Elliot, A. J. (1995). Are racial stereotypes really fading? The Princeton trilogy revisited. *Personality and Social Psychology Bulletin, 21,* 1139–1150.

Devine P. G., & Monteith, M. J. (1993). The role of discrepancy associated affect in prejudice reduction. In D. M. Mackie & D. L. Hamilton (Eds.), *Affect, cognition, and stereotyping: Interactive processes in intergroup perception* (pp. 317–344). San Diego: Academic Press.

Devine, P. G., Monteith, M. M., Zuwerink, J. R., & Elliot, A. J. (1991). Prejudice with and without compunction. *Journal of Personality and Social Psychology, 60,* 817–830.

Devine, P. G., Plant, E. A., Amodio, D. M., Harmon-Jones, E., & Vance, S. L. (2002). The regulation of explicit and implicit race bias: The role of motivations to respond without prejudice. *Journal of Personality and Social Psychology, 82,* 835–848.

Devine, P. G., & Vasquez, K. A. (1998). The rocky road to positive intergroup relations. In J. L. Ebberhardt & S. T. Fiske (Eds.), *Confronting racism: The problem and the response* (pp. 234–262). Thousand Oaks, CA: Sage.

Dovidio, J. F., & Gaertner, S. L. (1986). Prejudice, discrimination, and racism: Historical trends and contemporary approaches. In J. F. Dovidio & S. L. Gaertner (Eds.), *Prejudice, discrimination, and racism* (pp. 1–34). San Diego: Academic Press.

Dovidio, J. F., Kawakami, K., & Gaertner, S. L. (2002). Implicit and explicit prejudice and interracial interaction. *Journal of Personality and Social Psychology, 82,* 62–68.

Dovidio, J. F., Kawakami, K., Johnson, C., Johnson, B., & Howard, A. (1997). On the nature of prejudice: Automatic and controlled processes. *Journal of Experimental Social Psychology, 33,* 510–540.

Dunton, B. C., & Fazio, R. H. (1997). An individual difference measure of motivation to control prejudiced reactions. *Personality and Social Psychology Bulletin, 23,* 316–326.

Duval S., & Wicklund, R. A. (1972). *A theory of objective self-awareness.* San Diego, CA: Academic Press.

Elliot, A. J. (2006). The hierarchical model of approach-avoidance motivation. *Motivation and Emotion, 30,* 111–116.

Elliot, A. J., & Church, M. A. (1997). A hierarchical model of approach and avoidance achievement motivation. *Journal of Personality and Social Psychology, 72,* 218–232.

Elliot, A. J., Gable, S. L., & Mapes, R. R. (2006). Approach and avoidance motivation in the social domain. *Personality and Social Psychology Bulletin, 32,* 378–391.

Elliot, A. J., & Harackiewicz, J. M. (1996). Approach and avoidance achievement goals and intrinsic motivation: A mediational analysis. *Journal of Personality and Social Psychology, 70,* 461– 475.

Esses, V. M., Haddock, G., & Zanna, M. P. (1993). Values, stereotypes, and emotions as determinants of intergroup attitudes. In D.M. Mackie & D. Lewis (Eds.), *Affect, cognition and stereotyping: Interactive processes in group perception* (pp. 137–166). San Diego: Academic Press.

Fazio, R. H., Jackson, J. R., Dunton, B. C., & Williams, C. J. (1995). Variability in automatic activation as an unobtrusive measure of racial attitudes: A bona fide pipeline? *Journal of Personality and Social Psychology, 69,* 1013–1027.

Feather, N. T. (1967). Level of aspiration and performance variability. *Journal of Personality and Social Psychology, 6*, 37 – 46.

Galinsky, A., & Moskowitz, G. (2000). Perspective taking: Decreasing stereotype expression, stereotype accessibility, and in-group favoritism. *Journal of Personality and Social Psychology, 78*, 708–724.

Gaertner, S. L., & Dovidio, J. F. (1986). The aversive form of racism. In J. F. Dovidio & S. L. Gaertner (Eds.), *Prejudice, discrimination, and racism* (pp. 61–89). San Diego: Academic Press.

Greenwald, A. G., McGhee, D., & Schwartz, J. (1998). Measuring individual differences in implicit cognition: The implicit association test. *Journal of Personality and Social Psychology, 74*, 1464–1480.

Guimond, S., Dambrun, M., Michinov, N., & Duarte, S. (2003). Does social dominance generate prejudice? Integrating individual and contextual determinants of intergroup cognitions. *Journal of Personality and Social Psychology, 84*, 697–721.

Haddock, G., Zanna, M. P., & Esses, V. M. (1993). Assessing the structure of prejudicial attitudes: The case of attitudes toward homosexuals. *Journal of Personality and Social Psychology, 65*, 1105–1118.

Hembree, R. (1988). Correlates, causes, effects, and treatment of test anxiety. *Review of Educational Research, 58*, 47 – 77.

Higgins, E. T. (1987). Self-discrepancy: A theory relating self and affect. *Psychological Review, 94*, 319–340.

Higgins, E. T., & Friedman, R. S. (1998). Performance incentives and means: How regulatory focus influences goal attainment. *Journal of Personality and Social Psychology, 74*, 285–293.

Katz, D., & Braly, K. (1933). Racial stereotypes of one hundred college students. *Journal of Abnormal and Social Psychology, 28*, 280–290.

Katz, I., & Hass, R. G. (1988). Racial ambivalence and American value conflict: Correlational and priming studies of dual cognitive structures. *Journal of Personality and Social Psychology, 55*, 893–905.

Kinder, D. R., & Sears, D. O. (1981). Prejudice and politics: Symbolic racism versus racial threats to the good life. *Journal of Personality and Social Psychology, 40*, 414–431.

Kruglanski, A. W., & Freund, T. (1983). The freezing and unfreezing of lay-inferences: Effects on impressional primacy, ethnic stereotyping, and numerical anchoring. *Journal of Experimental Social Psychology, 19*, 448–468.

Leary, M. R. (1983). Social anxiousness: The construct and its measurement. *Journal of Personality Assessment, 47*, 66–75.

Macrae, C. N., & Bodenhausen, G. V. (2000). Social cognition: Thinking categorically about others. *Annual Review of Psychology, 51*, 93–120.

Mahone, C. H. (1960). Fear of failure and unrealistic vocational aspiration. *Journal of Abnormal and Social Psychology, 60*, 253–261.

Martin, J. G., & Westie, F. R. (1959). The tolerant personality. *American Sociological Review, 24*, 521–528.

McConahay, J. G. (1986). Modern racism, ambivalence, and the modern racism scale. In J. F. Dovidio & S. L. Gaernter (Eds.), *Prejudice, discrimination, and racism,* (pp. 91–125). San Diego, CA: Academic Press.

McConahay, J. G., Hardee, B. B., & Batts. V. (1981). Has racism declined? It depends on who's asking and what is asked. *Journal of Conflict Resolution, 25*, 563–579.

McGregor, J. (1993). Effectiveness of role playing and antiracist teaching in reducing student prejudice. *Journal of Education Research, 86*, 215–226.

McHoskey, J. W. (1996). Authoritarianism and ethical ideology. *Journal of Social Psychology, 136*, 709–717.

Mischel, W., & Shoda, Y. (1995). A cognitive-affective system theory of personality: Reconceptualizing situations, dispositions, dynamics and invariance in personality structure. *Psychological Review, 102*, 246–268.

Mischel, W., & Shoda, Y. (1998). Reconciling processing dynamics and personality dispositions. *Annual Review of Psychology, 49*, 229–258.

Monteith, M. J. (1993). Self-regulation of prejudiced responses: Implications for progress in prejudice-reduction efforts. *Journal of Personality and Social Psychology, 65*, 469–485.

Monteith, M. J., Ashburn-Nardo, L., Voils, C. I., & Czopp, A. M. (2002). Putting the brakes on prejudice: On the development and operation of cues for control. *Journal of Personality and Social Psychology, 83*, 1029–1050.

Monteith, M. J., Sherman, J., & Devine, P. G. (1998). Suppression as a stereotype control strategy. *Personality and Social Psychology Review, 2*, 63–82.

Monteith, M. J., Voils, C. I., & Ashburn-Nardo, L. (2001). Taking a look underground: Detecting, interpreting, and reacting to implicit racial biases. *Social Cognition, 19*, 395–417.

Ostrom, T. M., & Sedikides, C. (1992). Outgroup homogeneity effects in natural and minimal groups. *Psychological Bulletin, 112*, 536–552.

Plant, E. A., & Devine, P. G. (1998). Internal and external motivation to respond without prejudice. *Journal of Personality and Social Psychology, 75*, 811–832.

Plant, E. A., & Devine, P. G. (2003). The antecedents and implications of interracial anxiety. *Personality and Social Psychology Bulletin, 29*, 790–801.

Plant, E. A., & Devine, P. G. (2004). Unpublished data.

Plant, E. A., & Devine, P. G. (in press). Approach and avoidance motives in intergroup processes. In A. Elliot (Ed.), *Handbook of approach and avoidance motivation*. Hillsdale, NJ: Erlbaum.

Plant, E. A., & Devine, P. G. (2007). Intentions to be free of bias or hide bias: The roles of external and internal motivation to respond without prejudice. Unpublished manuscript, Florida State University.

Richeson, J. A., & Shelton, J. N. (2003). When prejudice doesn't pay: Effects of interracial contact on executive function. *Psychological Science, 13*, 287–290.

Rokeach, M., & Mezei, L. (1966). Race and shared belief as factors in social choice. *Science, 151*, 167–172.

Sedikides, C. (1997). Differential processing of ingroup and outgroup information: The role of relative group status in permeable boundary groups. *European Journal of Social Psychology, 27*, 121–144.

Shah, J., Higgins, T. E., & Friedman, R. S. (1998). Performance incentives and means: How regulatory focus influences goal attainment. *Journal of Personality and Social Psychology, 74*, 285–293.

Shelton, J. N. (2003). Interpersonal concerns in social encounters between majority and minority group members. *Group Processes and Intergroup Relations, 6*, 171–185.

Sidanius, J., & Pratto, F. (1999). *Social dominance: An intergroup theory of social hierarchy and oppression*. Cambridge, MA: Cambridge University Press.

Snyder, M., & Gangestad, S. (1986). On the nature of self-monitoring: Matters of assessment, matters of validity. *Journal of Personality and Social Psychology, 51*, 125–139.

Stangor, C., & Duan, C. (1991). Effects of multiple task demands upon memory for information about social groups. *Journal of Experimental Social Psychology, 27*, 357–378.

Stephan, W. G., & Stephan, C. W. (1985). Intergroup anxiety. *Journal of Social Issues, 41*, 157–175.

Stephan W. G., & Stephan, C. W. (1989). Emotional reactions to interracial achievement outcomes. *Journal of Applied Social Psychology, 19*, 608–621.

Swann, W. B. (1983). Self-verification: Bringing social reality into harmony with the self. In. J Suls & A. Greenwald (Eds.), *Psychological perspectives on the self* (Vol. 2, pp. 33–66). Hillsdale, NJ: Erlbaum.

Swann, W. B. (1985). The self as architect of social reality. In B. Schlenker (Ed.), *The self and social life* (pp. 100–125). New York: McGraw-Hill.

Swann, W. B., & Selye, C. (2005). Personality psychology's comeback and its emerging symbiosis with social psychology. *Personality and Social Psychology Bulletin, 31*, 155–165.

Tajfel, H., & Turner, J. C. (1986). The social identity theory of intergroup behavior. In S. Worchel & W. G. Austin (Eds.), *Psychology of intergroup relations* (pp. 7–24). Chicago, IL: Nelson-Hall Publishers.

Watson, D., & Friend, R. (1969). Measurement of social-evaluative anxiety. *Journal of Consulting and Clinical Psychology, 33*, 448–457.

Vorauer, J. D., Hunter, A. J., Main, K. J., & Roy, S. A. (2000). Meta-stereotype activation: Evidence from indirect measures for specific evaluation concerns experienced by members of dominant groups in intergroup interactions. *Journal of Personality and Social Psychology, 78*, 690–707.

Vorauer, J. D., & Kumhyr. S. M., (2001). Is this about you or me? Self- versus other-directed judgments and feelings in response to intergroup interactions. *Personality and Social Psychology Bulletin, 27*, 706–709.

Vorauer, J. D., Main, K. J., & O'Connell, G. B. (1998). How do individuals expect to be viewed by members of lower status groups? Content and implications of meta-stereotypes. *Journal of Personality and Social Psychology, 75*, 917–937.

Westie, F. R., & DeFleur, M. L. (1959). Autonomic responses and their relationship to race attitudes. *Journal of Abnormal and Social Psychology, 58*(3), 340–347.

Word, C. O., Zanna, M. P., & Cooper, J. (1974). The nonverbal mediation of self-fulfilling prophecies in interracial interaction. *Journal of Experimental Social Psychology, 10*, 109–120.

Zinner, L. R., & Devine, P. G. (2007). The regulation of prejudiced emotion. Unpublished data, University of Wisconsin.

10

Social Psychological Processes Linking Personality to Physical Health
A Multilevel Analysis With Emphasis on Hostility and Optimism

BERT N. UCHINO, ALLISON A. VAUGHN, and SONIA MATWIN

University of Utah

OVERVIEW AND INTRODUCTION

> The concept that certain personality types are predisposed to certain diseases has been ever present in medical thought. When medicine was based on clinical observation alone the frequent occurrence of certain diseases in persons of definite physical or mental habitus was often noted by observant physicians. The significance of this fact, however, was completely unknown. (Alexander, 1950, p. 71)

Personality has long been suspected as a factor influencing physical health outcomes (Alexander, 1950). One of the earliest of such accounts had its roots in the theorizing of Hippocrates around 400 BC. Hippocrates is widely regarded as the father of modern medicine. He proposed that the body was composed of four primary humors, and it was the balance of these that maintained health. This thinking dominated early medical thinking, but it was Galen, around

160 AD,, who further elaborated on the "temperaments" potentially associated with these four humors. These humors were thought to be associated with traits such as irritability, sadness, enthusiasm, and apathy. This work formed one of the earliest attempts to explain disease based on personality processes that might be evident to the "observant physician."

More recent frameworks for an analysis of personality and physical health have their origins with the psychoanalytic tradition (Alexander, 1950; Dunbar, 1943). In one classic analysis, Dunbar (1954) described the coronary-prone patient as follows: "Compulsively consistent action" and "Conversations an instrument of domination and aggression" (pp. 746–747, Table insert). Of course, one critique of such early accounts is that it was often difficult to determine if these personality traits were causes or outcomes of disease (or due to some other factor). Nevertheless, such hypothesizing generated increased interest in questions linking personality processes to physical health.

We now have much more data on the links between personality and disease. The above historical observations are now supplemented by interdisciplinary research from diverse fields (e.g., Psychology, Medicine, Epidemiology, Sociology). For many literatures linking personality to physical health, the first generation of questions is still focused on whether or not such a link can actually be demonstrated empirically. For some personality factors (e.g., hostility, optimism), however, there is now solid evidence linking them to physical health (Smith & Gallo, 2001). The next generation of questions for these more advanced literatures has in common the goal of identifying the mechanisms potentially responsible for links between personality and physical health (Cohen & Herbert, 1996). Such progress has been slowed, however, by the complexity of the phenomena that are linked to multiple levels of analyses.

In order to foster more comprehensive accounts linking personality to physical health outcomes, we will focus our review on the mechanisms that might be operating at different levels of analysis. We will be focusing on a multilevel perspective that bridges the social and biological levels (Berntson & Cacioppo, 2000; Cacioppo & Berntson, 1992; Engel, 1977). Due to the importance of social-cognitive and biological processes in links between personality and physical health, we believe a multilevel perspective to be critical in organizing research on the question at hand (Cacioppo, Petty, & Tassinary, 1989).

Before addressing these questions, we first discuss some basic issues that need consideration when linking personality to health outcomes, including the issues of defining personality and the disease processes of interest. We next provide a brief review of studies linking the personality factors of hostility and optimism to cardiovascular disease. We focus on these personality processes because they (a) are more firmly linked to physical health outcomes and (b) represent examples of "negative" and "positive" personality profiles. A general social-cognitive model linking personality to disease via relevant physiological processes is then proposed, along with empirical evidence relevant to the model. We conclude by elucidating important but largely unexamined mechanisms based on a multilevel perspective of health and disease.

Preliminary Questions

What Is Personality? A comprehensive review of the question: "What is personality?" is, of course, beyond the scope of the present review. However, there are several perspectives in the literature that bear on this review. Briefly, personality represents those characteristics of the person that account for patterns in behavior (Pervin, 1970). While the ways in which these patterns are defined may vary across theories (i.e., intra-, inter-individual), there is general consensus in the understanding of personality as that which gives organization and consistency to "you." In this regard, there have been several research traditions that have examined this basic question that differ in their assumptions and approach.

One conception of personality is in terms of traits, such that certain dispositions would predispose individuals to engage in relevant behaviors (McCrae & Costa, 1997). Simply stated, it is assumed that there exists a direct relationship between a trait and its behavioral expression, a relationship with cross-situational and temporal consistency. In some cases it is thought that a set number of traits exist, although trait theorists differ in the extent to which they endorse certain traits as central (e.g., Cloninger, Svrakic, & Przybeck 1993; McCrae & Costa, 1997; Rothbart, Ahadi, & Evans, 2000).

Of course, the link between personality traits and behavior has historically been an issue of strong debate, following the seminal review by Mischel (1968). As a result, trait researchers sought out stronger evidence for cross-situational consistency to bolster assumptions regarding stability in behavioral dispositions that were thought to underlie personality (Bem & Allen, 1974; Epstein, 1979). While this approach yielded a number of important insights (e.g., aggregation), one of the basic issues of concern to social psychologists was that it treated the situation as "error variance" and hence ignored the potential coherence in person X situation interactions (Mischel, 2004; Mischel & Shoda, 1995).

The social psychological approach to personality is often called the social-cognitive perspective (e.g., Cervone, 2004; Mischel, 2004; Mischel & Shoda, 1995). Thus, a second means of studying personality has been to conceptualize it in terms of activated intra-individual processes, such that the relationship between behavioral expressions and personality traits is no longer assumed to be direct, but rather is reflected as relevant person X situation processes. In other words, personality may be studied by examining the dynamic and meaningful interactions among processes operating within the person and situation (Cervone & Shoda, 1999). For instance, Mischel and Shoda (1995) have provided empirical evidence for intra-individually stable situation-behavior relations and have suggested that these patterns may represent signatures of personality. Cervone (2004) has also built on this research by explicitly drawing a distinction between structure (i.e., knowledge) and process (i.e., appraisals) to better specify intra-individual personality coherence.

As noted by Mischel (2004), the trait and social-cognitive approach to personality are not necessarily incompatible (also see Kagan, 2003). Each can explain a portion of the personality puzzle. The focus of this review will be on a mix of these two approaches, given the empirical database available. The prior research on personality and health has typically examined a limited set of personality traits thought to directly influence health-relevant processes (e.g., hostility). However, some of this research also highlights the importance of person X situation interactions because repeated transactions with the environment in health relevant ways (e.g., exposure to stress) are thought to provide the most plausible link to the development of diseases with a long-term etiology (Krantz & Manuck, 1984). The features of such health-relevant situations and how they relate to social-cognitive structures will thus also be examined as part of this review (e.g., see Allred & Smith, 1991; Rhodewalt & Smith, 1991; Smith & Anderson, 1986).

What Disease Is of Interest? An analysis of personality and physical health is inherently an interdisciplinary endeavor. Thus, an equally important question relates to the disease process of interest. It is important to understand that each major disease has a unique natural progression that ultimately compromises physical health (see Uchino, Smith, Holt-Lunstad, Campo, & Reblin, 2007). For instance, the antecedent processes (e.g., behaviors, pathophysiology) that give rise to cardiovascular disease are distinct from those involved in cancer, and this level of specificity needs strong consideration in research linking personality to health. Of course, this level of specificity is also critically important in designing focused interventions.

Researchers examining the links between personality and physical health will also need to consider the stage of disease impacted. Does personality actually influence the development of disease, or is it primarily a factor after the medical diagnosis of disease when individuals are attempting to cope with disease-specific stressors and challenges? As an example, can optimism influence cardiovascular diseases that take decades to become clinically significant? Or is it the case that optimism is mostly effective after one is diagnosed with cardiovascular disease and faced with life changing (e.g., diet, exercise) and stressful (e.g., threats to self) circumstances? This information would again be extremely important in the design of appropriate interventions.

As noted earlier, we will focus primarily on links between hostility and optimism with cardiovascular disease. As background, cardiovascular disease is a broad term used to cover several diseases of the cardiovascular system, including coronary artery disease (CAD) and hypertension. It is by far the leading cause of death in the United States and most industrialized countries (American Heart Association, 2004). In fact, it typically accounts for about as many deaths as the next five or six leading causes of death combined. It is estimated that if all major forms of cardiovascular disease were eliminated, life expectancy would be raised by about 7 years. This stands in comparison to a life expectancy gain of 3 years if all forms of cancers were eliminated (American Heart Association, 2004).

CAD is a condition in which the coronary arteries become narrowed, ultimately resulting in decreased blood flow to the heart. The pathological change in the coronary arteries is due to a process called atherosclerosis, which is a progressive build-up of fatty deposits within the arterial walls. This build-up is not a passive process that simply occurs with the passage of time. Recent research suggests that inflammation (e.g., macrophage activity, cytokine release) may play a key role in the progression of CAD (Libby, 2002; Ross, 1999). The end result of this process is the formation of arterial lesions and narrowing of the arteries. These processes increase the chance that a blood clot will form, thereby heightening the risk of blocking the arterial passage. Although most people think of CAD as occurring in older adults, it is important to note that this atherogenic process starts very early. For instance, the beginnings of arterial plaque can be found in children, with some young adults already evidencing advanced lesions. Of course, only when the disease is in its later stages (as is often the case with older adults) does it result in clinical symptoms. Thus, CAD is generally considered a disease with a long-term developmental history.

Hypertension is another leading cardiovascular disorder and is a condition of elevated blood pressure (SBP $\geq$ 140 mmHg or DBP $\geq$ 90 mmHg). However, there is also increasing appreciation for the health relevance of blood pressure previously labeled as normal. Recent guidelines suggest that SBP between 120-139 mmHg and/or DBP between 80-89 mmHg be considered "pre-hypertension" (AHA, 2004). In about 5 to 10% of cases, the cause of high blood pressure can be determined and is labeled secondary hypertension (e.g., kidney problems). However, in the vast majority of cases the cause of elevated blood pressure is unknown and is labeled essential or primary hypertension. Due to the heightened workload within the cardiovascular system, as well as the increased pressure in various organ systems, the consequences of hypertension can include kidney damage and increased risk of myocardial infarction (MI), stroke, and heart failure.

Besides practical considerations (i.e., available database), there are several important advantages of focusing on cardiovascular disease. First, the disease context is relatively well-specified. This will allow us to consider (a) connections with existing data linking behavioral risk factors to heart disease, (b) appropriate statistical controls, and (c) the challenges faced by individuals with this chronic condition. Second, given the long-term pathophysiology of cardiovascular disorders, one can examine the potential stage of disease that personality factors might impact. For these reasons we will focus on cardiovascular diseases but will conclude with the implications of these findings for links between personality and other specific disease processes (i.e., cancer, infectious diseases).

Personality and Cardiovascular Disease

In this section we will provide a brief review of evidence linking the personality factors of hostility and optimism to cardiovascular disease. In the following section, we propose a general social-cognitive model detailing the potential mechanisms responsible for associations between personality and cardiovascular risk at differing levels of analysis. Evidence for this model is then reviewed, along with future research directions.

Trait Hostility and Cardiovascular Disease. Although specific definitions of trait hostility differ, it is generally thought to contain three important components (Barefoot, 1992). It is a personality factor characterized by cognitive (e.g., negative attitudes/beliefs regarding others), affective (e.g., tendency towards feelings of anger), and behavioral (e.g., aggression) aspects (Barefoot, 1992; Smith,

1992). Although many researchers emphasize the cognitive component of hostility (e,g., cynicism, mistrust), there are empirical problems in trying to separate out these processes as they tend to be correlated across assessment devices (Miller, Smith, Turner, Guijarro, & Hallett, 1996).

One important issue in studying the influence of trait hostility on health is related to the assessment of hostility (Miller et al., 1996). A widely used scale to assess the links between trait hostility and physical health is the Cook-Medley scale (Barefoot, 1992). However, this scale has a relatively poor internal structure and tends to be more highly related to measures of neuroticism than other measures (e.g., Barefoot, Dodge, Peterson, Dalstrom, &Wiliams, 1989). In addition, some hostility assessments appear more sensitive to physical health outcomes than others. Trait hostility has been assessed using behavioral measures, self-reports, and other reports (e.g., spouse), with some evidence indicating stronger associations between hostility and physical health using behavioral measures obtained during structured interviews (Miller et al., 1996).

Despite these issues, epidemiological studies paint a consistent picture of links between trait hostility and physical health outcomes such as cardiovascular disease. In an early review, Booth-Kewley and Friedman (1987) examined 12 studies and documented a statistically significant positive relationship between hostility and cardiovascular disease (also see Matthews, 1988). A meta-analysis by Miller and colleagues (1996) looked specifically at hostility and its links to physical health more generally in 45 studies. They found that hostility was related to all-cause mortality, including cardiovascular disease (also see Suls & Bunde, 2005).

Importantly, hostility may have an influence on both the development of cardiovascular disease and its associated clinical course (Smith & MacKenzie, in press). For instance, Niaura and colleagues (2002) studied initially healthy men (ages 21-80) from the Normative Aging Study. At a 3-year follow-up, hostility significantly predicted the incidence of cardiovascular disease (also see Chang, Ford, Meoni, Wang, & Klag, 2002; Irribarren et al., 2005). Similarly, recent studies have suggested links between hostility and mortality in cardiac patients (Boyle et al., 2004; Matthews, Gump, Harris, Haney, & Barefoot, 2004; Olson et al., 2005), although such links appear weaker compared to studies utilizing healthy populations (Suls & Bunde, 2005).

Optimism and Cardiovascular Disease. Optimism is a more recent personality process thought to influence physical health outcomes (Carver & Scheier, 2002; Smith & Gallo, 2001). Optimism has been defined and examined in at least two ways (Peterson, 2000). One definition emphasizes optimism as a personality characteristic marked by generalized positive expectations for the future (Carver & Scheier, 2002). The other perspective comes from the Abramson, Seligman, and Teasdale (1978) model of explanatory style. This perspective emphasizes the characteristic attributions that individuals make about negative events that are associated with feelings of helplessness or optimism (Peterson, 2000). Although there is some evidence linking the explanatory style approach to health outcomes (e.g., Peterson, Seligman, Yurko, Martin, & Friedman, 1998), most of the research has been examined from the generalized expectancy approach of Carver and Scheier

(2002). As a result, we mainly focus on this conceptualization and operationalization of optimism in our review.

We should mention that within this approach there are two related issues that are of importance in examining its associations with physical health outcomes. One of these relates to the possibility that optimism is associated with other personality processes, such as neuroticism, that might explain associations with health outcomes (Smith, Pope, Rhodewalt, & Poulton, 1989). For instance, Smith and colleagues (1989) found that statistically controlling for neuroticism eliminated the link between optimism and symptom reports/certain coping behaviors, whereas the reverse was not true. In response, Scheier, Carver, and Bridges (1994) revised the Life Orientation Test (LOT-R) to eliminate several potential problematic items. Although studies suggest that optimism continues to predict certain outcomes even when controlling for neuroticism, it is clear that such associations are typically attenuated (Chang, 1998a; Mroczek, Spiro, Aldwin, Ozer, & Bosse, 1993; Scheier et al., 1994). Less research has examined this issue within the physical health domain, but one study found that although links between optimism and lower ambulatory SBP were eliminated when controlling for neuroticism, associations with ambulatory DBP were not (Raikkonen, Matthews, Flory, Owens, & Gump, 1999).

A second general issue concerns the extent to which optimism/pessimism represent opposite ends of a continuum or are separable dimensions (Chang, 1998a). To this point, studies suggest that the optimism and pessimism subscales of the LOT-R are separable, as shown via exploratory and confirmatory factor analyses (Marshall, Wortman, Kusulas, Hervig, & Vickers, 1992; Robinson-Whelen, Kim, MacCallum, & Kiecolt-Glaser, 1997). More recently, Chang (1998a) has suggested that confounding with other personality factors may not be as prevalent using this two-factor structure, although more data will be needed on this point.

Compared with trait hostility, there is considerably less epidemiological research examining the links between optimism and physical health outcomes. Part of this reflects the different origins of these literatures as well as the relative recency of the proposed links between optimism and health (Smith & Gallo, 2001). In one study, dispositional optimism was linked to lower cardiovascular disease mortality in a 9-year follow-up of a Dutch population-based cohort (Giltay, Geleijnse, Zitman, Hoekstra, & Schouten, 2004). However, the specific stage of disease by which optimism might influence cardiovascular mortality is unclear. The few available prospective studies do suggest that lower optimism predicts the development of cardiovascular disease. In the Normative Aging study, Kubzansky, Sparrow, Vokonas, and Kawachi (2001) found that healthy adult men who endorsed a more optimistic explanatory style were at less risk for the development of coronary disease 10 years later, even after statistically controlling for a number of standard biomedical controls (e.g., smoking, cholesterol levels). These data are consistent with a recent imaging study showing that optimism predicted less of an increase in carotid intima thickness across a 3-year period (Matthews, Raikkonen, Sutton-Tyrrell, & Kuller, 2004).

Several studies have examined the link with optimism following the diagnosis of cardiovascular disease (Leedham, Meyerowitz, Muirhead, & Frist, 1995; Scheier et al., 1989; Shen, McCreary, & Myers, 2004). In an early study, Scheier and colleagues (1989) examined the influence of optimism in patients who underwent coronary artery bypass surgery. During the study, optimists showed a faster rate of physical recovery in the hospital and a quicker return to life activities following discharge. Middleton and Byrd (1996) also studied older adults who had been admitted to and discharged from a hospital due to cardiovascular disease. Optimism was related to fewer cases of unexpected readmissions to the hospital. These studies suggest that optimism may also play a protective role in the clinical course of diagnosed cardiovascular disease.

Modeling the Social-Cognitive Influences of Personality on Disease

There is ample evidence linking the personality processes associated with hostility and optimism to cardiovascular disease. At this point, we would like to outline a general social-cognitive model that might be used to systematically investigate the influence of personality on health. This model is informed by the prior literature and highlights different links that may need further investigation, depending on the personality process of interest. It also emphasizes the type of multilevel research strategy that we believe has been useful in informing our present work on psychosocial risk factors for disease (see Uchino, Holt-Lunstad, Uno, Campo, & Reblin, 2007).

As shown in Figure 10.1, we believe that personality has a "cascading" influence on a number of processes, once activated. Of these, social (e.g., interpersonal

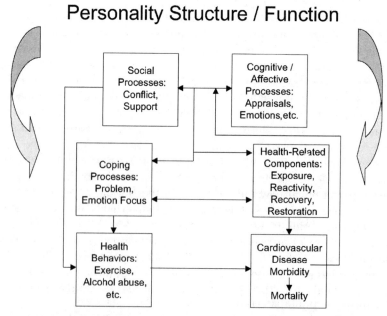

Figure 10.1 General social-cognitive model highlighting potential intra- and interpersonal pathways linking personality with cardiovascular disease.

interactions), cognitive/affective (e.g., appraisals, emotion), behavioral (e.g., health behaviors), and physiological (e.g., cardiovascular stress reactivity) processes appear especially promising as mediators for links between personality and physical health outcomes such as cardiovascular disease. At the core of these associations are the social and cognitive/affective links associated with personality. Although there are several social (interpersonal) processes that appear important in explaining links between personality and health (Smith & Gallo, 2001), two important factors in this regard relate to interpersonal stress (conflict) and social support processes. Exposure to these social situations results in the activation of relevant cognitive/affective processes (e.g., attributions, appraisals, emotion; Mischel & Shoda, 1995). We have included bi-directional links between the social and cognitive/affective processes, as there is evidence for such influences. For instance, it is also the case that cognitive schemas can influence one's interpretation of social situations (E. R. Smith & Zarate, 1992; Swann & Read, 1981). For instance, hostile individuals are more likely to make unfriendly attributions for relatively ambiguous social behavior, thus shaping the potential for social conflict (Smith & Gallo, 2001). These social-cognitive processes appear to form a central set of organizing mechanisms that then have an influence on health-relevant processes further down stream.

The combination of these social and cognitive/affective processes can directly influence health-related component processes. Cacioppo and Berntson (2007) propose that there are at least four health-relevant stress components that need consideration. These health-relevant components include stress exposure, stress reactivity, stress recovery, and restoration. Exposure refers to the number of "toxic" situations (i.e., stressors) that an individual experiences, reactivity refers to the strength of an individual's physiological reaction in any given event, whereas recovery refers to how long it takes an individual to return to "baseline" following stressors. Restoration is a relatively unique aspect of this perspective that focuses on anabolic processes that refresh or repair the organism, given that threatening situations may directly impede our ability to perform these functions (e.g., disturbed sleep, impaired wound healing). As will be covered below, there is evidence linking personality to these component stress-related processes. For instance, due to their mistrustful schemata, hostile individuals may interpret ambiguous social information as more threatening and thus increase their exposure to stress (Smith, 1992).

As detailed in 10.1, social-cognitive processes associated with personality can also influence these components indirectly via behavioral coping strategies as the individual attempts to manage life's stressors and challenges. A primary/broad coping taxonomy includes the distinction between problem- and emotion-focused coping strategies. Problem-focused coping is more concerned with directly altering the source of stress (e.g., planning), whereas emotion-focused coping attempts to minimize the negative affect associated with stress (Carver, Scheier, & Weintraub, 1989). In general, problem-focused coping strategies appear to be linked to better adjustment compared to emotion-focused strategies (Suls & Fletcher, 1985). If applied to inappropriate situations (e.g., uncontrollable stressors), however, the use of problem-focused coping strategies may be linked to greater stress exposure and may lessen recovery from the stressor via rumination. Over the long-term, coping strategies that are linked to appropriate situations (e.g., acceptance for uncontrollable stress, active planning for controllable stress; Scheier, Weintraub, & Carver, 1986) may foster adaptation via relevant health components such as stress exposure and ample opportunity for restoration.

It is important to note that health behaviors may also explain part of the link between personality and disease. The two salient pathways involve a direct path from social processes as well as through coping processes. Social processes may play a direct role on health behaviors via social control (Lewis & Rook, 1999; Umberson, 1987). According to this view, social processes related to relationships are health-promoting because they facilitate healthier behaviors, such as exercise, eating right, and not smoking. This can happen in a direct (e.g., health-related informational support) or indirect (e.g., life meaning) fashion (Umberson, 1987). Likewise, social conflict may also have a detrimental influence on health behaviors in itself (Burg & Seeman, 1994), or when considered with relevant indices of social support (Cohen & Lichtenstein, 1990). Finally, if coping responses do not terminate or alleviate the source of stress, then this may adversely influence health behaviors such as exercise, diet, and smoking (Ng & Jeffery, 2003; Stetson, Rahn, Dubbert, Wilner, & Mercury, 1997).

The health-related components of exposure, reactivity, recovery, and restoration are next predicted to have direct effects on cardiovascular disease morbidity and mortality. There are reliable links between these stress-related component processes and cardiovascular disease morbidity/mortality, although less evidence exists on links between recovery and restoration and such physical health outcomes (see review in Uchino et al., 2007). For instance, the reactivity hypothesis of cardiovascular disease assumes that both stress reactivity and exposure are important for the development of cardiovascular disease (Krantz & Manuck, 1984; Manuck, 1994). There is evidence consistent with the reactivity hypothesis in predicting coronary outcomes (Treiber et al., 2003). As noted above, less evidence is available on links between recovery and restoration and disease, and future research will need to more firmly establish these links, as well as how the different components are related over time (Uchino et al., 2007).

Finally, it is important to distinguish between disease morbidity and mortality for several reasons. First, as shown in 10.1, disease morbidity may trigger relevant social, cognitive, and affective processes (Nicassio & Smith, 1995). For instance, the diagnosis of a chronic condition can influence social processes, such as mobilization of support and/or potential increases in social conflict (Bolger, Foster, Vinokur, & Ng, 1996; Helgeson, 1993; Stephens, Kinney, Norris, & Richie, 1987). Chronic diseases are also associated with increases in threat and associated negative emotions (Nicassio & Smith, 1995). Of course, it is important to note that some chronic disease patients may experience positive social, cognitive, and emotional experiences such as deepening relationships and a greater sense of life meaning (Holahan & Moos, 1990). Second, the distinction between disease morbidity and mortality is important so that theoretical models can consider the stage of disease potentially impacted by the personality process of interest. This point is highlighted by work suggesting that trait hostility predicts cardiovascular mortality in healthier populations (suggesting links to disease development; Miller et al.,

1996), whereas more mixed evidence is available for populations with diagnosed cardiovascular disease (Suls & Bunde, 2005).

The distinction between stages of disease is also necessary because different biological processes are salient in the development versus exacerbation of existing cardiovascular disease. For instance, the role of stress reactivity in the development of disease highlights the role of endothelial injury due to mechanical (e.g., shear force) or chemical (e.g., catecholamines) factors as important precipitating events (Krantz & Manuck, 1984). More recent research is focusing on the possibility that, following endothelial injury, inflammatory processes take center stage due to the migration of macrophages/T-cells and the release of cytokines (Libby, 2002; Ross, 1999). Cytokines are glycoprotein hormones produced by cells of the immune system and serve to regulate diverse aspects of immunity, including inflammation (Dinarello & Mier, 1987).

In comparison, the mechanisms linking stress to the exacerbation of disease may be related more to the induction of myocardial ischemia, arrhythmias, and thrombosis (Rozanski, Blumentha. & Kaplan, 1999). Acute stress may precipitate ischemia due to hemodynamic changes in blood pressure (Rozanski et al., 1988), perhaps due to stress-induced increases in endothelial dysfunction and subsequent vasoconstriction (Goldberg et al., 1996; Yeung et al., 1991). Acute stress may cause changes in the autonomic nervous system that lead to arrhythmia and sudden cardiac death (Kamarck & Jennings, 1991). Thus, chronic processes are salient in the development of cardiovascular disease, whereas in theory, acute events in and of themselves may be sufficient to induce problems in cardiac patients.

Evidence for the Model

We have outlined a broad, multilevel model that highlights social-cognitive processes as critical mediators of links between personality and health. In the following section we review existing evidence on aspects of these proposed links. We should note, however, we are aware of no study that has assessed the full model, and future research will be needed to determine the plausibility of the combined pathways. We again focus on trait hostility and optimism to illustrate the utility of the proposed model.

Potential Social Processes Linking Personality to Disease. As noted earlier, two important social processes explaining links between personality and health are social conflict and social support (Smith & Gallo, 2001). In one prospective study, changes in trait hostility from college to midlife predicted exposure to negative changes in family, work, and economic life (Siegler et al., 2003; also see Miller et al., 1995). Individuals high in trait hostility are also more likely to create interpersonal stressors across both work and home contexts (transactional model; Smith & Frohm, 1985; Smith, Pope, Sanders, Allred, & O'Keeffe, 1988). More recent evidence from daily experience sampling methodologies is consistent with these prior studies. Brondolo and colleagues (2003) examined both the frequency and intensity of daily negative and positive interactions as a function of trait hostility. These researchers found that trait hostility was associated with greater exposure to negative interpersonal exchanges, although such exposure did not predict ABP.

Exposure to interpersonal stress for hostile individuals is, in turn, related to greater cardiovascular reactivity with both strangers (Powch & Houston, 1996; Suarez & Williams, 1989) and close ties (Smith & Gallo, 1999). For instance, Suarez and Williams (1989) had participants perform cognitive stressors under differing conditions of experimenter harassment. These researchers found that hostility was related to greater cardiovascular reactivity during cognitive stressors, but only under harassment conditions (Suarez & Williams, 1989). It is worth highlighting that the increased cardiovascular reactivity in hostile individuals is relatively specific to interpersonal stress and not stress more generally (Suls & Wan, 1993).

Hostile individuals who experience interpersonal stress also appear to have slower cardiovascular recovery and less effective restoration, although more evidence is needed linking personality to these processes (Brissette & Cohen, 2002; Broadwell & Light, 2005). For instance, hostility was associated with poorer reported sleep quality; an effect that was related to interpersonal conflict from the prior day (Brissette & Cohen, 2002). Taken together, these data are consistent with associations between trait hostility and stress exposure and reactivity that may in turn be related to disruptions in restorative processes.

In contrast, there is evidence linking optimism to decreased exposure to interpersonal stressors (Lepore & Ituarte, 1999; Raikkonen et al., 1999). For instance, a 3-day diary study examined the links between optimism and exposure to negative interpersonal interactions (Raikkonen et al., 1999). These researchers found that optimism was related to less exposure to negative social exchanges during the course of the study. Similarly, Lepore and Ituarte (1999) found optimism in cancer patients to be related to fewer negative interactions. They further found that the lower interpersonal stress experienced by optimists was a statistical mediator of links between optimism and negative/positive affect (Lepore & Ituarte, 1999).

Although the results above are consistent with decreased exposure to interpersonal stress in optimists, there are complicating factors that have conceptual implications for this issue and more general associations with stress exposure. Segerstrom (2005) has proposed an "engagement hypothesis" to address some discrepancies in the literature examining optimism and aspects of immune function. Segerstrom (2005) proposes that, due to the greater use of problem-focused coping strategies by optimists, when the stressor is more easily addressed, optimism should be related to better immune function because these coping strategies can effectively terminate the stressor (Segerstrom, 2005). On the other hand, when the stressor is complex and difficult, optimism may be related to lower immune function in the short-term because of persistent attempts to engage the stressor. The greater persistence in optimists may be related to increased stress exposure, at least relative to their pessimistic counterparts, who may disengage and attempt to cope through emotion-focused coping avenues. However, it is unclear if the predicted stress exposure for optimists in this context has long-term health consequences, as it may eventually resolve the stressor (Carver & Scheier, 2002; Segerstrom, 2005). In addition, although these coping strategies might seem to put optimists at risk during more uncontrollable stress (e.g., bereavement), it does appear that optimists are better at discriminating when to disengage under such circumstances (Aspinwall & Richter, 1999; Scheier, Weintraub, & Carver, 1986).

There are several studies consistent with the engagement hypothesis (Segerstrom, 2005). In one study, optimists showed greater autonomic nervous system (ANS) and endocrine reactivity to an anagram stressor task (Solberg, Segerstrom, & Sephton, 2005). Of course, this pattern is the opposite of would be expected if reactivity was a mechanism linking optimism to better health. This pattern of findings, however, is consistent with the engagement hypothesis proposed by Segerstrom (2005). It is important to note that the reactivity hypothesis assumes that lab-based assessments generalize to real world contexts. As noted by Aspinwall and Taylor (1999), lab-based stressors might misrepresent the effective coping strategies of optimists due to unfamiliarity with the coping context. In fact, in the presence of alternatives optimists appear to disengage earlier, and this should be related to decreases in physiological reactivity during stress (Aspinwall & Richter, 1999).

The data linking personality processes to interpersonal conflict is important because social stress appears to have particularly negative influences on psychological and physical health outcomes (Bolger, DeLongis, Kessler, & Schilling, 1989; Kiecolt-Glaser & Newton, 2001). In fact, conflictual interactions may be especially powerful due to a negativity bias (Taylor, 1991). There is consistent evidence linking conflict in close relationships (i.e., marriage) to negative health profiles, including cardiovascular and endocrine function (Kiecolt-Glaser & Newton, 2001). Bolger and colleagues (1989) also found in a daily diary study that social stress was associated with greater "carryover" effects on negative mood than other types of stress. The adverse effects of social stress have been shown in both animal and human models of stress processes (Herbert & Cohen, 1993; Cohen et al., 1998; Padgett et al., 1998). For instance, Padgett and colleagues (1998) exposed latently infected Herpes Simplex Virus (HSV) rats to either social stress (i.e., social group reorganization) or physical stress (i.e., restraint stress). Results revealed that only social stress was associated with significant reactivation of HSV (i.e., over 40% of socially stressed animals), although both sources of stress activated the hypothalamic-pituitary–adrenal (HPA) axis. Cohen and colleagues (1998) also reported that the effects of longer-term stressors (e.g., 1 to 6 months) on susceptibility to the common cold were associated primarily with interpersonal and work stressors. Such data suggest that interpersonal conflict may be one important pathway linking relevant personality processes to cardiovascular disease.

A second major social process potentially linking personality to health involves its association with social support. Importantly, trait hostility has been linked to lower perceptions of social support (Smith, 1992), and longitudinal changes in trait hostility are associated with social isolation and inadequate social support (Siegler et al., 2003). Optimists also report using more social support in response to stressors (Scheier, Weintraub, & Carver, 1986), and optimism is a prospective predictor of increased social support over time (Brissette, Scheier, & Carver, 2002).

These links are important because social support is a consistent predictor of lower rates of cardiovascular disease (Berkman, Glass, Brissette, & Seeman, 2000; Cohen, 1988; Uchino, 2004). Models of social support processes suggest that health benefits may be derived from at least two stress-related pathways (see Uchino, 2004): stress prevention (reduced exposure) and stress-buffering (reduced stress reactivity). Although less data exists on the stress prevention pathway, Russell and Cutrona (1991) found that social support was prospectively related to less stress exposure over a subsequent six-month period in an older adult sample. The mechanisms related to this effect may be due to support-related identity processes or the provision of support resources that help individuals proactively cope in ways that decrease stress exposure (Aspinwall & Taylor, 1997; Thoits, 1995).

The stress-buffering process is the other social support mechanism of relevance to personality and health links. According to this hypothesis, social support is beneficial because it decreases the harmful influences of cardiovascular reactivity during stress (Cohen & Wills, 1985; Kamarck, Manuck, & Jennings, 1990). Consistent with this perspective, studies that manipulate the supportive functions of relationships (e.g., emotional support) show clear reductions in cardiovascular reactivity during stress (e.g., Gerin et al., 1992; Lepore, 1995; Thorsteinnsson, James, & Gregg, 1998). Based on the evidence reviewed above, it would be expected that hostile individuals, due to their cynical/distrustful schemata, might not benefit from the stress-reducing properties of social support whereas optimists, given their greater openness to support resources, might benefit more than pessimists. We are aware of no study that has examined this link for optimism, but several studies are consistent with the predicted influence on trait hostility. In one study, Lepore (1995) utilized a confederate to provide emotional support to individuals during a stressful task. Results showed that individuals low in trait hostility showed reductions in cardiovascular reactivity when provided with support. However, individuals high in trait hostility failed to show a reduction in cardiovascular reactivity to support (also see Christensen & Smith, 1993).

When attempting to model the influence of these social processes on personality and health links, it is also important to note that social conflict and social support tend to be separable constructs (Finch, Okun, Barrera, Zautra, & Reich, 1989; Newsom, Nishishiba, Morgan, & Rook, 2003; Pierce, Sarason, & Sarason, 1991; Rook, 1984). Thus, high levels of social support do not imply low levels of social conflict, etc. As a result, separate assessments of support and conflict are needed to determine their links to personality and the conditions under which these social processes have beneficial and/or deleterious influences on cardiovascular disease.

Potential Cognitive, Affective, and Behavioral Processes Linking Personality to Disease. The other important factors involve the intra-personal cognitive/affective processes potentially linking personality to disease outcomes. As noted earlier, trait hostility is linked to greater interpersonal conflict. This increased exposure/reactivity to interpersonal stress may be due to cognitive processes, as hostile individuals are more likely to attribute hostile intentions to others (Smith, 1992). In fact, hostile individuals tend to make more negative attributions for other's behaviors across a number of contexts, including those involving competition and conflict (Pope, Smith, & Rhodewalt, 1990).

The cognitive processes associated with hostility may in turn be linked to the experience of negative emotions, especially anger. Hostile individuals have been found to experience greater levels of anger during conflict (Allred & Smith, 1991), and anger is linked to greater rumination and slower cardiovascular recovery (Anderson, Linden, & Habra, 2005; Rusting & Nolen-Hoeksema, 1998; Schwartz, Gerin, Christenfeld, Davidson, & Pickering, 2000). Consistent with this line of reasoning, several studies have found trait hostility to be associated with slower cardiovascular recovery following stress (Broadwell & Light, 2005; Fredrickson et al., 2000; Neumann, Waldstein, Sollers, Thayer, & Sorkin, 2004). In one study, Fredrickson and colleagues (2000) asked participants to recall an anger-inducing personal event and examined cardiovascular reactivity and recovery. Results of this study revealed that when such cognitive-affective processes were activated, hostile individuals evidenced greater blood pressure reactivity during the anger recall task. Importantly, these investigators also found that hostile individuals took longer to recover from the anger-inducing event, as evidenced by a slower DBP return to baseline (also see Broadwell & Light, 2005; Neumann et al., 2004).

It is also evident that optimists engage in cognitive appraisals, which result in emotional processes that may facilitate coping and relevant health outcomes (Aspinwall & Taylor, 1997; Carver & Scheier, 2002). At one level, optimists appear more likely to unconsciously process positive stimuli, in contrast to pessimists who tend to unconsciously process more negative stimuli (Segerstrom, 2001a). Such a link may explain associations between optimism and greater experiences of positive affect (Chang & Sanna, 2001; Marshall et al., 1992). It is important to emphasize that the association between optimism and the unconscious processing of positive stimuli does not mean that optimists *consciously* ignore negative stimuli. Aspinwall and Brunhart (1996) have shown that when information is self-relevant, optimists tend to pay greater attention and recall more health risk information. These results are consistent with studies showing that optimists have more adaptive health beliefs and behavioral risk profiles (Radcliffe & Klein, 2002).

Theoretically, optimism might be expected to have an effect on appraisal processes that, in turn, influence perceptions of stress (Lazarus & Folkman, 1984). Although more data are needed, one study found that optimism was related to more adaptive secondary appraisals, but no differences in primary appraisals, in response to examination stress (Chang, 1998b). In addition, optimists do appear to engage in more adaptive reappraisal patterns in response to chronic conditions (e.g., cancer). For instance, Sears, Stanton, and Danoff-Burg (2003) examined the association between optimism and reappraisal processes in a study of early-stage cancer patients. These researchers found that optimism was related to positive reappraisals, which in turn was related to positive mood, perceptions of better health, and psychosocial growth 3 to 12 months later.

It is important to emphasize the links between optimism and the experience of positive affect (Chang & Sanna, 2001; Marshall et al.,1992). This affective pathway may be a function of the cognitive processes associated with optimism but may also be linked to social and behavioral (e.g., coping) processes (Aspinwall & Taylor, 1997; Folkman & Moskowitz, 2000). The implications of these links are illustrated by Fredrickson's (2001) broaden-and-build model. In this model, positive emotions serve important adaptive functions by broadening thought-action repertoires (e.g., coping) in ways that facilitate the building of resources that can be accessed during times of need (Fredrickson, 2001). For instance, positive affect is a predictor of faster cardiovascular recovery following stress and is a statistical mediator of the links between individual differences in resiliency and physiological recovery (Tugade & Fredrickson, 2004).

The cognitive and affective processes associated with personality are also important because they motivate individuals to engage in certain behavioral strategies that have implications for disease outcomes. Given the cynical attribution style of hostile individuals, one might expect them to be less likely to utilize social support as a coping option. Several studies are consistent with this possibility (Mao, Bardwell, Major, & Dimsdale, 2003; Shen et al., 2004). More generally, hostile individuals appear to engage in more negative coping strategies such as behavioral disengagement, self-blame, and denial (Mao et al., 2003; Shen et al., 2004).

The cognitive-affective processes associated with optimism may also drive coping responses in ways that facilitate adjustment. Consistent with their more adaptive appraisal patterns, there is strong evidence linking optimism to more problem-focused coping strategies (Aspinwall & Taylor, 1992; Chang, 1998b; Scheier et al., 1986; Scheier et al., 1994). In fact, the problem-focused coping style of optimists may promote greater knowledge and flexibility about the conditions under which particular coping strategies work best (Aspinwall, Richter, & Hoffman, 2001). Consistent with this suggestion, optimists appear adaptively flexible in their coping approaches as they tend to use other coping strategies, such as acceptance, when situations are relatively uncontrollable (Scheier et al., 1986). Carver and colleagues (1993) also found that the use of more active and fewer passive coping strategies statistically mediated the optimism–distress link in early stage cancer patients.

Although these studies suggest that appraisal processes and coping may be driving much of the adjustment associated with optimism, some studies suggest that they provide only a partial explanation. Aspinwall and Taylor (1992) found that optimism was related to more effective coping strategies. However, coping strategies were only a partial mediator of the optimism-adjustment link. Chang (1998b) similarly showed that although optimism was related to appraisals and coping, controlling for these factors revealed that optimism was still related to adjustment. Thus, the processes outlined provide only a partial explanation, and simultaneously modeling the social processes (e.g., conflict, social support) may provide a more comprehensive explanation of personality–health links.

We should note that there are other mechanisms that might have more complex or perhaps independent effects on cardiovascular disease outcomes, depending on the personality process of interest. According to the health behavior model of trait hostility, such individuals are also more likely to engage in health damaging behaviors, as well as fewer health protective behaviors (Smith, 1992). For instance, several longitudinal studies suggest that trait hostility is linked to heavy drinking, smoking, less exercise, and higher fat diets (Miller, Markides, Chiriboga, & Ray, 1995; Siegler et al., 2003). Given optimists' greater knowledge and processing of personally relevant health messages (Aspinwall & Brunhart, 1996; Radcliffe & Klein, 2002), it might be predicted that optimists engage in healthier behaviors. Some studies have found optimism to be associated with positive health behaviors, including preventive dental care (Ylostalo, Ek, & Knuuttila, 2003), exercise and nutrition during high risk pregnancy (Lobel, DeVincent, Kaminer, & Meyer, 2000), and health-promoting behaviors more generally (Mulkana, & Hailey, 2001). These health behaviors might explain, at least in part, the links between personality and health outcomes (Giltay et al., 2004).

It is also important to emphasize, however, that these links between personality and health behaviors may be directly linked to the social-cognitive mechanisms detailed above. For instance, stress has been associated with poorer health behaviors, so these effects might be due to the increased interpersonal stress experienced by hostile individuals. Likewise, the lower social support associated with trait hostility may be linked to less effective social control that appears to have a beneficial influence on health behaviors (Lewis & Rook, 1999; Umberson, 1992). Optimism has also been linked to (a) lower conflict, (b) greater social support, and (c) use of problem-focused coping, all factors that should promote healthier behaviors in both healthy and chronic disease populations (Burg & Seeman, 1994; Uchino, 2004). Thus, researchers should not consider health behaviors simply as statistical control variables, as they have conceptual links to personality that become evident when examining their influence across levels of analysis.

Towards an Integrative Multilevel Analysis of Personality and Physical Health

In this chapter we have reviewed evidence linking personality to cardiovascular disease and highlighted the social-cognitive mechanisms potentially responsible for such links. The pathways modeled in this review appear a result of complex but orderly intra- and interpersonal processes that vary systematically as a function of distinct personalities. These events unfold in the context of multifaceted biological processes that influence susceptibility to diseases. Due to this complexity, it should be evident that an examination of personality and health inherently involves differing levels of analysis (Cacioppo & Berntson, 1992; Engel, 1977).

There are several important advantages to a multilevel perspective on personality and physical health. First, depending on the specific personality process of interest, different research strategies become salient. For literatures attempting to make potential links between personality and physical health, an important first step is to demonstrate links between personality and conceptually relevant biological assessments. Indices such as cardiovascular reactivity/recovery, ABP, resting blood pressure levels, cardiovascular imaging (e.g., computed tomography scans of coronary arteries), and restoration can serve as more "intermediate" outcomes. For literatures that have made such links, the simultaneous collection of data on mechanisms (see Figure 10.1) can further elucidate important pathways at multiple levels of analysis, thus highlighting potential entry points for interventions. In general, such an approach can help guide a research program based on the levels of analysis that are likely to be of immediate and/or longer-term conceptual importance (Cacioppo & Berntson, 1992).

A second advantage of a multilevel approach is that it can make salient the importance of an integrative approach to examining mechanisms. An examination of multilevel pathways is generally considered a primary research agenda in linking psychosocial risk factors to physical health (Berkman et al., 2000). The simultaneous collection of such information can provide a powerful means of testing multiple linkages between different pathways that can then inform theoretical models of specific personality processes and disease. The model depicted in Figure 10.1 can be used as a general framework for future studies examining such processes.

However, an examination of mechanisms should not be limited to those depicted in Figure 10.1 because these are simply the most salient based on prior research. A multilevel perspective also highlights the importance of complementary levels of analyses (Cacioppo & Berntson, 1992; Engel, 1977). Of the different levels of analyses, higher level sociocultural processes need greater consideration. Such sociocultural factors provide the important context for interpreting and shaping links between personality and health outcomes. For instance, examining the role of socioeconomic status (SES) may be informative because there is strong evidence that socioeconomic status is in itself a risk factor for disease (Ader, Felten, & Cohen, 2001). Modeling the combination of SES with personality processes may thus provide greater predictability in explaining links to complex health outcomes (Williams, Barefoot, & Schneiderman, 2003). In addition, based on models of personality (e.g., Mischel, 2004), SES sets the stage for transactions with the environment in health-relevant ways and can guide the development of more precise models. That is, a low SES environment may include greater exposure to financial stress, violence, and riskier health norms that provide the backdrop for understanding the development and maintenance of personality processes (Kagan, 2003).

A third advantage of a multilevel perspective is an emphasis on the critical biological pathways (Berntson & Cacioppo, 2000), as well as the importance of a full conceptual consideration of such mechanisms in the study of personality and disease. It is important to emphasize that physiological indicators are not simply outcomes; they are an integral part of the theoretical modeling of the phenomenon of interest. In the present review, we have focused on changes that occur within the cardiovascular system that may have relevance to cardiovascular disease. However, there are other important biologic alterations detailed below that may have implications for cardiovascular disease, as well as additional disease processes.

In this regard, potential links between personality and immune function would be particularly important, as the immune system is the primary mechanism of defense against infectious and malignant diseases (Abbas & Lichtman, 2003). Researchers interested in such questions typically draw a distinction between enumerative and functional immune measures (see Kiecolt-Glaser & Glaser, 1995 for a review). Enumerative assays provide information on the number or percentage of certain cell populations (e.g., helper T-cells, natural killer cells), whereas functional measure provide information on the performance of the immune cells under conditions of challenge (Herbert & Cohen, 1993). Functional measures are generally considered more health-relevant because they model the ability of the immune system to generate a response, although cell numbers or percentages are of importance depending on the population of interest (e.g., HIV+ individuals; Kiecolt-Glaser & Glaser, 1995). Thus, an association between personality and immune measures, in theory, may provide a link to cancer and/or infectious diseases (Abbas

& Lichtman, 2003; Dunn, Bruce, Ikeda, Old, & Schreiber, 2002). However, it would also be important for researchers to utilize paradigms that directly examine the biological relevance of such links (e.g., common cold paradigm of Cohen and colleagues, 1991, 1998).

The literature linking personality to immune function is just emerging; however, there is some evidence for such links that are of potential relevance to this review. These associations are hypothesized to be a direct result of the social-cognitive processes detailed in Figure 10.1, although direct modeling of such associations will be needed. For instance, hostility has been linked to changes in natural killer cell activity following exposure to acute laboratory stress (Miller, Dopp, Myers, Felton, & Fahey, 1999). Optimism has also been related to higher CD4+ cells and greater delayed type hypersensitivity (indicative of a stronger cellular immune response) under easier circumstances (Segerstrom, 2001b). However, under more difficult circumstances, optimism may be related to negative immune outcomes, at least in the short-term, due to greater engagement with the stressor (Segerstrom, 2005). Optimism has also been associated with greater cytokine production following an influenza vaccination (Kohut, Cooper, Nickolaus, Russell, & Cunnick, 2002) and in lymphocyte cell cultures stimulated with the influenza virus (Costanzo et al., 2004).

As is the case for cardiovascular disease, it is important to emphasize that personality can play a role either in the development or the progression of clinical significant immune-mediated diseases. The most direct evidence for such a link comes from studies that have examined the health-related component processes we propose to be activated by relevant social-cognitive mechanisms. In terms of malignant diseases, damaged cells may become cancerous following changes to their DNA (Abbas & Lichtman, 2003). However, the cell is usually repaired or dies off before it replicates (i.e., apoptosis). There is a small literature indicating that exposure to stress may influence both of these processes. In studies of medical students during high stress (i.e., exams), apoptosis of blood leukocytes in response to gamma irradiation is impaired (Tomei, Kiecolt-Glaser, Kennedy, & Glaser, 1990). In addition, rats exposed to rotational stress showed lower levels of a DNA repair enzyme in response to carcinogens (Glaser, Thorn, Tarr, Kiecolt-Glaser, & D'Ambrosio, 1985).

Different aspects of the immune response appear important in detecting and eliminating some forms of cancer (Dunn et al., 2002). The elimination phase of cancer immunoediting is characterized by immune processes that actively prevent and eliminate tumors (Dunn et al., 2002). Importantly, there is strong evidence indicating that exposure to stress can influence aspects of both innate and adaptive immunity (Herbert & Cohen, 1993; Segerstrom & Miller, 2004). Stress exposure/reactivity has also been directly linked to decreased immunity in cancer patients and hence may theoretically play a role in disease progression, depending on the stage and time course of disease (Kiecolt-Glaser & Glaser, 1995). For instance, Andersen and colleagues (1998) examined whether perceptions of cancer-related stress had an influence on immune measures following surgical treatment. Cancer-related stress in these patients had uniform effects on immunity as it was related to lower NK cell activity, proliferative responses to mitogens, NK cell activation via interferon-γ, and T-cell proliferation to antibody (Ab) directed at the T-cell receptor. This study is consistent with the results of interventions suggesting that stress-reduction may improve immune function in cancer patients, with potential beneficial influences on survival (Fawzy et al., 1993).

It should be noted that despite the above evidence, links between psychosocial factors and cancer are controversial (Fox, 1998). However, we believe an examination of the different levels of analysis indicted in Figure 10.1 may help researchers better understand the reasons for such discrepancies. In some cases, extending one's perspective over the relevant levels of analysis can shed light on apparent inconsistencies. In an illustrative study, Haber and Barchas (1983) examined the influence of amphetamines on the social behavior of monkeys. At first, the effects of the drug on behavior seemed chaotic. However, extending their analysis to the social level revealed greater order as dominant behaviors were increased in monkeys high in the social hierarchy, whereas submissive behavior increased in those lower in the social order (Haber & Barchas, 1983).

It is also possible that personality may influence susceptibility to infectious diseases. Again, factors that influence disease susceptibility and progression are important to separate for theoretical reasons. In the context of HIV it is possible that personality may influence exposure or risk for HIV infection (Baum & Posluszny, 1999). This is salient because the primary route of HIV infection is behavioral in nature (Kelly, Murphy, Sikkema, & Kalichman, 1993). Stress is linked to changes in health behaviors, including alcohol and drug use (Testa & Collins, 1997). In addition, conflictual interactions are an important determinant of alcohol and drug use, whereas social support appears a protective factor (Burg & Seeman, 1994; Wills et al., 2000). The use of alcohol and illicit drugs may in turn increase risky sexual behavior due to processes such as disinhibition and facilitation of sexual arousal (McCarty et al., 1982; O'Keeffe et al., 1990).

For some infectious diseases, vaccination can provide an effective means for decreasing susceptibility (e.g., flu vaccine). However, factors highlighted in Figure 10.1 can influence the integrity of the immune system in ways that impact its effectiveness. For instance, stress has been linked to a lower immune response to influenza (Kiecolt-Glaser, Glaser, Gravenstein, Mularkdy, & Sheridan, 1996; Miller et al., 2004; Vedhara et al., 1999), hepatitis B (Jabaaij et al., 1993; Glaser et al., 1992), meningitis C (Burns, Drayson, Ring, & Carroll, 2002), and pneumococcal pneumonia (Glaser, Sheridan, Malarkey, MacCallum, & Kiecolt-Glaser, 2000) vaccinations. Consistent with such links, several studies suggest that optimism is related to a better immune response following vaccination (Costanzo et al., 2004; Kohut et al., 2002). It is also possible that personality can influence whether one chooses to be vaccinated in the first place (e.g., optimism and preventive health practices), although we know of no direct data on this issue.

Once an infectious disease is contracted, the immune system again becomes important in the resolution of the infection. However, some viruses (e.g., EBV) avoid elimination by going latent and "hiding," relatively inactive, in certain cells. The exposed individual is infected for life, but the cellular immune response is usually successful at keeping the virus in check. However, individuals with compromised cellular immune processes (e.g., HIV+ populations, patients on immunosupressive therapies) may experience reactivation of one or more of these latent viruses. In such cases, increased Ab titers to latent viruses suggest poorer cellular immunity because the reactivation of the virus triggers the humoral arm of adaptive immunity. Importantly, there is strong evidence from both animal and human studies that the proposed health-related component processes detailed in Figure 10.1 (e.g., stress exposure) can reactivate latent viruses (Padgett et al., 1998). Keeping the integrity of the immune system may be particularly important for HIV+ individuals, and preliminary evidence suggests that optimism is related to better immunity in such individuals (Byrnes et al., 1998).

It should also be noted that there are extensive interactions between the nervous system and immunity (see Ader et al., 2001). These connections form the basis for the interdisciplinary field of psychoneuroimmunology (PNI). Evidence suggests that nerve fibers from the autonomic nervous system directly innervate lymphoid organs (Felton, Ackerman, Weigand, & Felton, 1987). Moreover, lymphocytes have functional receptors for a variety of endocrine hormones, including EPI, norepinephrine, ACTH, cortisol, opioids, growth hormone, prolactin, and estrogen (Plaut, 1987; Sanders, Kasprowicz, Kohm, & Swanson 2001;). Thus, earlier evidence linking personality to activation of the autonomic and endocrine system has direct implications for relevant immune-mediated disease states. Such research is starting to shed a more integrated light on how different biological systems may be coordinated to influence physical health.

There is also recent research on cardiovascular disease that further highlights the importance of a more integrated perspective across different physiological systems. Of these, the recent emphasis on atherosclerosis as an immune-mediated inflammatory disease is important (Ross, 1999; Libby, 2002). Immune processes are now implicated in just about every stage of atherogenesis, and the release of inflammatory cytokines from immune cells (e.g., macrophages, T-cells) appears particularly important to model (Libby, 2002). One of the earliest events in the atherogenic process is endothelial damage (Ross, 1999). At early stages of damage, the endothelium begins to express adhesion molecules, such as vascular adhesion molecule-1, that help in the binding of immune cells to the vasculature. Monocytes and T-lymphocytes are then recruited to sites of inflammation and migrate into vessel walls via various chemokines (e.g., MCP-1) that are released from vascular cell walls (Charo & Taubman, 2004). Chemokines are cytokines that activate and attract various leukocyte populations (Murdoch & Finn, 2000). Once inside vessel walls, these immune cells proliferate and release a variety of growth factors (e.g., platelet-derived growth factors) and cytokines (e.g., IL-1) characteristic of the inflammatory response (Libby, 2002). Immune events at later stages can lead to the rupture of such plaques. For instance, macrophages are common in vulnerable plaques and can produce enzymes (e.g., metalloproteinases) that degrade the fibrous cap, while T-lymphocytes release interferon-γ that can impede collagen formation (Libby, 2002).

Importantly, the health-related pathways in Figure 10.1 postulated to play an important role in links between personality and disease can directly lead to the release of cytokines, which are crucial mediators of the cardiovascular inflammatory response (Black & Garbutt, 2002; Kop & Cohen, 2001). Animal models show that stress increases the release of inflammatory cytokines, such as IL-1 and tumor necrosis factor-α (TNF-α), as well as subsequent acute phase proteins, such as C-reactive proteins (CRP) (Black & Garbutt, 2002). Thus, inflammatory processes provide a new and exciting set of biological pathways to model in links between personality and cardiovascular disease.

A final point we would like to emphasize is that a multilevel perspective on personality and health can foster the development of more focused but comprehensive interventions aimed at reducing disease risk. Although personality processes can be stable, there is evidence that psychosocial interventions may modify these "traits" with beneficial influences on health outcomes. In the important Recurrent Coronary Prevention Project (RCPP), Friedman and colleagues (1986) conducted a large clinical trial on the modification of the Type A personality profile in coronary patients. They demonstrated that modifying components of the Type A personality (e.g., hostility, time urgency) via multiple social-cognitive pathways (e.g., modification of social/work environments, cognitive restructuring, relaxation) was related to a 44% reduction in disease reoccurrence 4.5 years later, compared to a control condition.

The data from the RCPP were important, not only due to its impressive results, but because it suggested that personality processes could be modified via psychosocial interventions. Smaller interventions have similarly shown trait hostility can be modified in health-relevant ways (Gidron, Davidson, & Bata, 1999). For instance, Gidron and colleagues (1999) developed a brief intervention to reduce the cognitive, affective, and behavioral components of hostility in cardiovascular disease patients. Results of this multilevel intervention revealed reductions in hostility levels, as well as resting DBP 2 months later. These data suggest that personality processes are amenable to change, and such alterations may be beneficial in chronic disease populations. In fact, an examination of 10.1 reveals multiple potential entry points for interventions. Cognitive-behavioral interventions address many of these pathways (e.g., stress management via coping and effective use of social support) and thus could be adapted based on the personality process of interest. Of course, given the different levels of analyses represented in links between personality and health, the most effective interventions are likely those that comprehensively address these multilevel pathways.

Conclusions

There are promising data linking some personality processes (i.e., hostility, optimism) to physical health outcomes such as cardiovascular disease. The only other literature with sufficient evidence includes the personality trait of neuroticism, and similar general mechanisms as covered in 10.1 appear salient (Bolger, 1990; Smith & Gallo, 2001; Suls & Martin, 2005). However, progress on understanding links between personality and disease has been slowed by the complexity of the phenomenon at the social, psychological, and biomedical levels of analysis. In this chapter, we provided an integration of these literatures with one that more fully elucidates important social-cognitive pathways, thereby providing a broad framework for investigating links between personality processes and health outcomes.

Overall, the data and model reviewed in this chapter represent only the first wave of research linking personality to health outcomes. Future research will be critical to provide stronger tests of how specific personality processes influence particular stages of disease, along with additional levels of analyses that might be relevant based on the ability to shed conceptual light on this important phenomenon. The next decade of research holds much promise due to emerging interdisciplinary perspectives and the resulting emphasis on bringing together all of the pieces of the puzzle in ways that foster an appreciation for the complex whole. Such research will be critical to the formation of comprehensive theories that can serve as guides to the design of much needed interventions.

ACKNOWLEDGMENTS

Preparation for this chapter was generously supported by grant number R01 HL68862 from the National Heart, Lung, and Blood Institute. Correspondence concerning this article should be addressed to Bert N. Uchino, University of Utah, Department of Psychology, 380 S. 1530 E. Rm. 502, Salt Lake City, Utah 84112, or via e-mail (bert.uchino@psych.utah.edu).

REFERENCES

Abbas, A. K., & Lichtman, A. H. (2003). *Cellular and molecular immunology.* Philadelphia: Saunders.

Abramson, L. Y., Seligman, M. E. P., & Teasdale, J. D. (1978). Learned helplessness in humans: Critique and reformulation. *Journal of Abnormal Psychology, 87,* 32–48.

Ader, D. L. Felten, S. Y., & Cohen, N. (2001), *Psychoneuroimmunology* (3rd ed.). New York: Academic Press.

Alexander, F. (1950). *Psychosomatic medicine: Its principles and application.* New York: W.W. Norton.

Allred, K. D., & Smith, T.W. (1991). Social cognition in cynical hostility. *Cognitive Therapy and Research, 15,* 399–412.

American Heart Association. (2004). *2004 Heart and stroke statistical update.* Dallas, Tex.: American Heart Association.

Andersen, B. L., Farrar, W. B., Golden-Kreutz, D., Kutz, L. A., MacCallum, R., Courtney, M. E., & Glaser, R. (1998, January). Stress and immune responses after surgical treatment for regional breast cancer. *Journal of the National Cancer Institute, 90,* 30–36.

Anderson, J. C., Linden, W., & Habra, M. E. (2005). The importance of examining blood pressure reactivity and recovery in anger provocation research. *International Journal of Psychophysiology, 57,* 159–163.

Aspinwall, L. G., & Brunhart, S. M. (1996). Distinguishing optimism from denial: Optimistic beliefs predict attention to health threats. *Personality and Social Psychology Bulletin, 22,* 993–1003.

Aspinwall, L. G., & Richter, L. (1999). Optimism and self-mastery predict more rapid disengagement from unsolvable tasks in the presence of alternatives. *Motivation and Emotion, 23,* 221–245.

Aspinwall, L. G., Richter, L., & Hoffman, R.R. (2001). Understanding how optimism "works": An examination of optimists' adaptive moderation of belief and behavio In E. C. Chang (Ed.), *Optimism and pessimism: Theory, research, and practice* (pp 217–238). Washington: American Psychological Association.

Aspinwall, L. G., & Taylor, S. E. (1992). Modeling cognitive adaptation: A longitudinal investigation of the impact of individual differences and coping on college adjustment and performance. *Journal of Personality and Social Psychology, 63*, 989–1003.

Aspinwall, L. G., & Taylor, S. E. (1997). A stitch in time: Self-regulation and proactive coping. *Psychological Bulletin, 121*, 417–436.

Barefoot, J. C. (1992). Developments in the measurement of hostility. In H. Friedman (Ed.), *Hostility, coping, and health* (pp. 13–31). Washington, DC: American Psychological Association.

Barefoot, J. C., Dodge, K. A., Peterson, B. L., Dahlstrom, W. G., & Williams Jr., R. P. (1989). The Cook-Medley hostility scale: Item content & ability to predict survival *Psychosomatic Medicine, 51*, 46–57.

Baum, A., & Posluszny, D. M. (1999). Health psychology: Mapping biobehavioral contributions to health and illness. *Annual Review of Psychology, 50*, 137–163.

Bem, D. J., & Allen, A. (1974). On predicting some of the people some of the time: The search for cross-situational consistencies in behavior. *Psychological Review, 81* 506–520.

Berkman, L. F., Glass, T., Brissette, I., & Seeman, T. E. (2000). From social integration to health: Durkheim in the new millennium. *Social Science and Medicine, 51* 843–857.

Berntson, G. G., & Cacioppo, J. T. (2000). Psychobiology and social psychology: Past, present, and future. *Personality and Social Psychology Review, 4*, 3–15.

Black, P. H., & Garbutt, L. D. (2002). Stress, inflammation and cardiovascular disease *Journal of Psychosomatic Research, 52*, 1–23

Bolger, N. (1990). Coping as a personality process: A prospective study. *Journal of Personality and Social Psychology, 59*, 525–537.

Bolger, N., DeLongis, A., Kessler, R. C., & Schilling, E. A. (1989). Effects of daily stress on negative mood. *Journal of Personality and Social Psychology, 57*, 808–818.

Bolger, N., Foster, M., Vinokur, A. D., & Ng, R. (1996). Close relationships and adjustment to a life crisis: The case of breast cancer. *Journal of Personality and Social Psychology, 70*, 283–294.

Booth-Kewley, S., & Friedman, H. S. (1987). Psychological predictors of heart disease: A quantitative review. *Psychological Bulletin, 101*, 343–362.

Boyle, S. H., Williams, R. B., Mark, D. B., Brummett, B. H., Siegler, I. C., Helms, M. J., & Barefoot, J. C. (2004). Hostility as a predictor of survival in patients with coronary artery disease. *Psychosomatic Medicine, 66*, 629–632.

Brissette, I., & Cohen, S. (2002, September). The contribution of individual differences in hostility to the associations between daily interpersonal conflict, affect, and sleep *Personality and Social Psychology Bulletin, 28*, 1265–1274.

Brissette, I., Scheier, M. F., & Carver, C. S. (2002). The role of optimism in social network development, coping, and psychological adjustment during a life transition. *Journal of Personality and Social Psychology, 82*, 102–111.

Broadwell, S. D., & Light, K. C. (2005). Hostility, conflict and cardiovascular responses in married couples: A focus on the dyad. *International Journal of Behavioral Medicine, 12*, 142–152.

Brondolo, E., Rieppi, R., Erickson, S. A., Bagiella, E., Shapiro, P. A., McKinley, P., & Sloan, R. P. (2003). Hostility, interpersonal interactions, and ambulatory blood pressure. *Psychosomatic Medicine, 65*, 1003–1011.

Burg, M. M., & Seeman, T. E. (1994). Families and health: The negative side of social ties. *Annals of Behavioral Medicine, 16,* 109–115.
Burns, V. E., Drayson, M., Ring, C., & Carroll, D. (2002). Perceived stress and psychological well-being are associated with antibody status after meningitis C conjugate vaccination. *Psychosomatic Medicine, 64,* 963–970.
Byrnes, D., Antoni, M. H., Goodkin, K., Efantis-Potter, J., Simon, T., Munajj, J., Ironson, G., & Fletcher, M.A. (1998) Stressful events, pessimism, natural killer cell cytotoxicity, and cytotoxic/suppressor T-cells in HIV+ Black women at risk for cervical cancer. *Psychosomatic Medicine, 60,* 714–722.
Cacioppo, J. T., & Berntson, G. G. (1992). Social psychological contributions to the decade of the brain: Doctrine of multilevel analysis. *American Psychologist, 47,* 1019–1028.
Cacioppo, J. T., & Berntson, G. G. (2007). Balancing demands of the internal and external milieu. In H. S. Friedman & R. Cohen Silver (Eds.), *Oxford Handbook of Health psychology* (pp. 73–91). New York: Oxford University Press.
Cacioppo, J. T., Petty, R. E., & Tassinary, L. G. (1989). Social psychophysiology: A new look. *Advances in Experimental Social Psychology, 22,* 39–91.
Carver, C. S., Pozo, C., Harris, S. D., Noriega, V., Scheier, M. F., Robinson, D. S., Ketcham, A. S., Moffat Jr., F. L. & Clark, K. C. (1993). How coping mediates the effect of optimism on distress: A study of women with early stage breast cancer. *Journal of Personality and Social Psychology, 65,* 375–390.
Carver, C. S., & Scheier, M. F. (2002). Optimism. In C. R. Snyder and S. J. Lopez (Eds.), *Handbook of positive psychology* (pp. 231–243). New York: Oxford University Press.
Carver, C. S., Scheier, M. F., & Weintraub, J. K. (1989). Assessing coping strategies: A theoretically based approach. *Journal of Personality and Social Psychology, 56,* 267–283.
Cervone, D. (2004). The architecture of personality. *Psychological Review, 111,* 183–204.
Cervone, D., & Shoda, Y. (1999). Social-cognitive theories and the coherence of personality. In D. Cervone & Y. Shoda (Eds.), *The coherence of personality: Social-cognitive bases of consistency, variability, and organization* (pp. 3–36). New York: Guilford Press.
Chang, E. C. (1998a). Distinguishing between optimism and pessimism: A second look at the optimism-neuroticism hypothesis. In R. R. Hoffman, M. F. Sherrick, & J. S. Warm (Eds.), *Viewing psychology as a whole: The integrative science of William N. Dember* (pp. 415–432). Washington, DC: American Psychological Association.
Chang, E. C. (1998b). Dispositional optimism and primary and secondary appraisal of a stressor: Controlling for confounding influences and relations to coping and psychological and physical adjustment. *Journal of Personality and Social Psychology, 74,* 1109–1120.
Chang, P. P., Ford, D. E., Meoni, L. A., Wang, N., & Klag, M. J. (2002). Anger in young men and subsequent premature cardiovascular disease: The precursors study. *Archives of Internal Medicine, 162,* 901–906.
Chang, E. C., & Sanna, L. J. (2001). Optimism, pessimism, and positive and negative affectivity in middle-aged adults: A test of a cognitive-affective model of psychological adjustment. *Psychology and Aging, 16,* 524–531.
Charo, I. F., & Taubman, M. B. (2004). Chemokines in the pathogenesis of vascular disease. *Circulation Research, 95,* 858–866.
Christensen, A. J., & Smith, T. W. (1993). Cynical hostility and cardiovascular reactivity during self-disclosure. *Psychosomatic Medicine, 55,* 193–202.
Cloninger C. R., Svrakic D. M., & Przybeck T. R. (1993). A psychobiological model of temperament and character. *Archives of General Psychiatry, 50,* 975–990.
Cohen, S. (1988). Psychosocial models of the role of social support in the etiology of physical disease. *Health Psychology, 7,* 269–297.

Cohen, S., Frank, E., Doyle, W. J., Skoner, D. P., Rabin, B. S., & Gwaltney, Jr., J. M. (1998). Types of stressors that increase susceptibility to the common cold in healthy adults. *Health Psychology, 17,* 214–223.

Cohen, S., & Herbert, T. B. (1996). Health psychology: Psychological factors and physical disease from the perspective of human psychoneuroimmunology. *Annual Review of Psychology, 47,* 113–142.

Cohen, S., & Lichtenstein, E. (1990). Partner behaviors that support quitting smoking. *Journal of Consulting and Clinical Psychology, 58,* 304–309.

Cohen, S., Tyrrell, D. A. J., & Smith, A. P. (1991). Psychological stress and susceptibility to the common cold. *New England Journal of Medicine, 325,* 606–612.

Cohen, S., & Wills, T. A. (1985). Stress, social support, and the buffering hypothesis. *Psychological Bulletin, 98,* 310–357.

Costanzo, E. S., Lutgendodrf, S. K., Kohut, M. L., Nisly, N., Rozeboom, K., Spooner, S., Benda, J., & McElhaney, J. E. (2004). Mood and cytokine response to influenza virus in older adults. *Journal of Gerontology: Medical Sciences, 59A,* 1328–1333.

Dinarello, C.A., & Mier, J.W. (1987). Lymphokines. *New England Journal of Medicine, 317,* 940–945.

Dunbar, H. F. (1943). *Psychosomatic diagnosis.* New York: Hoeber.

Dunbar, H. F. (1954). *Emotions and bodily changes.* New York: Columbia University Press.

Dunn, G. P., Bruce, A. T., Ikeda, H., Old, L. J., & Schreiber, R. D. (2002). Cancer immunoediting: From immunosurveillance to tumor escape. *Nature Immunology, 3,* 991–998.

Engel, G. L. (1977). The need for a new medical model: A challenge for biomedicine. *Science, 196,* 129–136.

Epstein, S. (1979). The stability of behavior: I. On predicting most of the people much of the time. *Journal of Personality and Social Psychology, 37,* 1097–1126.

Fawzy, F. I., Fawzy, N. W., Hyun, C. S., Gutherie, D., Fahey, J. L., & Morton, D. (1993). Malignant melanoma: Effects of an early structured psychiatric intervention, coping, and affective state on recurrence and survival six years later. *Archives of General Psychiatry, 50,* 681–689.

Felton, D. L., Ackerman, K. D., Wiegand, S. J., & Felton, S. Y. (1987). Noradrenergic sympathetic innervation of the spleen: I. Nerve fibers associate with lymphocytes and macrophages in specific compartments of the splenic white pulp. *Journal of Neuroscience Research,* 18: 28–36.

Finch, J. F., Okun, M. A., Barrera, M., Zautra, A. J., & Reich, J. W. (1989). Positive and negative social ties among older adults: Measurement models and the prediction of psychological distress and well-being. *American Journal of Community Psychology, 17,* 585–605.

Folkman, S., & Moskowitz, J. T. (2000). Positive affect and the other side of coping. *American Psychologist, 55,* 647–654.

Fox, B. H. (1998). Psychosocial factors in cancer incidence and prognosis. In J. C. Holland (Ed.), *Psycho-oncology* (pp. 110–124). New York: Oxford University Press.

Fredrickson, B. L. (2001). The role of positive emotions in positive psychology: The broaden-and-build theory of positive emotions. *American Psychologist, 56,* 218–226.

Fredrickson, B. L., Maynard, K. E., Helms, M. J., Haney, T. L., Siegler, I. C., & Barefoot, J. C. (2000). Hostility predicts magnitude and duration of blood pressure response to anger. *Journal of Behavioral Medicine, 23,* 229–243.

Friedman, M., Thoresen, C. E., Gill, J. J., Ulmer, D., Powel, L. H., Price, V.A., Brown, B., Thompson, L., Rabin, D., Breall, W. S., Bourg, E., Levy, R., & Dixon, T. (1986). Alteration of type A behavior and its effect on cardiac recurrences in post-myocardial infarction patients: Summary results of the Recurrent Coronary Prevention Project. *American Heart Journal, 112,* 653–662.

Gerin, W., Pieper, C., Levy, R., & Pickering, T. G. (1992). Social support in social interaction: A moderator of cardiovascular reactivity. *Psychosomatic Medicine, 54,* 324–336.

Gidron, Y., Davidson, K., & Bata, I. (1999). The short-term effects of a hostility-reduction intervention on male coronary heart disease patients. *Health Psychology, 18,* 416–420.

Giltay, E. J., Geleijnse, J. M., Zitman, F. G., Hoekstra, T., & Schouten, E. G. (2004). Dispositional optimism and all-cause and cardiovascular mortality in a prospective cohort of elderly Dutch men and women. *Arch Gen Psychiatry, 61,* 1126–1135.

Glaser, R., Kiecolt-Glaser, J. K., Bonneau, R. H., Malarkey, W., Kennedy, S., & Hughes, J. (1992). Stress-induced modulation of the immune response to recombinant hepatitis B vaccine. *Psychosomatic Medicine, 54,* 22–29.

Glaser, R., Sheridan, J., Malarkey, W. B., MacCallum, R. C., & Kiecolt-Glaser, J. K. (2000). Chronic stress modulates the immune response to a pneumococcal pneumonia vaccine. *Psychosomatic Medicine, 62,* 804–807.

Glaser, R., Thorn, B. E., Tarr, K. L., Kiecolt-Glaser, J. K., & D'Ambrosio, S. M. (1985). Effects of stress on methyltransferase synthesis: An important DNA repair enzyme. *Health Psychology, 4,* 403–412.

Goldberg, A. D., Becker, L. C., Bonsall, R., Cohen, J. D., Ketterer, M. W., Kaufman, P. G., Krantz, D. S., Light, K. C., McMahon, R. P., Noreuil, T., Pepine, C. J., Raczynski, J., Stone, P. H., Strother, D., Taylor, H., & Sheps, D. S. (1996). Ischemic, hemodynamic, and neurohormonal responses to mental and exercise stress: Experience from the psychophysiological investigations of myocardial ischemia study (PIMI). *Circulation, 94,* 2402–2409.

Haber, S. N., & Barchas, P. R. (1983). The regulatory effect of social rank on behavioral after amphetamine administration. In P. Barchas (Ed.), *Social hierarchies: Essays towards a sociophysiological perspective* (pp. 119–132). Westport, CT: Greenwood Press.

Herbert, T. B., & Cohen, S. (1993). Stress and immunity in humans: A meta-analytic review. *Psychosomatic Medicine, 55,* 364–379.

Helgeson, V. S. (1993). Two important distinctions in social support: Kind of support and perceived versus received. *Journal of Applied Social Psychology, 10,* 825–845.

Holahan, C. J., & Moos, R. H. (1990). Life stressors, resistance factors, and improved psychological functioning: An extension of the stress resistance paradigm. *Journal of Personality and Social Psychology, 58,* 909–917.

Irribarren, C., Jacobs, D. R., Kiefe, C. I., Lewis, C. E., Matthews, K. A., Roseman, J. M., & Hulley, S. B. (2005). Causes and demographic, medical, lifestyle and psychosocial predictors of premature mortality: The CARDIA study. *Social Science and Medicine, 60,* 471–482.

Jabaaij, L., Grosheide, P. M., Heijtink, R. A., Duivenvoorden, H. J., Ballieux, R. E., & Vingerhoets, A. J. J. M. (1993). Influence of perceived psychological stress and distress on antibody response to low dose fDNA Hepatitis B vaccine. *Journal of Psychosomatic Research, 37,* 361–369.

Kagan, J. (2003). Biology, context, and developmental inquiry. *Annual Review Psychology, 54,* 1–23.

Kamarck, T. W., & Jennings, J. R. (1991). Biobehavioral factors in sudden cardiac death. *Psychological Bulletin, 109,* 42–75.

Kamarck, T. W., Manuck, S. B., & Jennings, J. R. (1990). Social support reduces cardiovascular reactivity to psychological challenge: A laboratory model. *Psychosomatic Medicine, 52,* 42–58.

Kelly, J. A., Murphy, D. A., Sikkema, K. J., & Kalichman, S. C. (1993). Psychological interventions to prevent HIV infection are urgently needed: New priorities for behavioral research in the second decade of AIDS. *American Psychologist, 10*, 1023–1034.

Kiecolt-Glaser, J. K., & Glaser, R. (1995). Psychoneuroimmunology and health consequences: Data and shared mechanisms. *Psychosomatic Medicine, 57*, 269–274.

Kiecolt-Glaser, J. K., Glaser, R., Gravenstein, S., Malarkey, W. B., & Sheridan, J. (1996). Chronic stress alters the immune response to influenza virus vaccine in older adults. *Proc. National Academy of Science, 93*, 3043–3047.

Kiecolt-Glaser, J. K., & Newton, T. L. (2001). Marriage and health: His and hers. *Psychological Bulletin, 127*, 472–503.

Kohut, M. L., Cooper, M. M., Nickolaus, M. S., Russell, D. R., & Cunnick, J. E. (2002). Exercise and psychosocial factors modulate immunity to influenza vaccine in elderly individuals. *Journal of Gerontology: Medical Sciences, 57A*, M557–M562.

Kop, W. J., & Cohen, N. (2001). Psychological risk factors and immune system involvement in cardiovascular disease. In R. Ader, D. L. Felten, & N. Cohen (Eds.), *Psychoneuroimmunology*, (Vol. 2, 3rd ed., pp. 525–544). New York: Academic Press.

Krantz, D. S., & Manuck, S. B. (1984). Acute physiologic reactivity and risk of cardiovascular disease: A review and methodologic critique. *Psychological Bulletin, 96*, 435–464.

Kubzansky, L. D., Sparrow, D., Vokonas, P., & Kawachi, I. (2001). Is the glass half empty or half full? A prospective study of optimism and coronary heart disease in the normative aging study. *Psychosomatic Medicine, 63*, 910–916.

Lazarus, R. S., & Folkman, S. (1984). *Stress, appraisal, and coping*. New York: Springer-Verlag.

Leedham, B., Meyerowitz, B. E., Muirhead, J., & Frist, W. H. (1995). Positive expectations predict health after heart transplantation. *Health Psychology, 14*, 74–79.

Lepore, S. J. (1995). Cynicism, social support, and cardiovascular reactivity. *Health Psychology, 14*, 210–216.

Lepore, S. J., & Ituarte, P. H. G. (1999). Optimism about cancer enhances mood by reducing negative social relations. *Cancer Research Therapy and Control, 8*, 165–174.

Lewis, M. A., & Rook, K. S. (1999). Social control in personal relationships: Impact on health behaviors and psychological distress. *Health Psychology, 18*, 63–71.

Libby, P. (2002). Inflammation in atherosclerosis. *Nature, 420*, 868–874.

Lobel, M., DeVincent, C. J., Kaminer, A., & Meyer, B. A. (2000). The impact of prenatal maternal stress and optimistic disposition on birth outcomes in medically high-risk women. *Health Psychology 19*, 544–553.

Manuck, S. B. (1994). Cardiovascular reactivity in cardiovascular disease: "Once more unto the breach". *International Journal of Behavioral Medicine, 1*, 4–31.

Mao, W.-C., Bardwell, W. A., Major, J. M., & Dimsdale, J. E. (2003). Coping strategies, hostility, and depressive symptoms: A path model. *International Journal of Behavioral Medicine, 10*, 331–342.

Marshall, G. N., Wortman, C. B., Kusulas, J. W., Hervig, L. K., & Vickers, Jr., R. R. (1992). Distinguishing optimism from pessimism: Relations to fundamental dimensions of mood and personality. *Journal of Personality and Social Psychology, 62*, 1067–1074.

Matthews, K. A. (1988). Coronary heart disease and type A behaviors: Update on and alternative to the Booth-Kewley and Freidman (1987) quantitative review. *Psychological Bulletin, 104*, 373–380.

Matthews, K. A., Gump, B. B., Harris, K. F., Haney, T. L., & Barefoot, J. C. (2004). Hostile behaviors predict cardiovascular mortality among men enrolled in the Multiple Risk Factor Intervention Trial. *Circulation, 109*, 66–70.

Matthews, K. A., Raikkonen, K., Sutton-Tyrrell, K., & Kuller, L. H. (2004). Optimistic attitudes protect against progression of carotid atherosclerosis in healthy middle-aged women. *Psychosomatic Medicine, 66,* 640–644.
McCarty, D., Diamond, W., & Kaye, M. (1982). Alcohol, sexual arousal, and the transfer of excitation. *Journal of Personality and Social Psychology, 42,* 977–988.
McCrae, R. R., & Costa Jr., P. T. (1997). Personality trait structure as a human universal. *American Psychologist, 52,* 509–516.
Middleton, R A., & Byrd, E. K. (1996). Psychosocial factors and hospital readmission status of older persons with cardiovascular disease. *Journal of Applied Rehabilitation Counseling, 27,* 3–10.
Miller, G. E., Cohen, S., Pressman, S., Barkin, A., Rabin, B. S., & Treanor, J. J. (2004). sychological stress and antibody response to influenza vaccination: When is the critical period for stress, and how does it get inside the body? *Psychosomatic Medicine, 66,* 215–223.
Miller G. E., Dopp, J. M., Myers, H. F., Felten, S. Y., & Fahey, J. L. (1999). Psychosocial predictors of natural killer mobilization during marital conflict. *Health Psychology, 18,* 262–271.
Miller, T. Q., Markides, K. S., Chiriboga, D. A., & Ray, L. A. (1995). A test of the psychosocial vulnerability and health behavior models of hostility: Results from an 11-year follow-up study of Mexican Americans. *Psychosomatic Medicine, 57,* 572–581.
Miller, T. Q., Smith, T. W., Turner, C. W., Guijarro, M. L., & Hallett, A. J. (1996). A meta-analytic review of research on hostility and physical health. *Psychological Bulletin, 119,* 322–348.
Mischel, W. (1968). *Personality and assessment.* New York: Wiley.
Mischel, W. (2004). Toward an integrative science of the person. *Annual Review Psychology, 55,* 1–22.
Mischel, W., & Shoda, Y. (1995). A cognitive-affective system theory of personality: Reconceptualizing situations, dispositions, dynamics, and invariance in personality structure. *Psychological Review, 102,* 246–268.
Mroczek. D. K., Spiro, III, A., Aldwin, C. M., Ozer, D. J., & Bosse, R. (1993). Construct validation of optimism and pessimism in older men: Findings from the normative aging study. *Health Psychology, 12,* 406–409.
Mulkana, S., & Hailey, B. J. (2001). The role of optimism in health-enhancing behavior. *American Journal of Health Behavior, 25,* 388–395.
Murdoch, C., & Finn, A. (2000). Chemokine receptors and their role in inflammation and infectious diseases. *Blood, 95,* 3032–3043.
Neumann, S. A., Waldstein, S. R., Sollers, III, J. J., Thayer, J. F., & Sorkin, J. D. (2004). Hostility and distraction have differential influences on cardiovascular recovery from anger recall in women. *Health Psychology, 23,* 631–640.
Newsom, J. T., Nishishiba, M., Morgan, D. L., & Rook, K. S. (2003). The relative importance of three domains of positive and negative social exchanges: A longitudinal model with comparable measures. *Psychology and Aging, 18,* 746–754.
Ng, D. M., & Jeffery, R. W. (2003). Relationships between perceived stress and health behaviors in a sample of working adults. *Health Psychology, 22,* 638–642.
Niaura, R., Todaro, J. F., Stroud, L., Spiro, A., Ward, K D., & Weiss, S. (2002). Hostility, the metabolic syndrome, and incident coronary heart disease. *Health Psychology, 21,* 588–593.
Nicassio, P. C., & Smith, T. W. (1995). *Psychosocial management of chronic illness.* Washington, DC: American Psychological Association.
O'Keeffe, M. K., Nesselhof-Kendall, S., & Baum, A. (1990). Behavior and prevention of AIDS: Bases of research and intervention. *Personality and Social Psychology Bulletin, 16,* 166–180.

Olson, M. B., Krantz, D. S., Kelsey, S. F., Pepine, C. J., Sopko, G., Hangberg, E., Rogers, W. J., Gierach, G.L., McClure, C. K., & Merz, C. N. B. for the WISE Study Group (2005). Hostility scores are associated with increased risk of cardiovascular events in women undergoing coronary angiography: A report from the NHLBI-sponsored WISE study. *Psychosomatic Medicine, 67,* 546–552.

Padgett, D. A., Sheridan, J. F., Dorne, J., Berntson, G. G., Candelora, J., & Glaser, R. (1998, June). Social stress and the reactivation of latent herpes simplex virus type 1. *Proc. National Academy of Science, 95,* 7231–7235.

Pervin, L. A. (1970). *Personality: Theory, assessment, and research.* Oxford, UK: Wiley.

Peterson, C. (2000). The future of optimism. *American Psychologist, 55,* 44–55.

Peterson, C., Seligman, M. E. P., Yurko, K. H., Martin, L. R., & Friedman, H. S. (1998). Catastrophizing and untimely death. *Psychological Science, 9,* 127–130.

Pierce, G. R., Sarason, I. G., & Sarason, B. R. (1991). General and relationship-based perceptions of social support: Are two constructs better than one? *Journal of Personality and Social Psychology, 61,* 1028–1039.

Plaut, M. (1987). Lymphocyte hormone receptors. *Annual Review of Immunology, 5,* 621–669.

Pope, M. K., Smith, T. W., & Rhodewalt, F. (1990). Cognitive, behavioral, and affective correlates of the Cook and Medley hostility scale. *Journal of Personality Assessment, 54,* 501–514.

Powch, I. G. & Houston, B. K. (1996). Hostility, anger-in, and cardiovascular reactivity in caucasian women. *Health Psychology, 15,* 200–208.

Radcliffe, N. M., & Klein, W. M. P. (2002). Dispositional, unrealistic, and comparative optimism: Differential relations with the knowledge and processing of risk information and beliefs about personal risk. *Personality and Social Psychology Bulletin, 28,* 836–846.

Raikkonen, K., Matthews, K. A., Flory, J. D., Owens, J. F., & Gump, B. B. (1999). Effects of optimism, pessimism, and trait anxiety on ambulatory blood pressure and mood during everyday life. *Journal of Personality and Social Psychology, 75,* 104–113.

Rhodewalt, F., & Smith, T. W. (1991). Current issues in type A behavior, coronary proneness, and coronary heart disease. In C. R. Snyder and D. R. Forsyth (Eds.), *Handbook of social and clinical psychology: The health perspective* (pp. 197–220). New York: Pergamon Press.

Robinson-Whelen, S., Kim, C., MacCallum, R. C., & Kiecolt-Glaser, J. K. (1997). Distinguishing optimism from pessimism in older adults: Is it more important to be optimistic or not to be pessimistic? *Journal of Personality and Social Psychology, 73,* 1345–1353.

Rook, K. S. (1984). The negative side of social interaction: Impact on psychological well being. *Journal of Personality and Social Psychology, 46,* 1097–1108.

Ross, R. (1999, January). Atherosclerosis—An inflammatory disease. *The New England Journal of Medicine, 340,* 115–126.

Rothbart, M. K., Ahadi, S. A., & Evans, D. E. (2000). Temperament and personality: Origins and outcomes. *Journal of Personality and Social Psychology, 78,* 122–135.

Rozanski, A., Blumenthal, J. A., & Kaplan, J. (1999). Impact of psychological factors on the pathogenesis of cardiovascular disease and implications for therapy. *Circulation, 99,* 2192–2217.

Rozanski, A., Bairey, C. N., Krantz, D. S., Friedman, J., Resser, K. J., Morell, M., Hilton-Chalfen, S., Hestrin, L., Bietendorf, J., & Berman, D. S. (1988). Mental stress and the induction of silent myocardial ischemia in patients with coronary artery disease. *The New England Journal of Medicine, 318,* 1005–1012.

Rusting, C. L., & Nolen-Hoeksema, S. (1998). Regulating responses to anger: Effects of rumination and distraction on angry mood. *Journal of Personality and Social Psychology, 74,* 790–803.

Russell, D. W., & Cutrona, C. E. (1991). Social support, stress, and depressive symptoms among the elderly: Test of a process model. *Psychology and Aging, 6,* 190–201.

Sanders, V. M., Kasprowicz, D. J., Kohm, A. P., & Swanson, M. A. (2001). Neurotransmitter receptors on lymphocytes and other lymphoid cells. In R. Ader, D. L. Felten, & N. Cohen (Eds.), *Psychoneuroimmunology* (Vol. 1, 3rd ed., pp. 161–196). New York: Academic Press.

Scheier, M. F., Carver, C. S., & Bridges, M. W. (1994). Distinguishing optimism from neuroticism (and trait anxiety, self-mastery, and self-esteem): A reevaluation of the Life Orientation Test. *Journal of Personality and Social Psychology, 67,* 1063–1078.

Scheier, M. F., Matthews, K. A., Owens, J. F., Magovern, Sr., G. J., Lefebvre, R. C., Abbott, R. A., & Carver, C. S. (1989). Dispositional optimism and recovery from coronary artery bypass surgery: The beneficial effects on physical and psychological well-being. *Journal of Personality and Social Psychology, 57,* 1024–1040.

Scheier, M. F., Weintraub, J. K., & Carver, C. S. (1986). Coping with stress: Divergent strategies of optimists and pessimists. *Journal of Personality and Social Psychology, 51,* 1257–1264.

Schwartz, A. R., Gerin, W., Christenfeld, N. G., Davidson, K. W., & Pickering, T. G. (2000). Effects of an anger-recall task on poststress rumination and blood pressure recovery in men and women. *Psychophysiology, 37,* S12–3.

Sears, S. R., Stanton, A. L., & Danoff-Burg, S. (2003). The yellow brick road and the emerald city: Benefit finding, positive reappraisal coping, and posttraumatic growth in women with early-stage breast cancer. *Health Psychology, 22,* 487–497.

Segerstrom, S. C. (2001a). Optimism and attentional bias for negative and positive stimuli. *Personality and Social Psychology Bulletin, 27,* 1334–1343.

Segerstrom, S. C. (2001b). Optimism, goal conflict, and stressor-related immune change. *Journal of Behavioral Medicine, 24,* 441–467.

Segerstrom, S. C. (2005). Optimism and immunity: Do positive thoughts always lead to positive effects? *Brain, Behavior, and Immunity, 19,* 195–200.

Segerstrom, S. C., & Miller, G. E. (2004). Psychological stress and the human immune system: A meta-analytic study of 30 years of inquiry. *Psychological Bulletin, 130,* 601–630.

Shen, B. J., McCreary, C. P., & Myers, H. F. (2004). Independent and mediated contributions of personality, coping, social support, and depressive symptoms to physical functioning outcome among patients in cardiac rehabilitation. *Journal of Behavioral Medicine, 27,* 39–62.

Siegler, I. C., Costa, P. T., Brummett, B. H., Helms, M. J., Barefoot, J. C., Williams, R. B., Dahlstrom, W. G., Kaplan, B. H., Vitaliano, P. P., Nichaman, M. Z., Day, R. S., & Rimer, B. K. (2003). Patterns of change in hostility from college to midlife in the UNC alumni heart study predict high-risk status. *Psychosomatic Medicine, 65,* 738–745.

Smith, E. R., & Zarate, M. A. (1992). Exemplar-based model of social judgment. *Psychological Review, 99,* 3–21.

Smith, T. W. (1992). Hostility and health: Current status of a psychosomatic hypothesis. *Health Psychology, 11,* 139–150.

Smith, T. W., & Anderson, N. B. (1986). Models of personality and disease: An interactional approach to type A behavior and cardiovascular risk. *Journal of Personality and Social Psychology, 50,* 1166–1173.

Smith, T. W., & Frohm, K. D. (1985). What's so unhealthy about hostility? Construct validity and psychosocial correlates of the Cook and Medley ho scale. *Health Psychology, 4,* 503–520.

Smith, T. W., & Gallo, L. C. (1999). Hostility and cardiovascular reactivity during marital interaction. *Psychosomatic Medicine, 61,* 436–445.

Smith, T. W., & Gallo, L. C. (2001). Personality traits as risk factors for physical illness. In A. Baum, T. Revenson, & J. Singer (Eds.), *Handbook of health psychology* (pp 139–172). Hillsdale, NJ: Erlbaum.

Smith, T. W., & MacKenzie, J. (in press). Personality and risk of physical illness. *Annual Review of Clinical Psychology.*

Smith, T. W., Pope, M. K., Rhodewalt, F., & Poulton, J. L. (1989). Optimism, neuroticism, coping, and symptom reports: An alternative interpretation of the Life Orientation Test. *Journal of Personality and Social Psychology, 56,* 640–648.

Smith, T. W., Pope, M. K., Sanders, J. D., Allred, K. D., & O'Keeffe, J. L. (1988). Cynical hostility at home and work: Psychosocial vulnerability across domains. *Journal of Research in Personality, 22,* 525–548.

Solberg, L. N., Segerstrom, S. C., & Sephton, S. E. (2005). Engagement and arousal: Optimism's effects during a brief stressor. *Personality and Social Psychology Bulletin, 31,* 111–120.

Stephens, M. A., Kinney, J. M., Norris, V. K., & Ritchie, S. W. (1987). Social networks as assets and liabilities in recovery from stroke by geriatric patients. *Psychology and Aging, 2,* 125–129.

Stetson, B. A., Rahn, J. M., Dubbert, P. M., Wilner, B. I., & Mercury, M. G. (1997). Prospective evaluation of the effects of stress on exercise adherence in community-residing women. *Health Psychology, 16,* 515–520.

Suarez, E. C., & Williams, R. B. (1989). Situational determinants of cardiovascular and emotional reactivity in high and low hostile men. *Psychosomatic Medicine, 51,* 404–418.

Suls, J., & Bunde, J. (2005). Anger, anxiety, and depression as risk factors for cardiovascular disease: The problems and implications of overlapping affective dispositions. *Psychological Bulletin, 131,* 260–300.

Suls, J., & Fletcher, B. (1985). The relative efficacy of avoidant and nonavoidant coping strategies: A meta-analysis. *Health Psychology, 4,* 249–288.

Suls, J. & Martin, R. (2005). The daily life of the garden-variety neurotic: Reactivity, stressor exposure, mood spillover, and maladaptive coping. *Journal of Personality, 73,* 1–25.

Suls, J., & Wan, C. K. (1993). The relationship between trait hostility and cardiovascular reactivity: A quantitative review and analysis. *Psychophysiology, 30,* 615–626.

Swann, W. B., Jr., & Read, S. J. (1981). Self-verification processes: How we sustain our self-conceptions. *Journal of Experimental Social Psychology, 17,* 351–372.

Taylor, S. E. (1991). The asymmetrical impact of positive and negative events: The mobilization-minimization hypothesis. *Psychological Bulletin, 110,* 67–85.

Testa, M., & Collins, R. L. (1997). Alcohol and risky sexual behavior: Event-based analyses among a sample of high-risk women. *Psychol. Addict. Beh., 11,* 190–201.

Thoits, P. A. (1995). Stress, coping, and social support processes: Where are we? What next?. *Journal of Health and Social Behavior,* [extra issue], 53–79.

Thorsteinnsson, E. B., James, J. E., & Gregg, M. E., (1998). Effects of video-relayed social support on hemodynamic reactivity and salivary cortisol during laboratory-based behavioral challenges. *Health Psychology, 17,* 436–444.

Tomei, L. D., Kiecolt-Glaser, J. K., Kennedy, S., & Glaser, R. (1990). Psychological-stress and phorbol ester inhibition of radiation-induced apoptosis in human peripheral blood leukocytes. *Psychiatry Research, 33,* 59–71.

Treiber, F. A., Kamarck, T., Schneiderman, N., Sheffield, D., Kapuku, G., & Taylor, T. (2003). Cardiovascular reactivity and development of preclinical and clinical disease states. *Psychosomatic Medicine, 65,* 46–62.

Tugade, M. M., & Fredrickson, B. L. (2004). Resilient individuals use positive emotions to bounce back from negative emotional experiences. *Journal of Personality and Social Psychology, 86*, 320–333.

Uchino, B. N. (2004). *Social support and physical health: Understanding the health consequences of our relationships.* New Haven, CT: Yale University Press.

Uchino, B. N., Holt-Lunstad, J., Uno, D., Campo, R., & Reblin, M. (2007). The social neuroscience of relationships: An examination of health relevant pathways. In E. Harmon-Jones & P. Winkielman (Eds.), *Fundamentals of social neuroscience* (pp. 474–492). New York: Guilford.

Uchino, B. N., Smith, T. W., Holt-Lunstad, J. L., Campo, R., & Reblin, M. (2007). Stress and illness. In J. Cacioppo, L. Tassinary, & G. Berntson (Eds.), *Handbook of psychophysiology* (3rd ed., pp. 608–632). New York: Cambridge University Press.

Umberson, D. (1987). Family status and health behaviors: Social control as a dimension of social integration. *Journal of Health and Social Behavior, 28*, 306–319.

Umberson, D. (1992). Gender, marital status, and the social control of health behavior. *Social Science and Medicine, 34*, 907–917.

Vedhara, K., Cox, N. K. M., Wilcock, G. K., Perks, P., Hunt, M., Anderson, S., Lightman, S. L., & Shanks, N. M. (1999). Chronic stress in elderly carers of dementia patients and antibody response to influenza vaccination. *Lancet, 353*, 627–631.

Williams, R. B., Barefoot, J. C., & Schneiderman, N. (2003). Psychosocial risk factors for cardiovascular disease: More than one culprit at work? *JAMA, 290*, 2190–2192.

Wills, T. A., Gibbons, F. X., Gerrard, M., & Brody, G. H. (2000). Protection and vulnerability processes relevant for early onset of substance use: A test among African American children. *Health Psychology, 19*, 253–263.

Yeung, A. C., Vekshtein, V. I., Krantz, D. S., Vita, J. A., Ryan, Jr., T. J., Ganz, P., & Selwyn, A. P. (1991). The effect of atherosclerosis on the vasomotor response of coronary arteries to mental stress. *New England Journal of Medicine, 325*, 1551–1556.

Ylostalo, P., Ek, E., Knuuttila, M. (2003). Coping and optimism in relation to dental health behaviour-a study among Finnish young adults. *European Journal Oral Science, 111*, 477–482.

Author Index

A

Aarts, H., 98
Abbas, A. K., 268–269
Aboud, F. E., 180
Abrams, D. B., 23, 180, 182, 184, 188
Abramson, L. Y., 87, 256
Ackerman, K. D., 271
Ader, D. L., 268, 271
Adler, A., 3, 51, 86, 80
Adolphs, R., 156, 157
Adorno, T. W., 180, 182, 188., 224, 225
Ahadi, S. A., 253
Ainsworth, M. D. S., 117, 119, 122, 123, 126, 137, 138
Akhtar, S., 65
Albino, A. W., 129, 136
Aldwin, C. M., 257
Alexander, A. L., 162
Alexander, F., 251, 252
Alexander, R., 134
Allard, L., 136
Allen, A., 12, 253
Allen, E. A., 129
Allen, E. S., 130
Alliger, G. M., 199
Allison, T., 156
Allport, F. H., 180
Allport, G. W., 22, 150, 206, 226
Allred, K. D., 254, 261, 265
Alpert, N. M., 153
Altemeyer, B., 188, 225
American Heart Association, 254
American Psychiatric Association, 64–65
Ames, D. R., 159
Amodio, D. M., 226, 232
Anders, S. L., 121
Andersen, B. L., 269
Andersen, S. M., 5, 30, 31, 52, 72, 79, 80, 81, 82, 83, 84, 85, 87, 89, 90, 91, 92, 93, 94, 95, 96, 97, 99, 100, 103, 104, 105
Anderson, J. C., 265
Anderson, N. B., 254
Antoun, N., 157
Aron, A., 84, 85, 134, 162, 190
Aron, E. N., 84, 85
Aronson, J. A., 155, 161
Artistico, D., 22
Asch, S. E., 179
Asendorpf, J. B., 27, 28
Ashburn-Nardo, L., 226, 238

Ashmore, R. D., 82, 84
Ashton, M. C., 16
Aspinwall, L. G., 263, 264, 265, 266
Assanand, S., 58
Atkinson, J. W., 233
Avidan, S., 107, 127
Avihou, N., 107, 127
Avolio, B. J., 205
Ayduk, O., 27, 30, 32, 87, 95, 96, 165, 168
Ayman, R., 213

B

Baccus, J. R., 31, 32
Back, K., 180
Bacon, M. K., 82
Bader, P., 199
Baird, A. A., 155
Bakan, D., 86, 87
Baker, S. C., 155, 156
Baldwin, M. R., 52
Baldwin, M. W., 5, 30, 31, 32, 82, 84, 85, 90, 91, 94, 95, 97, 98, 105, 106, 242
Bales, R. F., 199, 204
Banaji, M. R., 62, 89, 155, 156
Bandura, A., 2, 11, 19, 20, 21, 22, 87, 212
Banse, R., 92
Barchas, P. R., 270
Barclay, L. C., 575, 60, 70
Barden, J., 244
Bardwell, W. A., 266
Barefoot, J. C., 255, 256, 257, 268
Bargh, J. A., 32, 63, 87, 90, 91, 92, 98, 99, 235
Barndollar, K., 87, 98, 235
Barnlund, D. C., 199
Baron, R. M., 179
Baron-Cohen, S., 155
Barrera, M., 264
Barrett, L. F., 128
Bartholomew, K., 120, 121, 126, 128, 132
Bartz, J., 105, 152
Bass, B. M., 205, 214
Bata, I., 272
Bateman, A. W., 155, 169
Batson, C. D., 86, 164
Batts. V., 229
Baucom, D. H., 130
Baum, A., 81, 82, 83, 84, 92, 103, 270
Baumeister, R., 10, 13, 32, 38, 50, 53, 57, 60, 71, 81, 86, 87, 164, 183
Beach, S. R. H., 123

285

Becker, E., 87
Becker, H., 188
Belanger,C., 135
Bell, G. B., 199
Belsky, J., 134
Bem, D. J., 12, 253
Benet-Martinez, V., 28
Bennett, M. R., 39
Berant, E., 125
Berenson, K., 91, 93, 95, 100, 105
Berger, J., 212
Berglas, S. C., 53, 70
Berk, M. S., 87, 89, 92, 96, 99, 102
Berkman, L. F., 33, 263, 268
Berns, G. S., 155
Berntson, G. G., 252, 259, 267, 268
Berridge, K. C., 29
Berscheid, E., 28, 96, 101
Biernat, M., 227
Bihrle, S., 154
Billig, M., 180, 182, 188
Binning, J. F., 210
Birnbaum, G., 105, 107
Black, P. H., 271, 272
Blair, I. B., 92
Blair, R. J., 154
Blakely, B. S., 129
Blalock, J., 139
Blascovich, J. J., 212, 213
Blatt, S. J., 79., 86
Blehar, M. C., 117, 119, 122, 123, 126
Blumenthal, J. A., 261
Boden, J. M., 53
Bodenhausen, G. V., 226
Bogaert, A. F., 134
Boldry, J., 125
Bolger, N., 260, 263, 270
Boncimino, M., 162
Bond, R. N., 90
Boniecki, K. A., 227
Bonnell, D., 130
Bono, J. E., 208
Bookwala, J., 132
Booth-Kewley, S., 256
Borgatta, E. F., 199
Borsboom, D., 19, 34
Bosse, R., 257
Bosson, J.K., 63
Botvinick, M., 156
Boucher, H. C., 242
Boudreau, L. A., 179
Bourhis, R. Y., 182
Bowlby, J., 51, 86, 117, 119, 119, 120, 121, 123, 125, 127, 132, 137, 138
Boyd, K. R., 81

Boyle, S. H., 256
Bradbury, T. N., 123, 135
Bradford, S. A., 128, 135
Bradshaw, D., 123
Braly, K., 226
Branscombe, N. R., 188
Brauer, M., 156
Brennan, K., 120, 121, 130, 140
Brewer, M. B., 159, 164, 186, 187, 190, 244
Bridges, M. W., 257
Brissette, I., 262, 263
Britt, T. W., 227, 232, 239
Broadwell, S. D., 262, 265
Brodish, A. B., 224, 226, 239, 241
Bromley, S., 225
Brondolo, E., 261
Brown, J. D., 100, 207
Brown, K. A., 214
Brown, L. M., 227
Brown, R. J.,63, 180
Bruce, A. T., 269
Brummett, B. H.,256
Bruner, J. S., 84, 87
Brunet, E., 155
Brunhart, S. M., 265, 266
Bryman, A., 188
Buchanan, T. W., 156
Bucholtz, I., 125, 126
Bunde, J., 256, 261
Burg, M. M., 260, 267, 270
Burge, D., 79
Burns, J. M., 204
Burns, V. E., 270
Buss, D. M., 67, 136
Buunk, B. P., 129
Bylsma, W. H., 120, 121, 156
Byrd, E. K., 258
Byrnes, D., 271

C

Cacioppo, J. T., 252, 259, 267, 268
Calder, A. J., 157
Caldwell, T. L., 2, 6, 9, 37, 38, 71
Callan, V. J., 130, 131
Campbell, J. D., 58
Campbell, L., 125, 128, 131, 132, 134, 135
Campbell, S. E., 11
Campbell, W. K., 67, 134
Campo, R., 254, 258
Canli, T., 151
Cantor, N., 2, 4, 5, 14, 19, 53, 55, 137, 178, 183, 206
Caprara, G. V., 11, 13, 39
Carlyle, T., 197
Carnelley, K. B., 132

Carr, L., 156, 157
Carrel, S. E., 3, 85, 91, 97, 98
Carroll, D., 270
Carroll, J. M., 162
Carson, R. C., 79
Carter, L. F., 199
Cartwright, D., 180
Caruso, D. R., 209
Carver, C. S., 18, 60, 87, 128, 229, 230, 233, 234, 241, 256, 257, 259, 260, 262, 263, 265, 266
Cassidy, J., 128
Castelli, F., 155
Cavanna, A. E., 156
Cervone, D., 2, 6, 9, 11, 13, 16, 17, 18, 19, 20, 21, 22, 23, 24, 25, 29, 33, 34, 37, 39, 71, 229, 253
Chan, D. W., 16
Chan, K., 209, 213
Chang, E. C., 256, 257, 265, 266
Charo, I. F., 271
Chartrand, T. L., 98, 99
Chase, S. K., 52
Chemers, M. M., 7, 197, 202, 203, 205, 210, 212, 213
Chen, S., 5, 72, 79, 80, 81, 82, 84, 85, 87, 89, 90, 92, 94, 92, 98, 99, 242
Cheney, S., 65, 67
Chiodo, L. M., 67
Chiriboga, D. A., 266
Christenfeld, N. G., 264
Christensen, A. J., 264
Church, M. A., 233
Clark, C., 120
Clark, L. A., 102
Clarke, M., 156
Clémence, A., 177, 179
Cloninger C. R., 11, 253
Clore, G. L., 21, 102
Cloutier, J., 156, 159
Coats, S., 81
Cobb, R. J., 126
Cohen, J. D., 155, 161
Cohen, N., 268, 271
Cohen, S., 33, 252, 260, 262, 263, 264, 268, 269
Cole, S. W., 81, 82, 83, 84, 87, 89, 91, 93, 94, 100, 104
Colletti, P., 154
Collins, N. L., 5, 101, 119, 120, 121, 124, 125, 126 127, 128, 130, 133, 135, 136, 137, 139
Collins, R. L., 270
Condor, S., 188
Conger, J. A., 188
Conklin, L., 163
Connelly, M. S., 209, 210

Cooley, C. H., 85
Coon, H. M., 186
Cooper, J., 223
Cooper, M. L., 129, 130, 136
Cooper, M. M., 269
Corcoran, K., 120, 131
Cosmides, L., 163
Costa Jr., P. T., 206, 253
Costa, P. T., 16, 19
Costall, A., 15
Costanzo, E. S., 269, 270
Courchesne, E., 161
Cowan, L. P., 134
Cowan, P. A., 134
Coyne, J. C., 139
Cozzarelli, C., 120, 121
Crandall, C. S., 228
Creasey, G., 131
Critelli, J. W., 65
Crits-Christoph, P., 82, 83
Crocker, J., 30, 50, 52, 63, 65, 71, 87, 98
Crosby, F., 225
Crouch, A. S., 199
Crowne, D. P., 229
Cunnick, J. E., 269
Cunniff, C., 150
Curran, M., 134
Cutrona, C. E., 264
Czopp, A. M., 226

D

D'Ambrosio, S. M., 269
Dakin, S., 154
Damasio, A. R., 156
Dambrun, M., 225
Dandeneau, S. D., 31
Danoff-Burg, S., 265
Dapretto, M., 152, 157–158
Darley, J., 223
Davidson, K. W., 264, 272
Davila, J., 79, 135
Davis, D., 129, 130
Davis, K. E., 120, 129, 130
Davis, M. H., 163
Davison, J., 69
Day, D., 209
De Cremer, D., 188
de Quervain, D. J., 161
de Raad, B., 14
De Vader, C. L., 199
Decety, J., 155, 156, 158
Deci, E. L., 86, 87
Deci, E. M., 52, 71
DeFleur, M. L., 224
DeLongis, A., 263

Deluga, R. J., 208
Dennett, D., 149
DeVincent, C. J., 267
Devine, P. G., 6, 89, 223, 224, 226, 227,228, 229, 231, 232, 233, 234, 239, 241, 243, 244, 345, 346, 347, 348
Dhamala, M., 155
Di Paula, A., 58
di Pellegrino, G., 156
Diamond, A., 15
Dick, W., 92
Digman, J. M., 3, 16
Dijksterhuis, A., 98
Dimaggio, G. 18
DiMatteo, M. R., 33
Dimsdale, J. E., 266
Dinarello, C. A., 261
Dion, K. K., 28, 128
Dodge, K., 80
Doise, W., 180, 182
Dolan, R. J., 155, 156, 160
Dollard, J., 180, 182
Donahue, E. M., 58, 59
Doob, L. W., 180, 182
Dopp, J. M., 269
Dovidio, J. F., 225, 226
Downey, G., 7, 18, 30, 32, 55, 87, 94, 95, 96, 98, 102, 149, 151, 152, 165
Downs, D. L., 87
Drasgow, F., 209, 213
Drayson, M., 270
Duan, C., 226
Duarte, S., 225
Dubbert, P. M., 260
Dubeau, M. C., 156, 157
Duemmler, S., 130, 131
Dukerich, J. M., 198
Dunbar, H. F., 252
Dunbar, R., 149
Dunn, G. P., 269
Dunton, B. C., 226, 228
Durkheim, E., 179
Dutton, D. G., 132
Duval S., 230
Dweck, C. S., 19, 21, 55, 70, 87, 137

E
Eddings, S., 65, 66, 68
Ee, J. S., 65
Egner, T., 151
Ehrenreich, J. H., 82, 83
Ehrlich, P., 25
Ehrlich, S. B., 198
Eid, M., 18
Ek, E., 267

Ellemers, N., 183
Elliot, A. J., 21, 63, 226, 233, 234, 236
Elliot, E. S., 70
Elms, A. C., 180, 181
Emmons, R. A., 68
Endler, N. S., 3
Eng, J., 158
Englis, B. G., 160, 163
Epley, N., 163
Epstein, S., 53, 55, 56, 60, 87, 268
Ernst, D., 190
Eshkoli, N., 107, 127
Eshleman, A., 228
Esses, V. M., 224, 225
Evans, D. E., 253

F
Fabian, S. A., 156
Fahey, J. L., 269
Fairbairn, W. R. D., 79, 86
Fairfield, M., 70
Farnham, S. D., 63
Farr, R. M., 179
Fawzy, F. I., 270
Fazio, R. H., 62, 63, 69, 223, 226, 228, 229, 232
Feather, N. T., 233
Feeney, B. C., 120, 121, 124, 126, 127, 128, 132, 135, 136, 139
Feeney, J. A., 121, 122, 125, 128, 129, 130, 131, 134, 135
Fehr, B., 85
Feick, D. L., 70
Feldman Barrett, L., 105, 131
Feldman, A., 134
Feldman, S. I., 55, 87, 94, 95, 96, 98, 102
Feldman, S., 30, 32, 95, 152
Felten, S. Y. , 268, 269, 271
Felton, D. L., 271
Ferentinos, C. H., 199
Festinger, L., 180
Fiedler, F. E., 7, 204, 208, 212, 213
Finch, J. F., 264
Fincham, F. D., 123, 135
Finley, E., 65, 67
Finn, A., 271
Fiori, M., 23
Fischer, G. W., 81
Fishtein, J., 131
Fiske, A. P., 79
Fiske, S. T., 5, 86, 93, 155
Fitzsimons, G. M., 31
Fitzsimons, G. M., 32, 87, 90, 92, 98, 99
Fleeson, W., 18
Fleischman, E. A., 210
Fletcher, B., 259

AUTHOR INDEX 289

Fletcher, P. C., 155, 156
Florian, V., 120, 121, 123, 125, 126, 134
Flory, J. D., 257
Fogassi, L., 157
Folkman, S., 87, 265
Fonagy, P., 155, 169
Ford, D. E., 256
Forsterling, F., 16
Foster, C. A., 134
Foster, M., 260
Foti, R. J., 199
Fox, B. H., 270
Fox, N. A., 14
Frackowiak, R. S., 155, 156
Fraley, R. C., 13, 120, 125, 130
Frankl, V. E., 97
Franks, M. M., 33
Fraser, C., 181
Fredrickson, B. L., 265, 266
Freitas, A. L., 96
French, R. L., 199
Frenkel-Brunswick, E., 180, 224
Freud, S., 3, 17, 34, 82, 91
Freund, T., 226
Friedman, H. S., 256
Friedman, M., 5, 51, 117, 128, 134, 272
Friedman, R. S., 230, 236
Friend, R., 229
Frist, W. H., 257
Frith, C., 155, 156, 160
Frith, U., 154, 155
Froehlich, M., 72
Frohm, K. D., 261
Fujita, K., 158
Funder, D. C., 10, 11, 12

G
Gabbard, G. O., 136
Gable, S. L., 234
Gabriel, M. T., 65
Gabrieli, J. D., 151
Gaertner, S. L., 225
Galinsky, A. D., 214, 226
Gallagher, H. L., 155
Gallant, M. P., 33
Gallese, V., 157, 158
Gallo, L. C., 252, 258, 262, 272
Gallois, C., 130
Galton, F., 197
Gangestad, S. W., 130, 229
Garbutt, L. D., 271, 272
Garcia, J. E., 208, 213
Garcia, M., 132
Gard, D. E., 29
Gard, M. G., 29

Gardner, W. L., 164, 186, 190.
Geertz, C., 15
Geleijnse, J. M., 257
Gentzler, A. L., 130
Gerberding, J. L., 32
Gergen, K. J., 180
Gerhardt, M. W., 208
Gerin, W., 264, 265
Ghera, M. A., 14
Gibb, C. A., 299
Gidron, Y., 272
Giere, R. N., 18
Gilbert, D., 150, 163, 187
Gilbert, J. A., 209
Gillath, O., 106, 107, 121, 127
Gilovich, T., 163
Giltay, E. J., 257, 267
Glaser, R., 268, 269, 270
Glass, T., 263
Glassman, N. S., 3, 81, 82, 83, 87, 89, 90, 91, 92, 94, 95
Gobbini, M. I., 161
Goddard, H. H., 198
Goel, V., 155
Gold, D., 81
Goldberg, A. D., 261
Goldberg, L. R., 3, 16, 17, 18
Goldman, B. M., 57, 60, 51
Goldsteen, K., 33
Goldwyn, R., 117
Gollwitzer, P. M., 87, 98
Gormley, B., 132
Gosling, S. D., 33
Gosselin, F., 156
Gotlib, I. H., 151
Gottlieb, G., 25
Gottman, J. M., 130
Grabill, C. M., 120
Grafman, J., 155
Grafton, S. T., 155
Grafton, S. T., 156
Grannemann, B. D., 57, 60, 70
Grant, H., 19, 21
Grant-Pillow, H., 55
Graumann, C. F., 180
Gravenstein, S., 270
Gray, J., 35, 38
Green, S. G., 204, 214\
Greenberg, J. R., 51, 71, 82, 86, 100
Greenson, R. R., 82, 83
Greenwald, A. G., 56, 60, 62, 63, 89, 232, 238
Gregg, M. E., 264
Grich, J., 125
Griffin, R. N., 214
Grishenkoroze, N., 16

Gruenfeld, D. H., 214
Guerrero, L. K., 129
Guijarro, M. L., 256
Guimond, S., 225
Guisinger, S., 86
Gump, B. B., 257

H
Haber, S. N. 270
Habra, M. E., 265
Hacker, P. M. S., 15, 39
Hackman, J. R., 204, 214
Haddock, G., 224, 225
Hadjikhani, N., 158
Hagendoorn, L., 188
Hailey, B. J., 267
Hains, S. C., 210
Haist, F., 161
Halevy, V., 107, 127
Hall, C. S., 66–67
Hallett, A. J., 256
Hallett, M., 155
Halpin, A. W., 200, 203
Hammen, C., 79
Haney, T. L., 257
Happe, F., 154, 155
Harackiewicz, J. M., 233
Hardee, B. B., 229
Hardin, C. D., 84
Harding, F. D., 210
Hardy-Bayle, M. C., 155
Harmon-Jones, E., 226, 232
Harré, R., 15, 17, 18
Harris, K. F., 257
Harris, L. T., 155
Harris, R. N., 69, 70
Harrison, T., 161
Haslam, N., 97
Haslam, S. A., 178, 184, 185, 186, 187, 188, 190
Hass, R. G., 225
Haxby, J. V., 161
Hazan, C., 120, 121, 123
Hazen, N., 134
Hazlett, S., 70
Heatherton, T. F., 155
Hedlund, J., 207
Heinicke, C. M., 134
Helgeson, V. S., 86, 260
Heller, W., 29
Helms, M. J., 256
Hembree, R., 233
Henderson, H. A., 14
Henderson, M. D., 158
Henson, R., 153
Herbert, T. B., 253, 263, 268, 269

Hermans, H. J. M., 15
Hervig, L. K., 257
Hesson-McInnis, M., 131
Hewstone, M., 177
Higgins, E. T., 12, 19, 20, 21, 30, 50, 53, 55, 56, 57, 80, 81, 84, 85, 87, 89, 92, 99, 101, 230, 234
Higgins, T. E., 236
Hill, S. K., 70
Hiller N., 209
Hinkle, S., 184
Hinkley, K., 66, 85, 87, 89, 90
Hirsch, J., 151
Hock, E., 130
Hoekstra, T., 257
Hoffman, E. A., 161
Hoffman, R. R., 266
Hoffman, S. G., 29
Hogan, R., 68
Hogg, M. A., 50, 72, 177, 178, 180, 181, 182, 183, 184, 185, 186, 187, 188, 210
Hohaus, L., 134, 135
Holahan, C. J., 260
Hollander, E. P. , 152, 210
Hollenbeck, J. R., 207
Hollist, C. S., 125
Holmes, J. G., 5, 100, 10, 139
Holt-Lunstad, J. L., 254, 258
Hong, Y., 13
Hopkins, N., 188
Horesh, N., 122
Horney, K., 79, 83, 86
Horowitz, L., 120, 121, 126, 128
Horowitz, M. J., 79, 83
House, J. S., 33
House, R. J., 204, 208, 214
Houser, D., 155
Houston, B. K., 262
Hovland, C., 210
Howard, A., 226
Hoyt, C., 212, 213
Hulley, S. B., 256
Hunh, S., 67, 68
Hunsberger, 225
Hunter, A. J., 227
Hynes, C. A., 155

I
Iacoboni, M., 151, 156, 157
Ickes, W., 164, 178, 186, 189
Idson, L. C., 162
Ikeda, H., 269
Ilgen, D. R., 207
Ilies, R., 208
Impett, E. A., 129, 130

AUTHOR INDEX 291

Irribarren, C., 256
Ituarte, P. H. G., 264

J
Jabaaij, L., 270
Jack, A. I., 155
Jackson, J. R., 226
Jackson, P. L., 155, 156, 158
Jacobs, D. R., 256
Jacobs, T. O., 210
Jacobvitz, D., 134
Jaffe, K., 132
James, J. E., 264
James, W., 49, 50
Janoff-Bulman, R., 87
Jaspars, J. M. F., 181
Jeffery, R. W., 260
Jencius, S., 33
Jennings, J. R., 261, 264
Jetten, J., 178
Jha, A. P., 156
Jiwani, N., 21
John, O. P., 16, 29, 33, 58, 59, 65, 178
Johnson, B., 226
Johnson, C., 226
Johnson, J. T., 81
Johnson-Frey, S. H., 156
Johnstone, T., 162
Joiner, T., 139
Jones, E. E., 53, 69, 70, 179
Jordan, C. H., 62, 63, 69
Joseph, R. M., 158
Judge, T. A., 208

K
Kagan, J., 11, 14, 17, 253, 268
Kahn, R. L., 204
Kalichman, S. C., 270
Kamarck, T. W., 260, 261, 264
Kaminer, A., 267
Kanungo, R. N., 183
Kanwisher, N., 155
Kaplan, J., 261
Kappen, D. M., 188
Kapuku, G., 260
Karpinski, A., 52
Karylowski, J. J., 81, 89, 92
Kashy, D. A., 125
Kasprowicz, D. J., 171
Kassel, J., 22
Kasser, T., 58, 59
Katerlos, T. E., 135
Katz, D., 204, 225, 226
Kaube, H., 156
Kawachi, I., 257

Kawakami, K., 226
Kazén, M., 11, 18
Keane, J., 157
Keczkemethy, C., 105
Keedian, E., 85
Keelan, J. P. R., 82, 85, 90, 105, 106, 128, 129
Keinonen, M., 16
Kelley, H. H., 69
Kelly, G., 55, 80, 84, 206
Kelly, J. A., 270
Keltner, D. J., 21, 214
Kemmelmeier, M., 186
Kemp, C., 199
Kennedy, S., 269
Kenny, D. A., 199
Kernberg, O., 83
Kernis, M. H., 52, 55, 57, 60, 61, 67, 68, 69, 70
Kerns, K. A., 120, 130
Kessler, R. C., 263
Keysar, B., 163
Keysers, C., 156, 157
Khouri, H., 95, 96
Kiebel, S. J., 160
Kiecolt-Glaser J. K., 33, 257, 263, 268, 269, 270
Kiefe, C. I., 256
Kiesler, D. J., 3, 4
Kihlstrom, J. F., 4, 14, 1, 183
Kilcullen, R., 209
Kilpatrick, S. D., 68
Kim, H., 162
Kim, M., 96
Kinder, D. R., 225
King, G., 80, 81
Kinney, J. M., 260
Kipnis, D., 214
Kirkpatrick, L. A., 130, 132
Kitayama, S., 87
Klag, M. J., 256
Klein, W. M. P., 265, 266
Klinger, E., 87
Knoops, T. B., 32
Knowles, M., 164
Knuuttila, M., 267
Kobak, R. R., 119, 120, 130, 131, 133
Koestner, R., 63
Kohm, A. P., 271
Kohut, H., 52, 83
Kohut, M. L., 269, 270
Kooij, C. S., 5, 52, 79
Konarzewski, K., 81, 89, 92
Koole, S. L., 11, 18
Kop, W. J., 271
Kosaka, H., 161
Kosslyn, S. M., 153
Kouznetsova, L., 16

Krantz, D. S., 254, 260, 261
Kreindler, S. A., 189
Kring, A. M., 29
Krokoff, L. J., 130
Kross, E., 151
Kruglanski, A. W., 87, 226
Krull, D., 150
Kubzansky, L. D., 257
Kuhl, J., 11
Kuller, L. H., 257
Kumhyr. S. M., 227
Kunce, L. J., 127
Kusulas, J. W., 257

L
LaCasse, L., 154
Lambert, L., 92,
Langeheine, R., 18
Lanigan, L., 129
Lanzetta, J. T., 160, 163
Larsen, G., 35, 38
Larsen, R. J, 102
Laurenceau, J-P., 128
Laureys, S., 156
Lawrence, P. R., 203
Lazarus, R. S., 19, 20, 265
Leary, M. R., 49, 50, 53, 57, 71, 87, 91, 86, 164, 229
Leary, T., 79
Leavitt, H. J., 204
Lebolt, A., 96
LeBon, G., 179
LeDoux, J., 21
Lee, K., 16
Lee, S. S., 152
Lee-Chai, A., 87, 98
Leedham, B., 257
Lefcourt, H. M., 34
Leggett, E. L., 19, 70, 87, 137
Leibenluft, E., 161
Leicht, C., 18
Lencz, T., 154
Lenzi, G. L., 156, 157
LePine, J. A., 207
Lepore, S. J., 262, 264
Lerner, J. S., 21
Leslie, A. M., 154
Leslie, K. R., 154, 156
Levin, S., 189
Levinson, D. J., 180, 224
Levy, M. B., 120, 121
Levy, R., 265
Lewin, K., 17, 180, 185, 206
Lewis, C. E., 256
Lewis, M. A., 260, 267

Leyens, J., 159
Libby, P., 254, 261, 271
Liberman, N., 158
Lichtenstein, E., 33, 260
Lichtman, A. H., 269–269
Light, K. C., 262, 265
Linden, W., 265
Lindsey, S., 62
Linville, P. W., 58, 59, 81
Little, B. R., 26
Litwin, G. H., 233
Lloyd, D., 156
Lobel, M., 267
Logel, C. E. R., 62, 63
Lombardi, W. L., 90
London, B. E., 30, 32
Lopez, D. F., 31, 85, 91, 97, 98
Lord, R. G., 199, 209, 210, 212
Lorenzi-Cioldi, F., 177, 179
Lorsch, J. W., 203
Luborsky, L., 82, 83
Luce, C., 163
Lugenbuhl, J., 70
Lussier, Y., 135
Lydon, J. E., '05

M
MacCallum, R. C., 257
MacKenzie, J., 256
Macrae, C. N., 155, 156, 159, 226
Maddux, W. W., 244
Madrian, J. C., 65, 67
Magee, J. C., 214
Magnusson, D. , 3, 26, 27, 28, 39
Maher, K. J., 210, 212
Mahone, C. H., 233
Main, K. J., 31, 227
Main, M., 117
Mainguy, N., 135
Major, J. M., 266
Malarkey, W. B., 270
Mallinckrodt, B., 120, 131
Malone, P. S., 187
Manes, F., 157
Manicas, P. T., 179
Mann, R. D., 198
Mansfield, E., 15
Manuck, S. B., 254, 260, 261, 264
Manzella, L. M., 82
Mao, W.-C., 266
Mapes, R. R., 234
Marcaurelle, R., 135
Marchand, A., 130, 132, 135
Mark, D. B., 256
Markides, K. S., 266

AUTHOR INDEX

Marks, J. S., 32
Markus, H., 19, 21, 22, 55, 57, 87, 97, 183, 188
Marlow, D., 229
Marques, J. M., 184, 188
Marshall, G. N., 257, 265
Marshall, M. A., 207
Marshall, P. J., 14
Martin, A. M., 128
Martin, C. L., 60.
Martin, J. G., 224
Martin, L. R., 256
Martin, R. A., 34, 35, 38, 177, 272
Mashek, D. J., 162
Mason, I., 210
Mason, M. F., 155, 159
Matthews, G., 11
Matthews, K. A., 256, 257
Matwin, S., 7, 251
Mauricio, A. M., 132
May, S., 212
Mayer, J. D., 209
Mayseless, O., 133
Mazziotta, J. C., 156, 157
McAdams, D. P., 15, 86
McBain, L., 134
McCabe, K., 155
McCarthy, G., 156
McCarty, D., 270
McClelland, D. C., 63
McClure, S. M., 155
McConahay, J. G., 225, 229
McCrae, R. R., 16, 19, 178, 206, 253
McCreary, C. P., 258
McCullough, M. E., 68
McDougall, W., 179
McGarty, C. A., 185, 187
McGhee, D., 232, 238
McGowan, S., 107
McGregor, J., 226
McHoskey, J. W.225
McLaughlin-Volpe, T., 190
Mead, G. H., 85
Meesters, C., 121
Meindl, J. R., 198
Mellenbergh, G. J., 19, 34
Meltzoff, A. N., 156
Mendoza-Denton, R., 87, 95
Meoni, L. A., 256
Mercury, M. G., 260
Messick, D. M., 214
Metcalfe, J., 18, 60, 151
Metzner, H. L., 33
Meunier, J., 31, 95
Meyer, B. A., 267
Meyerowitz, B. E., 257

Mezei, L., 226
Michaelis, B., 96
Michinov, N., 225
Mickelson, K. D., 30
Middleton, R A., 258
Mier, J. W., 261
Mikulincer, M., 30, 105, 106, 107, 120, 121, 122, 123, 125, 126, 127, 134, 136, 139
Miller, G. E., 269, 270
Miller, L. C., 18
Miller, N. E., 180, 182
Miller, R. B., 125
Miller, T. Q., 256, 260–261, 266
Miranda, R., 30, 84
Mirowsky, J., 33
Mischel, W., 2, 5, 6, 11, 12, 17, 18, 26, 29, 30, 32, 37 53, 60, 71, 80, 85, 87, 94, 95, 98, , 137, 150, 151, 155, 162, 165, 229, 231, 241, 253, 268, 269
Mitchell, J. P., 7, 149, 155, 156, 160
Mitchell, S. A., 51, 82, 86
Mitchell, T. R., 204, 214
Mohamed, A. A. R., 11
Mokdad, A. H., 32
Montague, P. R., 155
Monteith, M. J., 226, 234, 238, 284
Mooney, C. N., 68
Moorman, L., 121
Moos, R. H., 260
Morf, C. C., 11, 18, 53, 55, 64, 65, 66, 67, 68, 69, 70, 71, 100
Morgan, D. L., 264
Morgan, M., 18, 121
Morris, C. G., 214
Morris, J. P., 156
Morris, K. A., 120, 121, 140
Morrison, I., 156
Morrison, M. S., 18
Moscovici, S., 177
Moskowitz, D. S., 18
Moskowitz, G. B., 87, 92, 150, 226
Moskowitz, J. T., 265
Motes, M., 81, 89, 92
Mougios, V., 30, 32
Mowrer, O. H., 180, 182
Mroczek. D. K., 257
Muirhead, J., 257
Mulkana, S., 267
Mumford, M. D., 209, 210
Muraven, M., 60
Murdoch, C., 271
Muris, P., 121
Murphy, D. A., 270
Murphy, J., 81
Murray, H. A., 17

AUTHOR INDEX

Murray, S. L., 5, 100
Myers, D., 1
Myers, H. F., 258, 269

N

Nachmias, O., 105, 107
Nachson, O., 121, 128
Nelligan, J. S., 120, 125, 126, 127, 128
Nelson, G., 84, 85
Neumann, R., 156
Neumann, S. A., 265
Newcomb, T. M., 12
Newman, L. S., 69, 70
Newsom, J. T., 264
Newton, T. L., 33, 263, 269
Ng, D. M., 260
Ng, R., 260
Ng, S. H., 188
Niaura, R., 23, 256
Nicassio, P. C., 260
Nichols, K. E., 14
Nickolaus, M. S., 269
Nisbett, R. E., 12., 80
Nishishiba, M., 264
Nitschke, J. B., 161
Nitzberg, R. A., 127
Nixon, M., 199
Nolen-Hoeksema, S., 265
Noller, P., 125, 128, 129, 130, 131, 132, 133, 134
Norris, V. K., 260
Nosek, B. N., 92
Novacek, J., 68
Nowak, A., 18, 72
Nurius, P., 55, 57
Nystrom, L. E., 155, 161

O

O'Brien, L., 228
O'Connell, G. B., 227
O'Connor-Boes, J., 209
O'Doherty, J., 156
O'Keeffe, J. L., 261
O'Keeffe, M. K., 270
Oakes, P. J., 180, 184, 185, 187
Ochsner, K. N., 151, 153., 155, 156
Ogilvie, D. M., 82, 84
Ognibene, T. C., 125, 126
Okun, M. A., 264
Old, L. J., 269
Oldham, G. R., 214
Olson, M. B., 69, 256
Onorato, R. S., 187
Onorato, S., 187
Orbach, I., 120

Orcutt, H. K., 132
Oriña, M. M., 122, 164
Orom, H., 2, 6, 9, 22, 33, 71
Ostrom, T. M., 226
Otten, S., 184
Owens, J. F., 257
Oyserman, D., 186
Ozer, D. J., 12, 28, 257

P

Packer, D. J., 31
Padgett, D. A., 263, 270
Paetzold, R. L., 5, 51, 149
Páez, D., 184, 188
Pagnoni, G., 155
Paley, B., 79, 135
Palmer, R., 70
Park, C. L., 87
Park, L. E., 30, 50, 63, 71
Park, R. D., 27
Parker, C. W., 209
Paulhus, D. L., 60, 67
Paunonen, S. V., 16
Pavelchak, M., 86, 93
Peake, P. K., 12, 87, 95
Pelham, B. W., 65, 150
Pelphrey, K. A., 156
Pennebaker, J. W., 87
Pennisi, E., 25
Pensky, E., 134
Peplau, L. A., 129, 130
Pereg, D., 30
Pervin, L. A., 1, 33, 49, 253
Peterson, B., 3, 49, 65, 66
Peterson, C., 130, 256
Petty, R. E., 244, 252, 267, 268
Phelps, E. A., 21
Phillips, D.122, 127
Pickering, T. G., 264, 265
Pickett, C. L., 164, 166, 187
Pickett, S. M., 132
Pienta, A. M., 33
Pieper, C., 265
Pierce, G. R., 264
Pierce, K., 161
Pierce, T., 105
Pietromonaco, P. R., 105, 131, 132
Pincus, A. L., 4, 16
Pistole, M. C., 125, 128, 129, 130, 131, 132
Pittman, T. S., 53
Plant, E. A., 224, 226, 227, 228, 229, 230, 231, 232, 234, 235, 236, 237, 238
Platow, M. J., 188
Plaut, M., 271
Pomerantz, E., 25

AUTHOR INDEX 295

Poole, J. A., 126
Pope, M. K., 259, 261, 264
Posluszny, D. M., 270
Postmes, T, 178, 184
Poulton, J. L., 259
Powch, I. G., 262
Pratto, F., 189, 225
Prentice, D., 81
Price, J. M., 80
Priel, B., 126
Prkachin, K. M., 156
Przybeck T. R., 253
Puce, A., 156
Puhlik-Doris, P., 35, 38
Pyszczynski, T., 71, 100

Q
Quinn, D. M., 52

R
Radcliffe, N. M., 265, 266
Rahn, J. M., 260
Raikkonen, K., 257, 262
Raine, A., 154
Raskin, R., 66–67, 68
Ray, L. A., 266
Read, S. J., 18, 119, 125, 140, 259
Reblin, M., 254, 258
Reich, J. W., 264
Reicher, S. D., 184, 188
Reid, S. A., 188
Reis, H., 149
Rempel, J. K., 79, 83
Rentfrow, P. J., 33
Repetti, R. L., 168
Reynolds, K. J., 178, 184, 186, 188, 189
Reznik, I., 79, 81, 82, 87, 89, 92, 95, 97, 99, 100, 103, 104
Rhodewalt, F., 1, 2, 3, 11, 18, 25, 49, 53, 55, 60, 64, 65, 66, 67, 68, 69, 70, 100, 223, 254, 259, 264
Rholes, W. S., 3, 26, 51, 117, 119, 120, 122, 125, 126, 127, 128, 134, 135, 136
Richeson, J. A., 232
Richter, L., 263, 266
Ridgeway, C. L., 187
Rilling, J. K., 155, 161
Rincon, C., 96
Ring, C., 270
Ritchie, S. W., 260
Rizzolatti, G., 157
Robbins, C., 33
Roberts, P. W., 13, 25, 58, 59
Roberts, N., 125, 132, 133, 156
Robins, R. W., 58, 59, 61

Robins, R., 65
Robinson, T. E., 29
Robinson-Whelen, S., 257
Rockloff, M., 72
Rodriguez, M., 87, 95
Roepstorff, A., 155
Rogers, C., 49, 86
Rokeach, M., 226
Rook, K. S., 260, 264, 267
Ropp, S. A., 190
Roseman, J. M., 256
Ross, C. E., 12, 33
Ross, L., 80, 198
Ross, R., 254, 261, 271
Rothbart, M. K., 253
Rothschild, L., 190
Rotter, J. B., 206
Rovine, M. J., 128
Roy, S. A., 227
Rozanski, A., 261
Rush, M. C., 210
Russell, D. R., 269
Russell, D. W., 264
Russell, J. A., 19, 162
Rusting, C. L., 102, 265
Ryan, L., 132, 155
Ryan, M. K., 188
Ryan, R. M., 52, 71, 87

S
Saarela, M. V., 156
Sabourin, S., 135
Sadato, N., 155
Sadava, S., 134
Safran, J. D., 79, 86
Saklofske, D. H., 11
Salovey, P., 209
Sanbonmatsu, D. M., 70
Sanders, J. D., 261
Sanders, V. M., 271
Sanfey, A. G., 155, 161
Sanford, R. M., 180
Sanford, R. N., 224
Sanna, L. J., 265
Sarason, B. R., 264
Sarason, I. G., 264
Sarfati, Y., 155
Saribay, S. A., 5, 52, 79, 84
Saucier, G., 17
Saunders, K., 132
Saxe, L., 225
Saxe, R.155, 158
Sceery, A., 119, 120, 133
Schachner, D. A., 129, 130
Schachter, S., 180

AUTHOR INDEX

Scheier, M. F., 18, 60, 87, 229, 233, 234, 241, 256, 257, 258, 259, 260, 262, 263, 265, 266
Schein, E. H., 202
Schilling, E. A., 263
Schimek, J., 82
Schleicher, D., 209
Schlenker, B. R., 53
Schmitt, M. T., 188, 189
Schneiderman, N., 260., 268
Schooler, T. Y., 62
Schouten, E. G., 257
Schreiber, R. D., 269
Schroder, H. M., 59
Schwartz, A. R., 264
Schwartz, J., 232, 238
Schwarz, N., 21, 102
Schwean, V. L., 11
Schyns, P., 156
Scott, W. D., 21
Searle, J. R., 14, 19, 20
Sears, D. O., 225
Sears, R. R., 180, 182
Sears, S. R., 265
Sedaghat, F., 161
Sedikides, C., 186, 188, 226
Seeman, T. E., 168, 260, 263, 267, 270
Segal, Z. V., 79
Segerstrom, S. C., 262, 265, 269
Seidel, M., 85
Seligman, M. E. P., 87, 256
Selye, C., 1, 244
Semerari, A., 18
Sephton, S. E., 262
Serôdio, R., 184, 188
Seymour, B., 156
Shadel, W. G., 22, 23, 24, 33
Shah, J. Y., 30, 32, 87, 90, 92, 98, 99, 100, 236
Shallice, T., 156
Shamai, D., 126
Shaver, P. R
Shaver, P. R., 30, 106, 120, 121, 122, 123, 125, 127, 129, 130, 136
Shaw, M. E., 180, 182
Sheffield, D., 260
Sheldon, K. M., 58, 59
Shelton, J. N., 227, 232
Shen, B. J., 258, 266
Sheridan, J., 270
Sherif, M., 182
Shi, L., 131
Shoda, Y, 2, 5, 6, 11, 18, 19, 30, 32, 37, 39, 80, 85, 98, 137, 150, 155, 229, 231, 24, 253, 269
Showers, C. J., 58, 59
Showers, C., 100
Shweder, R. A. 26, 27

Sidanius, J., 189, 225
Siegler, I. C., 256, 261, 263, 266
Siemionko, M., 223
Sigman, M., 152
Sikkema, K. J., 270
Silver, M. D., 187
Silver, R. C., 87, 127
Simon, B., 186
Simonds, J., 17
Simpson, J. A., 119, 120, 122, 125, 126, 127, 128, 129, 131, 134, 135, 141, 164
Sinclair, L., 5, 30, 31, 94, 95
Singer, J. L., 82, 83
Singer, T., 156, 160, 161, 166
Sivers, H., 151
Skelton, A., 53
Slater, P. E., 204
Smart, L., 53
Smith T. W., 25
Smith, A., 163
Smith, D. S., 70
Smith, E. R., 81, 87, 259
Smith, J. R., 184
Smith, R. E., 23
Smith, T. W., 2, 252, 254, 256, 258, 259, 260, 261,262, 264, 265, 272
Smith, V., 155
Snyder, C. R., 69, 70
Snyder, J., 158
Snyder, M., 53, 96, 176, 178, 182, 188, 189, 213, 229
Solberg, L. N., 263
Solomon, P. E., 156
Solomon, S., 71
Somerville, L. H., 162
Sorrow, D., 60, 64, 66, 68
Spangler, W. D., 208
Sparrow, D., 257
Spears, R., 184
Spencer, S. J., 62, 63
Spiro, III, A., 257
Srivastava, S., 16
Sroufe, L. A., 120
St. Aubin, E., 15
Stangor, C., 226
Stanton, A. L., 265
Starzomski, A., 132
Steele, C. M., 100
Steiner, I. D., 180, 202
Stephan, C. W., 227
Stephan, W. G., 227
Stephens, M. A., 260
Stern, W., 39
Sternberg, R. J., 203, 210
Stetson, B. A., 260

Stewart, T., 156
Stogdill, R. M., 198, 199
Strack, F., 156
Streufert, S., 59
Strickland, L. H., 180
Stroup, D. F., 32
Strube, M. J., 70, 186, 188
Suarez, E. C., 262
Suedfeld, P., 59
Suedfeld, P., 59
Sugiyama, L. S., 14
Sullivan, H. S., 4, 27, 51, 79, 86, 87, 82, 91
Sullivan, M., 27
Suls, J., 256, 259, 261, 262, 272
Sumer, N., 120, 121
Sutton-Tyrrell, K., 257
Svrakic D. M., 253
Swann, W. B., 1, 4, 27, 52, 62, 63, 244
Swann, W. B., Jr., 33, 65, 140, 259
Swanson, M. A., 271
Syme, S. L., 33

T

Tager-Flusberg, H., 158
Tajfel, H., 177, 180, 181, 182, 183, 185, 210, 226
Tambor, E. S., 87
Tangney, J. P., 49
Tanke, E. D., 96
Tapias, M. P., 242
Tarr, K. L., 269
Tarrant, N., 132
Tassinary, L. G., 252, 267, 268
Taubman, M. B., 271
Taylor, D. M., 180
Taylor, S. E., 100, 168, 263, 264, 265, 266
Taylor, T., 260
Teasdale, J. D., 87, 256
Terdal, S. K., 87
Terman, L. M., 198
Terry, D. J., 130, 187
Terry, H., 67
Tesser, A., 53, 66
Testa, M., 270
Tetlock, P. E., 59
Thoits, P. A., 187, 264
Thomas, J. C., 210
Thompson, D. W., 85
Thompson, J. A., 65
Thompson, J. C., 156
Thompson, W. L., 153
Thor, K., 209
Thorn, B. E., 269
Thornhill, R., 130
Thorsteinnsson, E. B., 264
Thrash, T. M., 63

Tice, D.M., 60, 70
Tissaw, M. A., 18
Todorov, A., 155
Tomei, L. D., 269
Törestad, B., 26
Torquati, J. C., 130
Tota, M. E., 90
Toulmin, S., 14, 15, 28
Tracy, J. L., 61, 129, 130
Tragakis, M., 53, 65, 66, 67, 68, 70
Tran, S., 126, 128, 134
Tranel, D., 156
Trapnell, P. D., 4, 207
Treiber, F. A., 260
Trimble, M. R., 156
Trope, Y., 158
Trötschel, R., 87, 98
Trouard, T., 155
Troy, A. B., 128
Trzebinski, J., 16
Tschanz, B., 70
Tucker, P., 121, 134
Tudor, M., 84, 85
Tugade, M. M., 266
Turgeon, C., 135
Turner, C. W., 256
Turner, J. C., 177, 178, 180, 182, 183, 184, 185, 186, 187, 188, 189, 210, 226
Tweed, R. G., 132
Twenge, J. M., 1314
Tyler, T. R., 216

U

Uchino, B. N., 7, 251, 254, 258, 260, 263, 264, 267
Uleman, J. S., 150
Umberson, D., 33, 260, 267
Unckless, A., 209
Uno, D., 258

V

Vallacher, R. R., 18, 72
Van Boven, L., 163
van Heerden, J., 19, 34
van Knippenberg, B., 188
van Knippenberg, D., 184, 188, 210
Van Mechelen, I., 18
Vance, S. L., 224, 226, 232, 241
Vansteelandt, K., 18
Vasquez, K. A., 223, 227, 241, 244
Vaughn, A. A., 7, 251
Vaux, A., 126
Vazsonyi, A. T., 130
Vedhara, K., 270
Veenstra, K. E., 178, 184, 186

Verkuyten, M., 188
Vernon, M. L., 129, 130
Vescio, T. K., 227
Vickers, Jr., R. R., 257
Vinokur, A. D., 260
Virshup, L. K., 187
Vogeley, K., 156
Vogt, B. A., 156
Vogt, L., 156
Vohs, K. D., 32, 60
Voils, C. I., 226, 238
Vokonas, P., 257
Vollm, B. A., 155, 160
Vonnegut, K., 149
Vorauer, J. D., 227
Vroom, V. H., 204

W

Wachtel, P. L., 4, 5, 82, 83
Wadas, R. F., 69, 70
Wall, S., 117, 119, 122, 123, 126
Wallace, J. L., 126
Waller, S., 70
Walster, E., 28
Wan, C. K., 262
Wang, A. T., 152
Wang, N., 256
Waters, E., 117, 119, 120, 122, 123, 126
Watson, C. B., 212
Watson, D., 102, 229
Weick, K., 214
Weigold, M. F., 53
Weinberger, J., 63
Weintraub, J. K., 259, 260, 263
Weir, K., 35, 38
Weiss, W., 210
Wekerle, C., 132, 133
Weller, A., 125, 126
Westen, D., 65, 82, 83
Westie, F. R., 224
Westin, D., 136
Westmaas, J. L., 127
Wetherell, M. S., 184
Whalen, P. J., 162
White, K. M., 187
White, L., 209
White, R. W., 87
Whitfield, S. L., 151
Wicker, B., 156
Wicklund, R. A., 230
Wiegand, S. J., 271
Wiggins, J. S., 4, 16, 207

Williams, C. J., 226
Williams, D., 209
Williams, E. L., 63
Williams, K. D., 178, 182, 186
Williams, R. B., 252, 256, 268
Wills, T. A., 264, 270
Wilner, B. I., 260
Wilpers, S., 27, 28
Wilson, C. L., 126, 127, 134
Wilson, T. D., 62
Winer, B. J., 200, 203
Winston, J. S., 160
Winter, L., 150
Wittgenstein, L., 15
Woddis, D., 105, 107
Wolfe, C. T., 50, 52, 65, 71, 87, 98
Wolfe, D. A., 132, 133
Wong, R. Y., 13
Wood, R. E., 21, 214
Woods, F. A., 197
Woolsey, L. K., 134
Word, C. O., 223
Wortman, C. B., 87, 257
Woycke, J., 208
Wray, L. A., 33
Wright, J., 5
Wright, S. C., 190
Wundt, W., 179
Wurf, E., 19, 2, 97

Y

Yetton, P. W., 204
Yeung, A. C., 261
Ylostalo, P., 267
Young, A. W., 157
Yuki, M., 186
Yurko, K. H., 256

Z

Zaccaro, S. J., 199, 207, 209, 210, 213
Zaki, J., 7, 149
Zanna, M. P., 62, 63, 223, 224, 225
Zarate, M. A., 81, 259, 264
Zdaniuk, B., 132
Zeigler-Hill, V., 58, 59, 63
Zelditch, M., 212
Zimbardo, P. G., 184
Zinner, L. R., 243
Zitman, F. G., 257
Zuroff, D. C., 18, 79
Zuwerink, J. R., 226

Subject Index

Page numbers in italic refer to figures or tables

A
Adler, Alfred, style of life, 3–4
Adult attachment style, relationship satisfaction, 117–118, 123–141
Agency, 4
Agreeableness, 3
Anger, 138–139
  attachment style, 121–123
Anxiety, 4
  attachment style, 106, 119–120
  interracial interactions, 232–233
  proximity, 120
  separation, 120
  trust, 120
Appraisals
  defined, 19–20
  Knowledge-and-Appraisal Personality Architecture (KAPA), 19–20
  self-schemas, 22
  speed, 22–23
Attachment style, 119–123
  anger, 121–123
  anxiety, 106, 119–120, 120–121, 123–141, *124*
  avoidant, 119–120, 120–121, 123–141, *124*
  global positive affect, 105–106
  hostility, 106–107, 121–123
  relationship satisfaction
    conflict, 130–132
    difficult life circumstances, 134–136
    giving care and support, 125–135
    intimacy, 128–130
    perceiving care and support, 125–135
    research, 136–141
    risk factors, 125–135
    seeking care and support, 125–135
    self-disclosure, 128–129
    sexuality, 129–130
    transition to parenthood, 134–135
    violence, 132–133
  secure, 119, 121
  self, 51
  transference, 105–107
Attachment theory, 5, 118–123
  evolution, 118–119
Attribution, 214–215
Augmentation, 69
Authoritarianism, 224–225
Autism, 154
  false belief task, 154

Automaticity, 150
  transference
    efficiency, 91–92
    unconscious activation, 91–92
Autonomy, 121
Avoidance, 120–121
  attachment style, 119–120

B
Borderline personality disorder, 154–155
Brain regions
  social cognition, *155*, 155–158, *157*
  theory of mind, *155*, 155–158, *157*

C
Cardiovascular disease, 254
  hostility/optimism, 255–256
    evidence for model, 261–267
    potential affective processes linking, 264–267
    potential behavioral processes linking, 264–267
    potential cognitive processes linking, 264–267
    potential social processes linking, 261–264
    social-cognitive influence modeling, *258*, 258–261
    stress, 258–267
  personality, 255–258
Categorization
  prejudice, 226
  stereotyping, 226
Coaching, 214–216
Cognition
  leadership, 206–208
  uniquely social, 152
Cognitive-Affective Personality System (CAPS) model, 150
  personality architecture, 18
    dispositional tendencies, 18
    patterns of behavior, 18
  theory, 85–86
Cognitive-Experiential Self Theory, 52, 62–63
Cognitive psychology, 5
Communion, 4
Competitiveness, social cognition, 160–161
Conflict, 130–132
Contextualized personality signatures, 150
Cooperativeness, social cognition, 160–161

299

SUBJECT INDEX

Coronary artery disease, 254–255
  processes, 254–255
Cross-situational coherence, Knowledge-and-Appraisal Personality Architecture (KAPA), 22–24
  knowledge, 22–23
  nomothetic methods, 22–23
  patterns of consistency, 22–23
  vs. traditional inter-individual difference categories, 22–23

D

Delay of gratification tasks, 32
Depersonalization, 184
Depressed mood, 104
Design stance, 150
Discounting, 69
Discrimination, 223–244
Disposition, 10–11
  dispositional constructs, 2
    variability in responding across situations, 2
  as *if-then* contingencies, 5
  integrating individual differences, 165–168
  predicting behavior, 10
  social cognition, 166–169
    lability, 168
    link to personality dispositions and disorders, 166–168, *167*
    set points, 168
    social-cognitive space, *167*
    three-factor model, 165–168
Dyadic interactional perspective, 4

E

Egoism, 138–139
Emotion, 86–88, 101–102
Emotional intelligence, leadership, 209–210
Empathy, 152
  neuroimaging, *155*, 155–158, *157*
Evaluative standards, 20

F

Facial affect, transference, 93–94
Fairness, 215–216
False belief task, autism, 154
Familiarity, social cognition, 161–162
Freud, Sigmund
  psychosexual development, 3
  theory of psychosexual development, 3

G

Global positive affect, attachment system, 105–106
Gossip, 149
Group norms, 184

H

Health behavior, relationships, 32–33
Hostility, 104–105
  attachment style, 121–123
  attachment system, 106–107
  cardiovascular disease, 255–256
    evidence for model, 261–267
    potential affective processes linking, 264–267
    potential behavioral processes linking, 264–267
    potential cognitive processes linking, 264–267
    potential social processes linking, 261–264
    social-cognitive influence modeling, *258*, 258–261
    stress, 258–267
Humor assessment, 34–38
  contextualizing intra-individual strategies, 34–36
  global inter-individual strategies, 34–36
  HSQ, 35–36
  personality architecture, strategy, 37–38
  SHRQ, 34–35
  structure-process distinction, 36–37
Hypertension, 255

I

Ideal selves, 104
Idiographic-nomothetic distinction, 80
If-then model
  patterns, 30
  self-other links, 85–86
  situation-behavior patterns, 150
Image management, leadership, 205, 210–213
  desirable leadership prototype, 211
  observer bias in prototype perception, 212
  person/situation fit, 212–213
    moderators, 213
  prototype characteristics, 210–211
  prototype expression, 212–213
Independence, 4, 121
Individuality
  characterized, 186–187
  defined, 178
  influence, 187–188
  leadership, 197–198
  personality, 182–183
  prototypicality, 187–188
  self-categorization theory, 183–187
  social identity, 182–183
Inference, transference, 89–91
  chronic accessibility, 90–91
  transient contextual cueing, 90

SUBJECT INDEX

Influence
　individuality, 187–188
　prototypicality, 187–188
Intentionality, Knowledge-and-Appraisal Personality Architecture (KAPA), 19
Intentional stance, 150
Interactionist frameworks, 2
Intergroup relations, self-regulation, 226–229
Inter-individual differences, personality, 16–17
　taxonomies, 16–17
　theoretical constructs, 16
Interpersonal acceptance
　expectancies, 94–96
　relational self, 94–96
Interpersonal behavior
　self, connections, 50
　self-esteem, connections, 50
　Sullivan, Harry Stack, 4
　transference, 96
Interpersonal self-regulation
　elements, 56–63
　Knowledge-Organization System, 56–59
　　self-knowledge content, 57–58
　　self-knowledge organization, 57–58
　Regulation-Action System, 59–61
　self-esteem, 61
Interracial interactions, 223–244
　personality, process modeling, 239–241, *240*
　prejudice
　　anxiety, 232–233
　　approaching egalitarianism, 232–239
　　avoiding overt bias, 232–239
　　external motivation to respond without prejudice, 227–239
　　goals, 233–239
　　internal motivation to respond without prejudice, 227–239
　　likelihood of meeting standards, 231–239
　　outcome expectancies, 231–239
　　self- vs. other-imposed standards proscribing prejudice, 230–231
　　strategies, 233–239
　self-regulation, process modeling, 239–241, *240*
Intimacy, 128–130
Intra-individual personality architecture, 9–39,
　see also Personality architecture

J

James, William, 49–50
Judgment, 214–215
Justice, 215–216

K

Knowledge
　defined, 19–20

Knowledge-and-Appraisal Personality Architecture (KAPA), 19–20
Knowledge-and-Appraisal Personality Architecture (KAPA)
　appraisals, 19–20
　cross-situational coherence, 22–24
　　knowledge, 22–23
　　nomothetic methods, 22–23
　　patterns of consistency, 22–23
　　vs. traditional inter-individual difference categories, 22–23
　intentionality, 19
　knowledge, 19–20
　personality, views complementary to, 25–27
　personality architecture, 19–24
　　knowledge *vs.* appraisal differentiation principle, 19–20
　　principle differentiating among alternative forms of knowledge and appraisal, 20
　　relations among knowledge and appraisal mechanisms, 20–21, *21*
　　system of social-cognitive personality variables, 19–20
　persons-in-situations, 21–25
　　literature review, 26–27
　　synthetic accounts, 26
　smoking, *23*, 23–24
Knowledge-Organization System
　interpersonal self-regulation, 56–59
　self-knowledge content, 57–58
　self-esteem, 53–55, *54*

L

Lability, 168
Leadership, 197–216
　characterized, 200–205
　cognition, 206–208
　conventional wisdom, 197–200
　effectiveness
　　characterized, 201–202
　　elements, 210–216
　emotional intelligence, 209–210
　empirical study, 198
　expertise, 210
　five-factor model of personality, 206, 208
　function, 202–203
　great man theory of leadership, 197–198
　image management, 205, 210–213
　　desirable leadership prototype, 211
　　observer bias in prototype perception, 212
　　person/situation fit, 212–213
　　person/situation fit moderators, 213
　　prototype expression, 212–213
　　prototypical characteristics, 210–211
　individual difference models, 206–210

Leadership (continued)
  individualism, 197–198
  motivation, 208–209
  organizational functions, 202–203
  personality, 206–208
  person-oriented explanations, 197–198
  problem-solving, 210
  processes, 204–205
    historical overview, 204–205
    integrative approach, 205
  relationship development, 205, 214–216
    attribution, 214–215
    coaching, 214–216
    fairness, 215–216
    judgment, 214–215
    justice, 215–216
    leader behavior, 214
    situational moderators, 214
  research methods, 200
  resource deployment, 205
  rotational designs, 199–200
  self-monitoring, 209–210
  social appraisal skills, 209–210
  social intelligence, 209–210
  status, 200–201
  tacit knowledge, 210
  trait determinants, 198–199
Linkage model, 85–86

M

Memory effects, transference, 89–91
  chronic accessibility, 90–91
  transient contextual cueing, 90
Mental state inference, 150, 152
  neuroimaging, *155*, 155–158, *157*
Model of relational schemas, 85
Motivation, 86–88
  to achieve success, 233–234
  to attend to social cues, 152
  to avoid failure, 233–234
  leadership, 208–209
  self-regulation, 98–105
    activating approach-avoidance motivation, 98–99
    activating other-protective self-regulation, 100–101
    activating self-protective self-regulation, 100
    activating self-regulation, 99–102
    activating self-regulatory focus, 99–100
    approach-avoidance motivation, 98–99
    calm, lack of, 104–105
    chronically unsatisfied goals, 102
    chronic need violation, 102
    chronic self-induced violation of own standards, 102–103
    contextually-based expectancy violation through interpersonal roles, 103
    depressed mood, 104
    disrupting positive affect, 102–103
    emotions, 101–102
    hostile mood, 104–105
    self-discrepancies from parent's perspective, 104–105

N

Narcissism
  interpersonal self-esteem regulation, 64–69
  Knowledge-Organization System, *54*, 65
  Regulation-Action System, 66
  social feedback, 68
  social inclusion, 68–69
Neuroimaging, 151
  empathy, *155*, 155–158, *157*
  mental state inference, *155*, 155–158, *157*
  modularity, 152–153
  shared representations, *155*, 155–158, *157*
  situational accessibility, 152–153
  social cognition, modularity, *155*, 155–158, *157*

O

Object-relations perspective, self, 51–52
Optimal distinctiveness theory, 187
Optimism, cardiovascular disease, 256–258
  evidence for model, 261–267
  potential affective processes linking, 264–267
  potential behavioral processes linking, 264–267
  potential cognitive processes linking, 264–267
  potential social processes linking, 261–264
  social-cognitive influence modeling, *258*, 258–261
  stress, 258–267
Ought selves, 104

P

Parents, 104–105
  relationship satisfaction, 134–135
Personality
  alternative conceptions, 16–24, 24–29
  assessment, case example, 33–38
  cardiovascular disease, 255–258
  characterized, 186–187, 253–254
  cognitive substrate, 5
  combined idiographic-nomothetic approach, 80
  constructs, 10–11, 16
  contextual variability, 79–108

SUBJECT INDEX   303

defined, 1–2, 16, 178
  two distinct classes of referents, 15
dispositional perspectives, 178
individuality, 182–183
interactional perspective, 178
inter-individual differences, 16–17
  taxonomies, 16–17
  theoretical constructs, 16
interpersonal perspective, 3–4
interracial interactions, process modeling, 239–241, *240*
intra-individual differences
  person effects, 24–25
  situation effects, 24–25
  Knowledge-and-Appraisal Personality Architecture (KAPA), views complementary to, 25–27
leadership, 206–208
narrative, 9–10
  deconstructing, 13–15
  rewritten, 12–15
personality variable, 10–11
physical health
  disease selection, 254–255
  historical aspects, 251–252
  integrative multilevel analysis, 267–272
  interdisciplinary research from diverse fields, 252
  multilevel perspective, 252
  psychoanalytic tradition, 252
  social psychological processes linking, 251–273
prejudice, 188–189, 241–244
preoccupation with other people's minds, 149–150
relational representations, 29–33
relational self, 84–85
situational perspective, 178
social behavior, overview, 1–7
social cognition, 29–30
  research agenda, 169
social-cognitive neuroscience perspective, 149–169
social identity, 182–183
social psychology
  balkanization, 2
  difference between, 38–39
  emerging symbiosis, 1
  structural approach, 150
  trait approach, 150
  types of units, 5
Personality architecture, 17–24
  Cognitive-Affective Personality Systems (CAPS) model, 18
  dispositional tendencies, 18

  patterns of behavior, 18
  humor assessment, strategy, 37–38
  implications, 10–12
  inter-individual conception
    assessing person effects, 27–29
    assessing situation effects, 27–29
  intra-individual architecture of cognitive and affective systems, 11–12
  intra-individual structure and dynamics, 19–24
  Knowledge-and-Appraisal Personality Architecture (KAPA), 19–24
    knowledge *vs.* appraisal differentiation principle, 19–20
    principle differentiating among alternative forms of knowledge and appraisal, 20
    relations among knowledge and appraisal mechanisms, 20–21, *21*
    system of social-cognitive personality variables, 19–20
  model, 11–12
  overview, 10–12
  principles, 18
Personality disorders, social cognition deficits, 154–155
Personality psychology
  alternative perspective, 10
  defined, 11
  resurgence, 17–18
Person effects, inter-individual personality architecture, 27–29
Persons
  contextualized person constructs, 14–15
  defined, 10, 11
  situation-free attributes, 14–15
  social behavior, relative size, 12–13
Person–situation debate, 2–3
Philosophy of mind, 20
Physical health, personality
  disease selection, 254–255
  historical aspects, 251–252
  integrative multilevel analysis, 267–272
  interdisciplinary research from diverse fields, 252
  multilevel perspective, 252
  psychoanalytic tradition, 252
  social psychological processes linking, 251–273
Predictions, 28
  vs. understanding, 28
Prejudice, 223–244
  categorization, 226
  early social psychological approaches, 224–227
  interracial interactions

Prejudice (*continued*)
    anxiety, 232–233
    approaching egalitarianism, 232–239
    avoiding overt bias, 232–239
    external motivation to respond without prejudice, 227–239
    goals, 233–239
    internal motivation to respond without prejudice, 227–239
    likelihood of meeting standards, 231–239
    outcome expectancies, 231–239
    self- *vs.* other-imposed standards proscribing prejudice, 230–231
    strategies, 233–239
    more symbolic, modern, or ambivalent forms, 225
    personality, 188–189, 241–244
    prejudiced personality, 224–225
    self-regulation
        anxiety, 232–233
        approaching egalitarianism, 232–239
        avoiding overt bias, 232–239
        external motivation to respond without prejudice, 227–239
        goals, 233–239
        internal motivation to respond without prejudice, 227–239
        likelihood of meeting standards, 231–239
        outcome expectancies, 231–239
        self- *vs.* other-imposed standards proscribing prejudice, 230–231
        strategies, 233–239
Prototypicality
    individuality, 187–188
    influence, 187–188
Proximity, anxiety, 120
Psychological attributes, 14
Psychopathy, 154
Psychosexual development, Freud, Sigmund, 3

R
Racism, 223–244
    more symbolic, modern, or ambivalent forms, 225
Reciprocal interactionist views, 2
Reductionism, 180–182
Regulation-Action System
    interpersonal self-regulation, 59–61
    narcissism, 66
    self-esteem, 53–55, 54
Rejection
    expectancies, 94–96
    relational self, 94–96
Rejection sensitivity, 31–32, 95–96
Relational representations, 29–33

activation, 31
changing interpersonal expectancies, 31–32
construct applications, 31–32
training procedures, 31–32
Relational schemas, 30–31
    activation, 31
    defined, 30
Relational self, 5, 79–80, 186
    evidence for, 94–96
    interpersonal acceptance, 94–96
    personality, 84–85
    rejection, 94–96
    social behavior, 84–85
    theoretical framework, 84–85
Relationship development, leadership, 205, 214–216
    attribution, 214–215
    coaching, 214–216
    fairness, 215–216
    judgment, 214–215
    justice, 215–216
    leader behavior, 214
    situational moderators, 214
Relationships
    health behavior, 32–33
    personality, relational representations, 29–33
    self-regulation, 32–33
    smoking, 33
Relationship satisfaction, attachment style, 117–118, 123–141
    conflict, 130–132
    difficult life circumstances, 134–136
    effects of partner insecurity, 135–136
    giving and seeking care and support, 125–135
    intimacy, 128–130
    perceptions of availability of support, 125–135
    research, 136–141
    risk factors, 125–135
    self-disclosure, 128–129
    sexuality, 129–130
    transition to parenthood, 134–135
    violence, 132–133
Resource deployment, leadership, 205
Risk regulation system, 5
Role identities, 187
Rotational designs, leadership, 199–200

S
Security, 4
Self
    attachment style, 51
    defined, 49
    fragile, 63–64
    interpersonal behavior, connections, 50

SUBJECT INDEX

interpersonal process model, 49–50
literature review, 50–52
multi-faceted view, 97
object-relations perspective, 51–52
principle organizing function in human behavior, 49
psychodynamic perspective, 51
self-esteem, connections, 50
social behavior, 49–73
symbolization, 49
Self-categorization theory, individuality, 183–187
Self-concept, transference, 97–98
Self-disclosure, 128–129
Self-esteem
  interpersonal behavior, connections, 50
  interpersonal self-regulation, 61
  Knowledge-Organization System, 53–55, 54
  narcissism, interpersonal self-esteem regulation, 64–69
  regulation-action system, 53–55, 54
  self, connections, 50
  self-handicapping, 69–71
  self-regulation, 53–55, 54
  self-system, 52
  social feedback, 53–55, 54
  standards, 52–53
Self-evaluation, transference, 97–98
Self-handicapping, self-esteem, 69–71
Self-knowledge content, 57–58
Self-knowledge organization, 58–59
Self-monitoring, leadership, 209–210
Self-other links, if-then model, 85–86
Self-regulation, 86–88, *see also* Interpersonal self-regulation
  defined, 50
  intergroup relations, 226–229
  interracial interactions, process modeling, 239–241, 240
  motivation, 98–105
    activating approach-avoidance motivation, 98–99
    activating other-protective self-regulation, 100–101
    activating self-protective self-regulation, 100
    activating self-regulation, 99–102
    activating self-regulatory focus, 99–100
    approach-avoidance motivation, 98–99
    calm, lack of, 104–105
    chronically unsatisfied goals, 102
    chronic need violation, 102
    chronic self-induced violation of own standards, 102–103
    contextually-based expectancy violation

    through interpersonal roles, 103
    depressed mood, 104
    disrupting positive affect, 102–103
    emotions, 101–102
    hostile mood, 104–105
    self-discrepancies from parent's perspective, 104–105
  prejudice
    anxiety, 232–233
    approaching egalitarianism, 232–239
    avoiding overt bias, 232–239
    external motivation to respond without prejudice, 227–239
    goals, 233–239
    internal motivation to respond without prejudice, 227–239
    likelihood of meeting standards, 231–239
    outcome expectancies, 231–239
    self- vs. other-imposed standards proscribing prejudice, 230–231
    strategies, 233–239
  relationships, 32–33
  self-esteem, 53–55, 54
Self-schemas
  appraisals, 22
  situational beliefs, 22
Self-system, self-esteem, 52
Self-with-other representations, 30
Separation, anxiety, 120
Set points, 168
Sexuality, 129–130
Shared representations, neuroimaging, 155, 155–158, 157
SHRQ, humor assessment, 34–35
Significant-other representations
  idiographic nature, 80
  transference, 81–82
Situational beliefs, self-schemas, 22
Situation effects, inter-individual personality architecture, 27–29
Situations
  predicting behavior, 10
  social behavior, relative size, 12–13
Skewed interactionism, 4
Smoking
  Knowledge-and-Appraisal Personality Architecture (KAPA), 23, 23–24
  relationships, 33
Social appraisal skills, leadership, 209–210
Social behavior
  narrative, 9–10
    deconstructing, 13–15
    rewritten, 12–15
  personality, overview, 1–7
  persons, relative size, 12–13

Social behavior (*continued*)
  relational self, 84–85
  self, 49–73
  situations, relative size, 12–13
Social categorization, psychological salience, 185–186
Social cognition, 5
  brain regions, *155*, 155–158, *157*
  competitiveness, 160–161
  contextual influences, 158–162
  cooperativeness, 160–161
  disposition, 166–169
    lability, 168
    link to personality dispositions and disorders, 166–168, *167*
    set points, 168
    social-cognitive space, *167*
  effect of relationship between self and others, 159–162
  effects of in- *vs.* out-group membership of other, 159–162
  familiarity, 161–162
  modular nature, 152–153
  neuroimaging, modularity, *155*, 155–158, *157*
  perceiver features, 162–165
    cognitive busyness, 163
    perceiver expectancies, 162–163
    relational motivation, 163–165
    stress, 163
  personality, 29–30
    research agenda, 169
Social-cognitive model of transference, 5
  historical roots, 82–83
Social-cognitive processes, situational influences, 153
Social-cognitive space, *167*
Social construct theory, transference, 84
Social dominance, 188–189
Social feedback
  narcissism, 68
  self-esteem, 53–55, *54*
Social identity
  individuality, 182–183
  personality, 182–183
Social identity theory, European metatheory, 180–182
Social inclusion, narcissism, 68–69
Social intelligence, leadership, 209–210
Social psychology
  defined, 1–2
  dual-process models, 62–63
  European, 180–182
  individual *vs.* collective, 179–180
  personality
    balkanization, 2
    difference between, 38–39
  emerging symbiosis, 1
  research, prototypical three-study package, 6
Social relationships
  preoccupation with other people's minds, 149–150
  social-cognitive neuroscience perspective, 149–169
Stereotyping, 184, 223–244
  categorization, 226
  early social psychological approaches, 224–227
  implicit priming, 226
Stress, 163, 258–267
Style of life, 51
  Adler, Alfred, 3–4
Sullivan, Harry Stack, interpersonal behavior, 4
Symbolization, self, 49

T
Theory of psychosexual development, Freud, Sigmund, 3
Traits as Situational Sensitivities (TASS) model, 207
Trait theory, 2
Transference, 5
  assumptions, 81–85
  attachment system, 105–107
  automaticity
    efficiency, 91–92
    unconscious activation, 91–92
  cognitive bases, 83–84
  conceptualization, 81–85
  evaluation effects, 92–93
  facial affect, 93–94
  historical roots, 82–83
  inference, 89–91
    chronic accessibility, 90–91
    transient contextual cueing, 90
  interpersonal behavior, 96
  memory effects, 89–91
    chronic accessibility, 90–91
    transient contextual cueing, 90
  methodology, 87–88
  self-concept, 97–98
  self-evaluation, 97–98
  significant-other representations, 81–82
  social-cognitive process, 79–80
  social construct theory, 84
Trust, anxiety, 120

V
Violence, 132–133

W
Wachtel, Paul, 4, 5